G000320426

COMPUTER GRAPHICS

Edward Angel

University of New Mexico

Addison-Wesley Publishing Company

Reading, Massachusetts • Menlo Park, California • New York
Don Mills, Ontario • Wokingham, England • Amsterdam • Bonn
Sydney • Singapore • Tokyo • Madrid • San Juan

Cover art courtesy of LINKS Corporation.

James T. DeWolf	Sponsoring Editor
Karen Myer	Production Supervisor
Patsy DuMoulin	Production Coordinator
Joseph K. Vetere	Technical Art Consultant
Rose Mary Molnar	Artist
Lyn Duprè	Copyeditor
Jean Seal	Cover Design
Jean Hammond	Interior Design
Melinda Grosser	Four-Color Insert Design

Library of Congress Cataloging-in-Publication Data

Angel, Edward.
Computer graphics / Edward Angel.
      p.   cm.
Includes index.
ISBN 0-201-13548-5
1. Computer graphics.   2. C (Computer program language)
I. Title.
T385.A513   1990

006.6–dc19   89-332
                                                                                                     CIP

ABCDEFGHIJ-HA-89

■ **To Rose Mary**

P R E F A C E

The past few years have seen a revolution in the way computer graphics is practiced. Computer graphics, while still an area of much activity in computer science, is also an area of great importance to students and practitioners of engineering, science, business, and mathematics. The advances in both hardware and software have led to the modern graphics workstation as a standard tool. These workstations include not only the hardware for high-resolution, bit-mapped displays but also the necessary software tools that allow users to develop their own applications. Thus, we are seeing the electrical engineer writing her own interface to a circuit-analysis package and mechanical engineers writing menu-driven CAD packages. For the computer scientist, computer graphics has expanded to include a wealth of new and exciting problems from the generation of photorealistic displays to the design of software tools.

This book is intended for use in a first course in computer graphics for computer scientists and engineers. Although such a course is normally taught for seniors, the only prerequisites assumed are good programming skills (equivalent to CS 2 in the ACM model curriculum) and trigonometry.

There are four fundamental precepts on which the book is based. First, with the availability of present software and hardware tools, it is both possible and important that students get working on significant *applications* of computer graphics early in the course. Hence, I have adopted a top-down approach that attempts to get students working on projects using Graphical Kernel System (GKS)—or any other available system—before we spend significant time on the standard graphics algorithms, such as line drawing and fill. This approach is in contrast to most books that use a bottom up approach that begins with pixels and works up through lines and eventually gets to applications.

Second, the adoption of GKS as the standard graphics language is of great significance to the teaching of computer graphics. In spite of its faults, GKS provides a conceptual basis for the teaching of computer graphics that is shared by many systems and allows us to teach using tools that can easily be transported to other systems. Just as we do not teach our own locally-developed programming language to our beginning students, I believe we should avoid teaching home-grown graphics software in a first graphics course.

Third, the increased programming skills of both engineers and computer scientists has had a significant effect on this book. Material such as modeling with hierarchical data structures, which most texts leave to the end or completely omit, is well within the abilities of sophomores and juniors in computer science and engineering. The chapters on transformations and hierarchical modeling are core to this book and appear early.

Finally, the expansion of our knowledge in computer graphics has made it likely that there will be at least two courses in computer graphics within most computer science departments. The first will be an introduction covering the range of the field with a significant emphasis on the systems and software engineering aspects of computer graphics. Follow-on courses will emphasize algorithms, geometric modeling, ray tracing, and computational geometry. This book is designed for such a first course.

The choice of the C language and the level of detail on GKS were decisions made after great thought and with the input of a number of people. C provides a nice balance between the desire to provide some abstraction while still being close enough to the machine that implementation issues can be discussed. The fact that it is presently the language of choice by implementors of graphics systems is an added benefit. The level of C used should not present any serious problems to students who know only Pascal or FORTRAN. The level of detail on the GKS C language binding may be more controversial. My experience with other books has been that a lot of class time has been wasted clarifying or correcting sketchy material on some particular graphics language used by the text. I have tried to strike a balance by using a subset of GKS but providing the details for the functions used. Even in courses that do not have an available GKS implementation, I believe it is important to see the details even if the students write no code. For those with other software systems such as PHIGS or some of the commercial systems, the changes necessary to convert the GKS code should be minor.

The first eight chapters form the basis of a one-semester senior course, primarily for computer scientists and computer engineers. The book can be used for a two-semester course by going into more depth on some of the algorithms and doing more than surveying the final two chapters. For courses with a heavy project emphasis, a two-semester (or two quarter) sequence can be obtained by using Chapters 1–5 for the first course and Chapters 6–10 for the second. Chapters 1–4 and probably 5 should be studied in order. Chapters 6–7 and 8–10 are fairly independent of each other.

The book should also be accessible to professional programmers, engineers, computer scientists, and others. The notes that preceded this book are the basis for two four-day intensive short courses, one a survey of computer graphics and the other on GKS, which have been taught to thousands of programmers, engineers, and scientists in the United States and Europe.

I would like to acknowledge a number of people who have helped me not only with this book but also in learning computer graphics. This book started when I returned from sabbatical in 1982 to find there was no one available to teach computer graphics in my department. I thank the University of New Mexico for providing me with that opportunity and the facilities to develop a laboratory in computer graphics. David Collins, Eric Garen, and Anders Amundson of Learning Tree International, Inc. (formerly Integrated Computer Systems, Inc.) gave me the chance to create two short courses. Instructors, including Jim Burk, Mark Henderson, Mike Bailey, and Kelly Booth, and the thousands of participants in these courses provided significant feedback. Many students contributed to early versions of the programs and diagrams in this book. In particular, I wish to thank Mark McLaughlin, Dan Shawver, Mathew Nordhaus, and Joe Higgins. Of the many reviewers of various versions of the manuscript, George Grinstein, University of Lowell; Michael J. Zyda, Naval Postgraduate School; Lewis Hitchner, University of California, Santa Cruz; Spencer W. Thomas, The University of Michigan; Mark Henderson, Arizona State University; and Steve Wampler, Northern Arizona University provided particularly helpful comments. My colleagues John Brayer, Dick Nordhaus, and Bernard Moret were both knowledgeable and patient in filling in gaps in my knowledge in subjects as diverse as TEX, data structures, and architecture (both computer and building design). Rab Hagy and George Schaeffer provided me with the latest versions of the GKS and PHIGS C language bindings at a crucial time. Professors Michael Duff of University College London and Mike Godfrey of Imperial College were extremely generous in providing me with friendship and facilities during my recently completed sabbatical leave.

A few comments on the illustrations in this book are appropriate. Early in this project, Jim DeWolf, of Addison-Wesley, and I agreed that a book on computer graphics should use computer graphics to generate all the figures and that all the figures must be of high quality. With the exception of the color plates, all diagrams were produced on an Apple Macintosh SE by Rose Mary Molnar. Tools range from the use of Aldus Freehand (for most figures), to Super 3D, to the direct production of PostScript files from C programs. A few images, such as the pixel image of my cat Mongo, were created using a Thunder Scanner on an ImageWriter. Hopefully the figures are both informative and illustrate the quality of interactive graphics software presently available. Writing programs to generate the images in some of the figures or to create the kinds of drawing tools needed to produce such images can lead to innumerable interesting programming projects for students.

The people at Addison-Wesley, especially Karen Myer and Mona Zeftel, could not have been more helpful. I will have no author horror stories to share with my colleagues. A final thank you is due to Bob Drake. While Bob was at Addison-Wesley, he promised to (and did) call me once a month to convince me to do this book.

At this point, most authors thank their wives for their patience during the writing of their books. When your spouse is the illustrator of the book, patience is only one of many important and necessary characteristics. Fortunately for me, Rose Mary has so many wonderful qualities we were able to survive this experience.

Edward Angel
University of New Mexico

CONTENTS

9 Working with Polygons   351

OVERVIEW

Introduction

The development of science, technology, the arts, business, and industry has always been dependent on our ability to communicate information, whether via transmission of bits stored on a microchip or through voice conversation. Humans are fortunate to have developed a highly complex visual system. The adage "one picture is worth 10,000 words" is certainly as valid today as it was 100 years ago. It is thus not surprising that almost as soon as the digital computer appeared, researchers attempted to use it to produce images on the screen of a cathode-ray tube. Over the 40 years during which electronic digital computers have evolved, our ability to produce computer-generated images has increased to the point that now even the most basic of computers have some graphics capabilities.

The use of computer graphics pervades many diverse fields. Applications range from the production of charts and graphs, to the generation of realistic images for television and motion pictures to the interactive design of mechanical parts. To encompass all these uses, we can adopt a simple definition:

> *Computer graphics* is concerned with all aspects of using a computer to generate images.

Under this definition, computer graphics includes the design of hardware such as displays, the algorithms that are necessary to generate lines on these displays, the software that is used by both the graphics-system programmer and the application programmer, and the applications of computer-generated images.

We can take many approaches to the study of computer graphics, ranging from examining graphics hardware to study only the use of computer graphics in a specific area, such as very-large-scale-integrated circuit (VLSI) design. Our approach will be to look at the field from the perspective of the application programmer. As better and better hardware and software have become available, the study of computer graphics has become as important to the user of computer graphics as it is to the designer of the graphics system. The modern graphics workstation allows the user to design her own applications using sophisticated graphics systems, rather than having to call on a software wizard. Conversely, the same approach is often valuable to the hardware designer and systems programmer, as they must implement functions that arise from the demands of the application.

Generally, we cannot write applications programs that use computer graphics without some knowledge of implementation issues, lest we expect more from a system than it can produce. We must have an idea of the complete picture: hardware, software, algorithms, and applications. We shall start with the development of user programs, and shall use these as a basis for our discussions of implementation issues.

1.1
Applications of Computer Graphics

We can classify applications of computer graphics into four main areas:

- Display of information
- Design
- Simulation
- User interfaces

Although many applications span two, three, or even all of these areas, the development of the field was based, for the most part, on separate work in each domain.

1.1.1 Display of Information

Graphics has always been associated with the display of information. Examples of the use of orthographic projections to display floorplans of buildings can be found on 4000-year-old Babylonian stone tablets [Carl78]. Mechanical methods for creating perspective drawings were developed during the Renaissance. Countless engineering students have become familiar with interpreting data plotted on log paper. More recently, software packages that allow interactive design of charts incorporating color, multiple data sets, and alternate plotting methods (see Color Plate 1) have become the norm. In fields such as architecture (see Color Plate 2) and mechanical design (see Color Plate 3), hand drafting is being replaced by computer-based drafting systems using plotters and workstations. Medical imaging (see Color Plate 4) uses computer graphics in a number of exciting ways.

Recently there has been great interest in problems of scientific visualization. Although researchers are now using supercomputers to solve formerly intractable problems in fields such as fluid flow (see Color Plate 5) and molecular biology (see Color Plate 6), they need new display techniques to interpret the results of analyzing the vast quantities of multidimensional data generated.

1.1.2 Design

Professions such as engineering and architecture are concerned with design. Although their applications vary, most designers face similar difficulties and use similar methodologies. One of the principal characteristics of most design problems is the lack of a unique solution. Hence, the designer will examine a potential design and then will modify it, possibly many times, in an attempt to achieve a better solution. Computer graphics has become an indispensable element in this iterative process.

Consider for example how computer graphics might enter into the design of an electronic circuit (see Color Plate 7). The designer is seated at a graphics workstation with a graphical input device, such as a mouse, with which she can indicate locations on the display. The initial display screen might consist of the various elements that can be used in the circuit and an empty area in which the circuit will be "constructed." The designer will then use the input device to select and move the desired elements into the design and to make connections between elements. To form this initial design, the system makes sophisticated use of computer graphics. Circuit elements are drawn, and perhaps are moved about the screen. A graphical input device is used to indicate choices and positions. A number of aids may be used to help the designer position the elements accurately and to do automatically such tasks as routing of wires.

At this point, the designer probably will want to test her design. The circuit will be tested by an analysis program, which will display its results (e.g., graphs of voltages versus time) on the workstation. Now the designer can modify the design as necessary, try another design, or accept what has already been done. The designer never had to write a graphics program or even to know much about computer graphics; yet, without computer graphics, this design process would not be possible.

1.1.3 Simulation

Some of the most impressive and familiar uses of computer graphics can be classified as simulations. Video games demonstrate both the visual appeal of computer graphics and our ability to generate complex imagery in real time. The insides of an arcade game reveal state-of-the-art hardware and software. Computer-generated images are also the heart of flight simulators (see Color Plate 8), which have become the standard method for training pilots. The savings in dollars and lives realized from use of these simulators has been enormous. The computer-generated images we see on television and in movies (see Color Plate 9) have advanced to the point that they are almost indistinguishable from real-world images.

1.1.4 User Interfaces

The interface between the human and the computer has been radically altered by the use of computer graphics. Consider the electronic office. The figures in this book were produced through just such an interface (see Color Plate 10). A secretary sits at a workstation, rather than at a desk equipped with a typewriter. This user has a pointing device, such as a mouse, that allows him to communicate with the workstation. The display consists of a number of icons that represent the various operations the secretary can perform. For example, there might be an icon of a mailbox that, if pointed to and clicked on, causes any electronic-mail messages to appear on the screen. An icon of a wastepaper basket allows the user to dispose of unwanted mail, whereas an icon of a file cabinet is used to save letters or other documents.

A similar graphical interface would be part of our circuit-design system, discussed in Section 1.1.2. Within the context of this book, we see these interfaces as being obvious uses of computer graphics. From the perspective of the secretary using the office-automation system or of the circuit designer, however, the graphics is a secondary aspect of the task to be done. Although they never write graphics programs, multitudes of computer users use computer graphics.

1.2
The Development of Computer Graphics

1.2.1   1950 to 1960

The first examples of computer graphics appeared in the earliest days of the modern computer era. In the early 1950s, workers at the Massachusetts Institute of Technology used a computer to control the deflection of an electron beam in a cathode-ray tube (CRT). A simplified picture of a CRT is in Figure 1.1 When electrons strike the phosphor coating on the tube, light is emitted. The position of the beam is controlled by two pairs of deflection plates. The output of the computer is converted, by digital-to-analog converters, to voltages across the x and y deflection plates. Light can be made to appear on the surface of the CRT by directing a sufficiently intense beam of electrons at the phosphor. If the voltages steering the beam change at a constant rate, the beam will trace a straight line, visible to a viewer. This device is known as the *random-scan* or *calligraphic* CRT because the beam can be moved directly from any position to any other position. If the beam intensity is turned off, the beam can be moved to a new position without causing any visible display.

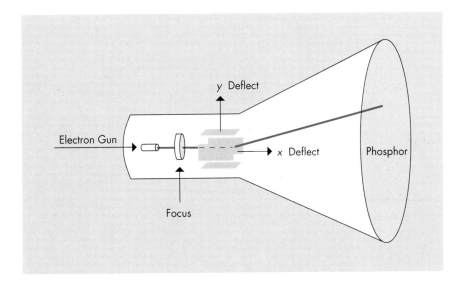

Figure 1.1
The Cathode Ray Tube

The CRT will emit light for only a very short time after the phosphor is excited by the electron beam. For a human to see a steady image on most CRT displays, the same path must be followed by the beam at least 50 times per second. Early digital computers could not compute the necessary voltages fast enough to generate complex pictures. This limitation, coupled with the high cost of early computers, at first stymied the development of computer graphics; subsequent developments, however, have made the CRT the standard output device on most systems.

1.2.2 1960 to 1970

During the 1960s a number of events dramatically changed the picture. The direct-view storage tube (DVST) became the standard low-cost output device. The DVST, although not a permanent storage device, could retain an image on its screen for hours, thus relieving the computer of the necessity of updating the display continually. This device was packaged as a terminal that used special character sequences to invoke its graphics capabilities. The device's relatively low cost and its portability as a terminal allowed the development of basic graphics packages, such as PLOT10, which could be transported from system to system.

The DVST is not a real-time device. Just like a line drawn on a piece of paper remains there until it is erased, all the output of a DVST is retained until the screen is completely cleared. Altering parts of an image, or animating them, is not possible with such a device. The development of the *display processor* allowed the generation of interactive real-time graphics on the random-scan CRT. The display processor is a special-purpose computer with a limited set of instructions that it can execute quickly. Primary among its tasks is to keep

Figure 1.2
Display Processor
Architecture

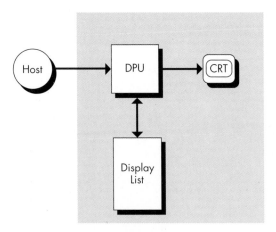

the CRT refreshed at a rate that makes the display appear smooth and flicker-free. Graphical entities that are defined on the host are placed in a special memory called the *display memory* or *display file*, which is accessed by the *display processing unit* (DPU), as in Figure 1.2. The host computer then needs to define graphical primitives only once. Once these primitives are sent on to the display processor, the host is free for other tasks. The functions of the display processor are incorporated in most present graphics systems, although advances in technology have allowed the functionality of the earliest systems to be reduced to one or two chips.

The display processor made possible other tasks, such as a user's interaction with the displayed image. Project Sketchpad [Suth63] demonstrated the potential of such a system, and researchers began a thorough examination of the issues involved. The importance of data structures for graphics was recognized, algorithms were developed, and the paradigms that characterize modern computer graphics were formulated.

1.2.3 1970 to 1980

The next era of computer graphics, which corresponds roughly with the 1970s, was characterized by the advent of *raster graphics*. Reductions in the cost of solid-state memory made it feasible to construct systems that used a raster-scan CRT. In raster graphics, the image is stored as an array of picture elements, or *pixels* (Figure 1.3), rather than as a set of line segments, as it is with random-scan displays. The pixels are stored in a special memory area, known as the *frame buffer*. The display hardware scans the frame buffer, usually at a rate of 50 to 70 scans per second, refreshing the display line by line, much in the way commercial television images are produced. Graph-

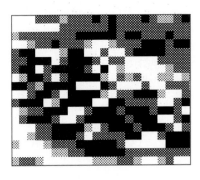

Figure 1.3
Pixels

ical output primitives, such as line segments and text, are displayed by turning on or off pixels in the frame buffer that approximate the primitive. This process is known as *scan conversion* or *rasterization*. Many scan-conversion algorithms were developed during this period.

The ability to build fast small computers at a low cost resulted in the *personal computer* and the forerunners of the modern workstation. In these architectures, the frame buffer was part of the memory of the computer, so the graphics display, rather than being a peripheral device, became an integral part of the computer. The ability to network these machines opened up many new possibilities in both hardware and software. Special-purpose systems for computer-aided design (CAD) became widespread. New ways of interacting with the computer, such as through mouse-controlled menu-driven interfaces, were developed in the 1970s.

The widespread use of computer graphics sparked considerable interest in the development of a standard graphics programming language. Two groups were formed, both of which issued draft standards in 1977 and second versions in 1979. The European group produced the Graphical Kernel System (GKS); the United States group developed the CORE system. The culmination of these projects came when GKS was adopted by the International Standards Organization (ISO) [GKS84] in 1984. Formal adoption of GKS by the American National Standards Institute (ANSI) followed soon after. We shall use GKS for our programming examples.

1.2.4 1980 to the Present

During the 1980s, the focus shifted somewhat. Powerful graphics workstations have become the standard tool of engineers, scientists, graphic artists, and architects. Such workstations not only place enormous computing power in the hands of the user, but also provide a powerful set of graphical tools—such as libraries of graphics routines and easy-to-use visual interfaces—and access to diverse capabilities through networking. Workstations used for scientific visualization can produce images from simulations at speeds close to those previously associated with supercomputers. Users of CAD systems now work with interactive solid modelers. Animators and commercial artists can produce photorealistic images using commercially available hardware and software.

Although progress continues in algorithm development, in software standards, in hardware capabilities, and in many other areas of computer graphics, there is general acceptance of the theoretical and practical foundations of the field. We anticipate many new and exciting developments, yet we pursue our applications with the confidence that our basic tools are well established and will continue to be relevant in the future.

1.3
A Basic Graphics System

Let us consider the organization of a typical graphics system we might use. As our initial emphasis will be on how the applications programmer sees the system, we shall omit details of the hardware. A block diagram of our system is shown in Figure 1.4. There are four key types of elements in our system:

- A processor
- Memory
- Output devices
- Input devices

The model is general enough to include workstations, personal computers, terminals attached to a central time-shared computer, and sophisticated image-generation systems. In most ways, this block diagram is that of a standard computer. How each element is specialized for computer graphics will characterize this diagram as one of a graphics system, rather than one of a general-purpose computer.

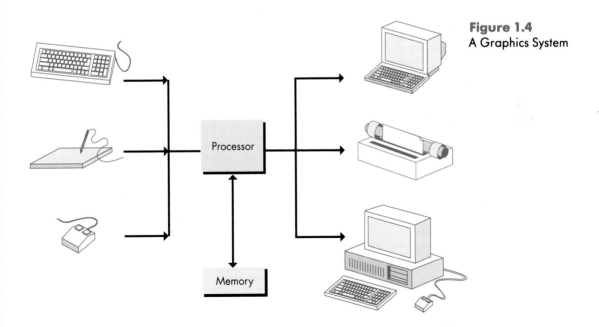

Figure 1.4
A Graphics System

1.3.1 The Processor

Within the processor box, two types of processing take place. The first is *picture formation* processing. In this stage, the user program or commands are processed. The picture is formed from the elements (lines, text) available in the system using the desired attributes, such as line color and text font. The user interface is a part of this processing.

The picture can be specified in a number of ways, such as through an interactive menu-controlled painting program or via a C program using a graphics library. The physical processor used in this stage is often the processor in the workstation or host computer.

The second kind of processing is concerned with the *display of the picture*. In a raster system, the specified primitives must be scan converted. The screen must be refreshed to avoid flicker. Input from the user might require objects to be repositioned on the display. The kind of processor best suited for these jobs is not the standard type of processor found in most computers. Instead, special boards and chips are often used. As we have already noted, one of the elements that distinguishes real-time graphics systems is their use of display processors. Since we have agreed to stay at the block-diagram level for now, however, we shall not explore these architectures in any detail until later.

1.3.2 Memory

There are often two distinct types of memory employed in graphics systems. For the processing of the user program, the memory is similar to that of a standard computer, as the picture is formed by a standard type of arithmetic processing. Display processing, however, requires high-speed display memory that can be accessed by the display processor, and, in raster systems, memory for the frame buffer. This display memory usually is different in both its physical characteristics and its organization from what is used by the picture processor. At this point, we need not consider details of how memory can be organized. You should be aware that the way the internals of our processor and memory boxes are organized distinguishes a slow system from a real-time picture-generating system, such as a flight simulator. However, from our present perspective, we shall emphasize that all implementations have to do the same kinds of tasks to produce output.

1.3.3 Output Devices

Our basic system has one or more output devices. As raster displays are the dominant type, we shall assume there is a raster-scan CRT on our system. We shall consider the frame buffer to be part of the display memory. In a self-contained system such as a workstation, the display is an integral part of the system, so the transfer of information from the processor to the display will happen rapidly. When the display is separate, such as with a graphics terminal, the speed of the connection is much slower. Terminals with raster displays usually must have their own frame buffers, so the displays can be refreshed locally. In our simple system, we might also have other displays, such as a plotter, to allow us to produce hardcopy.

1.3.4 Input Devices

A simple system may have only a keyboard to provide whatever input is necessary. Keyboards provide digital codes corresponding to sequences of keystrokes by a user. These sequences are usually interpreted as codes for characters. If individual keystrokes or groups of keystrokes are interpreted as graphical input, the keyboard can be used as a complex input device. For example, the "arrow" keys available on most keyboards can be used to direct the movement of a cursor on the screen. Most graphics systems will provide at least one other input device. The most common are the mouse, the lightpen, the joystick, and the data tablet. Each can provide positional information to the system and each usually is equipped with one or more buttons to provide signals to the processor.

From the programmer's perspective, there are numerous important issues with regard to the input and output devices. We must consider how the program can communicate with these devices. We must decide what kinds of input and output can be produced. We will be interested in how to control multiple devices, so that we can choose a particular device for our input, and can direct our output to some group of the available output devices.

1.4
Graphics Software

Since our initial focus is writing graphics programs, we shall address a number of software-related issues. How does an application user access the software in a graphics system? What jobs must the software do? We will consider these questions initially from the point of view of an applications programmer who may want to write a plotting program or to design a circuit-layout package.

There are a number of possible configurations for a graphics system. Each will affect the kind of software that can be developed, and how this software must be written. The three major types of systems, all of which have the elements described in the previous section, are terminals connected to a host; self-contained units, such as personal computers and workstations; and special-purpose high-speed systems, such as flight simulators.

1.4.1 Terminal-Based Software

Until recently, most computer graphics was produced using graphics terminals connected to a host computer. Perhaps the most important characteristic of such a configuration is the slow path between the host and the display. Slow graphical output devices, such as film recorders and plotters, have many of the same characteristics. On such systems, images cannot be constructed or altered quickly, so our ability to do real-time interactive graphics is limited. Raster operations are also limited by the time it takes to send large groups of pixels to the display. It is still possible to receive input from most devices, as this input is not very dense—for example, it might be a location received from a data tablet.

The user software for such systems is most often in the form of a library of functions or procedures that can invoke the basic capabilities of the input and output devices. For example, there are procedures that draw lines and circles, read the position of a mouse, and clear the screen. Users construct graphics programs by invoking procedures from a library. Consider a C program with a statement in it such as

```
plot(x_array,y_array,n);
```

This procedure might plot two n-dimensional arrays, `x_array` and `y_array`. The arrays would be formed and scaled in the part of the user program preceding such a call. The procedure call

```
mouse(x,y);
```

might return the position of the mouse, which could then be used in the program. The user program sees the graphics only through these procedures. A programmer could either use these library functions in her main program or create higher-level programs or subprograms that would be based on what is in the graphics library. For example, in Chapter 3, we shall develop a self-scaling plotting procedure that takes user data, axis labels, and a title, and builds an x,y plot. This procedure is invoked by a single user call, but is built on the lower-level functions in the graphics library.

1.4.2 Turnkey Software

Much graphics software is now completely *turnkey*. The user does not need to write a program. Instead, the user interacts with a display that consists of menus, icons, work areas, and other information. The user constructs graphical displays by using an input device, such as a mouse, to communicate with the system. Such an interface has significant benefits as compared to the traditional methods, such as writing programs. Much of the use of computer graphics on workstations and on other self-contained units is done in this way. As the display must be changed constantly, this type of graphics is not possible on terminal-based configurations. On specialized high-speed systems such as video games and flight simulators, the user interface with the system is similar: It consists of an interaction between the user and the graphics display, rather than the processing of programs written by the user. However, from our perspective, we must recognize that someone must write an interactive graphics program, which is the turnkey program that other people will use. To write this program, we will have to use tools such as a graphics library. The graphics libraries on such systems include procedures to access the special features of these systems.

1.5 The Rest of the Book

In the next chapter, we shall discuss fundamental ideas underlying modern computer graphics. Then, we shall look at computer graphics as applications programmers and as users. Chapters 3 and 4 will provide the basics for writing two-dimensional programs—first with only output, then with interaction. We shall use GKS for our examples, but will emphasize the similarities between GKS and other modern graphics systems. In discussing writing applications using a high-level device-independent system, usually we shall not distinguish between the writer of the application and the user of the program. In studying computer graphics, the two are often the same person.

Chapter 5 focuses on transformations. Transformations not only provide the basis for high-level applications involving interactive graphics, but also are crucial for implementing graphics systems. We shall discuss the use of hierarchical models to represent relationships in an application, and shall introduce the PHIGS system.

In Chapter 6, we shall turn to the implementation of graphics systems. Our approach will be to follow a primitive from its definition within an application program to its display on a hardware device, such as a CRT. We shall examine those operations from previous chapters that are transparent both to the user and to the writer of an application program. We shall discuss how simple hardware devices operate, and how the hardware and software communicate.

Our discussion of raster systems in Chapter 7 includes both implementation and application issues. If we are to make full use of such systems, we cannot, at least at this time, separate certain device-specific properties from the writing of application programs. We shall also examine aspects of human vision—in particular, color perception—so that we can make better use of the color available on many raster workstations.

The presentation of three-dimensional graphics in Chapter 8 will be based on extending the results of the previous chapters. Our emphasis will be on writing application programs with three-dimensional device-independent software. However, in order to write such programs, first we must develop a three-dimensional viewing model and a three-dimensional transformation capability. We will examine also the relationship between traditional viewing and computer graphics.

The final two chapters provide an introduction to advanced topics in computer graphics. We discuss how to provide realism both in the graphics produced and in the underlying application models. Chapter 9 works primarily with polygons, and uses them to produce approximations to realistic scenes that require hidden-surface removal and rendering. Chapter 10 examines what happens when we move away from linear entities, such as lines and planes, and work with curves and surfaces.

Although the C language is used for all codes, we have attempted to keep the examples as clear and simple as possible, even where more efficient code could have been written. The details of the C language binding of GKS, including the necessary structures, are presented in Appendices A and B.

▰▰ 1.6
▰▰ Suggested Readings

Computer graphics books reflect the development of the field. The text by Newman and Sproull [New73] was the first to incorporate most of the modern viewpoint on computer graphics. It was followed by the book by Foley and Van Dam [Foley82], which was the standard text for many years. Hearn and Baker's work [Hearn86] reflects some of the more recent advances and the influence of GKS. Image generation systems such as flight simulators are surveyed in [Sch83]. A guide to the literature until the early 1980s is presented in [Mach83], and yearly bibliographies are published in *Computer Graphics* [CG]. Readers unfamiliar with C should consult [Ker88] or one of a multitude of C books. The book by Tufte [Tufte83] provides a fascinating introduction to the graphical display of information.

■ Exercises

1.1 Identify a problem in your own field that could be solved in part with computer graphics. You must choose the properties that your graphics system will have. Describe a set of graphical primitives that would help you solve the problem.

1.2 The choice of a set of primitives for a graphics systems usually is based on the *principle of orthogonality,* which states that we should not be able to construct any primitive from the others. Does a system whose primitives include lines, characters, polygons, and circles obey this principle?

1.3 In computer programs written in high-level languages, such as FORTRAN or C, any required user input is normally in the form of strings of characters. For a program using computer graphics, what other forms of input would you consider appropriate?

1.4 Suppose we have a screen that can display 256 colors simultaneously and that is 512 by 512 pixels. How much memory is required to make full use of this display? How does the required memory change as we increase the resolution (number of pixels per row or column) of the display? If the screen has to be redrawn 60 times per second, at what rate must pixels be processed by the display processor?

1.5 An active area of computer research is parallel architectures. In a parallel system, there are multiple processors concurrently working on the same user program. Where do you think parallelism might enter in computer graphics?

2

FUNDAMENTAL Ideas

Introduction

In this chapter, we shall introduce the conceptual foundations of modern computer graphics. Some of the notions are mathematical, others are philosophical. Some you will recognize, others will be new. As a whole, they will provide the basis for developing not only the Graphical Kernel System (GKS), which we shall introduce in the following chapter, but also most modern graphics systems.

2.1
A Simple Plotting Procedure

We start by considering the output of the plotting procedure we shall develop in Chapter 3. Typical output is shown in Figure 2.1. The program will take the form of a function `plot,` which will allow a user

Rain in Spain

Altitude

Rainfall

Figure 2.1
Plot Program Output

to enter n points of x,y data, labels for the axes, and a title for the plot. A skeleton for this procedure simulates what we might do if we were to sketch the plot by hand using pencil and paper:

```
plot( n, x, y, xlabel, ylabel, title)

int n; /* number of points*/
float *x, *y; /* x and y data arrays */
char *xlabel, *ylabel, *title;
{
        draw_axes(.....);
        plot_data(.....);
        label_axes(.....);
        draw_title(.....);
}
```

To write this function, we must first address three underlying issues:

- With what primitives do we work?

- How do we describe and manipulate these primitives?

- How do we describe the picture we would like to produce?

In this simple example, we can restrict ourselves to two primitives: line segments and strings of characters. We can use line segments for our axes and to connect the data points. Some calculations are necessary to fit the plot into the desired area on the display and to compute the positions of various line segments. We need some mathematics to do these calculations, and we shall develop what we need.

First we must solve the even more fundamental conceptual problem of deciding how to envision the process of forming a picture. In our plotting example, we start with data. These data are given as pairs of numbers in a coordinate system that depends on the original problem that generated them. To form a picture or image, we must scale the data to fit in the desired part of the display. The titles may also have to be scaled to fit in the picture. Since the picture eventually appears on a physical device, such as a CRT or a plotter, there must be a coordinate conversion from the units of the problem to the units of the output device. Since our picture is composed of various distinct elements, we also need a method to describe and manipulate these objects to form our picture. This need is common to both traditional and computer graphics.

2.2
Image Formation

Both traditional and computer graphics are concerned with the creation of pictures. We shall extend standard image-formation techniques to our study of computer graphics. The connection between
modern computer graphics and the more traditional methods of picture formation such as painting and photography is a strong one.
Consider the making of a photograph, as in Figure 2.2. We have two
distinct entities in the process: the world, which consists of objects
such as the house, the trees, and grass; and the viewer of these objects,
the camera. What is in our photograph will be determined only when
we know everything about both the camera (where it is, what lens
is on it, and in what direction it is pointing) and the objects (their
positions, their orientations, and their surface properties). If we move
the camera, the picture recorded on the film must change, as it will if
we move any of the objects.

The result of the picture-formation process is an image that appears on the film. A similar process will be involved in describing
the image formed by a painter or what we find in the image plane of
a telescope. The mathematics of how objects that exist in a three-
dimensional world and a viewer that has to be positioned in this world

Figure 2.2
Making A Picture

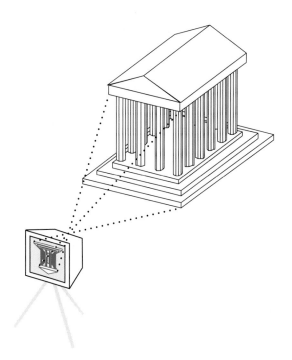

are combined to form an image that is two-dimensional will be discussed in Chapter 8, and need not concern us yet.

Classical graphics starts with the two entities: the world of objects, and a viewer who wishes to form an image of these objects. In Figure 2.3 we picture this image-formation process for a human observer, rather than for a camera. Little has changed, except that the optics of the eye replace those of the camera. The image is formed on the retina, a sensing structure located at the back of the eye. Both the retina and the film at the back of our camera have a finite size. The image that is formed cannot be infinite in extent. For human vision, what we see in the image is everything that lies in a cone whose apex is at the eye. For the camera, the cone of vision is replaced by a pyramid, since the back of the camera is a rectangle.

A slightly different conceptual view of image formation is in Figure 2.4, where now the image plane has been moved in front of the camera. The major difference here is that the image is now right side up, which is often easier to conceptualize. The image can be thought of as being formed by lines drawn from the apex of the viewing pyramid—known as the *center of projection*—to all points on the object. Where one such line, called a *projector*, intersects the image plane, or *projection* plane, is where the image of the point on the object is located, as in Figure 2.5. An equivalent picture is shown

Figure 2.3
Human Image Formation

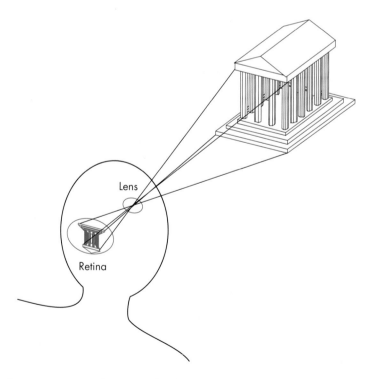

Lens

Retina

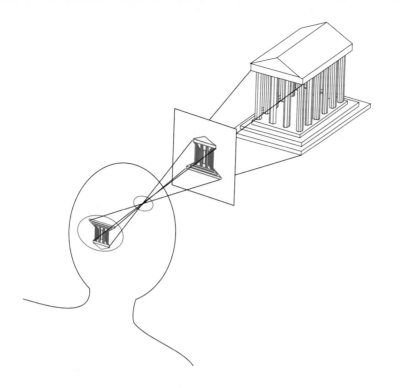

Figure 2.4
Moving the Projection
Plane

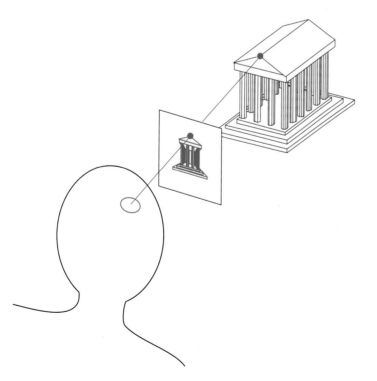

Figure 2.5
Images and Projections

2.2   Image Formation   21

Figure 2.6
Windows

Figure 2.7
Changing the Window

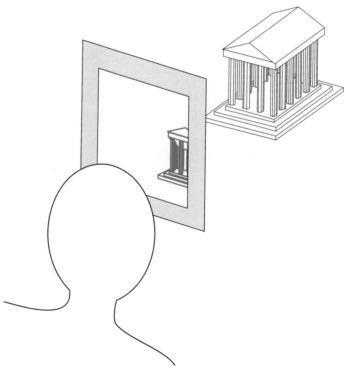

in Figure 2.6, where we see that this viewing procedure is similar to simply looking through a window. What we see in the window must be finite; when we move either the viewer or the window, a different image appears in the window (Figure 2.7). Making a picture with a computer follows a procedure so similar to the one we have just described that it has become known in computer graphics as the *synthetic camera analogy.*

2.3
The Synthetic Camera

2.3.1 Separating the Viewer from the Objects

When we think of taking a picture with a camera, and of other picture-formation processes (such as painting, using a telescope, or simply looking at something with the eye), we may think of imaging as combining objects with a viewer. It was not clear in the early days of computer graphics how to apply this notion to the writing of graphics programs. Early graphics-programming languages required that the user specify the picture directly through functions that emulated the actual drawing of the picture. A program fragment for a pen plotter looked something like

```
pen_up();
move_pen(x1,y1);
pen_down();
move_pen(x2,y2);
```

The two locations (x_1, y_1) and (x_2, y_2) were in units of the pen plotter (centimeters or inches). The program caused the plotter to lower the pen. Then, by moving the pen from (x_1, y_1) to (x_2, y_2), a line segment was drawn connecting these points, as in Figure 2.8.

Figure 2.8
Pen Plotter Model

If we return to Figure 2.2, we can see some of the problems that this mechanism left to the programmer. The objects are in a three-dimensional world, as is the camera. To compute the positions (x_1, y_1) and (x_2, y_2) the programmer had to work through the mathematics of projection or image formation. Thus, to draw a simple line, she had to do complex trigonometric calculations. Leaving this calculation to the user not only required that the user add a considerable amount of code, but also was a conceptually poor way to go about developing graphics software. Consider for example, what happens if we move the camera in such a system. The application program has to calculate all new positions in units of the pen plotter. So the simple conceptual idea of letting the camera roam about the scene became potentially a laborious task.

2.3 The Synthetic Camera   23

Figure 2.9
Moving Both Objects and
the Viewer

The alternative is to use the synthetic camera analogy and to provide a graphics system that treats the viewer and the objects separately. Of course, the calculations to find where on the pen plotter the lines will appear will have to be done. In the modern systems, however, they are done within the graphics system. This is the importance of the synthetic camera analogy: The applications programmer specifies independent object and viewing conditions. Picture formation, which combines these specifications, is the job of the graphics system.

The body of a graphics program consists mainly of two distinct kinds of statements: those that describe the viewer and those that describe the objects. Even though we have not yet presented a single actual graphics function, you should be able to envision the structure of a program that yields successive images of a moving object, such as a car, taken by a viewer located on another moving object, such as a bicycle. A sequence of pictures might appear as shown in Figure 2.9. The pseudocode might be something like

```
describe_bicycle(); /* the viewer */
describe_automobile(); /* a moving object */
describe_background(); /* non-moving objects */
while(desire_new_images)
{
 move_bicycle();
 move_automobile();
 output_new_image();
}
```

The output_new_image function tells the graphics system to take the present object and viewer specifications and to combine these data to produce a new image on the display. The details of how this combining is done are transparent to the applications program.

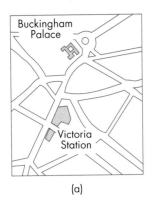  

Figure 2.10
Two Dimensional Viewing
(a) Two Dimensional
World. (b) World Through
Window. (c) Image.

(a)   (b)   (c)

2.3.2 Two-Dimensional Viewing

In two dimensions, the viewing problem is easier, both conceptually and mathematically. Objects can all be considered to exist in a flat, two-dimensional world. Line segments are then specified by their endpoints, (x_1, y_1) and (x_2, y_2). There is no notion of an object (or part of an object) being in a plane farther away from the viewer than is another object, since all objects are in the same plane. Viewing reduces to specifying what part of the object plane the viewer can see. We can envision this operation by considering a wall between the viewer and the object plane, as in Figure 2.10, with a rectangular opening called a *window* placed in the wall. Whatever is visible to the viewer through this window is part of the picture or image. If the window is made bigger, more of the object plane will be visible, possibly bringing additional objects into the picture. If it is shifted, a different part of an object or different objects may appear in the picture, as in Figure 2.11. The two fundamental procedures in a user program are a function `line`, which allows us to describe simple objects, and a function `window`, which allows us to specify a rectangular window, by giving its lower-left and upper-right corners. A program thus has the form

```
window(xmin, xmax, ymin, ymax);
line( x1, y1, x2, y2);
line( x2, y2, x3, y3);
line( x4, y4, x5, y5);
        .
        .
        .
        .
line( xN, yN, xN, yN);
```

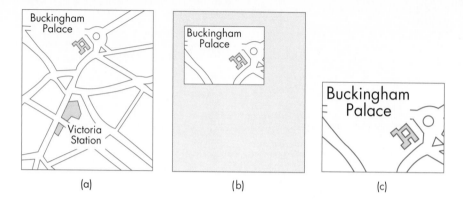

(a)   (b)   (c)

2.3.3 Device Independence

Another notion that follows from the synthetic camera analogy is
that of *device independence*. In our first example, we used a single
function, move_pen. Although this approach might seem better than
using two functions, window and line, on closer examination we see
that it is not. The function move_pen combines the viewing and object
specifications in a single command. The units of the parameters x and
y are those of the output device. We noted then that a user must do all
the calculations necessary to compute these values. If a new display
with a different size, or one that works in different units, is employed,
these calculations must be changed in the user's program.

Contrast this process to what happens when we use window and
line. Here, the parameters in these functions are those of the problem. The image-formation process that takes these parameters (which
are in the units of the problem), and constructs the picture (which
is in the coordinates of the output device), is done by the graphics
package and is not the concern of the user program. Not only has
this programming paradigm saved the user considerable work, but in
addition, since nowhere in the user program is there anything that is
in units of the output device, this program is *device independent*. The
program not only can be written more easily, as it is in the units natural to the particular problem, but also is transportable, as it contains
nothing specific to any output device that might be on the particular
system used.

2.4
Device-Independent Software

The synthetic camera analogy makes it possible to write a device-
independent graphics package. In this section, we shall examine the
structure of such a package in more detail. We shall describe the

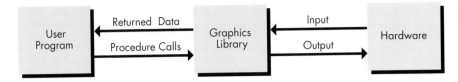

Figure 2.12
The Programmer's Model

kinds of functions that should be available, and implications of device independence for these functions.

Our model of a graphic program is that of a user-written application program that uses a graphics library, as in Figure 2.12. We have introduced two types of functions: object specification and viewing. In a complete package, we will need more. There will be control functions to initialize and terminate the graphics system and its devices. There will be functions that allow us to alter how primitives are displayed. We have not discussed input functions, which must be present if we are to write interactive programs. Functions of these types will be available, and even necessary, in most graphics packages. For now, however, we can restrict ourselves to the viewing and object functions, since they form the core of the graphics code in simple programs.

One benefit of the synthetic camera analogy is that it allows us to have the coordinates of our function expressed in the units of the user's problem. Because these functions describe objects and a viewer that exist in the world of the problem, this user coordinate system is known as the *world coordinate* (WC) system. In our previous example, parameters in both the `line` and `window` procedures were expressed in world coordinates. An important observation is that, in most systems, world coordinates must be real or floating-point numbers, to allow users to employ units ranging from microns (as in a VLSI design problem) to meters (as in an architectural layout). The use of floating-point numbers can have a significant effect on the implementation of the system.

At the output end are the physical devices, such as graphics terminals and plotters. These devices must be given the correct signals to enable them to produce graphical output. As these devices differ from one another, we should not be surprised that the values that describe positions to these devices differ from device to device. For instance, a raster terminal would have positions on its screen described by integer locations in its frame buffer, whereas a pen plotter might require its input to be in inches. The coordinate system for the output (and input) devices is called the *device coordinate* (DC) system, and may differ for each device.

A coordinate transformation is required to map values specified by the user (in WC) to device coordinates. This is one of the internal jobs of the graphics system. Since, in general, a real system will have a variety of output and input devices, it might appear that the

Figure 2.13
Coordinate
Transformations

graphics package is internally keeping track of many DC systems. The approach taken in most implementations is to use an intermediate coordinate system, known as the *normalized device coordinate* (NDC) system, for most of the work.

We can understand the use of NDC by considering the advantages of designing a graphics package for a single output device. A single device allows us to have a single transformation from the user coordinate system to device coordinates. Software can be developed for this device and transported to other installations. Pictures that are represented in terms of this device's coordinate system can be stored and transported in pictorial form, rather than the programs that produced the pictures being transported. Of course, the problem is that real output devices have many different coordinate systems. However, if we pick one theoretical or *virtual* device, we can write most of the necessary software in terms of this virtual device. The usual virtual device is a unit square in NDC space, which has its lower-left corner at the origin (Figure 2.13).

Values in units of the virtual device are transformed to values in the DC system at the last stage of processing. This final transformation from the NDC of our virtual device to DC is done in a piece of software known as a *device driver*. In a well designed system, as new devices are added or old ones replaced, it is relatively easy to add a new device driver without altering the body of the graphics package. We now have two layers of transformations, as in Figure 2.13, the first from the user's WC system to NDC, and the second from NDC space to DC. The example demonstrates a physical device in which the y direction is ordered from top to bottom, a not-uncommon choice in raster systems. When we consider graphical input, we shall reverse the transformations. Physical input will be in DC. This input will be transformed first to NDC space and then to WC.

2.5
Windows and Viewports

A position that is specified in WC will be mapped or transformed to a corresponding point in NDC. The necessary information to construct this transformation is contained in the specification of the window we introduced in Section 2.3. Before we derive the necessary equations, we shall add some flexibility to our graphics through the use of a *viewport*. We shall consider a two-dimensional world for now.

We often want to display more than a single picture on our output device. We have already seen examples where parts of the display are used for the user interface, and other parts are used for the graphics

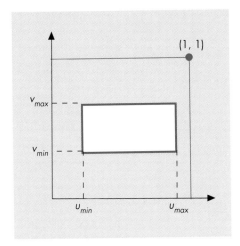

Figure 2.14
The Viewport

the user will generate. The desire to use only part of the screen for a given image can affect the WC-to-NDC mapping in a number of ways. One approach is to alter this mapping such that objects are mapped to a part of NDC space that will be mapped to the desired part of the output device. This method can be somewhat unwieldy, and also tends to be incompatible with our device-independent approach. A better technique is to specify which part of the screen we wish to allocate for a given image, independently of the WC window.

A viewport is a subarea of NDC space. A window in WC is mapped to a viewport in NDC, as in Figure 2.14. The viewport is specified by a function such as

```
viewport(u_min, u_max, v_min, v_max);
```

This is a second viewing procedure. Unlike in the **window** function, the parameters for the viewport are specified in NDC space. The four values must satisfy

$$0 \le u_{min} < u_{max} \le 1,$$
$$0 \le v_{min} < v_{max} \le 1,$$

since the virtual screen in NDC space is a unit square with the origin in the lower-left corner.

We can now derive the mapping that corresponds to this program fragment:

```
window(x_min, x_max, y_min, y_max);
viewport(u_min, u_max, v_min, v_max);
line( x1, y1, x2, y2);
```

Figure 2.15
Mapping a Line Segment

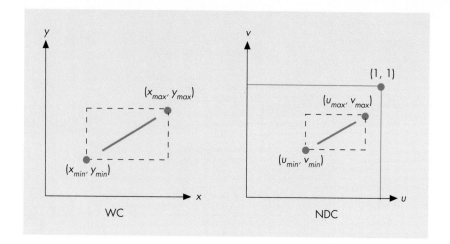

Although only the `window` and `viewport` functions determine the transformation, it is the line segment between (x_1, y_1) and (x_2, y_2) that must be transformed to a line segment between (u_1, v_1) and (u_2, v_2) in NDC space, as shown in Figure 2.15.

For a given window–viewport pair, the transformation will be the same for all WC points. We can derive the transformation by considering a generic point, (x, y), in WC, and by mapping that point to its image, (u, v), in NDC, as in Figure 2.16. We must maintain the same proportions in both spaces. A point in the middle of the WC window must be mapped to the midpoint of the viewport. The equations of proportionality can be written independently in the x and y directions:

$$\frac{x - x_{min}}{x_{max} - x_{min}} = \frac{u - u_{min}}{u_{max} - u_{min}},$$
$$\frac{y - y_{min}}{y_{max} - y_{min}} = \frac{v - v_{min}}{v_{max} - v_{min}}.$$

These equations can be solved for (u, v), yielding

$$u = u_{min} + \frac{u_{max} - u_{min}}{x_{max} - x_{min}}(x - x_{min}),$$
$$v = v_{min} + \frac{v_{max} - v_{min}}{y_{max} - y_{min}}(y - y_{min}).$$

Each point in a `line` procedure is transformed by these equations to determine a line segment in NDC space. We considered the simplest

Figure 2.16
The WC to NDC Mapping

case in Figure 2.16, where both endpoints of the line segment lie inside the window. If one or both endpoints of the line segment lie outside the window, as in Figure 2.17, we must decide what to do. In virtually all graphics systems, the part of the line that lies outside the window is discarded in the display process. We say the line is *clipped* to the window. Later, we shall develop algorithms for clipping. For now, you should assume that all primitives will be clipped automatically, as one of the functions the graphics system must perform for the user.

A similar pair of equations describes the transformation of the point (u, v) to a point (r, s) in DC for a particular output device. For example, suppose we have a raster display whose lower-left corner has coordinates (r_{min}, s_{min}) and whose upper-right corner has coordinates (r_{max}, s_{max}), as in Figure 2.18. The mapping to device coordinates is then

$$r = r_{min} + \frac{r_{max} - r_{min}}{u_{max} - u_{min}}(u - u_{min}),$$

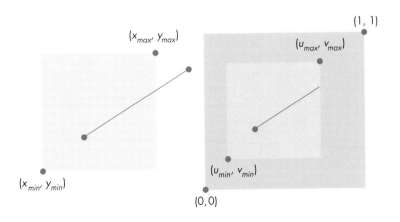

Figure 2.17
Clipping

2.5 Windows and Viewports **31**

Figure 2.18
The Mapping to Device
Coordinates

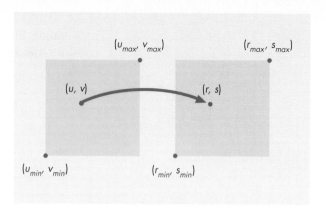

$$ s \;=\; s_{min} + \frac{s_{max} - s_{min}}{v_{max} - v_{min}}(v - v_{min}). $$

There are many aspects of these equations that are important to the implementor, such as how we use them most efficiently and where in the process of producing an image they are applied. Such issues will be examined when we discuss implementation in Chapter 6.

2.6 Positioning

We now have the rudiments of a graphics package: a line function for object specification and window and viewport functions for specifying the desired viewing conditions. Before we move on to describing GKS, a powerful graphics system we can use to produce sophisticated inter-active programs, we shall find it beneficial to examine different ways to do a simple task such as specifying a line segment. One reason to pause at this point and to consider alternatives is that, once we begin to discuss a particular system (in our case, GKS), there is a tendency for readers to assume that its way of doing some operation is the only way. This assumption can limit us severely by making us not seek other, possibly better, alternatives for a particular problem.
    Consider the line function

```
line( x1, y1, x2, y2);
```

We have used this procedure to define a line segment from (x_1, y_1) to (x_2, y_2). There are two important points here. First, the position information is specified absolutely in WC. Second, all the information about the line is the single call to `line`. For a single line segment, these choices might seem natural. However, consider the specification of the box in Figure 2.19. The program fragment

```
line( x1, y1, x1, y2);
line( x1, y2, x2, y2);
line( x2, y2, x2, y1);
line( x2, y1, x1, y1);
```

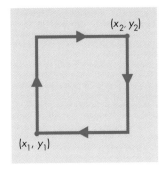

Figure 2.19
Box

describes the box by tracing its border in a clockwise direction. We see the repeated appearance of the data points, which might be a bit annoying, especially if we want to describe more complex objects. We can also see that, if we want to do something such as shifting our box to a new position, we will have to alter every call to `line`. These considerations lead us to inquire whether absolute positioning is either the most natural or the optimum way to describe our box—or any other object.

Now consider the street map in Figure 2.20. We could describe the path from any point to any other point as a sequence of lines, specified as in our `line` function. However, this path description is almost certainly not the way we would describe the path in words. More likely, if we were to give instructions to someone, we would say something like, "Go straight for two blocks, turn right, go ahead for three blocks, turn left,..." These instructions are all in *relative* rather than absolute form. Relative commands not only are most often the most natural way to describe an object, but also can be significantly easier to implement in both hardware and software.

Relative positioning specifies positional information in terms of where we are at the present; for example, "go forward six steps." The *current position* (CP) can be thought of as a graphics cursor in our WC space. At any time, CP gives the present location of this cursor. Since CP is a position in WC, it can be represented in two dimensions

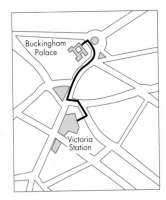

Figure 2.20
Street Map

$$CP = (CP_x, CP_y)$$

In three dimensions, we must add CP_z to obtain a three-dimensional CP. Our `line` function can be replaced by the function

```
line_to( x, y)
```

This procedure defines a line segment from (CP_x, CP_y) to (x, y). It also changes (CP_x, CP_y) from its current value to (x, y), so the next invocation of `line_to` will start where the last line segment ended. We now have a problem we did not have with `line`. We cannot define consecutive line segments that are not joined. The solution to this problem is to add a second function,

```
move_to( x, y)
```

whose sole function is to change (CP_x, CP_y) to (x, y). Another slight modification will increase the flexibility of our two new functions. We have defined move_to and line_to with (x, y) specified absolutely. In keeping with the spirit of relative positioning, we can add another function,

```
line_rel( dx, dy)
```

which defines a line segment from (CP_x, CP_y) to $(CP_x + dx, CP_y + dy)$, and moves CP to the new position. We can define move_rel in a corresponding manner. Now consider a simple function box(side), which defines a box centered at CP with a side of length side:

```
box(side)
float side;
{
      move_rel( -side/2, -side/2);
      line_rel( side, 0.0);
      line_rel( 0.0, side);
      line_rel( -side, 0.0);
      line_rel( 0.0, -side);
      move_rel( side/2, side/2);
}
```

Notice that the function leaves the original CP unchanged, which is probably a good general principle. The function needs no alteration for defining squares centered at various points in the world. All we have to do is to precede each call to box by a move_to to get the CP in the desired position. Whether box is used as a function or the equivalent code is placed in line, a single statement is all that needs to be altered to move or redefine a square. This simplicity was not possible with the absolute positioning we used with line.

The CORE system [GSPC79] and many others use this type of relative positioning. There are some problems with such a system. Consider what happens in the code fragment

```
move_to(x,y);
window(x1,x2,y1,y2);
line_to(a,b);
```

CP is set by `move_to`, but before a line segment can be fully defined by the call to `line_to`, the viewing conditions are changed. It is not clear how we can construct a line segment whose endpoints require two different transformations of the kind we developed in the previous section. This is one type of logical bind a relative positioning system can create. An absolute positioning system, such as is used in GKS, does not prevent an application programmer from creating her own positioning system using the given positioning system.

Another relative positioning system of some interest is that used in LOGO [Paper81]. Its graphics system is often called "turtle graphics" [Abel81]. The current position is regarded as a turtle who moves about the world with a pen fastened to his bottom. The turtle can move forward, turn right, or turn left. We also allow the turtle to lift and lower his pen. The position of the turtle acts as the CP, and graphical output is generated as the turtle moves about the world. We can get started by adding an initialization function that places our turtle at a specified position. We now have a graphics system based on the six functions:

```
initialize(x,y);
forward(distance);
right(degrees);
left(degrees);
pen_up();
pen_down();
```

In this system, a box can be defined starting at the location of the turtle by

```
for(i=0;i<4;i++)
{
        forward(side);
        left(90.0);
}
```

If we change the value of `side`, the number of degrees turned, and the number of times we go through the loop, the same code will generate approximations to circles and spirals. Some curves probably can be generated more easily by this kind of positioning system than by either the absolute positioning system as used in GKS or the relative positioning system in CORE. An interesting exercise is to create a turtle graphics system from either of the other systems.

2.7
Points, Lines, and Curves

We now turn to the problem of describing the entities our graphics system will employ. We shall describe these entities in two dimensions in this section, although we shall indicate what happens when we go to three dimensions where appropriate.

The dimensionality of an object can be thought of as the number of independent length measurements we can make on it. For example, a line has one dimension, since we can measure the length between any two points, but the line itself has no width. (Note that here we are talking about a mathematical line. A line as represented on the screen of a terminal or drawn with a pencil obviously has a nonzero width or we could not see it.) Curves, as represented in Figure 2.21, also have one dimension.

2.7.1 Points

Points, on the other hand, are zero-dimensional objects. A point has a location in space, but we can make no length measurements on it. Since we use points to define lines and curves, we first need a way to represent a point, as shown in Figure 2.22. The standard approaches

Figure 2.21
Curves

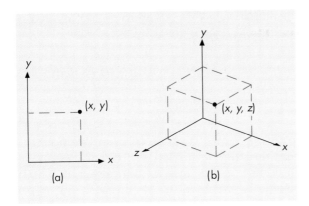

Figure 2.22
Point in (a) Two Dimensions
(b) Three Dimensions

are to represent a point either as the pair (x, y) or as a two-element column vector (or column matrix),

$$\mathbf{p} = \begin{bmatrix} x \\ y \end{bmatrix}.$$

This form is usually called a two-dimensional vector, since we are representing a point in a two-dimensional world. This terminology is not inconsistent with the fact that the point itself has no dimensionality. Points in three dimensions are natural extensions of the point in two dimensions,

$$\mathbf{p} = \begin{bmatrix} x \\ y \\ z \end{bmatrix},$$

as on the right side of Figure 2.22.

2.7.2 Vectors

In computer graphics, points are often associated with—and confused with—*vectors*. Either of the above representations of a point could be called a vector by a mathematician. The physicist, on the other hand, defines the vector as an entity with both direction and magnitude. Suppose we are drawing a sequence of line segments. Each segment has a direction and a length or magnitude. If a vector $\mathbf{v}$ is defined by

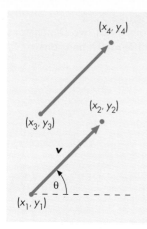

Figure 2.23
Defining a Vector

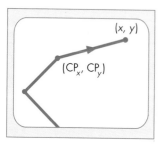

Figure 2.24
Random Scan Display

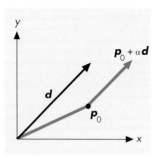

Figure 2.25
Vectors and Line Segments

the line segment between (x_1, y_1) and (x_2, y_2), as in Figure 2.23, its magnitude and direction are given by

$$|\mathbf{v}| = \sqrt{(x_1 - x_2)^2 + (y_1 - y_2)^2},$$

$$\tan \theta = \frac{y_2 - y_1}{x_2 - x_1}.$$

Thus, we see that a vector is obtained from two points.

This definition still will not satisfy the physicist, since magnitude and direction do not fix the position of the vector. The two vectors in Figure 2.23 would be identical to the physicist, but appear to be very different on the figure. To avoid confusion, vectors are used most often to describe directions, rather than locations. We shall follow this usage, especially when we deal with three-dimensional graphics in Chapter 8.

The original use of the term vector in computer graphics was to describe random-scan displays. A sequence of line segments was drawn, shown in Figure 2.24. At every endpoint of a segment, the direction (or vector) to the next endpoint had to be known for the hardware to draw the next segment. This requirement led people to describe such devices as *vector displays*.

This use of vectors and points is important, both for the hardware and for the underlying mathematics. Consider the diagram in Figure 2.25. We wish to describe the line segment from a point $\mathbf{p}_0$ to another point $\mathbf{p}_1$. The direction of this line segment is given by the vector $\mathbf{d}$, where

$$|\mathbf{d}| = \sqrt{(x_1 - x_0)^2 + (y_1 - y_0)^2},$$

$$\tan \theta = \frac{y_1 - y_0}{x_1 - x_0}.$$

Points on this line segment can now be described by the equation

$$\mathbf{p}(\alpha) = \mathbf{p}_0 + \alpha \mathbf{d}.$$

As α increases from zero, the point $\mathbf{p}(\alpha)$ emanates from $\mathbf{p}_0$ and goes in the direction $\mathbf{d}$ describing our line segment. You can easily calculate for what value of α the line segment passes through $\mathbf{p}_1$. This form can be used not only to describe the segment, but also to generate the line segment in hardware. It is an example of the parametric representation of a line. One conclusion we can draw from this example is that the term vector is best used to describe a direction. Alternate forms for representing curves are the topic to which we now turn our attention.

2.7.3 Curves

In computer graphics, we often find that the way we are accustomed to thinking of something is not necessarily the best way. The representation of curves is just such an example. A line is a special case of a curve—one that we shall use constantly. Since the types of representations we shall use for lines are similar to those for general curves, we shall describe general curves in two dimensions, then specialize to lines.

2.7.4 Explicit Curves

Probably the most familiar representation of a curve is the *explicit* form:

$$y = f(x).$$

The dependent variable y is given explicitly is terms of a formula that uses the independent variable x. Of course, a representation of the form

$$x = g(y),$$

is also explicit. The usual equations for the line and a circle centered at the origin are often written as

$$y = mx + h,$$
$$y = \sqrt{r^2 - x^2}.$$

They illustrate some of the problems with explicit representations. Both these equations, at best, yield incomplete representations.

    For the line in Figure 2.26, m is the *slope* and h is the y *intercept*. A problem arises for a vertical line. The slope is infinite, so there is no way to use the preceding equation. Of course, we could invert the equation and use

$$x = \frac{1}{m}(y - h),$$

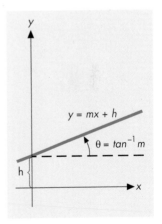

Figure 2.26
The Line

which works for vertical lines but fails for horizontal lines. We could attempt to use both forms simultaneously, but that is not very appealing, as our programs will be full of `if else` clauses to determine which form should be used. This particular problem is one variant of the problem of *axis dependence*, which characterizes explicit representations. Whenever one of the variables is given in terms of the other, we create a situation where, for some values of the independent variable, there may be no solution.

The explicit equation given for the circle shows two additional problems. First, the equation describes only the half of the circle above the x axis. The other half is given by

$$y = -\sqrt{r^2 - x^2}.$$

Now we have two equations for the circle, which, in a strict sense, is not an explicit representation. We can conclude that the circle does not have an explicit representation.

The other problem is a bit less obvious. When we look at the equations, we realize that both x and y must be in the range

$$-r \leq x, y \leq r.$$

If we are not careful to build these limits into any circle-definition routines in our computer programs, we are inviting trouble. Although using the limits might a bit time consuming, at least for the circle these limits are known. They might not be known for more complex curves.

2.7.5 Implicit Form

The equation of a circle centered at the origin is usually written as

$$x^2 + y^2 = r^2,$$

which is an example of the *implicit* representation of a curve

$$g(x, y) = 0.$$

This representation avoids many of the problems we encountered with the explicit representation. It is more useful as a test of whether or not a given point lies on the curve, however, than it is as a way of finding points on that curve.

In the general case, we have no analytic method for finding a point (x, y) that satisfies an arbitrary implicit equation. We must resort to numerical techniques, which are usually too slow to be useful in generating curves for graphics displays. Implicit forms are used, however— often in conjunction with other forms—to represent the polynomial curves and surfaces we shall discuss in Chapter 10. Here, real-time displays may not be an issue, and the special case of polynomial forms for $g(x, y)$ can keep the calculations within reasonable limits.

Returning to the line, we can examine its implicit representation,

$$ax + by + c = 0,$$

to describe a number of interesting properties. If either a or b is zero, we have a horizontal or a vertical line. We shall assume, for convenience, that neither of these terms is zero, even though the implicit form is valid in both these cases. If we divide by a or b, we can reduce the implicit to an explicit form. If we multiply the equation by any nonzero constant s, we obtain

$$sax + sby + sc = a'x + b'y + c' = 0,$$

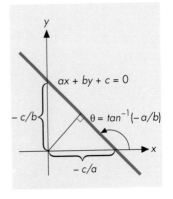

Figure 2.27
Implicitly Defined Line

which is an equivalent implicit form. Thus, even though this implicit form has three parameters, our multiplication by s shows that we can set one arbitrarily without changing the line. Often, we will pick s, so that the form is normalized to have

$$(a')^2 + (b')^2 = 1.$$

We can get a better understanding of the implicit form of the line from Figure 2.27. The following properties can be proved with a little trigonometry. The x and y intercepts of the line are at respective distances $-c/a$ and $-c/b$ from the origin. The slope of the line is $-a/b$. All lines with this slope are parallel. Any line with slope b/a is perpendicular (or normal or orthogonal) to the original line.

Consider the problem of finding the shortest distance from the origin to the line

$$ax + by + c = 0.$$

We know that the shortest distance from a point to a line is a perpendicular from the point to the line. Since our line has slope $-a/b$, the perpendicular line will have slope b/a. Since this perpendicular is drawn from the origin, the normal will satisfy the equation

$$bx - ay = 0.$$

We now have two equations in two unknowns, which we can solve to yield the point of intersection

$$x = -\frac{ac}{a^2 + b^2},$$

$$y = -\frac{bc}{a^2 + b^2}.$$

The distance from the origin to the line is then

$$d = \sqrt{x^2 + y^2} = \frac{c}{\sqrt{a^2 + b^2}}.$$

If the line has been normalized $(a^2 + b^2 = 1)$, we get some interesting insights. The point of intersection becomes

$$x = -ac,$$
$$y = -bc,$$

and it is a distance c from the origin. If, in our original equation, the line is normalized and has the form

$$ax + by + c = 0,$$

then the point (a, b) defines a unit normal from the origin, and c is the distance to the line. For unnormalized lines, the only difference is that we have to multiply the distance c by a constant $(1/\sqrt{a^2 + b^2})$ to obtain the distance from the origin to the line.

The relationship in the implicit form between a line and its normal arises repeatedly in computer graphics. In three dimensions, there is a similar relationship between a plane and its normal.

The implicit form of the line arises in a natural way in computer graphics. In most graphics applications, we are interested not in a line but rather in a line segment—the part of a line between two points, as opposed to the infinitely long line. For the explicit form, we can use a diagram such as Figure 2.28 to compute the slope and intercept from the endpoints (x_1, y_1) and (x_2, y_2). Noting the similarity of the triangles, the slope is

$$m = \tan \theta = \frac{y - y_1}{x - x_1} = \frac{y_2 - y_1}{x_2 - x_1}.$$

The two terms on the right can be cross-multiplied to obtain an implicit representation

$$(x_2 - x_1)y - (y_2 - y_1)x + x_1 y_2 - x_2 y_1 = 0.$$

This form is of particular importance in computer graphics since, if either endpoint of the segment is altered, as we might do in an interactive application, we have a direct method for changing all line segments that use the altered endpoint.

This is not the end of the story. The implicit form is not particularly useful for general curves; even for lines, it has some problems.

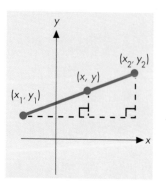

Figure 2.28
Computing The Implicit Form

One problem is that, even though the implicit form holds for both vertical and horizontal lines, without checking we cannot be sure whether we have either of these cases. Another problem is that we often want to know whether a given point is on a line segment connecting two other points. This problem arises, for instance, when we try to determine whether a line segment lies inside a window. The implicit form we derived previously is not particularly helpful in making this determination. A third problem arises when we consider what is the best form to represent a curve so that points along it can be generated by the hardware or software.

2.7.6 Parametric Form

The *parametric* representation avoids many of these problems. Rather that a single equation to describe a curve, we use two equations that are explicit in a parameter we call t:

$$x = x(t),$$
$$y = y(t).$$

For example, for the line connecting (x_1, y_1) and (x_2, y_2), we can use

$$x = (1 - t)x_1 + tx_2,$$
$$y = (1 - t)y_1 + ty_2.$$

We can verify the correctness of these equations by eliminating t and reducing them to the implicit form.

This pair of equations is not the only parametric representation of a line but, as evaluating the terms on the right side of the equations is easy, it is a useful one. For example, noticing that, for $t = 0$, the equations give us the point (x_1, y_1), and that for $t = 1$, we get (x_2, y_2), we can use the parametric form for a variety of operations involving line segments. If we interpret t as a time variable, by incrementing t in small steps, we can generate a sequence of points on the segment. These equations can be the basis of a hardware line generator.

As t goes from 0 to 1, we generate all points in the segment connecting (x_1, y_1) and (x_2, y_2). For values of t outside $(0, 1)$, we are still on the line, just not on the segment, as shown in Figure 2.29. This observation leads to the possibility of using the parametric form to decide whether two line segments intersect, as in Figure 2.30. This problem arises, as we have seen, when we try to decide whether a line segment lies inside a window, and in a number of other situations. Making this decision is much more difficult than is determining

Figure 2.29

Parametricly Defined Line

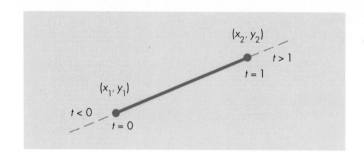

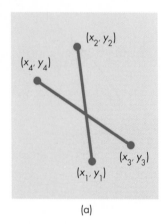

(a)

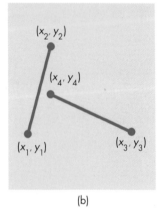

(b)

Figure 2.30

Intersecting Line Segments
(a) Segments Intersect (b)
Segments Do Not Intersect

whether two lines intersect, since lines will intersect as long as they are not parallel. We can obtain a straightforward method by writing the two line segments in parametric form. The first line segment is determined by

$$x = (1-t)x_1 + tx_2,$$
$$y = (1-t)y_1 + ty_2,$$
$$0 \geq t \geq 1.$$

For the second, we will use a parameter s to obtain the similar form

$$x = (1-s)x_3 + sx_4,$$
$$y = (1-s)y_3 + sy_4,$$
$$0 \leq s \leq 1.$$

The point of intersection is determined by a pair (s,t), which forces both sets of equations to yield the same (x,y). By setting the corresponding x and y equations equal to each other, we obtain the two equations for s and t:

$$(x_4 - x_3)s + (x_1 - x_2)t = x_1 - x_3,$$
$$(y_4 - y_3)s + (y_1 - y_2)t = y_1 - y_3.$$

It is easy to verify that, as long as the lines are not parallel, these equations can be solved for s and t. If both s and t are between zero and one, the segments intersect; otherwise, only the lines of which they are part intersect.

2.8
Portability Considerations

In this final section, we introduce some of the underlying principles involved in the software engineering of a device-independent graphics system. These principles are common to most large projects and thus may be familiar to you. Nonetheless, we wish to underscore a couple of points. One is the separation between the user of the device-independent package and the implementor. Although the notion of writing device-independent software making use of a standard graphics package is a good one, as we start writing programs, we shall encounter difficulties that indicate that achieving device independence is often, strictly speaking, not possible. The closer we get to a particular implementation of a device-independent package, the more we usually have to worry about device dependencies.

The second important issue is that of error tracking and checking. We will argue that error tracking is a necessity, and we shall examine its implications for the writer of user programs.

2.8.1 Functionality versus Format

The specification of a standard is usually a functional specification. It specifies what the standard will do and, in the case of a standard such as GKS, what procedures or functions are contained in the standard.[1] Other information, such as which errors will be recognized and what the minimal set of line types is, is also part of the standard.

There is still much more to be defined before an implementor can attempt to build the package. For example, consider the basic line-segment–defining procedure, polyline, which is present in most systems. This function defines a sequence of line segments from the first point to the second, from the second to the third, and so on. The functional specification tells us that this procedure has two inputs: the number of points, which is an integer greater than one; and the points, which are in WC. Although it may not be obvious, there are only two possible types of errors. One is that the graphics system is not in the proper state when the call to polyline is issued. For example, we might have not initialized the system correctly. The second is that the number of points is invalid—that is, less than two.

---

[1] In this book we shall use the terms *procedure* and *function* synonymously. Although the C language defines only functions, the manner in which we use these functions is analogous to the use of a graphics library as a procedural rather than a functional language.

This information does not give us the the name for the function call, which is certainly an important piece of information if we want to write a program. There are a number of obvious possible names for a C language binding. We could adopt the brief FORTRAN name GPL, but that is not consistent with present notions of good C programming style. We could use either of the clearer names `polyline` or `poly_line`. Actually, the choice was made by the GKS Standards Committee to use the name `gpolyline`, which uses the prefix g, as do all GKS functions; in PHIGS, the name `ppolyline` is used. We shall assume that the system is GKS, although the same issues apply to any system.

Now we can look at the parameters. The first is an integer, but is it of type `long` or `short`? If we set it to type `int`, we still risk different implementations using different lengths for `int`. The usual solution to this problem is to define data types for our implementation; these usually appear in an `include` file. Our programs will use a data type `Gint`; for example,

```
Gint num_pt;
```

for the `gpolyline` function. The implementor can decide how to implement the data type `Gint` and the other fundamental types `Gfloat` and `Gchar`. This information could be placed in `gks.h` or in another include file; either way, it will look something like

```
typedef int Gint;
typedef float Gfloat;
typedef char Gchar;
```

in a typical implementation. All the other GKS data types will be built on these three fundamental types.

Returning to our polyline functions, we find the issue of defining the data arrays for the polyline is more complex. In a language such as FORTRAN, there are few possibilities; in C, there are many. Since GKS is a two-dimensional standard, a point in two dimensions should be a basic data type; since we are working with WC, we should use the underlying type `Gfloat`. The point in the C binding is defined by the `typedef`

```
typedef struct
{
    Gfloat x;
    Gfloat y;
} Gpt;
```

and the input to the polyline function is a pointer to an array of points; that is,

```
Gint num_pt;
Gpt array_pt[NUM];
        .
        .
        .
gpolyline(num_pt, array_pt);
```

The C language binding thus consists of the names of the functions, their inputs and outputs, and the necessary data types, with the understanding that the lowest-level types, such as `Gint`, might be determined locally. This information is sometimes referred to as the *format* of the standard.

2.8.2 Defaults and Choices

A number of parameters that are inputs to graphics functions are best defined either by enumerated types or by use of the **define** facility in C. For example, our standard may require at least four different line types: solid, dashed, dotted, and dashed-dotted. These are specified by the integers 1, 2, 3, and 4. Rather than using these "magic numbers," we usually prefer to use something like

```
#define GLN_SOLID 1
#define GLN_DASH 2
#define GLN_DOT 3
#define GLN_DOTDASH 4
```

Such a method is especially useful when we have more types than the minimum required by the standard.

Enumerated types are useful for information that is discrete. For example, GKS defines four types of fills for solid areas through the enumerated type

```
typedef enum
{
    GHOLLOW, /* draw only the boundary */
    GSOLID,  /* fill with a solid color */
    GPAT,    /* fill with a pattern of colors */
    GHATCH   /* fill with cross hatched lines */
} Gfill_int_style;
```

We shall use uppercase character strings only for enumerated types and for strings declared in **define** statements. In general, this choice is a matter of good programming style and is not particular to our graphics system.

The use of defaults for many parameters, such as the foreground and background colors and line type, may be specified in the standard or may be up to the implementor. Thus, if we want to produce truly device-independent code, we should specify our default values.

Putting together all these rules and guidelines, we might expect to see code something like the following at the beginning of a GKS program

```
#include <gks.h> /* typedefs defined by standard */
#include <local_gks_typedefs.h>
#include <local_gks_defaults.h>
```

Once more, we emphasize that these issues are not particular to GKS; we should expect to face them whenever we use standards.

2.8.3 Error Handling

A program that uses a device-independent package will usually run slower than will one that is optimized for a single device. There are many reasons for this performance loss; a major one is the cost of error handling. The necessity for error tracking is an often overlooked and misunderstood aspect of device-independent software.

Consider our polyline function. It has two inputs and will produce output on display if the line segments are within the window and thus not clipped out. Other than this information, the function is a "black box," as shown in Figure 2.31. *Black box* is a term engineers use to describe a system specified only by its input/output properties. We do not know what goes on inside the box, we know only what output

Figure 2.31
Polyline as a Black Box

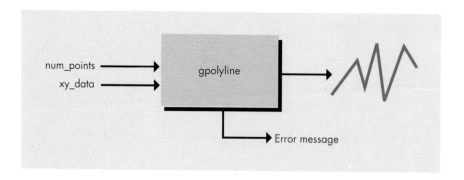

should be produced given certain inputs. In terms of software, we do not know how a given package implements its polyline function or any other function. Furthermore, we should not have to know this if the software really is standard.

Without some sort of error-tracking mechanism, however, this black-box point of view can present serious difficulties in debugging user programs. Suppose we write a user program and link it with our graphics package, and it crashes. Being sophisticated programmers, we run our debugger and receive a message such as, "Overflow in function gpolyline at address 1234." This information is of limited use to us, since gpolyline is a black box and we cannot go inside it to track down the problem. Thus, we cannot easily tell whether there is an error in our program, whether there is an error in the implementation of gpolyline, or whether we made an error during an earlier invocation of a graphics function. For example, an incorrect window specification can cause problems when we try to use the window to decide whether the line segments specified by a gpolyline will appear on our display. If such an incorrect specification was causing a problem, without an error-tracking mechanism, the error could easily manifest itself through an indication such as the obscure message "overflow in gpolyline," even though the parameters for the polyline were correct.

A partial solution to this difficulty is to require each function to check its input data and to produce an error message if an incorrect value is detected. Hence, if the error occurred during the execution because of an incorrect window specification, the window function would have produced an error message when it checked its input data. The usual mechanisms employed are either to have each function return an error code or to track errors by mapping them to a file or to the standard error-logging device. In GKS and PHIGS, error tracking is done by each function having a unique number and each possible error having its own number. For example, requesting a polyline consisting of one point would generate a message such as "error 100 in function 13." With this information, debugging, although still potentially painful, is far easier for users.

2.9
Suggested Readings

Much of the mathematics presented here can be found in either [Rog76] or [Bow83]. The most important mathematics for most work in computer graphics is trigonometry, about which there are many books.

The standard systems (CORE, GKS, PHIGS) share the synthetic camera model. The book [End84] discusses some of the software-engineering aspects of the GKS system.

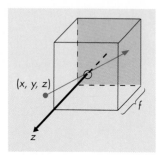

Figure 2.32
Pin Hole Camera

■ Exercises

2.1 The process of *zooming* makes an object appear larger or smaller on a display. Show how you could accomplish zooming by changing either the window size or the scaling of the object. Can you tell by observing a sequence of images on a display which method of zooming is being used? Does your answer depend on whether we are working in two or three dimensions?

2.2 We can construct a pinhole camera by punching a small hole in a box, as in shown in Figure 2.32. The *focal length f* of this camera is the distance from the pinhole to the film, which is placed at the back of the box. Suppose that the center of our coordinate system is at the opening, and that the z direction is along the optical axis, perpendicular to the film in the back of the box. Where on the film is the image of a point of light at (x, y, z)?

2.3 Suppose you are using a graphics system that has only absolute positioning. Create a relative positioning system; that is, construct procedures `move_to` and `line_to` that can call only `line`.

2.4 We allowed our window and viewport to have different aspect ratios, which could cause shapes to be distorted when they are mapped to NDC space. How would you change our mappings to force shapes to be preserved? Are there negative effects of adopting your suggestions? If there are, describe them.

2.5 Create a LOGO-like positioning system from an absolute positioning system.

2.6 An important feature of robust graphics systems is that each procedure checks its input data for errors. Rewrite the `box` procedure to incorporate error checking. For what kinds of errors should the procedure `line` check?

2.7 A circle with radius r centered at the origin can be described by the parametric equations $x = r \cos \theta$ and $y = r \sin \theta$. We can create a circle-generating algorithm by starting with a point on the circle—for example, $(r,0)$—and increasing θ in small steps. Derive such an algorithm. Then use approximations to sine and cosine for small angles to speed up the algorithm.

2.8 Surfaces in three dimensions can be described using two parameters

$$x = f(s,t),$$
$$y = g(s,t),$$
$$z = h(s,t).$$

Generate a set of parametric equations for a sphere. Can you find more than one parametric representation for the same sphere?

2.9 The parametric equations $x = x_0 + \alpha t$ and $y_0 + \beta t$ describe a line starting at (x_0, y_0). Relate the constants α and β to the slope of the line.

2.10 Many line-drawing methods in hardware use the parametric form in Exercise 2.9 to generate lines. However, devices such as the random-scan CRT move the beam at a constant speed v centimeters per second (cm/sec). Suppose we have a line segment connecting (x_1, y_1) and (x_2, y_2). Construct a parametric form such that, as t increases from 0 to 1, the beam moves at the same rate, independent of the slope of the line segment.

2.11 Curves in parameter space are often confused with spatial curves. Consider the parametric curve

$$x(t) = t(1 - t),$$
$$y(t) = t.$$

Plot these curves for a series of values of t between 0 and 1. Then sketch these curves in (x, y) coordinates by plotting values x, y from the x, t and y, t curves in parameter space.

2.12 Repeat Exercise 2.11 with

$$x(t) = t(1 - t),$$
$$y(t) = t(1 - t).$$

2.13 Consider a three-dimensional curve defined by the three functions

$$x(t) = \sin t,$$
$$y(t) = \cos t,$$
$$z(t) = t,$$

for $t \geq 0$. Sketch three parametric curves and the resulting curve in (x, y, z) space.

2.14 Given two points, $\mathbf{p}_0$ and $\mathbf{p}_1$, in two dimensions, write the line segment connecting them in the form

$$\mathbf{p}(\alpha) = \mathbf{p}_0 + \alpha \mathbf{d},$$

where $\mathbf{d}$ has unit length. Give the value of α that yields $\mathbf{p}_1$.

2.15 Propose two different data types for a window and two for a viewport.

2.16 For what kinds of errors should *window* and *viewport* procedures, which implement the window and viewport functions, check?

Two-Dimensional Graphics

Introduction

In this chapter, we construct our first complete graphics programs. They will use functions in a graphics library to provide the necessary interface to a graphics system. After overviewing the kinds of functions we would expect to find in any modern system, we shall concentrate on output-only programs of the type used to produce typical graphs. In the next chapter, we shall discuss programs that involve user interaction.

We shall use the Graphical Kernel System (GKS) to develop our programs. Although we will attempt to use GKS correctly, we will also attempt to avoid details particular to this system. Our programs should then be portable to other graphics systems with minimal changes. We will develop a simple self-scaling plotting procedure as an example of device independent graphics programming. We will also introduce metafiles that will allow us to transport graphical information between different programs and different systems.

▦ 3.1
▦ Device-Independent Graphics Standards

Diverse forces have led to the creation of standard graphics-programming languages. The motivations are similar to those for developing standard programming languages such as Pascal, C, and FORTRAN. Programmers want to write a program on one system and know that they can transport it to another system with virtually no knowledge of the hardware details of either system. They should not need to know the details of system-specific operations, such as input and output, to write most application programs. For example, in most high-level programming languages, input and output is done through standard logical units that are specified by a number or symbol; `printf` in C, or `WRITE(*,*)` in FORTRAN. Such programs are called *device independent*.

There are other advantages to standards. Sophistication of the language and the resulting code increases as more users become familiar with the system. Standard ways of performing tasks such as error handling develop. Better and less expensive hardware and software become available as the user community grows. Knowledge gained in one application is carried easily to the next. From a hardware perspective, there are many advantages to a standard software interface. In a graphics system, for example, the hardware designer will know what output primitives the hardware will be required to generate.

We shall use GKS both to develop our programs and to illustrate the capabilities of a modern graphics software package. GKS was developed with these ideas in mind. It is the culmination of work by a number of groups and of consideration of other proposed graphics languages, such as the CORE system. From the user's perspective, GKS is a set of functions that can be accessed from an application program. The user can use these functions to develop her own application or to serve as a basis for a new set of functions designed for a specialized user group, such as circuit designers or architects. The history of GKS and how it came to be adopted is documented elsewhere [End84]. It is interesting to see the difficulties involved, the issues raised, and the conflicting standards considered by the standards organizations. Since GKS has emerged from the process as the standard, however, we shall proceed from that point. Others programmer's standards, such as the Programmer's Hierarchical Interactive Graphics Standard (PHIGS) [Brown85], share a common framework with GKS; simple programs in one standard are virtually identical to simple programs in the others.

If we were to visualize GKS as simply a graphics library, we would miss many fundamental ideas incorporated in the system. Here the analogy with programming languages is particularly apt. How we solve a given problem can vary greatly, depending on what programming language we use. What we can do and how we do it in FORTRAN and LISP are different. The development of modern programming languages was due largely to the needs of the programmer and the computer scientist for more powerful tools with which to work. Such is the case with computer graphics systems. GKS and PHIGS incorporate many basic notions about how graphics programs should be developed. We have already seen some of these ideas, such as the synthetic camera analogy; others will be developed as we explore the systems.

The key features provided by modern graphics packages include

- Multiple logical workstations
- Segmentation and transformation of pictures
- Sophisticated control of workstation displays and input devices
- Storage and retrieval of graphical information
- User-controllable error handling

In this chapter, we shall introduce the lowest level of graphics programming. Our programs produce output based on direct use of the graphics primitives provided by the system. Input is not necessary, and the displays are generated only once. Such programs are used for plotting data, and the required graphics functions emulate a pen plotter. Simple graphics packages, often called graphics *toolkits,* are based on this model.

In the process of developing this model, we shall become familiar with output primitives, with their attributes, and with two-dimensional viewing. We make no claims as to completeness, although we develop correct programs. Our intention is to learn how to program simple graphics applications using a system such as GKS as a tool.

3.2 The Programmer's Model

When using a graphics system, the application programmer often uses a conceptual model of the architecture of the graphics system, such as that in Figure 3.1. The model includes the ability to have both graphical input and output devices, to have multiple devices under the control of a single user, and to save or transport graphical information. The model does not include any details of the implementation. These details are unnecessary, as the programmer accesses these

Figure 3.1
The Programmer's Model

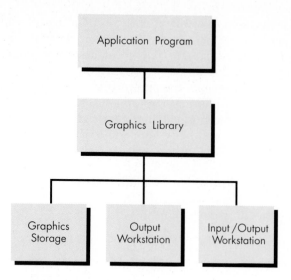

capabilities through procedure calls to the graphics system that are device independent. Hence, to the application programmer, graphics workstations are logical rather than physical units.

3.2.1 Logical and Physical Workstations

When we sit in front of a graphics terminal, a personal computer, or a sophisticated graphics workstation, we see a physical device that has a CRT display and one or more input devices, such as a keyboard and a mouse. Different workstation configurations have different physical properties. One may have a high-resolution monochrome display; another may have a low-resolution color display. Nonetheless, we want to develop device-independent software. We would like the same user program to work correctly on both of these displays; we do not want to have to alter it if a particular system has a data tablet instead of a mouse. One of the foundations of modern computer graphics is the use of logical rather than physical devices in user programs. *Logical workstations* allow us to develop application programs and to use graphics systems without worrying about the individual physical properties of specific devices.

A *logical device* is characterized by the functions it performs rather than by its physical characteristics. This concept should be familiar from standard programming languages. For example, the C input and output functions `read`, `write`, `printf`, and `scanf` refer to logical devices; the first two for binary data, the second pair for characters. In writing programs, we do not worry whether the input is coming from a terminal or from a file on a disk. The ability to redirect input and output from the terminal to files in many operating systems further illustrates that, within the user program, we are dealing with logical, not physical, devices.

In graphics, the use of logical workstations is bit more complex, as we want to provide a broad class of capabilities to the user. Some workstations are capable only of producing output, whereas others can both produce output and provide input to our programs. Other types of workstations may provide storage of our graphics and databases. For now, we shall consider three types of logical workstations: output, input, and input/output. A user program may control multiple logical workstations, whether or not these multiple workstations correspond to separate physical devices.

An *output workstation* has exactly one logical *display surface* on which graphical output can be placed. This display surface can display any of the primitives the system can produce, such as polylines and text. An *input workstation* has one or more logical input devices: devices that can provide graphical input to the application program. In the next chapter, we shall see that graphical input can take a number of forms. An input/output *workstation* has a single logical display surface and one or more logical input devices.

The decision as to how to organize logical workstations is often left to the applications programmer. For example, suppose we are designing an interactive painting program that will run on a personal computer. A typical personal computer will have a CRT display, a keyboard, a mouse, and a graphics plotter, as in Figure 3.2. Since we want to design a program with a helpful user interface, the display will show a number of menus and icons, as in Figure 3.3. For the most part, the user of this program will interact with the screen, sometimes using the mouse (e.g., to draw curves), and sometimes using the keyboard (e.g., to enter character strings for annotation). When hardcopy is desired, part of the CRT display (omitting the icons and menus) will be sent to the plotter.

In this example, we must have at least two logical workstations, since we have two physical displays to control. This logical division allows the programmer to control the two displays independently— an extremely desirable feature, since the graphical primitives we wish to send to the CRT are different from those we want to send to the printer.

The two input devices can be handled in a number of ways. Both can be associated with a single logical input workstation. Or we can associate both with one of the displays, thus creating a logical input/output workstation. Which one is actually used will be at the discretion of the programmer, and can be chosen to make the programming easy.

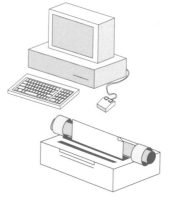

Figure 3.2
Personal Computer Configuration

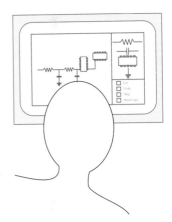

Figure 3.3
User Display

Figure 3.4
Display on Development
Workstation

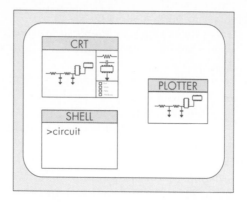

Although it might appear that there is a one-to-one correspondence between the logical and physical workstations, there need not be. For example, suppose we develop our painting program on a more powerful workstation, one with a high-resolution display and a capability for multiprocessing. On such a system, we can display both logical outputs on the single physical CRT (Figure 3.4), by assigning different parts of the physical CRT surface to the two logical workstations. Because logical devices can be reassigned to physical devices—by a simple mechanism we shall discuss later—the same software runs without alteration on both the personal computer and the development system.

3.2.2 Communicating with the Hardware

The user communicates with the physical devices only indirectly, through calls to graphics procedures. The physical workstation is seen as a logical device controlled by these calls. Since the user writes a program in some programming language, these calls are invoked through a set of standard names and calling conventions known as the *language binding*. The procedures are usually found in a library from which the necessary ones are extracted during the linkage of the user program. This is the level below the user program in Figure 3.1, and it is often all a user needs to know about the internal structure of the graphics system.

The interaction between the hardware and software can be pictured as in Figure 3.5. *Device drivers* provide the interface between the software and the hardware. Each physical device is controlled by its own driver, which can be either part of the software or contained in the hardware.

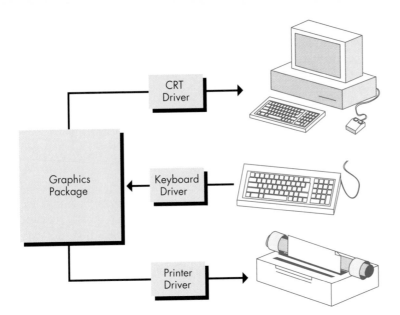

Figure 3.5
Hardware—Software
Interface

For our graphics system, output from the graphics package is produced in an NDC form. These data are converted to the correct commands and data for the physical devices in the drivers. Input is handled in the opposite way. Data from input devices are converted to an NDC form by the device drivers, and are sent to the graphics procedures. In a well-designed implementation, the device drivers will be the only device-dependent part of the system. Adding a new output or input device to a system should require only adding a proper device driver to the system.

3.2.3 Implementation Issues

The issues surrounding implementation are many and varied. They include how primitives are produced on a physical display, how the various input devices work, how software device drivers are written, and how a graphics package such as GKS is organized and written.

At this point, we profess to be developing device-independent graphics applications, which implies that we need not be concerned with implementation issues. We must recognize, however, that there is a difference between working on a terminal connected to a host by a serial interface and working on a color raster workstation.

We shall adopt an intermediate approach. When we are discussing application programs written in a system such as GKS, we shall ignore most implementation concerns. As we move to more sophisticated graphics in Chapter 5, we shall find we can no longer ignore implementation completely. In Chapters 6 and 7, we shall consider implementation more fully, and shall discuss in detail the issues involved with device drivers, device interfaces, and the use of real hardware.

3.3
Graphics Functions

Our model of the applications programmer using a graphics system has the programmer accessing the graphics through functions that comprise a library. A complete graphics package may contain hundreds of functions. A particular implementation may not need all possible functions. For example, applications such as desktop publishing may often take all their input from a simple text file, but they do require high-quality output. Other applications, such as flight simulators, may not require high-quality output, but certainly require sophisticated input. Requiring all implementations to realize all functions can lead to overly complex and slow implementations.

Rather than require that all systems implement all GKS functions, we can recognize various levels of implementation. For example, three different levels are recognized for output (0, 1, and 2) and three for input (a, b, and c). These levels in turn define nine levels of implementations as nine subsets of the approximately 200 GKS functions. We shall divide the functions into eight classes: output, control, attribute, transformation, input, segmentation, metafile, and inquiry.

3.3.1 Output Functions

A graphics system has a set of graphical primitives that it can display on its output devices. These primitives are the lowest-level entities with which a user program can work. The *output functions* define the "what" of a graphics system.

GKS has five primitives: polylines, text, polymarkers, fill areas, and cell arrays, which are shown in Figure 3.6. For each primitive, there is a corresponding output function, such as

```
gpolyline(num_points, array_of_points)
```

This set of primitives is fairly small. Of course, we can build more complex graphical entities by making our own functions using these primitives. We can also try to add more primitives. Candidates for inclusion, in two dimensions, might be polynomial curves, boxes, circles, and ellipses.

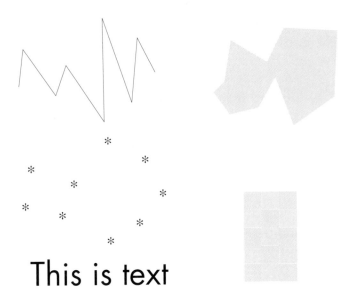

Figure 3.6
The GKS Primitives

The choice of the five primitives used in GKS was based on two factors. This set could reasonably be expected to be producible on virtually all hardware, and each primitive provides a capability unattainable from the others.

3.3.2 Control Functions

A number of *control functions* is necessary in a graphic system to control the workstation displays, the input devices, and the system state. For example, the system must be initialized, state tables set up, error files opened, and parameters set to their initial or default values. Decisions must be made as to how and when the displays on workstations are to be updated. An important characteristic of a well-designed system is the flexibility it gives a user through its control functions.

Many of the control functions, such as those involved in initializing and terminating a graphics program, are the same in virtually all programs. Thus, although we present them because they are necessary, we can then hide them within a few user written functions for use in later programs.

3.3.3 Attributes

Primitives can be displayed in a number of ways. A line can be thick or thin, solid or dashed, red or green. Characters can have different sizes, can be displayed horizontally or vertically, and can have different colors. The *attribute functions* define "how" the primitives are to be displayed.

3.3.4 Viewing and Transformation Functions

The *viewing functions* allow the viewer to specify the viewing parameters, or the "where" of the graphics systems. These functions specify what part of the world will appear on the displays, and where on the displays primitives will be shown. Thus, these functions include the window, viewport, and clipping functions of the graphics system. Since these functions determine the various mappings between coordinate systems—for example, WC to NDC, and NDC to DC—they determine certain transformations that the system must perform.

GKS provides two levels of viewing. The first determines what part of the WC system is to be mapped to a viewport in NDC space. The resulting transformation is known as the *normalization transformation*. Multiple normalization transformations can exist simultaneously, which, as we shall see, provides a useful facility to the user.

The second level of viewing is the workstation level; it permits the user to display different parts of NDC space on different workstations. This transformation, known as the *workstation transformation,* maps values in NDC space to DC. A workstation transformation exists for each output device.

Whereas the viewing operations define transformations between coordinate systems, we often want to make transformations within a single coordinate system; for example, when we rotate a line or move an object from one position to another, we are performing a transformation. Graphics systems usually provide some utility functions for this purpose.

Control, output, and transformation functions are necessary in any graphics program. The other classes (input, segmentation, metafile, inquiry) give the system its ability to provide the interactive and picture-manipulation capabilities we associate with modern computer graphics.

3.3.5 Input Functions

From the programmer's point of view, the *input functions* should be device independent, just as are the output functions. Graphical input is more varied than is input to standard programs, in that it comes in a number of forms. In a plotting program such as we shall develop later in this chapter, we might want the user to enter a title for the plot and labels for the axes; this is text input. If the user is to enter the data to be plotted, that input might take the form of locations on the screen. In a CAD application, we often want to move objects about the screen. Each of these is a separate form of logical input; it provides a completely different form of information to the user program, regardless of the physical device used to enter the input.

GKS defines six classes of logical input: locator, string, pick, choice, stroke, and valuator. Input can also occur in more than one mode. Consider, for example, a flight simulator, which must respond to the present state of its input devices at all times. In other situations, such as in most CAD applications, the user needs time to position a device or to type characters on a keyboard. In these applications, the user must issue a signal before the input is processed. GKS and PHIGS allow both types of input by allowing the programmer to specify the mode of input. In addition, there usually are some sort of initialization commands to control the input workstations. All these issues will be investigated in Chapter 4.

3.3.6 Segmentation Functions

Although primitives allow the user to describe sophisticated pictures, the simple sets of primitives in most graphics systems do not make this task easy. Most real applications work with entities far more complex than is a single polyline. For example, in a circuit-design problem, symbols for resistors, capacitors, and integrated circuits are used constantly, and the user does not want to have to redefine these elements repeatedly. At higher levels in this example, the user might want to work with entire subcircuits. The *segmentation functions* allow the user to form and manipulate identifiable groups of primitives called *segments*.[1]

Once a segment is defined, we can transform and change objects without worrying about individual low-level components. Thus, we will be able to rescale an entire user-defined structure, such as a plot or a circuit design, with a single command or action. On the input side, we can select an object on the screen of a display by pointing to any part of it, and we can communicate this information back to the user's program.

3.3.7 Metafiles

The *metafile functions* provide a mechanism for picture capture and recovery. We will be able to save a picture (or part of a picture) such that individual elements in the picture can be recovered by an application program. In addition, a picture can be stored on a file as

---

[1] GKS uses the term *segment;* PHIGS uses *structure,* a term possibly more pleasing to C programmers.

easily as it can be produced on a workstation—in fact, the conceptual mechanism is identical. Hence, rather than our having to transport or store a picture in hardcopy form or indirectly by the program that produced it, the metafile provides a third option.

3.3.8 Inquiry Functions

Although we usually want to write device-independent programs, we sometimes want to know something about either the hardware or what is going on within the graphics systems. For instance, although we can specify an arbitrary color for a line or fill area, we might want to know whether we are indeed working with a color system. If the system turns out to be monochromatic (e.g., a laser plotter), then we might want to replace our green lines by dotted lines and our solid red areas by cross-hatch–patterned ones. Consider another example. Most screens on terminals are not square, but they vary as to which side—horizontal or vertical—is longer. Depending on the *aspect ratio*, which is the ratio of these lengths, we will make different choices regarding the size and placement of graphical items such as menus. The *inquiry functions* allow the user to discover any of these properties of the workstation or of the internal state of the system.

3.4
A Simple Program

We start with a simple program that uses only a few of the output functions. Strictly speaking, such a program cannot work, because every program must have control statements and viewing conditions specified. We can avoid these issues for now by using our software design methodology and the default settings in our graphics system.

3.4.1 The Pen-Plotter Model

We shall examine a typical output-only offline program. This type of graphics programming is often called the *pen-plotter analogy,* because it corresponds to the style of computer graphics that preceded the modern interactive graphics workstation. Then, we produced graphics by writing a program that was submitted to a batch processor. If the program was correct, it was executed, and the graphics were produced some time later on a device such as a pen plotter. Thus, there was no interaction involved, and the commands available to the user were usually based on the kinds of entities that could be produced on a pen plotter: lines and text. The attributes associated with these primitives were also simple: a few types of lines, and perhaps a few text directions. An important aspect of this method of producing graphical output is that, once output is produced, there is no way of changing this output except by altering and rerunning the program. There also is no mechanism to recognize, for example, that a line might have been placed a bit to the right by the program, and that we thus might want to move it and to redraw the plot. To move the line, we must somehow enter the new position into the original program, rather than alter the output produced by that program. Most plotting applications are still of this form, even though we have more powerful hardware and software available to do the work.

This model of how computer-generated images can be produced is not far different from what we might do if we were to draw a picture by hand. Consider the following drawing procedure:

```
draw_picture()
{
    select_paper();
    orient_paper();
    select_pen();
    draw_lines();
    remove_paper();
}
```

In terms of graphics procedures, each of these steps corresponds to one of the classes of functions that we discussed in the preceding section. Step 1 is the initialization phase (control). Step 2, by a slight stretch of the imagination, corresponds to the selection of viewing conditions. We must decide which direction on the paper is up. We also may want to use only a part of the page, as we may add other pictures later, on other parts of the page. As our third step, we select a pen of the desired color and thickness. The color and thickness are attributes of the lines and text that we draw in step 4. Finally, we terminate (control again) the procedure in step 5. Thus, most output-only applications have a flow like this:

```
graphics_program()
{
    initialization();
    set_viewing_conditions();
    set_attributes();
    generate_primitives();
    termination();
}
```

The initialization and termination phases of most programs are virtually identical. We shall delay discussion of the necessary control functions by placing all these operations in two procedures called `init` and `finish`. Since we shall use these procedures repeatedly, we shall define them now as dummy procedures.

We can avoid the discussion of attributes and viewing conditions by using their default settings. If we were to examine the inside of the graphics library, we would find a number of tables and parameters. Some of these correspond to control conditions, such as which workstations are open and what the error state is. Others correspond to attributes (the current line width, the current text font) and the viewing conditions (the clipping window, the viewport). For many, but not all, of these conditions, most graphics systems set default values when the system is initialized. One of the advantages of using defaults is that not every program needs to set every parameter. Of course, these parameters must be set to "reasonable" default values if this facility is to be useful. For instance, a default line is usually solid and thin. If we fail to set parameters explicitly, we probably will be all right for our initial simple programs.

3.4.2 Polyline and Text

We start with two primitives, polyline and text. We use the default text style (face and font), character size, text direction (left to right), and default line type. The C names for these two procedures in GKS are `gpolyline` and `gtext`; they should be similar in other systems.

The *polyline* function is accessed by the procedure

```
void gpolyline( num_pt, array_pt);

Gint num_pt;
Gpt *array_pt;
```

`array_pt` is an array of `num_pt` points in two dimensions. The fundamental data type `Gpt` is defined by a pair of `Gfloat`s

```
typedef struct
{
    Gfloat x;
    Gfloat y;
} Gpt;
```

as in the preceding chapter.

Suppose the points in `gpolyline` correspond to specified x and y

values in the user program, such as through the code fragment

```
for(i=0; i<n,i++)
{
    points[i].x=x[i];
    points[i].y=y[i];
}
```

Hence, a call to gpolyline defines one line segment from the point[2] (x_0, y_0) to (x_1, y_1), another from (x_1, y_1) to (x_2, y_2), and so on, finishing with the line segment from (x_{n-1}, y_{n-1}) to (x_n, y_n). The values in the array points are in WC. Whether or not the defined polyline or any part of it will be displayed on a workstation depends on the viewing conditions in effect when the polyline is defined.

A minimal program might now look like this:

```
main()
{
    static Gpt data[2] = {{1.0, 1.0}, {2.0, 2.0 }};
    init();
    gpolyline(2, data);
    finish();
}
```

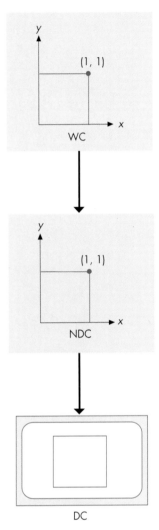

This program defines a single line segment from (1.0, 1.0) to (2.0, 2.0). However, if you were to run it, using the procedures init and finish discussed later in this chapter, you would find that the output is a blank page or empty screen. That result is due to the default viewing conditions. Because we did not specify a window and a viewport, GKS starts off with the default window and viewport. The default window is a unit square in WC, with the origin as its lower-left corner. The default viewport is a similar unit square in NDC. This region of NDC space is mapped to the largest square on the physical workstation, as in Figure 3.7. We can see from Figure 3.8 that, although the polyline we just defined is a perfectly reasonable polyline, it lies outside the window and does not generate any output. Of course, if we replace the initialization of data by

```
static Gpt data[2] = { {0.0, 0.0}, {1.0, 1.0 }};
```

we will see the polyline on our workstation.

Figure 3.7
Default Transformations

---

[2] The mathematical point (x_i, y_i), corresponds to the point defined by x[i] and y[i] in the C program.

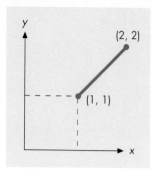

Figure 3.8
Polyline and Window

It is perfectly reasonable to construct other procedures using our polyline primitive. Consider for instance, the box procedure

```
box( xmin, xmax, ymin, ymax)
Gfloat xmin, ymin, xmax, ymax;
{
        Gpt points[5];
        points[0].x = xmin;
        points[0].y = ymin;
        points[1].x = xmax;
        points[1].y = ymin;
        points[2].x = xmax;
        points[2].y = ymax;
        points[3].x = xmin;
        points[3].y = ymax;
        points[4].x = xmin;
        points[4].y = ymin;
        gpolyline( 5, points);
}
```

To make our programs a little more interesting, we can add the text primitive through the procedure

```
gtext( start, string)
Gpt start;
Gchar *string;
```

Here **start** is the starting location of the text **string**. The point in **start** is in WC, and the default conditions are that characters in the string have a height of 0.05 units in WC, and the string goes left to right with the point **start** at the lower-left corner of the string.
Now a simple program might be

```
main()
{
    static Gpt start = { 0.25, 0.9 };
    init();
    box( 0.25, 0.75, 0.25, 0.75);
    gtext( &start, "Hello");
    finish();
}
```

Figure 3.9
Sample Output

which produces the output shown in Figure 3.9.
This all may seem simple. It is! With just two primitives, we can generate graphs, plots, flowcharts, and circuit diagrams. You might

want to consider how to center text, and to do other manipulations to make the output look nicer. What we shall find in the next few sections is that good graphics systems have many facilities to make the production of complex output easy to do.

3.5
Viewing

Viewing can be defined in terms of transformations between coordinate systems. We have already seen that the user works in WC. Internally, most systems use NDC, whereas each physical workstation uses its own DC system. Thus, as we have seen there are two transformations necessary; the first from WC to NDC (the *normalization transformation*), the second from NDC to DC (the *workstation transformation*). Each of these coordinate systems is two-dimensional and has its own origin, as illustrated in Figure 3.10.

3.5.1 The Normalization Transformation

We have not specified enough information to determine a unique transformation or mapping between any pair of these coordinate systems. We know that some part of the WC space will be mapped into some part of the NDC space, and that some of NDC space will be mapped to the workstation (DC). We are assuming here that there is only a single workstation to avoid confusion. In the preceding chapter, we looked at the NDC system as corresponding to a virtual screen. The display surface of this device is a square whose lower-left corner has NDC coordinates (0.0, 0.0), and whose upper-right corner is (1.0, 1.0). We can use any part of this area. The selected part is the viewport. In WC, we select an area (the window), to be mapped to this viewport.

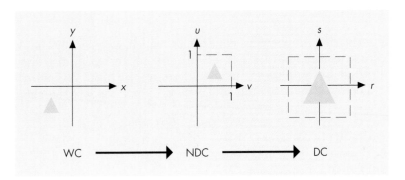

Figure 3.10
World Coordinates (WC) and Normalized Device Coordinates (NDC)

We specify both the window and viewport by giving the coordinates of the lower-left and upper-right corners of the rectangles they define. Hence, the window is a rectangle defined in WC that is mapped to a rectangle defined in NDC.

In many applications, it is convenient to be able to use more than one WC system and more than one viewport. For example, in a menu-driven interactive system, the menus and graphics output will appear in different viewports. Probably, each will be defined using whatever WC system is most natural to the problem. Thus, each distinct window and viewport will define a unique normalization transformation. Rather than having to redefine these transformations continuously within the program, we prefer to allow multiple normalization transforms to exist simultaneously. We accomplish this task by having an additional parameter, the *normalization transformation index*, in the specification of the window and the viewport. Thus, to define the window and viewport, we have the two procedures

```
void gset_win(trans_num, window)
void gset_vp(trans_num, viewport)

Gint trans_num;
Glim *window, *viewport;
```

Here `trans_num` is the *normalization transformation index*. Two pairs of coordinates, (x_{min}, y_{min}), (x_{max}, y_{max}), and (u_{min}, v_{min}), (u_{max}, v_{max}), define the window and viewport, shown in Figure 3.11, through two structures of the form

```
typedef struct
{
    Gfloat xmin;
    Gfloat xmax;
    Gfloat ymin;
    Gfloat ymax;
} Glim;
```

Usually, the default viewing conditions, which we used in the previous section, correspond to normalization transformation 0 being pre-defined (and unchangeable) as a unit square in both WC and NDC space. The effect is the same as it would be had we written the lines

```
static Glim window0 = { 0.0, 1.0, 0.0, 1.0};
static Glim viewport0 = { 0.0, 1.0, 0.0, 1.0};
gset_win(0, &window0);
gset_vp(0, &viewport0);
```

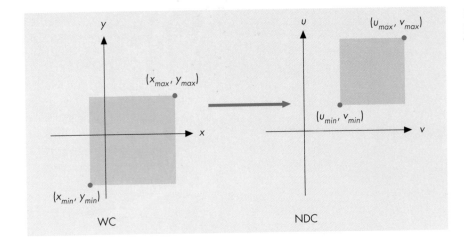

Figure 3.11
Defining the Normalization
Transformation

The desired window and viewport are selected through the function *select normalization transformation*

```
void gsel_norm_tran(trans_num)
Gint trans_num;
```

A transformation remains in effect until it is changed and the present normalization transformation is applied to all primitives. Thus, we can define a set of normalization transformations using `gset_win` and `gset_vp` at the beginning of a program, or within a procedure, and can move between them through `gsel_norm_tran`.

There is no constraint on the size of the world window. The viewport is constrained to lie within the bounds of the unit square defining NDC space. Primitives defined within the window will be mapped into a valid region of NDC space. These bounds do not necessarily preserve shapes, since the aspect ratio of the world window, $(y_{max}-y_{min})/(x_{max}-x_{min})$, need not match that of the corresponding viewport, $(v_{max}-v_{min})/(u_{max}-u_{min})$. Unless these two ratios are the same, an object must be stretched differently along its x and y axes to fit its assigned viewport. Although lines will still be preserved as lines, squares may be transformed into rectangles and circles into ellipses, as shown in Figure 3.12.

3.5.2 Clipping

Primitives that lie within the window will be mapped into the viewport, whereas those that are either partially or fully outside the window must be *clipped*. The process of clipping decides which part, if

Figure 3.12
Stretching to the Viewport

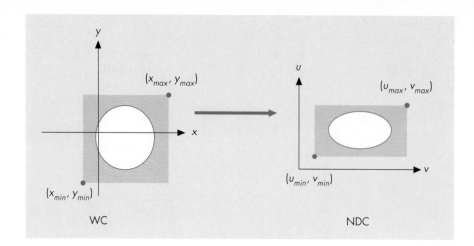

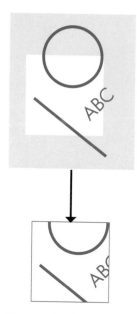

Figure 3.13
Clipping

any, of a primitive lies inside the window. When we clip, primitives that are outside the window are discarded, and primitives that are partially in the window are cut apart, so that only the parts inside are displayed, as in Figure 3.13. We shall discuss clipping algorithms when we consider implementation issues in Chapter 6. For the present, we need only to realize that clipping is a necessary internal operation of any graphics package.

Beginners often make the mistake of assuming that the hardware will take care of clipping. This assumption is usually based on the idea that a value outside a window is mapped to a value too large for the hardware, and that this value therefore will be limited automatically by the maximum or minimum values permitted by the hardware. There are two problems with this argument. First, the hardware may not be able to handle values that are too big or too small. In older hardware, values that were too large were "wrapped around" when they overflowed hardware registers, and that could cause primitives to appear in odd positions, as shown in Figure 3.14. Second, this ar-

Figure 3.14
Wrap Around Error

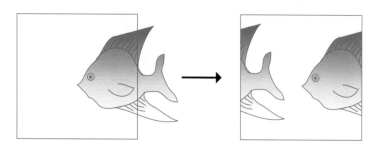

gument ignores the window-to-viewport mapping. For example, consider the line ABC in Figure 3.15. The segment AB lies inside the window and is mapped to the corresponding viewport. The segment BC lies outside the window and should be clipped out. However, since the viewport is smaller than the unit square defining our virtual screen, BC is mapped to a valid region of NDC space, even though this region is outside the desired viewport. This situation is one that usually cannot be left to the hardware. The hardware usually checks only whether a primitive lies in its own range, not whether the primitive lies within a user-defined viewport. Another way of looking at this situation is to recognize that many hardware devices, such as terminals, have no idea what a viewport is. Thus, the software must ensure that output primitives are clipped to the correct viewport before sending them to the hardware for display.

There are situations where, because clipping can be time consuming, we would like to turn the clipper off. For instance, we might be using hardware that understands windows and viewports, or we might know in advance that our primitives lie entirely inside the window and that clipping is therefore unnecessary. In these cases, a procedure that disables clipping is helpful and is incorporated in many graphics systems.

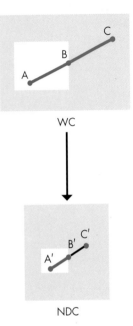

WC

NDC

Figure 3.15
Clipping to the Window

3.5.3 The Workstation Transformation

We can now discuss the second transformation, the workstation transformation. Objects in NDC space must be mapped to DC for us to create the display on our physical device(s). If we define only the world transformation, the default workstation transformation will map all of NDC space to the largest square that fits on the workstation display. This choice is a sensible one, since the aspect ratio will be preserved and there will be no distortion of objects between NDC space and the workstation (DC space). In many programs, we are content with this default. However, the flexibility to alter this choice can be helpful, as shown by the following example.

Consider again the circuit-layout program for which the display might be organized as shown in Figure 3.16. We allocate one area for a menu of the components we can use, another area for a control menu, and a large region for the actual layout. Although we cannot yet discuss how a user might interact with this picture, the first step in the writing of such a program is usually the design of the display the user will see on her terminal screen. We have already seen that, to the graphics system, this screen is a single logical workstation. At some point in the process, the user might want a hardcopy of her design. Usually, only the designed circuit and not the menus should be plotted. To the graphics system, our plotter is a second

Figure 3.16
Circuit-Layout Display

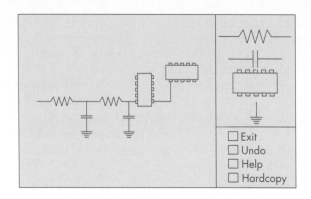

logical workstation. Hence, different displays should appear on the two workstations and, as far as the program is concerned, they should appear simultaneously. In addition, this program might use three different normalization transformations. The two menus are mapped from WC to two different viewports in NDC space, and the layout area uses a third viewport. These transformations are illustrated in Figure 3.17. In terms of what we see in NDC space, we want all of NDC mapped to the terminal workstation, but only part of it mapped to the plotter workstation.

The two procedures that define this mapping are *set workstation window* and *set workstation viewport:*

```
void gset_ws_win(wk_id, ws_window)
void gset_ws_vp(wk_id, ws_viewport)
```

Figure 3.17
Circuit-Design Mappings

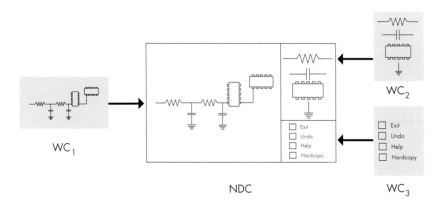

```
Gint wk_id;
Glim *ws_window;
Glim *ws_viewport;
```

gset_ws_win defines the *workstation window* for the workstation with the logical name wk_id. This workstation identifier will have been established in our initialization procedure init. This window defines the region of NDC space that will be mapped to the indicated workstation. gset_ws_vp defines a viewport on the workstation—an area to which the contents of the workstation window are mapped. Since the workstation window is an area of NDC space, its parameters are specified in NDC. The workstation viewport is on the workstation, so its coordinates must be specified in DC. For both the normalization transformation and the workstation transformation, a window in one space is mapped to a viewport in the next, as illustrated in Figure 3.18.

Returning to our example of a circuit-layout program, we can define two workstation transformations, as shown in Figure 3.19. However, there is a small problem. For the first time, we are confronted with parameters that have to be specified in DC. At this point, we could give up the notion of device independence and run to the manual to look up the size of our displays in DC. This research is not necessary, however; we can employ one of the *inquiry* functions to obtain this information. Since this information is available through the graphics system, we can still write our program in a device-independent manner.

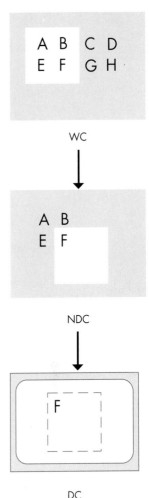

Figure 3.18
World and Workstation
Mappings

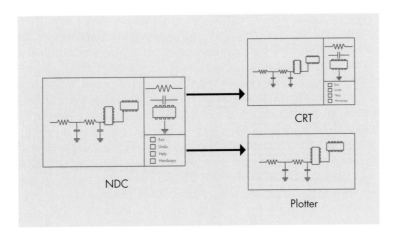

Figure 3.19
Workstation Mappings for
the Circuit-Layout Program

3.6
Control

The time has come to examine the contents of the `init` and `finish` procedures from our simple program in Section 3.4. In most systems, initialization and termination involve a number of steps. Although these steps may differ in specifics, and although the details may be hidden from the user, initialization and termination are nevertheless required for correct operation. We shall present the GKS procedures, but keep in mind that, having gone through these procedures once, we can place the steps in procedures such as `init` and `finish`, which will be used repeatedly. For other systems, we can replace the individual steps by their equivalents in the new system.

3.6.1 Initialization

Initialization performs a number of tasks that prepare the system for executing a user program. These tasks usually include

- Setting up state tables for the system
- Allocating memory
- Initializing error handling
- Allocating physical devices
- Initializing physical devices
- Linking logical devices to physical devices
- Setting default values

As we have argued, modern graphics systems do many jobs that once were considered the responsibility of the applications programmer. To do these jobs, the graphics system must initialize and keep track of many tables and parameters. Some values represent the internal state of the system, which, among other things, determines whether or not certain user operations are valid. For example, output primitives cannot be sent to workstations if no workstations have been defined, a fact that is determined by the state of the system. Memory will have to be allocated for storage of such entities as user-defined transformations and tables. As part of this process, the default values for attributes and such items as normalization transformation 0 are set.

Although error checking is an important part of the system, the user must decide what to do with error indications. We shall use the simple mechanism of writing errors in a file that must be initialized properly. Setting up any alternative error-handling mechanism is usually done as part of the initialization.

As part of the initialization process, logical devices must be mapped to physical devices in much the same way that a logical file is assigned to a physical file in a C program when the file is opened. The initialization of physical devices requires that they be available and be set up properly. For example, a pen plotter must have paper in it, whereas a CRT will have its screen cleared.

In GKS, these operations require at least four steps, as in this simple procedure:

```
init()
  {
      int fd;
      fd = creat( "errors", "w");
      gopen_gks(fd, BUFFER);
      gopen_ws(WS_ID, CON_ID, WS_TYPE);
      gactivate_(WS_ID);
  }
```

3.6.2 The Error File

The first significant action taken by the initialization procedure is to create a writable error file called **errors** as a standard C file with file descriptor **fd**. Since every graphics function can produce an error message, we must identify a place to store these errors before any graphics function is invoked. Each function has a unique number and each type of error also has a unique number identifying it. Although we can custom-tailor the error handler, for now we will accept the default, which is simply to write in our error file the number of the function in which the error occurred and the number of the error. We will then be able to examine the contents of this file after we run our program. Of course, we could use the standard output device or error device, rather than a file, to track the errors.

3.6.3 Opening the System

The second action we take is to open the graphics system. The procedure has two parameters. The first is the descriptor of the error file we just opened. The second is the amount of buffer storage needed. We will assume that this value has been set to some default value, either in our **define** file(s) or by the system. In general, there will be enough memory available (or allocatable by the system) to handle simple programs. For large programs, such as those that generate many large polylines or have many segments, we might have to request more memory by adjusting **BUFFER**.

3.6.4 Opening and Activating Workstations

Now we are ready to open one or more workstations. In the invocation of `gopen_ws`, we tie a logical workstation name that we will use in our program to a physical workstation on which the output will appear. After this call, we need to use only the names of logical workstations in our program. The first parameter, `ws_id`, is a number (of type `Gint`) that we choose to assign as the logical identifier of the workstation and that we will use in subsequent calls to refer to this workstation. The second two parameters establish the link to the physical workstation. Unfortunately, how this linkage is done varies from implementation to implementation. One way to define this link is to have `ws_type` refer to a particular physical workstation, and to have `con_id` select the device driver. Other implementations use these parameters to refer to entries in a file that contains the necessary information on physical workstations and device drivers. Since this one line contains the link between physical and logical workstations, it is usually the only line of code that will need to be altered to run our application on another system. For example, if we use symbolic names, which can easily be altered in an `include` file, then a typical invocation of `gopen_ws` might look like

```
gopen_ws(CRT ,CONN_ID_1, WK_TYPE_4105);
```

On a particular implementation, we might use

```
#define CRT 1
#define CONN_ID_1 "/dev/tty05"
#define WK_TYPE_4105 52
```

where the mnemonic `WK_TYPE_4105` might refer to a Tektronix Model 4105 graphics terminal, which in this implementation is workstation type 52. The connection identifier `/dev/tty05` will select the correct device driver for this terminal, and the user has chosen the integer 1 for the logical identifier of this workstation.

Finally, we can activate our workstation through the procedure `gactivate_ws`. Opening and activating a workstation are separate actions, as primitives will not be sent to an open but inactive workstation. Opening a workstation causes not only internal actions, such as setting values in state tables, but also some external actions, such as clearing the display surface of the workstation. Hence, if we want to impede primitives from going to the workstation but desire to reactivate the workstation later, we should keep it open; otherwise, we risk losing what is presently on the display.

Opening additional workstations can be included in `init`. For example, we can open and activate a plotter by adding the two lines

```
gopen_ws(PLOTTER,CONN_ID_2,WS_TYPE_PLOTTER);
gactivate_ws(PLOTTER);
```

where again these strings are assumed to be defined in our `include` files or in our program.

3.6.5 Termination

Termination is far simpler than initialization. We undo each action we took during initialization. Here is the `finish` procedure:

```
finish()
{
    gdactivatews(ws_id);
    gclosews(ws_id);
    gclosegks();
}
```

First, we deactivate the workstation; then, we close it. We do the same for any other active workstations. Once all workstations are closed, we can close the system. These actions cause a number of things to happen internally. What we shall probably see will be the clearing of the screen of our physical device or the ejection of the paper from our plotter. The error file can be closed as any normal C file would be, or it can be closed automatically on termination of the program. This file can be examined for any errors after the program has executed.

3.7
Polyline and Text Attributes

We now return to our primitives and to the problem of how they are displayed. So far, our only primitives are polyline and text, which are accessed through the procedures `gpolyline` and `gtext`. When we introduced them, we did not include any mechanism that allowed us to vary the color of the lines, the direction of the text, or any other properties of these entities. Here we will introduce most of the attributes of our two primitives. In the following two sections, we shall finally introduce the other GKS primitives, and we shall write a longer example program that uses some of these attributes.

Attributes define how a primitive is to be displayed: They specify its color, size, orientation. Some primitives, such as the polyline, have only a few attributes; others, such as text, need a large number of attributes to allow us to produce high-quality output. We shall introduce all the attributes in this section, but we shall not discuss each in detail. Our intention is to make you aware of what is possible. More detailed information on attributes and the necessary data types is given in Appendices A and B.

3.7.1 Geometric and Nongeometric Attributes

The setting of attributes can be done in a number of ways. If we see a green line on a display, we might ask ourselves whether the line is green because greenness is a property of the line, the way grass is green rather than blue. Or the line might be green simply because the programmer has decided to display it as green, whereas she just as easily could have made it red or blue. These two ideas reflect fundamentally different views of how attributes are associated with primitives. In one view, an attribute is bound to a primitive and can never be altered. In the other view, attributes can be changed during the execution of the program, usually at the workstation level. Either view can be correct within the context of a given problem. Fortunately, systems such as GKS give us a considerable amount of flexibility in how we handle attributes.

Primitive attributes—those bound to output primitives rather than to groups of primitives—are divided into two classes, *geometric* and *nongeometric*. Geometric attributes have size and are set explicitly in WC. For example, the height of a character is a geometric attribute. Geometric attributes are bound to the primitive and therefore are independent of the workstation used to display them.

All attributes that are not geometric are called nongeometric. For example, the type of line to be used by polyline (e.g., solid, dashed, or dotted) is a nongeometric attribute. Nongeometric attributes are set by indices into tables. Some entries in these tables are predefined. All can be set by the application programmer. Nongeometric attributes can be bundled and can be controlled at the workstation level, as described in the next section.

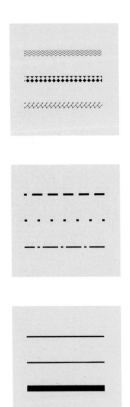

3.7.2 Polyline Attributes

The polyline has three attributes: line style, line color, and line width (Figure 3.20). None are geometric. The individual polyline attributes are set by the attribute procedures

```
void gset_linewidth(linewidth)
```

Figure 3.20
Polyline Width and Style

```
void gset_linetype(linetype)
void gset_line_colr_ind(line_colr_ind)
```

These procedures set the line-width scale factor, the line type, and the polyline color index, respectively.

The line-width scale factor is measured relative to a standard width for each workstation. A scale factor of 1.0 is the default line that the physical workstation will produce. The parameter `linewidth` multiples the thickness of this default line. The program cannot tell, without the use of an inquiry function, whether or not the physical device can produce lines of the requested thickness. Hence, we must realize that, although we can specify some desired value of an attribute, the physical limitations of the display will dictate that we will get a "best fit" to our request.

Line types are specified by the value of the index `linetype` in the procedure `gset_linetype`. The default is a solid line. Other indices give various dashed and dotted line types. Line color is specified through an index into a table of colors. GKS uses a three-color red–green–blue (RGB) system closely akin to the way most color monitors actually work. A color is formed by combining red, green, and blue primaries in adjustable amounts. Thus, the color table has three columns, as shown in Figure 3.21. The color index selects a row of the table, and the three column entries give the amount of red, green, and blue corresponding to this index. So that colors can be specified in a device-independent manner, the entries in the table are reals between 0.0 and 1.0, where 0.0 means that none of that primary, and 1.0 that the maximum amount of that primary is to be used. We shall discuss color and color systems in more detail in Chapter 7.

Index	R	G	B
0	0.0	0.0	0.0
1	1.0	1.0	1.0
2	1.0	0.5	0.5
.	.	.	.
.	.	.	.
.	.	.	.

Figure 3.21
The Color Table

The physical workstation interprets the specified RGB values as best it can. For example, a simple RGB color display might allow the user only the colors formed when each primary is either fully on or fully off. Such displays can produce eight colors: red, green, and blue (one color on and the other two off); black (all off); white (all on); cyan (blue and green on, red off), magenta (blue and red on, green off), and yellow (red and green on, blue off). In such a system, a value in the table of greater than 0.5 will cause the corresponding primary to be fully on, whereas a value of less than 0.5 will cause it to be off.

The entries in the color table are set to nondefault values on the (logical) workstation with identifier `ws_id` by the procedure, *set color representation*,

```
void gset_colr_rep(ws_id, colr_ind, colr_rep)
```

where `colr_ind` is the row of the table. The desired amounts of red, green, and blue are passed through the *color-bundle* structure

```
typedef struct
{
    Gfloat x;   /* red */
    Gfloat y;   /* green */
    Gfloat z;   /* blue */
} Gcolr_rep;
```

where `x`, `y`, and `z` determine the normalized red, green, and blue intensities, respectively. Thus, green and magenta can be defined on a workstation named CRT by

```
#define GREEN 1
#define MAGENTA 2
         .
         .
         .
static Gcolr_rep green = { 0.0, 1.0, 0.0 };
static Gcolr_rep magenta = { 1.0, 0.0, 1.0 };
         .
         .
gset_colr_ind( CRT, GREEN, &green);
gset_colr_ind( CRT, MAGENTA, &magenta);
```

Note that the same value of the index can be used to refer to different colors on different workstations. Hence, we can display the same primitive in different colors on two color workstations.

3.7.3 Text Attributes

Text attributes have become more important because the modern approach to the production of high-quality text in the printing industry is based on viewing each character as a graphical entity. Computer graphics were used for both diagrams and text in this book.

Modern graphics systems provide a variety of text attributes to allow the user to create high-quality text displays. These attributes include the size of the characters, their aspect ratio, their color, and the direction the text is produced on the screen. For applications that require precise text handling, we can control the spacing between characters and select from a variety of typefaces and fonts.

At this point, if you are anxious to proceed with the other aspects of computer graphics, you may want to skip the rest of this section. There are not only eight procedures in GKS to set our text attributes, but also a number of new data types. If you are interested at this point in writing programs that have at most simple annotation (i.e., text of a fixed height displayed from left to right), the default settings will probably work satisfactorily.

The GKS procedures for setting text attributes are

```
void gset_char_ht(char_ht)
void gset_expan(expan)
void gset_space(space)
void gset_text_colr_ind(colr_ind)
void gset_char_up_vec(char_up_vec)
void gset_text_path(text_path)
void gset_text_align(text_align)
void gset_fontprec(fontprec)
```

We fix the size of the characters by setting a character height, `text_ht`, in WC, in `gset_char_ht` and by choosing a scaling factor, `expan`, in the character-expansion procedure `gset_char_expan`, as in Figure 3.22. Additional spacing between characters can be provided by `gset_space`. The color for the text string is selected through an index into the color table via `gset_text_colr_ind`. We use the same color table as for our polyline colors, which were set by `gset_colr_rep`. However, even though we use a single color table, we can use different indices for text and polylines. Hence, more than one color can be in use at a time.

The usual way to put text on a page, at least in English prose, is from left to right. On even a simple graph, however, we usually want to be able to set labels and titles in other directions, such as parallel to the y-axis. The control of the direction is specified through

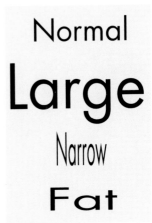

Figure 3.22
Setting Character Size

Figure 3.23
Character Up Vector

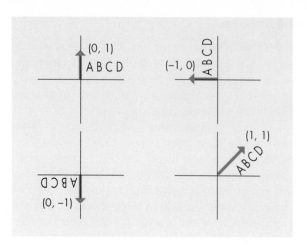

a vector called the *character up vector*, which is set by the function `gset_char_up_vec`. Some choices for this vector are indicated in Figure 3.23. We might also want to control the path characters follow once the direction is specified, as illustrated in Figure 3.24, which we do by setting the text path in `gset_text_path`. `Gtext_path` is an enumerated type that can take on the values `GRIGHT_PATH`, `GLEFT_PATH`, `GUP_PATH` and `GDOWN_PATH`.

Figure 3.24
Text Path

In the text function, we specify a position. In our simple example, this position was used in the default manner, which was assumed to be the lower-left corner of the string (in WC). This alignment choice is natural in many applications, but it makes careful placement of text on a page somewhat difficult. For example, if we want to center text at some point in WC, we might have to compute where to place this point. This calculation, if necessary, requires that we know the size of the characters, possibly for each physical workstation, and the characters spacing. Rather than requiring the application program to carry out this messy calculation, we can employ the text-alignment procedure `gset_text_align`. The choice of an alignment style can be done independently in the x and y directions. Alignment is specified by indices that reflect the properties of a string of characters. As we can see in Figure 3.25, there are four choices for horizontal alignment and six for vertical alignment. There are a greater number of choices for vertical alignment, as we have to consider letters with descenders (such as "g" or "p" or "y"), and the difference between uppercase and lowercase characters. `Gtext_align` contains a pair of enumerated types that specifies the desired alignment. For example, we can center a string through the function

```
static text_align={GCENTRE_HOR, GHALF_VERT};
```

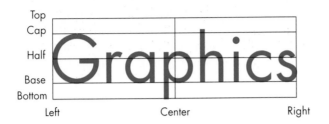

Figure 3.25
Text Alignment

The final procedure, `gset_fontprec`, allows us to choose a font and to select the precision we would like the hardware to use in producing our text. The data type `Gfontprec` has two components: the desired font, an integer and the desired precision, an ennumerated type. Text precision is related to the implementation issues we shall discuss in Chapter 6. The fundamental problem revolves around the difficulties in producing high-quality text. High-quality output requires sophisticated hardware and software. In addition, the system must do more work to produce characters with the specified attributes. Ensuring that characters are correctly mapped by graphics operations such as transformations further complicates the problem. By specifying the precision desired, we ask the system to work only as hard as necessary to generate output with the requested quality. Three levels of text precision are defined: *string, character,* and *stroke.* String precision is the lowest precision and thus allows the fastest production of text output. Stroke is the highest precision, and consequently is the slowest and most difficult to implement.

Numerous implementation issues arise as a result of this ability to specify accurate and varied types of text displays. As was the case with polyline attributes such as color and line width, specifying desired attributes in the user program does not guarantee that the hardware is capable of producing primitives displayed as requested. For attributes such as text color, we will see a best fit to the requested attribute. For other attributes, what is meant by a "best fit" may depend on the implementation. It is perfectly possible to specify text precisely in a program, only to find that the physical system cannot produce this quality and may produce no text output at all for a request it cannot handle. The avoidance of such an event may require careful use of manuals and inquiry procedures.

3.7.4 Bundled Attributes

A program can set nongeometric attributes either individually, as we have already discussed, or through *bundles*. In the first mechanism, each attribute is set to a nondefault value by a separate procedure call and, with the exception of its color, the primitive will have the same attributes on every workstation. Bundled attributes can be set in groups and provide a much more flexible mechanism. Bundled attributes can be used to make primitives appear in different ways on different workstations.

The importance of this mechanism can be seen in the following example. Consider our previous example of a user with a color CRT display and a plotter. The CRT can produce at least some colors, but the plotter can display only black lines on a white page. Suppose we wish to be able to distinguish between two different styles of lines. On the color display, we usually distinguish between two line styles by color. If we use this mechanism, the best the plotter can do will be to display both lines as black, thus making them indistinguishable. An alternative might be to make one line solid and the other dashed. Although that might solve the problem on the plotter, our user may find colored dashed lines less than appealing on the CRT. What we really would like is to have is different colors on the CRT and different line types on the plotter. Bundling attributes makes our wish possible.

For each nongeometric attribute, there is a flag called the *aspect source flag* that determines whether the attribute is bundled or individual. All told, there are 13 such attributes, and the flags form an array. The first three flags control the polyline attributes: line style, line-width scale factor, and color. We set an index for each workstation for each group of bundled polyline attributes through the *set polyline representation* procedure:

```
void gset_line_rep(ws_id, line_ind, line_rep)

Gint ws_id, line_ind;
Gline_rep *line_rep;

typedef struct
{
    Gint type;
    Gfloat width;
    Gint colr;
} Gline_rep;
```

Thus, we can create red and green solid lines on the CRT with indices one and two, but solid and dashed lines on the plotter with the same line indices, as in Figure 3.26. Within the program, the attributes are changed by the *set polyline index* procedure:

```
void gset_line_ind(line_ind)
```

Figure 3.26
Bundle Table

Index	WS	Type	Width	Color	
1	CRT	——	1	●——▶	(1., 0., 0.,)
1	Plotter	——	1	●——▶	(0., 0., 0.,)
2	CRT	——	1	●——▶	(0., 1., 0.,)
2	Plotter	– – –	1	●——▶	(0., 0., 0.,)

```
Gint line_ind;
```

Similar procedures hold for the other primitives (e.g., *set text representation* and *set text index*).

We shall assume that, by default or as part of the initialization, all attributes have been set to individual. However, the use of bundled attributes not only can give the programmer more flexibility, but also can clean up our programs by avoiding long series of repeated setting of attributes whenever we switch line or text styles. Bundle tables can be set once as part of initialization. Attributes are then manipulated in the program via a few indices.

3.8
Other Primitives

Although we could think of almost an infinite variety of additional primitives, ranging from various types of curves to sets of shapes, most systems provide a minimal set that should be supported on all implementations. GKS provides three primitives in addition to the polyline and text primitives: *polymarkers, fill areas,* and *cell arrays.* More sophisticated primitives can be generated through this set, possible through the use of approximations. For example, we might fit a curve with a polyline. We might also find "hooks" into a particular system, such as the generalized drawing primitive we shall discuss later in this section. These primitives have proven sufficient for most two-dimensional applications. In Chapter 8, we shall see how we can extend the two-dimensional primitives we develop here to a set of three-dimensional primitives.

3.8.1 The Polymarker

Markers are symbols, such as stars, crosses, dots, and pluses, often used in making plots. Although we could try to use single characters in text commands, this strategy is unwieldy. For instance, if we wish to change a plot that uses lines to join the data points through the polyline to a plot using a sequence of stars to mark the points, we would like this change not to alter the program significantly. The solution is the *polymarker* function:

```
void gpolymarker(num_pt, points)

Gint num_pt;
Gpt *points;
```

As with polyline, `points` is an array of `num_pt` points. The current marker is placed at each point in the array, where the values are in WC. The current marker symbol is established by the *set marker type* procedure

```
void gset_marker_type(marker_type)

Gint marker_type;
```

where `marker_type` is an index into a table of markers.

In addition to the marker type, the polymarker has a color attribute set and a marker-size scale-factor attribute.

3.8.2 The Fill Area

Fill areas in GKS are polygonal areas. We can define a polygon by giving an ordered list of points, or *vertices*. Successive vertices are connected by line segments called *edges*. The last vertex is connected to the first, thus creating a closed boundary. It might seem then that we could represent a polygon of n points as a polyline of $n+1$ points by adding an additional point to the polyline that is located at the same place as the first point is. This strategy would enable us to draw the boundary of a polygon. The name *fill area* is used, rather than *polygon*, to emphasize that a fill area has an interior, whereas the polygon formed by a closed polyline may not. The interior of a fill area can be colored or filled with a pattern. The choice of fill styles is an attribute of the fill area primitive. This important difference between a fill area and a closed polyline is illustrated in Figure 3.27. If two polylines define the triangle and the square, we get the image on the left. If we use fill areas, we can get either the image in the center or the one on the right, depending on the order in which the triangle and the square were placed on the display.

Figure 3.27
Polygon versus Polyline

A fill area is defined by the procedure

```
void gfill_area( num_pt, points)

Gint num_pt;
Gpt *points;
```

where `points` is an array of the `num_pt` vertices. GKS defines four styles for the interior of a fill area: hollow, solid, hatch, and pattern. These styles are illustrated in Figure 3.28. The selection of the style is made by the *set fill area interior style* procedure. A particular pattern or color (for solid fills) is selected by the *set fill area style index* procedure.

Filling the interior of a region defined by a set of vertices or edges with either a solid color or a pattern is virtually impossible to implement on anything but a raster system. We obtain hollow fills by drawing the edges of the fill area and not worrying about the interior, thus allowing fill areas to be displayed on random-scan systems. Hatch fills may also be producible on random-scan systems.

GKS defines the edge or boundary of a fill area to be inside the region. This choice is rather arbitrary and does not let us create a red solid with green edges except by using two primitives: a green fill area and a red polyline. Other systems, such as PHIGS, allow the user to work with the edge of a fill area independently of the fill area's interior.

The issue of what is inside and what is outside a fill area could be decided in a number of ways. GKS uses a scan-line method. Consider the fill area on the top of Figure 3.29. A raster system displays the contents of its frame buffer, line by line. Each of these horizontal lines

Figure 3.28
Fill Area Interior Styles

is known as a *scan line*. As we follow a scan line across a fill area, a point is considered inside the fill area if this line crosses an odd number of edges before reaching the point.[3] With this definition, the fill area is filled as shown on the bottom of the figure. The details of fill algorithms will be discussed in Chapter 7.

3.8.3 Cell Arrays

The *cell array* is a rectangular fill area where the user can define the fill pattern. It is accessed through the procedure `gcell_array`. This primitive defines a rectangular area in WC that is ruled into cells, as in Figure 3.30. Each cell is filled with a color whose index we obtain by cycling through an array specified in the parameter list.

The intention of the cell array was to provide the user with a raster-like primitive. However, since the cell array is defined in WC, as are all GKS output primitives, there are some problems in implementation. Random-scan systems may be unable to produce the patterns, and, in many raster systems, user-defined patterns may come out looking ragged when converted to DC. For these reasons, the cell array has not proved to be useful in many GKS applications.

Figure 3.29
Filling by Scan Lines

Figure 3.30
The Cell Array

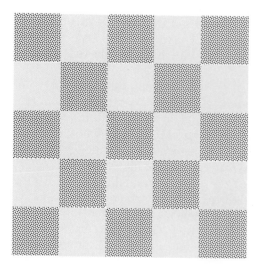

---

[3] As long as the line does not intersect any vertices, this definition will work equally well if we allow the line to cross the polygon in any direction.

3.8.4 Generalized Drawing Primitives

The generalized drawing primitive is accessed through the function

```
void ggdp(num_pt, points, gdp_id, gdp_data)

Gint num_pt;
Gpt *points;
Gint gdp_id;
Gdp_data *gdp_data;
```

This primitive allows direct access to specific hardware-generated output primitives such as circles, ellipses, and rectangles, illustrated in Figure 3.31, that are not defined within GKS. Since not all hardware can produce all these primitives, this procedure is device dependent, as is any program that uses it. The parameters of the call allow enough flexibility that a number of types of primitives can be accessed through ggdp.

Each available generalized drawing primitive will have an identifier gdp_id. A particular generalized drawing primitive will need num_pt points in the array points to define it uniquely. For example, num_id=1 might be a circle and num_id=2 an arc of a circle. The circle can be defined by two points—its center and a point on the circumference. The arc will need three points—for example, the center of the circle and two points on the circumference. The implementation-defined data record gdp_data may be necessary to define attributes of the primitive or any other information that the hardware may need. Alternately, attributes for the generalized drawing primitive can be obtained from the polyline or fill-area attributes. For example, a circle might use the current polyline attributes to draw its circumference, and the fill-area attributes to fill its interior. A circle centered at the origin with unit radius might be specified by the two lines

```
static Gpt circle_data[]={ {0., 0.}, {0., 1.} }
ggdp(2, circle_data, CIRCLE_ID, NULL);
```

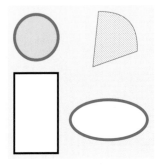

Figure 3.31
Generalized Drawing
Primitives

3.9
A Self-Scaling Plotter

As an example of many of the features we have just presented, we shall now design a self-scaling plotting function. The routine will plot a single curve of num_pt points, which are stored in an array pointed to by `xy_data`. We want labels on our plot for both the x and y axes, and a title on the top. These three strings or character arrays are denoted `x_label`, `y_label`, and `title`, respectively. Hence, the procedure will be accessed by code of the form:

```
Gint num_pt;
Gpt xy_data[NUM_POINTS];
Gchar *x_label, *y_label, *title;
            .
            .
            .
plot(num_pt, xy_data, x_label, y_label, title);
```

Before writing the code, let us examine some of the requirements of the procedure. Since we are passing only the data to the procedure, we must scale the plot so that it appears in the same area of the display, regardless of the values of the data. Therefore, our procedure must be self-scaling. We probably want to use some of our text attributes, because labels on graphs should be centered and, if possible, the y-axis label should have its text oriented along this axis. We might also attempt to make the output a little fancier than just a single polyline for the data and lines for the axes.

To scale the plot, we will have to find the maximum and minimum of the data points. Let us assume we have a procedure **bounds** that will return the maximum and minimum of the data. This procedure should be simple to write.

We already have written our initialization and termination procedures **init** and **finish**, which we can invoke here. Thus, the pseudocode of our procedure might incorporate these steps:

```
plot( num_pt, data, xlabel, ylabel, title)

Gint num_pt;
Gpt data[];
Gchar *xlabel, *ylabel, *title;
{
    init(.....);
    bounds(.....);
    set_up_normalization_transforms(.....);
    draw_axes(.....);
    plot_data(.....);
    draw_labels_and_title(....);
    finish(.....);
}
```

3.9.1 Setting Up the Normalization Transformations

We already have the routines for the first two steps. Setting up the normalization transformations takes planning. We will employ two transformations, one for the graph of the data and one for the labels and titles. We will form our final plot by overlaying the two parts. Using two normalization transformations ensures that the graph fits in the same area of the display, independent of the number of points or the range of the data, while still allowing us always to have characters of the same size in our labels and title.

Each normalization transformation requires the specification of a world window and of a corresponding viewport in NDC space. The procedure **bounds** returns four values, **xmin**, **xmax**, **ymin**, and **ymin**. The points (x_{min}, y_{min}) and (x_{max}, y_{max}) form the lower-left and upper-right corners of a rectangle that exactly fits all the data points. This rectangle, called either the *bounding box* or the *extent* of the data, is shown in Figure 3.32. Now the code

Figure 3.32
Bounding the Data

```
Glim window1;
window1.x1 = xmin;
window1.y1 = ymin;
window1.x2 = xmax;
window1.y2 = ymax;
gset_win( 1, &window1);
```

sets up half of our first normalization transformation: a window in WC that is the bounding box for the data. To complete this normalization transformation, we next have to decide where to place these data in NDC space. This decision is based on deciding where the labels and title should be placed and how large the characters should be. We will make the characters 5 percent of the screen size and attempt to center them in appropriate areas of the display. If we leave 10 percent of NDC space free on the bottom for the x label and 10 percent free on the left for the y label, the data will not overlap our text. If, as in Figure 3.33, we leave 10 percent free on the top in NDC space, we will have room for our title. An appropriate viewport for the data can now be defined by

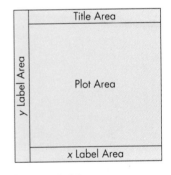

Figure 3.33
Display Layout for Plot Routine

```
Glim viewport1;
viewport1.x1 =  0.1;
viewport1.y1 =  0.1;
viewport1.x2 =  1.0;
viewport1.y2 =  0.9;
gset_vp( 1, &viewport1);
```

The second normalization transform will be used for both the labels and the title. Since characters can be declared to be of any size in WC, we can select any units we wish for this part of the problem. A convenient choice for situations like this is to use a normalization transformation whose window is the unit square defined by the points $(0.0, 0.0)$ and $(1.0, 1.0)$. With this choice, the specification of a character height (or of any geometric attribute) will thus be expressed as a fraction of the window dimension. Since the text will overlay the whole image, as shown in Figure 3.33, its appropriate viewport is all of NDC space. The window and viewport we just described are those of the default normalization transformation (0).

The axes can be drawn as a single polyline passing through the points (x_{min}, y_{max}), (x_{min}, y_{min}) and (x_{max}, y_{min}). The structure **axes** is used to hold these values. All the data can be plotted by a single call to polyline,

```
gpolyline( num_pt, data);
```

as can the axes.

Now we are ready to add the labels and titles. These will use normalization transformation 0, which must be selected by `gsel_norm_tran`. Remember we also had to use `gsel_norm_tran` to select transformation 1 before drawing the axes and data, or else we would still have been using the default transformation. The default for character direction is left to right, so we will add the x-axis label and the title on the top first. Two attributes must be set, the size of the characters and the alignment of the text. We can also choose a desired typeface and font. Since we decided that characters should be 5 percent of our window and the window is a unit square, we set the character height by

```
gset_char_ht(0.05);
```

We would like to have our strings centered in their assigned areas. We shall let GKS do the alignment by choosing to have strings centered both horizontally and vertically by

```
static Gtext_align center =
            { GCENTER_HOR, GHALF_VERT };
gset_text_align(&center);
```

A nondefault font is selected by `gset_fontprec`. Now we can add the x-axis label and the title by using `gtext`, giving the center of the allocated boxes in WC:

```
text_loc.x = 0.5;
text_loc.y = 0.05;
gtext( &text_loc ,xlabel);
text_loc.x = 0.5;
text_loc.y = 0.95;
gtext( &textloc, title);
```

We generate the *y*-axis label by setting the text path to be along the *y*- axis. We choose a text up vector that points to the left. Alignment has already been set, so we select the center of the allocated area as the text location

```
char_up.x = -1.0;
char_up.y =  0.0;
gset_charup(&charup);
text_loc.x = 0.05;
text_loc.y = 0.5;
gtext( &textloc, ylabel);
```

The plot formed as we have described is shown in Figure 3.34 for simple data. Although correct, it is not an exciting plot. To get an idea of how we can make it look a little flashier, let us make several small changes. We add color to the line and axes by setting colors in the table using `gset_colr_rep`, then changing colors for our polylines by `gset_line_colr_ind`. We employ thicker polylines via `gset_line_width` to emphasize the axes and curve. We fill in the area under the curve by forming a fill area whose top is the curve and whose

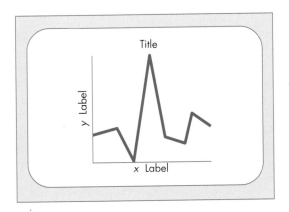

Figure 3.34
Plot Output: Simple Version

Figure 3.35
Sample Output

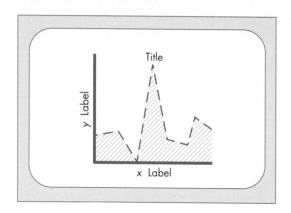

bottom is the x axis. We form this fill area by adding the two points (x_{max}, y_{min}) and (x_{min}, y_{min}) to the input data structure. We fill the fill area with a desired hatch pattern through `gset_fill_int_style` and `set_fill_style_ind`. Finally, we also use a polyline for the data to emphasize the top of the fill area. The resulting plot for a simple main program is shown in Figure 3.35. The full code of the procedure is given in Appendix C.

3.10
Metafiles

In this final section, we introduce metafiles as a method of storing and transporting graphical information. Our discussion of metafiles may seem unrelated to the rest of the chapter, but it is relevant. At this point, you should be capable of making use of a graphics software package. Once you start writing applications programs, you may want to send your results to a colleague, to make use of someone else's data, or to generate output on a high-quality device such as a film recorder, which might not be available locally. Metafiles provide a method of achieving these goals. We shall discuss two approaches: one within a particular system (in our case, GKS), and another that allows communication between different graphics systems.

Our approach to developing application programs has been to write a program without knowing the physical properties of any graphical devices or even the type of processor, and to use this program as our means of transporting graphical information. This approach should work if the recipient of our program is also using the same graphics system, has a C compiler, and has the C language binding of GKS. But he might not. In addition, he might not care to recompile and rerun a long program. He may care about only its output, or he may want to incorporate pieces of that output in his own display. If he is using GKS, the *GKS metafile* (GKSM) provides an additional method of storing and reading GKS output in a form that can be stored in a file or transported. The *Computer Graphics Metafile* (CGM), on the other hand, provides a metafile mechanism that can be applied to applications developed by almost any graphics package.

3.10.1 The GKS Metafile

The programs we have written can be looked at as containing two types of statements: GKS procedures and everything else. This seemingly silly statement is of great importance if we look at the execution of the program from the point of view of a logical workstation. Consider an active output-only workstation. It receives commands to display GKS primitives. It receives segments. It changes attributes. It may be asked to clear its display surface. All it sees is a sequence of GKS functions; it sees none of the other parts of the application program that were necessary to generate the data for these functions.

An appropriate conceptual model of a GKS workstation is a black box whose input is GKS functions and their parameters. Thus, this workstation could be given a list of GKS functions and data through means other than a program and could produce the same output. The GKS metafile is a mechanism for writing and reading this information such that that information can be transported easily.

The metafile is structured as in Figure 3.36. The format can vary from binary to ASCII and is an implementation issue that we shall not discuss. The file consists of a number of records, or *items*. The header items give the information about the file and its format. A terminator item is necessary to identify the end of the metafile. In between are other items (Figure 3.37), each of which corresponds to a GKS function a workstation might see. The function is identified by a number, which is followed by the data for the function.

The contents of a GKS metafile mirror the output functions a workstation would see. Hence, an output metafile should look like any other output workstation. We open a workstation whose type is metafile output. It is assigned a logical identifier, as is any other workstation. Now, as long as it is active, output will go to it, along

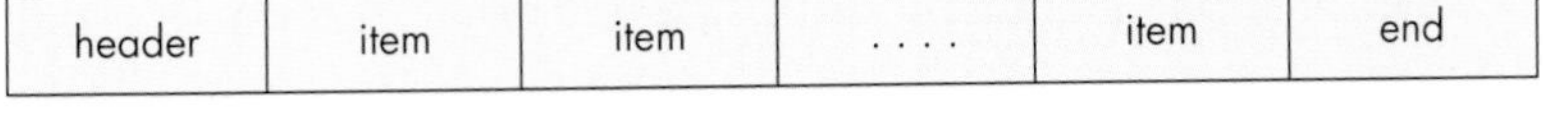

Figure 3.36
Metafile Structure

Figure 3.37
Metafile Item

item type	data length	data

with any other active workstations, and this output will be retained in the metafile.

Since all output goes to this metafile (if it is active), a GKS metafile provides a program trace. Consider the following code, which uses the *clear workstation* function:

```
init()

        .
        .
        .
gpolyline(....);

        .
        .
        .
gclear_ws(METAFILE);
finish();
```

Immediately before the metafile workstation is deactivated and closed by `finish`, we use the `gclear_ws` procedure to clear its surface. However, since the physical workstation is a file, the primitives generated by the polyline are in the file. When the metafile is closed, its contains all primitives that were displayed on it while it was active. A metafile input workstation could then extract primitives from this metafile that were placed there before the clear-workstation function. Thus, although the final display was empty, all primitives that were displayed on it are available in the metafile.

3.10.2 Interpreting A GKS Metafile

We read a GKS metafile by opening a workstation that is of type metafile input, then processing the items in the metafile. Making metafile input available through a normal GKS workstation is compatible with our workstation concept. However, we need special procedures for handling the items in the metafile, because they provide a new form of input to our programs. The three procedures required are *get item type from GKSM, read item from GKSM,* and *interpret item*

```
void gget_item_type( ws_id, item_type, item_data_length)
void gread_item(ws_id, max_item_data_length, item_data)
void ginterpret_item(item_type, item_length, item_data)

Gint ws_id;
Gint *item_type;
Gint *item_data_length;
Gint item_length;
Gint  max_item_data_length;
Gitem_data *item_data;
```

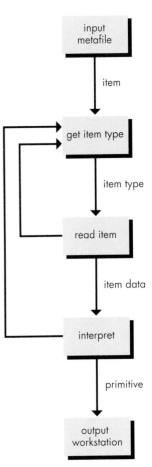

The flow of interpreting the file (Figure 3.38) begins with an open metafile with a file pointer pointed at some item. We use the procedure `gget_item_type` to tell us what this item is and what the length of its data record is. Note that the data record can vary for the same item type. For example, a polyline of three points and a polyline of 100 points are of the same type, but the second requires far more space for its data record. The file pointer is advanced automatically to the next item. After looking at the item type, we can either use it or go on to the next item in the file. Reading an item returns its data to the program in an implementation-dependent data structure `item_data`. These data are available for use by the application program.

We can obtain an item from our metafile and interpret it on all the active workstations through the procedure `ginterpret_item`. If the item read was a polyline and we decide to interpret it, the polyline will appear on all the active output workstations, including any active metafile output workstations. Thus, a program can go through the metafile and decide what to do with each item. Or it can read in an entire metafile at the beginning, then continue as follows:

```
/* After Opening Metafile */

gget_item_type(META_IN, item_type, item_data_length)
while(*item_type != END_METAFILE)
{
    gread_item(META_IN, MAX_LENGTH, item_data)
    ginterpret_item(item_type, item_length, item_data)
    gget_item_type(META_IN,item_type, item_data_length)
}

  /* Continue */
```

Figure 3.38
Interpreting the
GKS Metafile

In this way, metafiles could be used to provide building blocks for application programs that are independent of the code used to generate them.

3.10.3 The Computer-Graphics Metafile

Since the GKS metafile is a trace of a GKS program's execution, an interpreter of the metafile must be knowledgeable about GKS. Often, we desire to use a metafile only to transport our output to a high-quality output device, such as a film recorder. Such devices can be expensive and have only limited, if any, capability to process a user program that uses a particular graphics system, such as GKS. However, such a device will be able to generate the output primitives used in most systems. Such devices are usually run offline and must be made accessible to a wide variety of users, not just to those who use GKS.

What such a device needs as input is only the information necessary to produce pictures, such as a list of primitives and their attributes. The Computer Graphics Metafile [CGM86] was created as a standard way of storing this information. Its structure is similar to that of a GKS metafile, with header, terminator, and content records. The items that can be included are a little more general than are the GKS primitives. However, the CGM is only a description of a picture and does not provide the program trace capability of the GKSM.

The use of metafiles in graphics can be extended to solve other, more general portability problems. An application that uses graphics often needs to transport information other than graphical information. For example, if we design a mechanical part with an interactive CAD program, the design may include information such as the materials and tolerances. Our circuit-design examples may include element values and part numbers. A database must have an exchange method that can include, but is not restricted to, graphical information. The *Initial Graphics Exchange Standard* (IGES) [IGES86] is one such standard. Creation of these standards is an area of great activity, since, as the applications we use grow more sophisticated, we require more sophisticated database standards.

3.11
Suggested Readings

The ISO version of GKS is ISO 7492 [GKS84]; the ANSI version is ANSI X3.124-1985. The book [End84] provides additional information for people who might want to implement a system. It also explains the reasoning behind some of the decisions in GKS that you might find questionable. The books [Spr85] and [Hop83] contain further examples of GKS programs; [Har83] also has examples, but uses the older CORE system. The CGM and IGES are discussed in [Hend86] and [Smith84].

■ Exercises

3.1 GKS does not allow us to turn off clipping at the workstation-transformation level. Explain why clipping is still required in going from WC to NDC.

3.2 Applications such as the circuit-layout program use the same objects (e.g., resistors, capacitors) repeatedly to form a picture. For this example, or for any other you find interesting, define a set of appropriate *symbols*. Write procedures that generate these symbols using GKS primitives. Make the size and position of your symbols part of the calling parameters.

3.3 The graph-plotting program developed in this chapter is probably much simpler and less flexible than we would desire it to be. Using the procedures we have presented, implement a plotting procedure that allows (1) multiple plots, and (2) multiple ways of displaying the data (e.g., bar charts and pie charts).

3.4 Using GKS, create a turtle graphics procedure library. There should be five basic procedures: `place(x,y)` (to initialize the turtle's position), `forward(distance)`, `right(angle)`, `left (angle)`, and `pen(up_down)`. How do you choose an appropriate window? How do you treat a procedure call that attempts to move the turtle outside the window?

3.5 An interesting variant of Exercise 3.4 is to create a "reflecting turtle." Here, the turtle is placed in a fixed-sized box. It bounces off the sides as light bounces off a mirror, as shown in Figure 3.39.

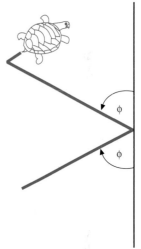

Figure 3.39
The Bouncing Turtle

3.6 Many people find the numerous text attributes one of the less appealing features of GKS. Identify a simpler set of text features, then write procedures to implement them, starting with the GKS procedures.

3.7 Suppose you are given text as an array in which each element is a single character. Write a procedure that will output the text

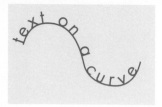

Figure 3.40
Following a Curved Path

along a curve described by a differentiable function $y = f(x)$, as in Figure 3.40.

3.8 Using the GKS text and attributes, construct a simple desk top publishing program. It should take an input file of ASCII characters and commands, and produce "typeset" output. You can place commands within the ASCII input by using the character \ as a prefix for commands (e.g., \font(font_num) or \vspace(vert_space)).

3.9 Boolean or logical expressions such as

$$f = (a + b)' \cdot (b' + c)$$

use three basic operators: AND ($\cdot$), OR ($+$) and NOT ('). We can display any Boolean expression using symbols (or gates), as is done in Figure 3.41. Write a program that will take an arbitrary Boolean expression and display it as a diagram.

Figure 3.41
Logic Symbols

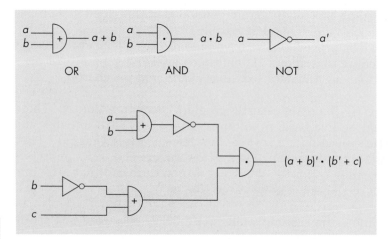

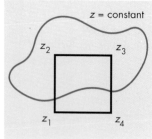

Figure 3.42
Contour Cells

3.10 The equation $z = f(x, y)$ describes a surface. One method of displaying this surface is to draw a series of *contours*. A contour is a closed curve of x, y values that satisfy the equation for a fixed value of z. Since this equation is implicit, one possible method is to generate a set of z values for x, y pairs on some grid forming a set of cells, as in Figure 3.42. For a given contour value of z—say between z_1 and z_2—we can interpolate along the edge of the cell to find a point on the contour. Write a program that generates the cells from a function $f(x, y)$ and then generates polylines that approximate contours. This exercise is difficult; a cell does not necessarily determine unambiguous contour crossings.

3.11 We defined the inside and outside of a polyline through a scan-line definition. Can you generalize this definition such that we do not have to refer to scan lines? What happens if a scan line passes through a vertex?

3.12 Our defintion of a fill area would cause a star pattern to be filled as shown on the top of Figure 3.43. How could we define a fill area so that the star pattern would be filled as on the bottom of the figure?

3.13 The *fill area set* primitive (Figure 3.44) has been added to many graphics systems. It is defined by a list whose elements point to lists of points. Each list of points defines a fill area. Can this primitive be constructed from the fill-area primitive?

3.14 An alternative definition technique for determining the inside of an area is to traverse its boundary in a clockwise manner, and to define *inside* as being to the right of our direction of travel. Is this a practical definition for computer graphics?

3.15 Often, when we generate numerous (one-dimensional) data, we display them as a cascade plot, like that in Figure 3.45. The first row contains the first k data points, the second row contains the next k points, and so on. Note than each row of data "hides" the data behind it. Write a program to generate such a plot.

Figure 3.43
Filling a Star

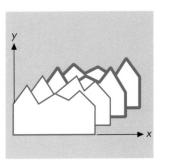

Figure 3.45
Cascade Plot

Figure 3.44
Fill Set

4

INTERACTIVE
GRAPHICS

Introduction

Any survey of the more sophisticated and exciting applications of modern computer graphics will reveal most of the following features: input and interaction, manipulation of pictures, and modeling of complex objects and phenomena. If a graphics software system is to be useful in the modern workstation environment, it must have capabilities to support these features.

4.1
Programming with Interaction

Consider, for example, an interactive CAD application such as might arise in the design of a mechanical part. In such applications, we work with models of three-dimensional objects. As part of the design process, we interactively add and modify elements in the model. We also change the view of the model to obtain access to other parts of the design. These operations require additional capabilities from our graphics system.

Although, in the long run, it will be important to understand what the mathematics of rotation are or how interactive hardware devices are built, the programmer does not explicitly need this knowledge to write a program. We do not mean to imply that you should not know this information. Rather, we are suggesting that we can start by studying the software functionality, independently of its implementation.

This chapter focuses on two aspects high-level interactive applications: *segmentation* and *input*. Segmentations allow us to group primitives into user-definable objects. Being able to work with objects, rather than with individual primitives, is the first step toward developing sophisticated interactive modeling techniques. We shall then develop the basic forms of graphical input, introducing both the devices and the input procedures. The addition of a transformation capability will be the subject of the following chapter.

As in the preceding chapter, we shall introduce the software using a simple but illustrative example: a shape-layout program. This application is conceptually similar to most painting programs, circuit-layout programs, and a host of other menu-oriented interactive applications.

▰ 4.2
▰ A Shape-Layout Program

Our choice of a shape-layout program allows us to illustrate not only the additional graphical features of a software package, such as input and segmentation, but also many of the standard design tools in user interfaces, such as menus, prompting, and icons. The example will be as simple as possible; you should feel free to experiment with many of the choices we have made. We shall address the design of the user interface at the end of the chapter, after we have explored the mechanics of writing interactive programs.

Our example will allow a user to form a picture consisting of shapes that will appear in a menu. She will also be able to add annotation (text) to the picture. The display presented to the user will provide prompts to help the user with the layout process. A typical application for this simple example might be to prepare flowcharts for programs. With a few simple modifications, it could become a circuit-layout or painting program.

Figure 4.1 shows the initial display presented to the user. The display has four areas, which correspond to four distinct viewports in our program. The upper-left area, which will be blank initially, will

Figure 4.1
Initial Display

be used for the picture the user will create. The allowable shapes will appear in a menu in the upper right. A message area will be placed on the bottom left for prompts to the user, such as one informing her what actions will be required next. The control area at the bottom right will be used for ending the program or clearing the work area.

There are a number of features missing that you might want to add later, such as a method of undoing actions and a way of producing output on a hardcopy device such as a printer.

Note that, in two of the viewports, we find *icons,* or pictures that represent possible actions. For example, the "X" is used as an icon that denotes the action of erasing the screen. This may be a poor choice of an icon, as "X" may not convey to a user that it symbolizes clearing the screen. We can use another symbol instead of the "X" in our design with only small changes to our program. The initial message displayed requests the user to select from the shape menu an item that will be placed in the drawing area. Once this action is complete, a new message will appear in this area.

4.2.1 Choosing Windows and Viewports

Our design starts with the layout of the display, which is similar to the procedure we followed with the plotting program. The following code contains our selections for the various windows and viewports. Later, we will place these procedures in a separate module. We use four normalization transformations, one for each of our viewports. Since this application has no natural world coordinate system associated with it, we can select each window and viewport pair with the same aspect ratio, and employ the WC system, in Figure 4.2.

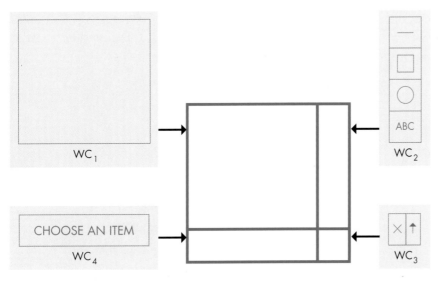

Figure 4.2
World Coordinate Systems

```
static Glim window1 = {0.0, 8.0, 0.0, 9.0};
static Glim viewport1 = {0.0, 0.8, 0.1, 1.0};
static Glim window2 = {0.0, 2.0, 0.0, 9.0};
static Glim viewport2 = {0.8, 1.0, 0.1, 1.0};
static Glim window3 = {0.0, 2.0, 0.0, 1.0};
static Glim viewport3= {0.8,1.0,0.0,0.1};
static Glim window4 = {0.0, 8.0, 0.0, 1.0};
static Glim viewport4 = {0.0, 0.8, 0.0, 0.1}

gset_win( DRAW_TRANS, &window1);
gset_vp( DRAW_TRANS, &viewport1);

gset_win( MENU_TRANS, &window2);
gset_vp( MENU,_TRANS &viewport2);

gset_win( CONTROL_TRANS, &window3);
gset_vp( CONTROL_TRANS, &viewport3);

gset_win( MESSAGE_TRANS, &window4);
gset_vp( MESSAGE_TRANS, &viewport4);
```

4.2.2 The Shape Menu

Our next step is to set up the object menu. We assume we have
available a generalized drawing primitive that draws a circle using
the present polyline attributes. The two data points we assume it
will take for its input are the center of the circle and any point on the
circumference. Since we will be surrounding our areas with rectangles,
we will employ a box-drawing procedure. However, if we wish to
draw boxes over each other, the last painting over the previous, we
can define a box that is actually a fill area in the background color,
followed by a polyline in the foreground color; for example,

```
fill_box( xmin, xmax, ymin, ymax)

Gfloat xmin, xmax, ymin, ymax;
{
    Gpt[5] box;
    box[0].x = box[3].x = box[4].x = xmin;
    box[1].x = box[2].x = xmax;
    box[0].y = box[1].y = box[4].y = ymin;
    box[2].y = box[3].y = ymax;
    gset_fill_area_int_style(GSOLID);
    gset_fill_area_colr_ind(BACKGROUND);
    gfill_area( 4, box);
    gset_linetype(SOLID)
```

```
        gset_line_colr_ind(FOREGROUND);
        gpolyline( 5, box);
    }
```

Using this procedure, we can now draw the shape menu area of the
display. The distances have been picked so that the shapes will be
centered in their boxes.

```
Gpt points[2];
Gpt loc;
static Gtext_align center = {GCENTRE_HOR, GHALF_VERT};

/* line icon */

fill_box( 0.0, 2.0, 6.75, 9.0);
points[0].x = 0.5;
points[0].y = 7.875;
points[1].x = 1.5;
points[1].y = 7.875;
gpolyline( 2, points);

/*rectangle icon */

fill_box( 0.0, 2.0, 4.5, 6.75);
fill_box( 0.5, 1.5, 5.0625, 6.1875);

/* Circle Icon (Using Implementation Dependent GDP) */

fill_box( 0.0, 2.0, 2.25, 4.5);
points[0].x = 1.0;
points[0].y = 3.375;
points[1].x = 1.0;
points[1].y = 2.5;
ggdp( 2, points, CIRCLE_ID, NULL)

/* Text Icon */

fill_box( 0.0, 2.0, 0.0, 2.25);
gset_text_align( &center);
gset_char_ht(1.0);
loc.x = 1.0;
loc.y = 1.125;
gtext( &loc, "ABC");
```

Similar code is used for the messages and for the control boxes.

4.3
Defining Objects

In our example, it will be far easier for a user to select an item from the menu if she can point to an area of the screen rather than to a single primitive such as a line segment. We prepared for this in our initial drawing of the menu by placing each item (the rectangle, the circle) over a solid fill area. Hence, we might consider the combination of this fill area defined by the `fill_box` procedure and the primitive to be a graphical *object*. If we can define such objects within our system, some problems of input may be eased. In addition, we might use such notions to facilitate operations such as redrawing the screen and moving groups of primitives to new locations.

4.3.1 Segments

Figure 4.3
Objects versus Primitives

A *graphical object* corresponds to what we might identify visually as an object on our displays or within our model of a particular application. For example, consider the simple diagram in Figure 4.3. If asked to describe what you see in the figure, you would probably answer "a box and a triangle," rather than "seven line segments." At a low level, however, the diagram is a collection of line segments or polylines. As application programmers, we have to define these entities in terms of the primitives of our system. Once they have been defined, we prefer to work with the groups of primitives.

Segments are groups of primitives. The choice of which primitives go into a segment is at the discretion of the application programmer. A good analogy to help us understand segments is to think of them as akin to simple files—that is, files whose components are graphical primitives.

Consider a standard file that we might define from a program. If we ask what can go in such a file, the answer is almost anything the programmer might want to put in it. Editors create text files; C programs can create data files; executable programs are themselves stored as binary files. We can create files whose contents are other files. Programs work with files routinely. When we "run" a user program, the operating system is actually reading a file that contains the executable code, and is manipulating any required input and output data files. Thus, we should find remarkable neither that files can hold graphical information, nor that a graphics programming language should contain functions that allow the user to define and manipulate such files. The GKS metafile in Chapter 2 is one such example. Segments, while not files, have many of their properties.

If we start with the notion of a C file we might create from a program, there are five necessary requirements: a beginning, an end, a way of naming or identifying the file, a way of putting things in the file, and a way of extracting information from the file. The same requirements hold for segments. We meet the first three requirements by creating (opening) and closing a segment. In GKS, a segment is initiated by the procedure *create segment,*

```
void gcreate_seg( seg_name )

Gint seg_name;
```

where `seg_name` is a positive integer that is used to identify the segment. In practice, a symbolic constant as in the code

```
#define CIRCLE 1
      .
      .
      .
gcreat_seg(CIRCLE);
```

is usually clearer. The segment is closed or ended by the *close segment* procedure:

```
void gclose_seg();
```

Since only one segment can be open at a time, no parameter is necessary in `gclose_seg`. Between the open and close, we can define primitives or use other procedures that do so. For instance, in our example, we will put all the messages the program might display to the user in segments, so we can easily manipulate them as necessary in our program. The initial message might form a segment such as

```
gcreate_seg(INITIAL_MESSAGE);
fill_box(0.0, 8.0, 0.0, 1.0);
gset_text_align(GCENTRE_HOR, GHALF_VERT);
gset_char_ht( 1.0);
gset_text_colr_ind(FOREGROUND);
loc.x = 4.0;
loc.y = 0.5;
gtext( &loc, "CHOOSE A SHAPE");
gclose_seg();
```

The segment is created. We use `fill_box` to fill the area with a solid color—the background color—painting over any graphics that may have already been in this area. Then, a polyline surrounding the area is drawn. The text, set to an appropriate height and color, is centered in the rectangle.

We should keep in mind that, when a primitive is defined in a segment, the present attributes of that primitive are used. Hence, if we omitted the setting of attributes in our example, the system would have used the last values that were set before the segment was created.

4.3.2 Segments and Program Flow

Where segments exist, and exactly when they exist, varies among graphics systems. In GKS, a segment is associated with all the workstations that are active at the time that segment is created. Primitives in the segment are displayed as soon as they are defined in the program. Segments cannot be modified after creation, although mechanisms exist to create new segments using parts of existing ones. There is no provision for altering or editing an existing segment. Systems such as PHIGS take a different approach. In PHIGS, *structures* (the PHIGS counterpart to the GKS segment) form part of a central database. The act of displaying these structures, called *posting*, is independent of their creation. One consequence of this separation between creation and display is that we can edit structures without inviting the concurrency problems inherent in the GKS view of segments. We shall further address modeling with GKS and PHIGS in the next chapter.

The flow of primitives from the application program to the display is such that both primitives defined outside of segments and those defined within segments appear on the display. The major difference in the handling of these primitives occurs when some action alters the screen (e.g., updates it) or when we cover something already on the display. Primitives outside of segments are sent to the display (after any necessary clipping) exactly once. Hence, if a primitive on the display is altered, as would happen if we placed a solid fill area over it, we cannot recover it, except by regenerating it from the user program. Segments, since they are stored, can be redisplayed, perhaps in new positions and with altered attributes. On the negative side, there is a fair amount of overhead associated with segmentation. A program that does not use segments will almost always run faster than will an equivalent program that does. If segmentation is supported directly in the hardware, this difference can be insignificant.

We now turn to how we can use segments. We cannot do much with our create and close commands alone. Returning to our analogy with files, we would like to be able to delete segments that are no longer necessary and to rename segments. These two operations are accomplished through the two procedures

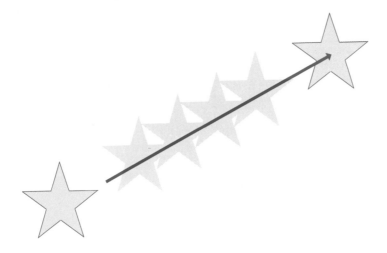

Figure 4.4
Buffering

```
void gdel_seg(seg_name)
void grename_seg(old_seg_name, new_seg_name)
```

4.3.3 Buffering

Deleting and renaming are at the heart of a simple buffering strategy that allows the user to control objects on the display. Suppose we have an object defined in a segment named STAR. In response to user input, such as via a mouse, we wish to move STAR to a new position, as in Figure 4.4. We could define a segment named NEWSTAR in the new position. We would delete the old segment STAR and, if our screen control and other parameters are set correctly, we might expect only the new segment to appear on the screen. However, this strategy creates a problem, since, for the rest of the program, we have to remember the new segment's name. Renaming solves this problem. The buffering code has the structure

```
gcreate_seg(NEWSTAR);

       .          /* create new segment elements */

       .
gclose_seg(NEWSTAR);
gdel_seg(STAR);
grename_seg(NEWSTAR, STAR);
```

This example does not tell us exactly when the changes will appear on the display. On a graphics system that is capable of redrawing all segments in one refresh cycle, typically one-sixtieth of a second, the sequence will be carried out virtually instantaneously and should require no user interaction. This automatic response is known as *implicit screen regeneration* and can be set up as part of our initialization procedure. On a slower system, implicit regeneration can be a detriment, since each change can force a complete redrawing of the display. Here, we would prefer *explicit screen regeneration*, which requires the user to take an explicit action before the screen is redrawn. A procedure such as *redraw all segments on workstation* allows the application program to redraw the display when necessary.

4.4
Segment Attributes

Since segments define graphical objects, their attributes are properties of the entire object. These include

- Visibility
- Priority
- Detectability
- Highlighting
- Transformation

Unlike many attributes of primitives, which can be bound to the primitive at the time of their creation, segment attributes are changeable during the execution of a program.

4.4.1 Visibility

A major feature of segments is that they can be removed from the display and can reappear later. In a complex application, we might want to define all the segments at the beginning, even though they may not be necessary at the time they are defined. That is our plan for the messages in our layout program. The *set visibility* procedure (`gset_vis`) makes this plan possible by allowing segments to be created that are initially not visible. This procedure usually is invoked directly after the segment is created and before any primitives are defined.

Consider the following fragment of code, which defines a second message for our layout program. The message asks the user to input the endpoint of a line segment; it will be displayed if the line icon in the menu was selected.

```
gcreate_seg(FIRST_END);
gset_vis(FIRST_END, GINVIS);
fill_box(0.0, 8.0, 0.0, 1.0);
gset_text_align{GCENTRE_HOR, GHALF_VERT};
gset_char_ht( 1.0);
gset_text_colr_ind(FOREGROUND);
loc.x = 4.0;
loc.y = 0.5;
gtext( &loc, "CHOOSE FIRST ENDPOINT OF LINE");
gclose_seg();
```

If we assume that the system has been configured to update itself as soon as possible, when an invisible segment is made visible, the segment is immediately drawn on the screen. This technique gives us a simple way of controlling the display of messages in our example. Rather than running through the primitives for the message repeatedly in response to user input, we instead define all necessary messages in initially invisible segments. We then alter their visibility as necessary.

4.4.2 Priority

Primitives outside segments are displayed only once, and the programmer can be fairly certain of the order in which they will appear. For primitives in segments, especially when screen regeneration is done implicitly, the situation is far less clear, due to implementation details such as the internal buffering strategy of each physical workstation. This uncertainty can be a serious problem. For example, as we saw in Chapter 3, the appearance of overlapping fill area primitives is dependent on the order in which they are drawn.

There are a number of possible ways of controlling the order in which segments are displayed. All have been used in various graphics systems. One simple method is to let the segment name, which is an integer, determine the order. Another is to use the original order of creation. We can also leave the order undetermined and let the hardware make the decision. Each method has its own advantages and disadvantages. GKS allows the user to determine the order, where necessary, by setting the priority of any segment through *set segment priority* procedure

```
void gset_seg_pri( seg_name, seg_pri)
```

The priority is a `Gfloat` between 0.0 and 1.0. The highest priority is 1.0. For the example of the triangle and box in Figure 4.5, if the

Figure 4.5
Temporal Priority

triangle is to appear on top of the box, the code might have the following form:

```
gcreate_seg(TRIANGLE);
triangle();  /* defines a filled triangle */
gclose_seg();
gcreate_seg(BOX);
box(); /* defines a filled box */
gclose_seg();

         .
         .

gset_seg_pri(TRIANGLE, FRONT);
gset_seg_pri(BOX, BACK);
gredraw_all_seg_ws(WS);
```

Another use of segment priorities occurs in input. Suppose we are using an input device known as a *pick*, which we shall discuss further in the next section, which locates a segment. What happens if, as in Figure 4.5, two segments overlap and the pick device is placed in the overlap area? It is possible that either segment can be selected by the pick device. As you might expect, we can resolve this conflict in a number of ways, or we can leave the decision to the implementation. GKS resolves the problem by using the priority of the segment, and returns the identifier of the highest-priority segment in the overlap region.

4.4.3 Other Attributes

Highlighting allows a segment to be displayed in an abnormal way; it is typically is used to attract a viewer's attention. In our layout program, we can use highlighting to direct the user's attention to the menu that is appropriate at a particular time.

Highlighting is a binary attribute that is set by the *set segment highlighting* procedure. Highlighting methods include making a segment blink or displaying it at increased brightness. Obviously, the method of highlighting will depend on the what the physical workstation can do and how the implementor has decided to implement this attribute.

The detectability attribute is also used in input. If a segment is undetectable, it cannot be selected by a pick device. This attribute is especially useful, as demonstrated in our layout program. Initially, we want the user to select one of the icons in the menu, and not to select the message segment. If we make the message segment undetectable, the graphics system will not accept this selection, even if the user erroneously attempts to choose it.

Segments can also be reoriented and moved about the screen by transformations. We can thus define a segment in a convenient position and with any desired size and orientation. We can then use a transformation on the segment to display the segment with another size, orientation, and position. This transformation will be described mathematically by an array or matrix that can be considered an attribute of the segment. To discuss transformations, we must first develop the necessary mathematics. We shall defer that discussion to Chapter 5.

4.5
Input

Returning to our layout program, we can now address the problems of interacting with the user. There are at least three different ways that input is required. First, when the user responds to the initial message to select an item from the shape menu, she points to an icon in that menu. The natural kind of input returned to the program from this choice should be the identifier of an object or segment. Suppose our user has selected the line icon. A message will come up asking her to enter one endpoint of the desired line segment. The required input is now a location. If our user had selected the text icon, she would have been prompted to enter a string, a third form of input.

Graphics systems recognize the need for different kinds of input. Rather than having the user write code to take a location and find the segment of which the location is part, modern systems provide procedures that provide the desired form of input directly. Not only does this facility ease the software problem, but also it allows special hardware to be used where available.

4.5.1 Logical versus Physical Input

Just as the programmer works with logical rather than physical displays, input is also logical. Logical input devices are defined by the kind of input or *measure* that is returned to the program.

Physical input devices include the mouse, the lightpen, the data tablet, and the keyboard of a terminal. Each can provide one or more of the logical classes of input. For example, a lightpen can be used to point to an icon in our menu, and later be used to indicate a position on the screen. A mouse can perform the same tasks. Neither could easily provide strings of characters to an application program. On the other hand, a standard keyboard with arrow keys can be used for all three jobs. Each of these three physical input devices has different capabilities. From the programmer's point of view, we prefer not to have to worry about these issues. We want to write a program that will not have to be altered if the physical devices are changed. The use of logical devices at the programmer's level avoids these problems. In writing an application program, we need to know only that the system supports all the necessary logical classes.

4.5.2 Logical Input Classes

GKS and many other systems recognize six logical classes of input:

- Pick
- Locator
- String
- Choice
- Stroke
- Valuator

The first three are those we need for our sample problem.

The *pick* (or pointing) device returns the identifier of a segment that is being pointed to by a physical input device, such as a mouse or a lightpen. In general, pointing close to any part of any primitive in the segment will return a segment identifier to the program.

The *locator* provides an x, y pair in WC in a two-dimensional system such as GKS. Certainly, a three-dimensional locator is a natural extension for three-dimensional graphics systems. Physical implementations of locators usually use the same device as the pick, which, as we shall see, can be a distinct advantage in many programs.

String input provides strings of characters. The usual physical implementation of this logical type is a keyboard, although we could use disk files to provide the characters. We could even put on the display a graphical keyboard that the user could operate with a mouse.

A *choice* device selects one of a number of possible selections and is the logical extension of a button. Physical implementations can range from keys on a keyboard to graphical buttons that are operated by a mouse or lightpen.

The *stroke* is used to obtain sequences of locations, such as would be needed in a painting application. In some ways, the stroke acts as a locator in a loop. Identifying it as a separate logical class allows us to implement the stroke function with a separate physical device and to implement the looping in hardware rather than in software.

Finally, the *valuator* allows the input of single real numbers. It acts as a dial. Physical implementations can range from an actual dial connected to our computer through an analog-to-digital converter to simple keyboard entry of the number.

4.5.3 Measure and Trigger

The relationship between logical and physical devices for output is fairly straightforward and one-directional. Output is defined logically and passes through a sequence of transformations to appear as physical output on a physical display. Except for some subtleties in the timing, such as determining exactly when a display is updated, the process is easy to visualize.

For input, the process is a bit more complex, since it covers multiple classes of input, different operating modes, and a two-directional transfer between the application program and the physical input devices. We can model this interaction through two processes: a *measure* process and a *trigger* process.

A logical input device is defined by a measure, a trigger, and a prompt/echo. The measure of a device is the set of logical values returned from the measure process running on the physical device. Thus, the measure of a pick device will include a segment identifier, whereas the measure of a locator includes a position in WC. Both also return a status measure.

An input procedure will initiate a measure process. As part of the initialization, a prompt, such as a cursor, may be placed on a display, and the initial value of the measure may be set. The current value of the measure may be echoed on the display. The measure process will exist until it is terminated either by the trigger process or by the user program.

The *trigger* of a logical device is a physical device that can generate signals (trigger events). Typical generators of trigger *firings* include a button on a mouse and the enter key on a keyboard. The trigger signal, like an interrupt, is an event that denotes a time. We can use the signal to terminate the input procedure by having the current state of the measure process be the required input, or we can use it to put the current measure into a queue. The exact use of trigger and measure processes will depend on the input mode.

4.5.4 Input Modes

When we write a simple C program that requires input such as through a scanf procedure

```
scanf("%d", number);
```

we make certain decisions about both the source and the timing of the input. The device is the standard input device, such as the terminal we are using. Actually, the standard device can be any of a variety of physical terminals, a disk file, or even the output of another program. This example is another in which we use a logical input device. The program comes to a halt while it waits for the necessary input. If the input comes from a terminal, the user will type in the characters and terminate the input by hitting the enter or return key. In this example, the measure process echoes the characters on the display. The trigger signal, the striking of the enter key, is required to inform the program that the input is complete and the program can resume execution.

There are other ways for a program to obtain character input. Often, the program requires a user to confirm a choice by printing a message such as "strike the Y key to continue"; as soon as this key is touched, the program proceeds. Here, the enter key is not required. These two examples demonstrates two different input modes.

In computer graphics, three input modes are important:

- Request

- Sample

- Event

The mode is selected through the *set input mode* procedure. *Request* mode is the simplest, and we shall use it for our layout program. On the execution of a request procedure, such as *request locator,* a measure process is initiated on the specified device. The trigger signal terminates this process and the current state of the measure process is returned to the program. At this point, the user program can proceed with the values returned. This sequence is shown in Figure 4.6. The advantage of request-mode input is that the device can be positioned or data entered at any time before the device is triggered. The user can correct keystrokes or carefully position the device as desired.

In *sample* mode, the input is taken from the device as soon as the input procedure is executed. The sample process takes the current measure without using the trigger signal, as shown in Figure 4.7. Hence, the program will see the input from the last action before the execution of the sample-mode input procedure. For a locator device, the physical input device must be positioned before the command. For a keyboard, the measure process will return the state of

Figure 4.6
Request-Mode Input

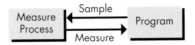

Figure 4.7
Sample-Mode Input

its buffer. Careful initialization is crucial in sample mode, because unlike in request mode, the user cannot carefully adjust or correct his actions.

In both request and sample mode, we ask for input from a specific device. Modern graphics systems usually possess a variety of input devices. Consider, for example, a flight simulator. The pilot sees images projected on screens. He has input devices such as a joystick, various dials, and switches. At any time, the program that controls the simulator must be able to react to input from any of the devices, since the pilot can initiate any of a number of actions at any time. Neither request nor sample mode input is well suited to this situation. The third type of input, *event* input, can be used for these situations.

In event-mode input (Figure 4.8), each time a trigger occurs, the current state of the measure process is put into an *event queue,* along with the necessary information to identify the type of measure and the logical device that generated it. Once the measure process is initiated, it continues until terminated by the program. Further trigger signals simply add additional events to the queue. The events placed in the queue can be examined by the application program, independently of the logging of the events.

As you might expect, event mode is more difficult to implement. Queues must be maintained and examined for which event, if any, has occurred. We shall examine event-mode input briefly at the end of this chapter.

4.5.5 Prompt, Echo, and Status Feedback

Effectively using input depends on supplying feedback to the user. When he indicates a location by positioning a mouse or moving the stylus on a data tablet, the user usually sees the position of the device indicated by a cursor on the display. Without this feedback, accurate positioning is very difficult to achieve. When we type characters on a

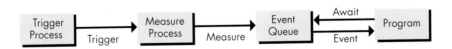

Figure 4.8
Event-Mode Input

keyboard, we virtually always see the string displayed as it is typed in. If you doubt the importance of this feedback mechanism, try to type this sentence without looking at the screen or the keyboard.

Three methods of obtaining feedback are of particular interest: *prompts, echoes,* and a *status* return. The prompt can be a cursor (or other marker) on the screen, or a line drawn from a fixed point to the logical location of the input device as mapped to the screen. Echoing can range from the copying of characters to the screen as they are entered to the flashing of a segment after it has been selected by the pick device. We can think of prompts and echoes as input attributes. They are implementation dependent, since the physical characteristics of a device will determine what prompts and echoes it can produce.

The return of a status variable in response to any attempt to use input provides a different form of feedback. Suppose a user triggers a pick device by pushing a button on the physical device but does not point at a segment. This situation might cause difficulties, because the user, having triggered his input device, may have trouble distinguishing whether he has missed pointing at the desired object or there is a problem in his program. A well-designed system should allow the programmer to write application programs that detect these kinds of situations and take appropriate action. In this example, a message such as "try again" might be displayed. Here, a returned status of GNONE, as opposed to GOK, allows the application program to detect that the device was triggered but no segment was being pointed at. We shall use returned status extensively to control the flow of our programs.

4.5.6 Programming Input

In some respects, input is conceptually like output, but the processing is reversed. The physical input device produces input in DC. For input from locator and stroke devices, the DC information is converted to NDC and then to WC. The programmer finally receives the input in the coordinate system that the application program is using.

To the applications programmer, input comes from logical workstations, which must be opened, activated, deactivated, and closed. We can do these operations from within our init and finish procedures. However, there are a few additional problems we have to worry about with input or input/output workstations. First, unlike an output workstation, which has a single display, the input or input/output workstation can have more than one input device of a given logical class. Hence, our functions to request or sample input must indicate not only which workstation but also which device on that workstation is to be used. Second, although input devices are available to the program when the workstations are opened and activated, the availability of prompts and echoes often makes it desirable to reinitialize input devices to change the location of the prompt or type of echo. We shall examine these issues when we return to our layout program. First, we examine physical input devices.

4.6
Physical Input Devices

Input from a variety of physical devices can be used to generate the logical input to our programs. Although programming with logical rather than physical devices allows the programmer the luxury of not having to worry about the availability or properties of particular physical devices, the differences among various physical devices are such that one may be far more suited to a particular application than is another. At this point, we shall take a small diversion to overview the more popular input devices.

4.6.1 The Keyboard

A keyboard, shown in Figure 4.9, provides codes for the standard characters to a system in response to the user striking keys. Special keys, such as the control key, allow the user to use character sets of up to 256 characters. The processor can also interpret individual keystrokes or sequences of keystrokes in special ways. For example, most keyboards now contain arrow keys. The graphics system can use these keys to move a cursor or to obtain other position information. Modern keyboards for graphics use often include thumb wheels and other accoutrements to increase flexibility.

When keystrokes occur, the identities of the keys struck are stored in a keyboard buffer in the processor. Initialization of the device can be used either to clear or to load this buffer. Request- and event-mode input is obtained from this buffer in response to a trigger signal, which is usually generated by the return or enter key.

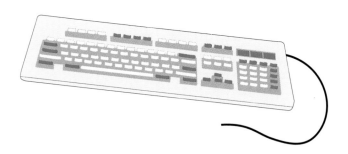

Figure 4.9
Keyboard

A keyboard can provide a number of different measures, depending on how the system interprets the contents of the buffer. Implementation of the logical string device is done by the standard interpretation of character codes. We can implement the choice device by interpreting character codes for the numeric keys as 10 choices, or by recognizing combinations, such as control key–number, for additional choices. We can implement a valuator device by simply typing in the number.

Locator and pick devices can be implemented by use of the arrow keys. When the logical device is initialized, the system sets a position to an initial location. Use of the arrow keys changes this location, which can be echoed back to the user by display of a marker or cursor.

Implementation of the pick requires computation by the implementation software or hardware. The keyboard can provide a position, but then the processor must find segments to which this position corresponds. This implementation issue can be difficult, depending on how close to an element in a segment we require a user to position a cursor. Exercises 4.3 and 4.4 explore approaches to this problem.

4.6.2 The Lightpen

The lightpen was the first of the special devices available for interactive computer graphics. In spite of the popularity of more recent innovations, the lightpen is still used in many applications. Figure 4.10 shows that the lightpen does not write (or emit) light, but rather reads (or senses) it. A threshold is set in the lightpen so that, when light intensity exceeds this threshold, an interrupt is generated. The processor knows exactly when this event occurs, and uses this time to compute the position of the lightpen on the face of the CRT.

One major problem with the lightpen is that there must be light for it to sense. Thus, if we use a lightpen for a pick device, we usually have to place the pen on an illuminated primitive. If this primitive is a thin line, the user may have difficulty positioning the lightpen

Figure 4.10
Lightpen

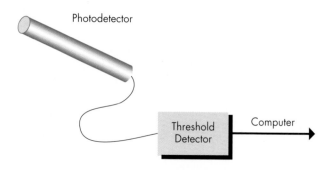

Figure 4.11
Lightpen on a Raster
Display

accurately. Other problems with the lightpen include the *vignetting* effect (there is less light at the edges of a display than at the center) and the rate at which light output from a CRT decays when it is no longer illuminated by its electron beam.

The handling of the triggering event is somewhat different in random- and raster-scan systems. A raster-scan system displays information line by line. Each refresh cycle begins at a precise time and proceeds line by line. By knowing when the triggering event occurred, the system can compute exactly where on the CRT face the lightpen was located at that time (Figure 4.11), so the use of the lightpen as a locator device is fairly easy. For a lightpen to be used as a pick on a raster system, the processor must use a position on the display to determine a segment.

On a random-scan system, the lightpen can be used most easily as a pick device. The displayed elements are in segments that comprise the display file (Figure 4.12). On each refresh of the display, which is initiated at a precise time, the system goes through the segments in the display file, displaying their primitives. When the trigger fires, we know which segment is being displayed, which provides the pick measure. Using the lightpen as a locator involves further calculation based on which primitive caused the trigger. For example, if the the threshold is exceeded while a line segment is being drawn, the processor can interpolate between the endpoints of the line segment to find the location of the lightpen at the time of the trigger firing.

We can make lightpens detect normally dark areas by periodically sweeping the surface of the display with a small spot. Since the light output from this spot is of short duration, the user will not see the spot, but the spot can be detected by the lightpen.

Figure 4.12
Lightpen on a Random-
Scan Display

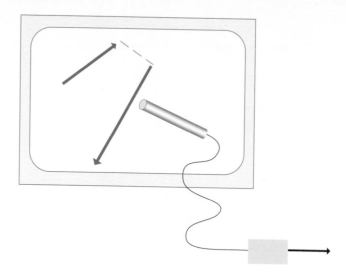

Lightpens often are constructed with a button. The user can activate it by pushing the lightpen onto the face of the CRT, if the button is on the tip of the pen, or by pushing it, if is located on the side of the pen. The button provides an alternate method of providing a trigger. The sensing of light then becomes part of the measure process.

4.6.3 The Joystick

Figure 4.13
Joystick

The joystick (Figure 4.13) is a device with two degrees of freedom. In the standard joystick, when the user moves the stick, he changes the settings on two potentiometers. This provides the processor with two independent values, which are stored in a pair of registers. Such a configuration makes the joystick a natural locator device. The trigger is usually provided by a button on the stick.

In addition, the joystick is often used in a somewhat different manner, which gives it unique advantages. When the joystick is constructed with mechanical elements such as springs, it can be give the user a natural "feel," like the control stick in an airplane. The joystick is usually constructed such that there is increasing resistance as the user pushes it farther from its resting position. It returns to the resting position when the user releases it.

With these mechanical properties, the joystick does not lend itself to use as a direct positioning device. Consider the modification in Figure 4.14, where the outputs of the potentiometers are integrated before they are stored in registers. This configuration allows us to

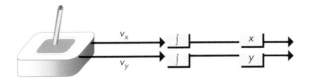

Figure 4.14
Joystick as a Velocity
Device

interpret the potentiometer outputs as velocities rather than as positions and converts the device into an incremental or relative device. If the stick is in its resting position, the x and y velocities are both zero, which does not alter the values in the registers. In addition, the device now has variable sensitivity. A small movement (low velocities) from the resting position causes small slow changes to the contents of the registers; a large movement from the resting position allows rapid but rough positioning.

4.6.4 The Trackball and the Mouse

Figure 4.15 shows a trackball, which, like the joystick, controls two potentiometers. In this case, the user changes the settings of the potentiometers by rolling the ball. The trackball is thus a relative-positioning device, where the velocity of the ball determines the change in position value stored in the processor's registers.

Figure 4.15
Trackball

If we take our trackball and turn it upside down, we have a device called a mouse (Figure 4.16). The user grasps the device and rolls the ball along a surface. One or more buttons on the device allow the user to generate trigger signals. Since the mouse is a relative-positioning device, the user can pick it up and move it to a new position without signaling any change to the processor. The mouse in Figure 4.16 is an electromechanical mouse: the motion is mechanical (the ball) and the sensing device is electrical (the potentiometers). Other popular mice are electro-optical and optical-mechanical.

The mouse is probably the most popular of the presently available input devices. It is inexpensive, reliable, and easy to use. Implementing a locator and a pick with the mouse is similar to implementing the joystick for these uses. With all these devices, however, it is difficult to obtain absolute positioning, which is necessary for tasks such as entering data from a map or a hand drawing.

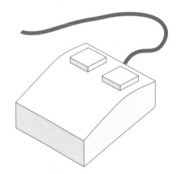

Figure 4.16
Mouse

4.6.5 Data Tablets

The data tablet (Figure 4.17) provides absolute positions to the processor. The user positions a stylus on the tablet. In a typical data tablet, the stylus can sense electromagnetic signals, which are sent out

Figure 4.17
Data Tablet

4.6 Physical Input Devices 127

over finely spaced wires in the tablet. These signals can be decoded to determine the position of the stylus with extreme accuracy. A button is provided either on the side or on the tip of the stylus for triggering.

How we can use the data tablet as a locator or stroke device is clear. Like our other devices, with some calculation, it can also be used as a pick. The absolute positioning of this device allows us to set aside areas of the tablet for special purposes. For example, we can create a string device by laying out a keyboard on part of the tablet. Devices such as touchpads are conceptually similar to the data tablet, but replace the stylus with the user's finger. Invisible touch screens can be placed over the face of a CRT, allowing the user to work directly on the screen image, albeit with resolution reduced to the size of her fingertip.

Figure 4.18
Light Buttons

4.6.6 Graphical Devices

The difference between logical and physical input devices is perhaps clearest when we use the graphics system to generate logical devices. These are implemented physically through the display and a single physical device such as a mouse. For example, consider implementing a choice device that can make three choices. We can have three physical buttons, or we can use three keys on our keyboard, or we can create a "device," such that as in Figure 4.18, which shows three *light buttons*. The user makes a choice by using the mouse, or whatever other pointing device is available, to move the cursor to the desired light button and clicking a button on the mouse as a trigger. A valuator is often implemented, as in Figure 4.19, where the mouse is slid

Figure 4.19
Graphical Valuator

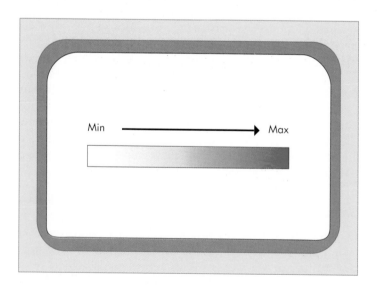

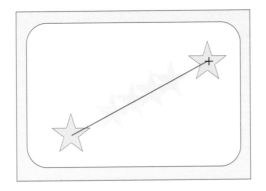

Figure 4.20
Dragging

along the display to indicate the desired value. Note how simply we can implement a nonlinear scaling and any desired range with such a device.

4.6.7 Dragging

The fact that the same physical device can be used as two different logical devices has interesting consequences. In a technique called *dragging,* we select an object, then move it to a new location by having it follow the movement of the cursor. We first use the physical device as a pick to select an object. Immediately after the completion of the pick operation, the same device is used (repeatedly) as a locator to give a new position for the picked segment. The segment appears to move, or to be dragged, across the display following the movement of the cursor, as in Figure 4.20. You might try to add this feature to our example program. Instead of prompting the user to enter location information, you could allow the user to drag a copy of the selected shape to the desired location. This technique probably will work better if we use the sample mode input discussed in Section 4.8.

4.7
The Pick

We shall now examine the programmer's interface to logical input devices. We shall consider the three devices we need for our shape-layout program: the pick, the locator, and the string devices. For the application programmer, the use of a device in sample and request modes is virtually identical. The procedures and their parameters are the same except for their names—for example, *request pick* and *sample pick*. Event-mode input will be presented after we finish with the layout program.

The logical pick device is a pointing device that returns to the user program the identifier of the segment at which the user is pointing when the trigger occurs (in request mode). The measure also includes a returned status and a *pick identifier*, which enable us to write simpler interactive programs without increasing the complexity of the hardware.

In the layout program, the user must first select an item from the menu of shapes. We designed the program so that the available shapes are displayed as icons. We placed these icons into segments, so that we could select an item by pointing to any part of it. We would like to give the user time to position a cursor on the desired icon, which dictates the use of request-mode input.

Since the contents of a segment are determined by the application program, we have considerable flexibility. One option is to use a separate segment for each icon. Another option, however—using pick identifiers—may be preferable. Either can be used through the *request pick* procedure:

```
void greq_pick( ws_id, pick_num, pick_st, req_pk)

Gint ws_id;
Gint pick_num;
Gin_st *pick_st;
Gpick *req_pick;
```

As usual, `ws_id` is our workstation identifier, as set in the opening of the workstation. `pick_num` is the number of the logical pick device on the workstation. A workstation may have more than one device in a given class. For instance, on a personal computer with a mouse attached, the keyboard and the mouse can both be used as logical pick devices. The numbering is set up locally and may have to be determined for each implementation you encounter, although 1 is always used to identify the first device of each class.

4.7.1 Using the Returned Status

The returned status, `pick_st`, is an enumerated type that returns one of the values GOK, GNONE, or GNO_IN. The same status type will be returned from all input procedures and is an important aid to the programmer. If the value returned is GOK, we know that the request has been processed, the device triggered, and a segment selected. However, we could have used our device correctly but not have been pointing at a detectable segment. In this case, the status GNONE is returned. Finally, something might have happened while the system was waiting for the user to trigger the device. For example, a special key or button is often reserved to allow the user to escape from an input request. In this case, the returned status is GNO_IN, which tells the program that no valid input has occurred.

We can see immediate possibilities for using the returned status in our program. The drawing area is not within a segment, so primitives in it cannot be picked. We decided to use segments for the messages so that we could bring them up on the display or remove them easily via the visibility attribute. Since there is no reason ever to pick the message area, we can make all these segments undetectable. Suppose we also make the control segments undetectable for now. The only segments that can be picked now are those that make up the menu of shapes. The initial loop can then have the form

```
do greq_pick( CRT_DEV, PICK_NUM, pick_st, req_pk);
   while( *pick_st != GOK);
```

The program will not proceed past the request until the user selects a visible segment. If each icon is a separate segment, the next step is to test which has been picked so that the appropriate next action can be initiated. This approach will work, but can be a bit unwieldy if there are multiple active menus displayed simultaneously. An alternative is to use the pick identifier.

4.7.2 Pick Identifiers

Assuming the returned status is GOK, we can examine the returned structure pointed to by req_pick. The returned structure consists of two parts:

```
typedef struct {
   Gint seg_name;
   Gint pick_id;
} Gpick;
```

The segment identifier, seg_name, is the identifier of the segment picked. The pick identifier, pick_id, is an attribute of primitives in a segment. It allows us to tag primitives within a segment with different labels. When we select a segment by pointing to a primitive in that segment, in addition to the name of the segment, we are given the pick identifier of this primitive. Pick identifiers provide considerable extra flexibility. In our layout program, we can put all the shape icons in a single segment and distinguish among them by looking at the pick identifier after a successful pick operation. The pick identifier is set by

```
void gset_pick_id(pick_id)
```

within the definition of the segment. Once this procedure has been executed, all subsequent primitives within this segment will carry the same pick identifier until it is changed by another call to **gset_pk_id**.

4.7.3 Setting Up the Menus

Here is the full code for setting up the menu segment that uses pick identifiers:

```
static Gpt line_pts[] = {{0.5; 7.875}, {1.5, 7.875}};
static Gpt circle_pts[] = {{1.0, 3.375},{1.0, 2.5}};
static Gpt text_loc = {1.0, 1.125};
static Gtext_align center = {GCENTRE_HOR, GHALF_VERT};

gopen_seg(MENU);

/* Use Previously Set Up
                Normalization Transformation */

gsel_norm_tran(MENU_TRANS) ;

/* line icon: draw a filled box as
background and then the line */

gset_pick_id(LINE);
fill_box(0.0, 2.0, 6.75, 9.0);
gpolyline( 2, line_pts);

/* use two filled boxes for the
rectangle icon */

 gset_pick_id(RECTANGLE);
 fill_box(0.0, 2.0, 4.5, 6.75);
 fill_box(0.5, 1.5, 5.0625, 6.1875);

/* circle icon using implementation dependent
 Generalized Drawing Primitive */

gset_pick_id(CIRCLE);
fill_box(0.0, 2.0, 2.25, 4.5);
ggdp( 2, &circle_pts, CIRCLE_NUM, NULL);
```

```
/* string icon */

gset_pick_id(TEXT);
fill_box(0.0, 2.0, 0.0, 2.25);
gset_text_align(&center);
gset_char_ht(1.0);
gtext( &text_loc, "ABC");
gclose_seg();

/* make segment detectable */

gset_det( MENU, GDET);
```

There are a few things to note here. Before the segment is created, we select the appropriate normalization transformation. After a segment is closed, it is set to be detectable via `gset_det`. The default of this attribute is undetectable, and undetectable segments cannot be picked. A segment must also be visible to be detectable, although the possibilities for what we could do with invisible detectable segments could be interesting.

Certain aspects of pick usage are implementation dependent. For example, we have used a solid fill as a "background" for each icon. The idea is to make the picking easier, since we can trigger the pick device at any location within the box. This strategy may not be possible with some systems, as the hardware may be unable to detect the inside of a dark region. Such is the case with many systems using random-scan CRTs. An alternative might be to use a solid fill area filled with a different color. Otherwise, the user may be forced to pick by pointing to either the outline of the box or the icon itself. The question of how close the user has to be to a segment (or element within a segment) to pick that segment is also an implementation-dependent one.

The control segment is set up in a similar manner. It contains two pick identifiers, so that we can distinguish between the "X" icon that is used to clear the screen and the arrow that is used to exit from the program. We shall discuss the use of more illustrative icons later in the chapter.

```
static Gpt x_pts_1[] = {{0.0, 0.0},{1.0, 1.0}};
static Gpt x_pts_2[] = {{1.0, 0.0},{0.0, 1.0}};
static Gpt arrow_pts_1[] = {{1.5, .75},{1.5, 0.25}};
static Gpt arrow_pts_2[] = {{1.25, 0.5},{1.5, 0.25}};
static Gpt arrow_pts_3[] = {{1.75, 0.5},{1.5, 0.25}};

gsel_norm_tran(CONTROL_TRANS);
```

```
gcreate_seg_(CONTROL);

/* the X */

gset_pick_id(CLEAR);
fill_box( 0.0, 1.0, 0.0, 1.0);
gpolyline(2, x_pts_1);
gpolyline(2, x_pts_2);

/* the arrow */

gset_pick_id(EXIT);
fill_box( 1.0, 2.0, 0.0, 1.0);
gpolyline(2, arrow_pts_1);
gpolyline(2, arrow_pts_2);
gpolyline(2, arrow_pts_3);

gclose_seg();

gset_det(CONTROL, GDET);
```

4.7.4 The Control Loop

The entire control loop of the program is now wonderfully simple.
We pick and check the segment name. If it is the control segment,
depending on the pick identifier, we either exit or clear the screen by
redrawing all visible segments. If we have selected the menu of shapes,
the pick identifier is used to select procedures that allow the user to
interactively enter the information necessary to draw the desired shape
in the drawing area. The code for this part of the program is

```
/* until exit picked */

do {

/* make initial message visible */

gset_vis(INITIAL_MESSAGE, GVIS);

/* request pick until segment selected */

do greq_pick(CRT_DEV, PICK_NUM, pick_stat, req_pick);
    while(pick_stat != GOK);

/* control segment picked */
```

```
        if(req_pick.seg_name == CONTROL)
            if(req_pick.pick_id == CLEAR)
                gredraw_all_seg_ws(CRT_DEV);
            else exit = DONE;

    /* else menu picked */

        else switch(req_pick.pick_id);
        {
                case(LINE):
                {
                    line();
                    break;
                }
                case(RECTANGLE):
                {
                    rectangle();
                    break;
                }
                case(CIRCLE):
                {
                    circle();
                    break;
                }
                case(TEXT):
                {
                    text();
                    break;
                }
        }
    }
    while(exit != DONE);
```

We will need locator and string input to position and draw the desired shapes when we write the procedures `line`, `rectangle`, `circle`, and `text`. These will be examined in the next two sections.

4.7.5 Mode Selection and Initialization

Let us fill out a few details of the pick operation. The sample pick command `gsample_pick` has exactly the same parameters as `greq_pick` does. Usually, we can use the logical device in either mode, or intermix the two. The *set pick mode* procedure enables us to switch between modes. We have used the pick in its default state. The *initialize pick* procedure can be used to set a number of parameters associated

Figure 4.21
Program Flow

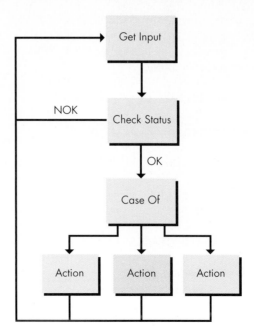

with the pick, such as the echo type. Many of these parameters will be similar to those for initializing the locator, so we shall delay our discussion of device initialization until we discuss the locator. The default echo and prompt are typically the tracking of the position of the device on the screen with a cursor and highlighting or flashing the picked segment.

4.7.6 General Program Flow

The flow of most interactive applications is similar to that of our layout program and can be described by a flowchart such as that in Figure 4.21. Whether the device is a pick, locator, or any of the other logical types, the program awaits input, then uses that input to select an action to be carried out. Once the action is complete, the program returns to its initial state and awaits more input. Of course, such a diagram must be interpreted recursively. Each action can begin with a request for input whose result then determines a number of possible subactions.

4.8
The Locator

Suppose our user selects the line icon. The message "CHOOSE FIRST ENDPOINT OF LINE" will appear on the screen. The user can now use a locator to provide this information. In most systems, the same physical device, such as a mouse, is used as both a pick and a locator. Again, we want to allow the user time to position the device before obtaining its measure. The *request locator* function, rather than the *sample locator* function, is appropriate.

4.8.1 Request Locator

Locator input is obtained by this function:

```
void greq_loc(ws_id,loc_num,in_st,norm_tran_num,loc_pos)

Gint ws_id;
Gint loc_num;
Gin_st *in_st;
Gint *norm_tran_num;
Gpt *loc_pos;
```

The first three parameters are the same as they are for the pick commands. We specify what the workstation identifier is and which device on the workstation we want to use. A status variable is returned. If the returned status is GOK, we can look at the other two returned variables: a normalization transformation number and a point in WC.

4.8.2 Inverting the Coordinate Transformations

Although the application program desires information in WC, input from the physical device is in DC at the level at which it is provided to the graphics system. Two coordinate transformations are necessary before any data received from a physical device can be used in an application program. First, the inverse of the workstation transform is performed to map the input data from DC into NDC. Since the request for input specified the workstation and the desired input device on this workstation, this transformation is well defined.

Next, these NDC values must be converted to WC. Here, we would like to use the inverse of the WC-to-NDC transformation. However, in our example, we defined a number of normalization transformations. Hence which one we should use may be ambiguous. The simplest

DC

$\downarrow$

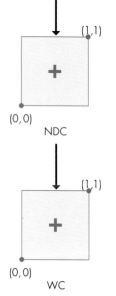

(1,1)

(0,0)

NDC

$\downarrow$

(1,1)

(0,0)

WC

Figure 4.22

Mapping Locator Input I

case is shown in Figure 4.22. In this situation, we have a single normalization transformation. If there is only a single transformation, it must be transformation 0, since that is predefined and always exists. This particular world window and viewport maps a unit square to all of NDC space. In this case, the position in NDC space is the same as the position in WC. The inverse of the workstation transformation provides the WC value returned by `greq_loc` in `loc_pos`. The value zero is returned in `norm_tran_num`, since this is the number of the normalization transformation used in the inverse mapping.

This process works well for the spot marked by the cross in Figure 4.22, but the location marked by the star presents a problem. This point lies outside the workstation viewport. In keeping with the requirements that primitives cannot be displayed outside their assigned viewports, the logical choice is to consider the star's position to be one that cannot be detected by a locator device. In this case `greg_loc` returns a status of **GNONE** after the trigger fires.

Now consider the more complex situation in Figure 4.23. Here we have two user-defined transformations, in addition to the predefined normalization transformation 0. There are three distinct situations. The cross is in the viewport of transformations 0 and 1; the star is in the viewports of transformations 0 and 2; the dot is in the viewports of all three transformations. There is now considerable ambiguity as to which transformation `greq_loc` should use to convert from values in NDC to values in WC. GKS makes this choice by *viewport priorities*. Each viewport can be assigned a priority by the *set viewport input priority* function:

```
void gset_vp_in_pri( tran_num, ref_tran_num, pri)

Gint tran_num;
Gint ref_tran_num;
Gpri pri;
```

The priority of a viewport, identified by its normalization-transformation number, is set higher (**GHIGHER**) or lower (**GLOWER**) than that of a reference viewport by the enumerated variable `pri`. With this procedure, the user can set up any desired ordering of normalization transformations.

4.8.3 Entering the Data

In our layout problem, we use the locator in the drawing area. Normalization transformation 1 was set up for this area in Section 4.2. Consider the code that reads in the first endpoint of the line segment:

Figure 4.23
Mapping Locator Input II

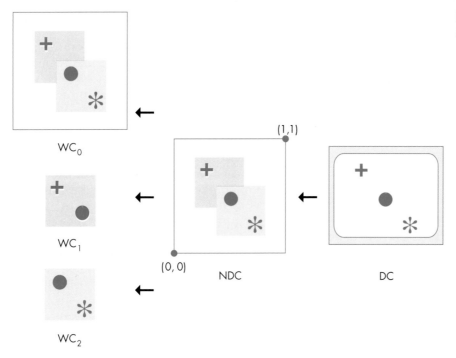

```
Gpt points[2], loc_pos;
Gin_stat status;
Gint tran_num;
            .
gset_vis( 4, GVIS);
            .
            .
            .
do greq_loc(CRTDEV, LOC_NUM, &status, &tran_num, &loc_pos)
    while((status != GOK)||(&tran_num != 1));
```

Segment 4 contains the message, "CHOOSE FIRST ENDPOINT OF LINE." We force this message to appear on the screen by making the segment visible. We then keep requesting locator input until we get a successful locate, and the normalization transformation for the drawing area (1) is returned. Note that a successful locate action is not enough; the availability of the number of the normalization transformation that the system used to return the location is now used to verify that these are the desired values. Successful completion of this action will lead to a similar piece of code that will allow the user to enter the second endpoint and draw the line. Now, initialization of the device, a topic we have ignored thus far, will be important.

4.8.4 Device Initialization

Initializing the locator is important for the clean operation of our program. Consider how we use the locator to define a line segment. When a request-locator function is executed, a prompt of some sort usually appears on the screen. Let us assume that this prompt is a cursor. The user then positions the cursor where desired and triggers the locator device. In the first request we discussed, there was an initial position for the cursor, and the user altered this position as she moved the device. When the device was triggered, one of two things happened. Either the returned status and normalization transformation index indicate a valid endpoint was entered, in which case we want to go on to select the second endpoint, or the status or transformation numbers indicate the program must reexecute the request. In either case, the *request locator* procedure was followed by another request for the locator. If we used the default initialization, the cursor would return to the same initial position each time. That would be annoying and also would waste the user's time, as she would have to keep repositioning the device. We prefer to leave the cursor unchanged after each request, allowing us to proceed from this position. The *initialize locator* function,

```
void gint_loc(ws_id, loc_num, init_norm_tran_num,
    init_loc_pos, pet, echo_area, loc_data)

Gint ws_id;
Gint loc_num;
Gint init_norm_tran_num;
Gpt *init_loc_pos;
Gint pet;
Glim *echo_area;
Gloc_data *loc_data;
```

allows us to place the cursor where desired before we use the device. Although this procedure has an annoying number of variables, in return we get a fair amount of control over how we use our device. The alternative, of course, is not to use initialization and to employ the default values.

As usual, `ws_id` and `loc_num` specify the device on our workstation. We select the initial position for the prompt by using normalization transformation `init_norm_tran_num` to map a cursor at `init_loc_pos` (in WC) to the screen. Thus, if these values are chosen as those returned by the previous use of the locator, the cursor position will remain unchanged as we go to the next request for locator input.

The variable `pet` selects a prompt/echo type. A number of types are possible, depending on the implementation. There has to be at least one available in every implementation. The most common prompt is a cursor placed at the current position of the locator. This cursor could use the current marker attributes or always be the same size and color. A second method is to employ a *rubberband* line, which is a line segment drawn from the initial position to the current position of the locator. The system redraws this line segment as the user moves the locator. A rubberband rectangle whose main diagonal joins the initial and current locator positions could also be used. A different approach might be to display on the screen a box whose content is the current cursor position.

For the more sophisticated prompt/echo types, some information may have to be passed to the system. The rectangle `echo_area` defines in DC the area on the screen that can be used for echoes, such as displaying the locator position as two numbers. We shall use such an area for echoing string input in the next section. The data record, `loc_data`, provides an implementation-dependent method for providing any other information a particular echo/prompt type might require, such as colors for the echo area or a particular line type for rubberbanding.

Initializing the pick device is virtually identical to initializing the locator, except that we provide an initial segment and pick identifier instead of the initial locator position and normalization transformation index.

4.9 String Input

We can now add the final pieces we need to complete our layout program. Using the locator, we can draw the line, rectangle, and circle shapes, since we can construct all these shapes by specifying a few points in WC. The text icon requires the use of string input. If the user selects this icon, she is prompted with a message to select the location in the drawing area where the text is to be placed. This selection is done, as before, using `ginit_loc` and `greq_loc`. When this operation is complete, the user is prompted to enter the string. The *request string* function is appropriate for this purpose:

```
void greq_string(ws_id, string_num, in_st, req_string)

Gint ws_id;
Gint string_num;
```

```
Gin_st *in_st;
Gchar *req_string;
```

The first three parameters serve the same purpose as in our other request procedures. A successful request returns the string input in `req_string`.

4.9.1 Using an Inquiry

We want to echo the characters we enter for string input as we type them in on a physical device such as a keyboard. We can use the echo area for this purpose. We have constructed a screen display that has certain areas we must protect, such as the layout we are designing with the program. We must place the echo area somewhere where it will cause no problems but still will be easily visible to the user. Although the initialization procedure allows us to select the echo area, unfortunately, unlike any other values we have encountered, the echo area must be specified in DC.

At this point, we can either stop the discussion and decide to use a local manual to find the necessary values for our particular display, or learn to find these values in a device-independent way through an inquiry procedure. We take this second approach.

Inquiry procedures can serve a number of purposes, ranging from finding the state of the system to finding the properties of the physical devices available to the program. The *inquire display space size* function returns the size of the physical display surface to the program as two reals that are the x and y dimensions of the display.

We can use these values to select an echo area for our text input. We choose to use a small part of the message area for the echo. If `min` is the smaller of the two values returned by the inquiry, then the region determined by

```
echo_area.xmin = 0.1*min;
echo_area.xmax = 0.8*min;
echo_area.ymin = 0.05*min;
echo_area.ymax = 0.1*min;
```

is within the message area. We use this area because the echoed string will be erased automatically by the next message, which appears as soon as the text input is received.

4.9.2 Pausing During Execution

We can use request-mode input to solve a problem that arises frequently even in programs that do not require input. Normally, programs continue until they are completed. Unless there is a request for input, the program continues its execution. Consider the self-scaling plotter we designed in Chapter 3. Immediately after drawing the specified primitives, the program moves on to the `finish` procedure. This procedure deactivates and closes the workstation, which clears the display surface. This shutdown happens before the user has even had an opportunity to absorb the graphical information that was just produced. The standard C solution to this problem is to insert the line

```
getchar();
```

just before `finish`. The idea is to stop execution of the program until the user hits the return or enter key. However, this technique may fail in a graphics application. If, as is often the case, the graphics system controls the input and output, normal C input may not work. The solution is to use the graphics system for the same purpose. Any request input procedure (e.g., `greg_string`) will pause the program until a trigger is fired.

4.9.3 Completing the Layout Program

At this point, we can put together all our pieces of code to compose the complete layout program. It is organized as series of functions in pseudocode form:

```
main()
{
    init();
    transforms();
    segments();
    loop();
    finish();
}
```

There should be no surprises here. The main program uses `init` to initialize the system, `transforms` to set up all all the necessary normalization transformations, and `segments` to define all the segments for our messages, menus, and control actions. Interaction is handled through `loop`, the various pieces of which we have written in the previous three sections. This procedure also includes the short drawing procedures `line`, `rectangle`, `circle`, and `text`. Termination is done by `finish` after the exit icon has been selected in `loop`.

This organization is not, of course, the only one possible for such a program. It does not make use of all the facilities of GKS, or of all those that might be available in another graphics system. However, it has a structure that should enable you to both modify this program and to write new ones for other purposes.

4.10
Event-Driven Input

With both sample- and request-mode input, the programmer identifies from which workstation and from which input device on that workstation the input should be taken. We may not wish to constrain our programs by making the choice of a device for the user. For example, some systems may have both a mouse and a data tablet attached. Either can be used for the locator, and different users may have different preferences.

An even more basic issue is that, with sample and request input, the flow of the program is much more rigid. For example, while we are waiting for a trigger from a request locator, input from all other devices will be ignored by the program. This situation is unacceptable in an application such as a flight simulator or a video game, where, at any time, the user can pick one of a variety of devices and can use that device to provide input.

In event-driven input, the input event can be used to control the flow of the program—an extremely powerful addition to our programming tools. Consider a system with a number of input devices of various logical types, all assumed opened as before. When these devices are triggered, their measures are placed in a data structure called an *event queue*. Included in the queue are the identity of the device that produced the event, the kind of event (locator, stroke, etc.), and the data from the event. The program can examine the queue through the *await event* function:

```
void gawait_ev( timeout, ws_id, class, input_num)
```

If there is an event in the queue, the procedure returns which workstation and device on the workstation produced the event and to which class (GLOC, GPICK, etc.) the event belongs. If the queue is empty, the program waits timeout seconds for an event to occur. If none occurs, class returns GNONE and the program continues.

If the event queue is not empty, gawait_ev removes the first event and the program can use the input associated with this event by a *get* function, such as *get pick:*

```
void gget_pick( pick_st, pick)
```

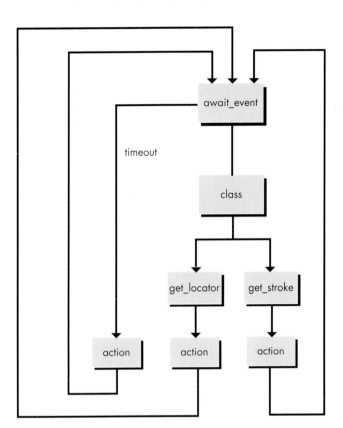

Figure 4.24
Program Flow for Event-Driven Programs

The returned information (status, segment number, and pick identifier) is exactly the same as that returned from sample pick and request pick. Using event input, the flow in our programs will follow a model such as that in Figure 4.24.

4.11
The User Interface

Now that we have some understanding of how to use input devices, we can look at how we can use interaction effectively. Since interaction involves a human as part of the graphics systems, the design of the user interface is of crucial importance to the functioning of our application.

The design of a user interface is important for all interactive computer applications, not just those using computer graphics. However, it is the advances in computer graphics, particularly the availability of input devices such as the mouse and the speed at which we can generate output on high-resolution displays, which have revolutionized the design of user interfaces. Without these advances, we might still be typing in individual commands at a keyboard rather than pulling down menus, clicking on icons, and using light buttons. Hence, this section is concerned with both how we write interactive graphics programs and how we apply computer graphics to user-interface design.

Any good user interface should demonstrate certain features. It should make possible actions clear, and help to lead the user through the application. The display should be informative without being distracting. User errors should be anticipated and mechanisms for graceful recovery built in. There are certain key elements that most experienced users and designers of user interfaces would agree are part of the interface:

- Menus

- Icons

- User feedback

- User aids

- Layout

- Color

We shall examine each of these briefly.

4.11.1 Menus

Control of the flow of an application program has changed over the past few decades. When interactive computer terminals became available, they allowed users to interact with a program, a great advance over having the flow of the program determined by the data fed in with the program on punched cards or magnetic tape. At first, users would enter data either on a command line, such as

```
run 3 2.0 37.5 6.5
```

or in response to simple prompting messages, such as

```
enter number of sides:
        .
        .
enter length in centimeters:
        .
        .
enter 1 to continue, 0 to exit:
```

Both methods had their defects. Command lines required expert knowledge by the user, whereas going through a series of simple commands could be tedious for experienced users.

An alternative arose, which was to put a menu of choices on the display. A user could enter data and control the program through the menu. Terminals with cursor control allowed the interaction to become fairly sophisticated, even without a graphics capability. Menus have proved to be an alternative that satisfies expert and novice users alike. With a graphics display, we can design menus involving text and icons. In addition, a graphics capability gives us precise control of the placement of the menus and the timing of their appearance.

In our layout program, we can identify a few ways to employ menus. In our initial design of the program, we forced the user to make the correct choices from a menu by making other actions impossible. When we wanted the user to select a shape from the menu, we made the other segments undetectable. An alternative is to alter the display to include only the menu of shapes. Since there is only one menu displayed, the user probably can do without the prompting messages. Once the choice of a shape has been made, the shape menu can disappear; it will "pop up" again when appropriate.

One criticism of this strategy is that a user may want to have more than one action possible at a time. In particular, we might want to have the ability to do a control action, such as terminating the program, at any time. Rather than have the control menu on the screen, we might employ a control bar, as in Figure 4.25. Each label

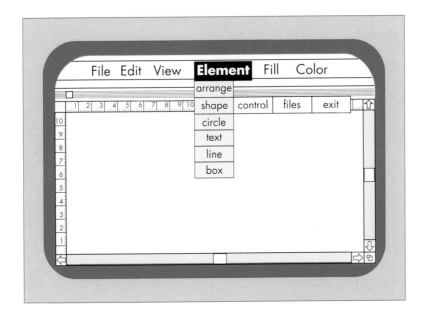

Figure 4.25
Using a Control Bar

Figure 4.26
Hierarchical Menus

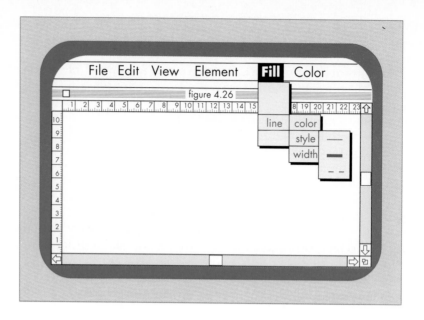

on the control bar refers to a menu, which is "pulled down" when the user points to the label. The menu is on the screen as long as a button on an input device is held down. The user chooses a menu item by sliding down the menu and releasing the button when the desired item is reached.

Menus offer a number of other possibilities. They can be used hierarchically. For example, suppose we want to add attributes, such as different line types and colors, to our layout program. One alternative is to have an attribute menu indicated on the control bar. Each item in this menu can bring up another menu, as illustrated in Figure 4.26.

The effective use of menus involves careful thought as to menu content (i.e., how many levels of hierarchy do we want?) and placement on the display, and as to the use of attributes to help the user. For example, we can show items in the control bar at diminished brightness if the they cannot be applied at the moment. We might highlight a menu item at which the user is pointing. We might also want to make available a wide selection of menus and to allow the user to configure the screen with the menus of her choice. This option is especially important where novices and experts might be using the same application program.

4.11.2 Icons

Icons are pictorial representations of actions or objects; they provide a visual method of communicating with our application. They have the

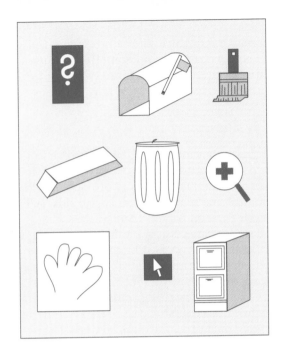

Figure 4.27
Icons

added advantage that the pictorial language is more universal than are our normal written languages. A program written using only icons to communicate with the user might be ported without alteration to another country, which would not be possible if the menus were in English or Japanese.

Our choice of icons is limited by their having to be represented as small pictures on the screen. For example, in many raster systems, icons are restricted to be no larger than 32 by 32 pixels. Simple shapes, however (such as our "X" to signify clearing the screen or arrow to signify exiting), do not directly represent those actions visually. Some standard icons are shown in Figure 4.27. We must be careful not to assume that icons such as the eraser will be understood universally. We might argue that the word "EXIT" conveys more information to an English-speaking user than does any icon for the action of leaving the program. Often, the user interface displays a choice in more than one way, much in the same way as road signs. In the United States, road signs provide three means of identification: stop signs are red (color) hexagons (shape) containing the word "STOP" (language) inside; yield signs are yellow triangles containing the word "YIELD."

Icons are also useful for cursors. Rather than having a single cursor, such as a cross or a small rectangle, we can employ a variety of cursors that can help to prompt the user or to indicate the status of the system. An arrow is helpful when the user is expected to enter a position, whereas a clockface or hourglass is often used to indicate the system is busy. An open hand sometimes is used to indicate the user has attempted an incorrect action.

4.11.3   User Feedback

In all applications, whether or not they involve computer graphics, a prime concern of the designer is to provide as much feedback to the user as possible. Menus and icons provide two types of feedback. Other types of user feedback include user aids (which we consider later), error handling, and a help facility.

The error-handling mechanism we discussed for GKS provides a beginning, and in many ways is a huge advance over earlier systems. In some of the earliest graphics systems, if the user attempted to move a cursor off the screen, the entire system crashed. The default mechanism in GKS handles this problem by detecting that the user has attempted to enter illegal data. The system reacts by refusing to execute the graphics procedure and entering this error in an error file. Although we have prevented a potential system crash, that may not help the user of our program, who may find that the application has terminated, so he may have to retry from the beginning. A more sophisticated mechanism is to have the application program deal with errors. In the example of attempting to enter incorrect data, the application can use either the data or the error message generated by the graphics system to correct the error. For incorrect data, the application can loop back and ask the user to reenter the data.

Any survey of applications software, CAD packages, and operating systems shows the importance of providing a help facility to the user. Often a user needs only to type in the command "help" or "?" to start the help facility. In a graphics application, help is normally provided by a help menu, which might always be referenced on the control bar. Help can range from a brief synopsis of a command to access to on-line manuals.

Another area where user feedback comes into play is to indicate to a user what he has done and to allow him to alter his most recent actions. For example, when a user picks an object on the screen, we usually use some form of highlighting, such as blinking the selected item, to indicate what the user has selected. If there is the possibility of user error, we might prefer to give the user the ability to alter his choice. One simple way to accomplish this is to highlight the indicated choice and require the user to indicate it a second time. If such user errors are unlikely, we might prefer to add a menu item that allows the user to backtrack one or more actions.

4.11.4 User Aids

One of the major uses of interactive graphics in CAD is the entering of data through the graphics system, rather than through typing of numbers into a keyboard or some other slow and error-prone method. The unaided human provides very low-resolution positioning to a graphical input device such as a mouse. We are both jittery and awkward. We can, however, use the graphics system to provide aids that get us around these difficulties. These aids can include slidebars, grids, relaxation, rubberbanding, variable sensitivity, and feedback. Such aids are important to virtually all computer applications. We shall discuss them in relation to entering positional information, such as in our layout program.

Suppose we are entering the position of the endpoint of a line segment. In our simple program, the user moves a device such as a mouse, following its location through a cursor on the display. When he is satisfied with the location, he pushes a button to generate a trigger signal to send the input to the program. Given the limited resolution of the display and the jitteryness of the user, obtaining an accurate and reproducible position is difficult without aids. One possible aid is to display the position of the cursor as coordinates in a viewport on the screen. Another is to put graphical rulers on the sides of the display. Often such rulers are used in conjunction with replacing the cursor with cross-hairs (Figure 4.28). Cross-hairs allow moderately

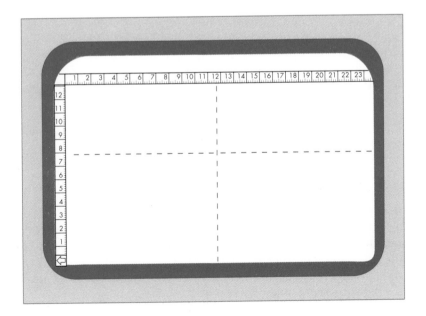

Figure 4.28
Rulers and Cross-hairs

independent motion in the x and y directions and are more valuable than a simple cursor as a visual indicator.

Rubberband lines are another alternative to cursors. Here, a line is drawn from some fixed initial point to the location indicated by the movement of the input device. As the device is moved, the line is redrawn from the same initial point to the new position. The line segment thus changes length and one endpoint in an elastic manner, following the user's motions. Other entities such as circles and rectangles can also be used in this technique. For example, one corner of a rectangle can remain fixed and the diagonally opposite corner can follow the user's motion.

Sometimes, placing a grid on the display is helpful to the user. In many situations, we know that only certain positions are valid. We may know that positions need only to be located at integer values in the WC system, or at equally spaced intervals. We can aid the user by creating a grid (possibly invisible) at the correct resolution. Values entered by the user are "snapped" or "relaxed" to the closest grid value.

Constraints can be enforced upon the user. For example, the program can prevent a user from moving the cursor out of a specified area on the display. Such a constraint can force the user to enter data only within a valid range.

The use of the graphics system to create graphical devices that perform the functions of any of the logical input devices provides many new possibilities. For example, we can create scales and slidebars to allow positioning to be done accurately (Figure 4.29). Since we can create virtually any mapping between position on the screen and real numbers through software, we can create scales with variable sensitivity. We can use the ends of the scale for rough positioning and the center for fine tuning.

Another important aid is to allow the user to work at different scales in the work area through zooming. By being able to switch between normal and zoomed views, the user can lay out a design roughly and then position it more precisely when necessary. Such techniques are especially valuable with large designs or where the user has a small, limited-resolution display.

4.11.5 Layout

The success of a user interface also depends on its visual appearance. A good user interface should be helpful without distracting the user. On one hand, we want to provide the user with all the information he might need; on the other hand, we want to leave the user some area in which to work. The use of a control bar, as we discussed, is one technique for saving space on the display surface.

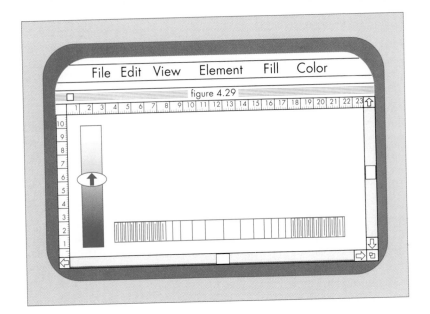

Figure 4.29
Scales and Slidebars

The style we used for our display in our shape-layout program employed fixed-size rectangles, or *tiles*, which did not overlap. The general form of such an interface is shown in Figure 4.30. Each tile corresponds to a viewport in our program. An alternative is to allow the viewports[1] to overlap (Figure 4.31). Menus are now hidden behind one another, but if we allow a top bar on each to be visible, the user is aware of which menus are available. When the user wants to use a particular menu, a click on the exposed part of the viewport will cause the system to display the selected menu by bringing it to the front. Such a strategy need not apply only to menus. We can employ overlapping viewports to allow a user to work on multiple diagrams concurrently.

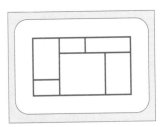

Figure 4.30
Tiling the Display

There is still much debate as to which of these forms is best. The answer certainly depends on the application, and also on the implementation. For example, drawing overlapping viewports might require the system to do more work than would tiling. We cannot determine whether this can be done without slowing down the application to the point where it is no longer useful, without considering algorithms and hardware for implementing the interface.

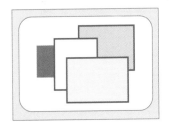

Figure 4.31
Overlapping Viewports

---

[1] Unfortunately much of the workstation community uses the term "window" rather than "viewport" in this context.

4.11.6 Color

Before we leave the subject of user interfaces, we shall comment on how color can affect the user interface. A more detailed discussion of color will be deferred until we discuss raster systems in Chapter 7.

Color CRT displays have progressed to the point that they are neither significantly more expensive nor lower in resolution than are monochrome displays. Color is both pleasing and informative to the viewer. We can use color in our graphics system by simply setting up color tables. The effective use of color, however, is dependent on aspects of the psychology of human vision.

One of the major problems with the use of color is overuse. Although a few colors improve the interface, use of more than five or six colors tends to distract and confuse the user. Humans interpret colors in a "thermal" manner. The cool colors (such as blue and green) are interpreted as conveying less important information than are the hot colors (such as red, white, and yellow).

Other factors governing the use of color are based on the physical properties of the sensing mechanism in the eye. For example, the lens in the eye is not color-corrected, as is a camera lens. It cannot focus simultaneously on frequencies on both ends of the visible spectrum. Displaying red and blue objects adjacent to each other can thus present problems to a viewer. In addition, the blue sensors in the eye are located primarily at the periphery of the retina. We should avoid using blue for small foreground objects, such as text. References to other important aspects of human color vision can be found in Section 4.13.

▬ 4.12
▬ The Burden of Interaction

We have introduced the mechanics of interaction in a graphics system and have examined how we might design interactive programs. We have not discussed the implementation issues. Interaction makes little sense if we cannot build a system that can interact with a user in real time. For an application user working with device-independent software, it is all too easy to overlook the tremendous burden that interactive graphics can place on the hardware.

Consider an interaction with a menu-based system employing overlapping viewports. Each time the user brings a menu to the front, a significant part of the screen must be redrawn. On a raster display, large areas must be filled. If we employ aids such as cross-hairs and rubberband lines, the system must attempt to draw and erase lines as fast as the user can move his input device. Movement of objects about the screen by dragging is another case where the display is altered almost continuously.

A related issue is whether standard graphics software packages can support the kinds of interactive techniques we have discussed. Certainly, many interactive programs can be developed with user programs using GKS and PHIGS. There are other cases, however, where it is not so clear that interaction is possible. For example, a user program based on random-scan (line-drawing) primitives, such as in GKS and PHIGS, cannot create a rubberband line.

Surveying the existing systems makes clear that it is possible to build highly interactive graphics systems. By studying implementation issues, we shall better understand where the limitations are, and shall discover what parts of the interaction should be part of the application program and which should be the implementor's responsibility. For now, you should be able to get started writing interactive programs and experimenting with the form and style of user interfaces.

4.13 Suggested Readings

Many of the issues involved in implementing user interaction are discussed in [Foley81]. Information on human vision and its influence on interactive graphics can be found in [Corn70] and [Murch85].

The present era of user interfaces and graphics workstations began with the work at the Xerox Corporation's Palo Alto Research Center (PARC) during the 1970s. Many of the techniques we have discussed were first used at PARC. Some references to designing and implementing user interfaces are [Gold83], [Ing81], [Myer88], [Sal87], [Schnei87], and [Smith82]. Information on the use of color in graphics can be found in [Krebs79] and [Wysz82]. Probably the best way to learn about graphical interfaces is to survey the available products, in particular those in the CAD community and on personal computers such as the Apple Macintosh.

■ Exercises

4.1 Consider the four basic operations with segments: create, close, delete, and rename. Compare linked-list and table-oriented implementations. Discuss the memory-management and timing problems with each type of implementation.

4.2 How would you go about adding a segment modification or editing facility to your solution to Exercise 4.1?

4.3 Consider the implementation of a stroke device through a physical device, such as a keyboard or data tablet, that can provide a location. One possibility is to associate a bounding box with each segment. Another is to use the display list. For each case, work out how to determine a segment identifier.

4.4 The definition of how close one must come to a primitive in a segment to pick the segment is left out in the specification of most graphics systems. In light of Exercise 4.3 and of what you know about input and output devices, come up with a reasonable definition for use with a particular physical device. Does it matter whether the display is random scan or raster scan?

4.5 Consider a standard CRT display as described in Chapter 1. Suppose a beam of electrons is focused ideally into a column of width w. At the center of the CRT, we will see a spot of width w. How do the width and intensity of the light output change as we move the beam across the CRT face? How does this change affect the selection of a threshold for a lightpen device?

4.6 Show that, if we use a joystick as a velocity device, we can replace the potentiometers with a pair of three-position switches.

4.7 A mechanical data tablet can be constructed as shown in Figure 4.32. The positions of the two angles are sensed by the graphics processor. Give the position of the stylus in terms of these angles (and the lengths of the arms). How does the sensitivity of this device change as we move the stylus about the surface?

4.8 Write procedures to implement graphically logical input devices, such as a choice and a valuator. How would you provide prompts and echoes?

4.9 The example of the shape-layout program used only request-mode input. A much nicer program can be obtained using sample and perhaps event input. Rewrite the program using one or both of these modes.

4.10 Given only a keyboard, how could you use it to provide all the logical input classes?

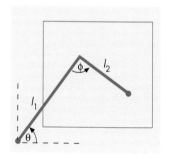

Figure 4.32
Mechanical Data Tablet

4.11 A variant of the shape-layout program occurs in making logic diagrams. We introduced the basic logical gates in Exercise 3.9. Expand that exercise to an interactive program for logic-circuit design. You might want to add an analysis capability where the designed circuit's Boolean equation is determined and a truth table is constructed.

4.12 The requirement that the aspect ratios of the workstation window and workstation viewport be the same often means that we use the largest square area on a rectangular display. This choice can result in our wasting considerable space on our output devices. Using the *inquire display space size* procedure, show how, for a given world window, we can select the world viewport, workstation window, and workstation viewport to use the entire display. Are there any unfavorable side effects? If there are, describe them.

4.13 The games of chess and checkers are played on an 8 by 8 board of black and white squares. The games can be simulated by computer graphics; two users move the pieces with an input device. Write such a program. Your program should also check for legal moves.

4.14 Using the standard input procedures we have discussed, derive input procedures for entering data with a locator. Include options for forcing the data onto a user-determined grid.

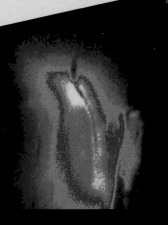

Pseudocolor enhanced display of autoradio-graph showing flow across membranes in the brain. (Courtesy of Departments of Computer Science and Neurology, University of New Mexico.)

Visualization of complex cube root function. (Courtesy of Ardent Computer Corp.)

Plate 1 Plotting

Three-dimensional display of data plotted using commercially available software. (Produced by Computer Associates International, Inc.)

Plate 2 Architecture

Computer renderings of computer-aided architectural designs. (Copyright 1987 and 1989 S. Kasahara-Kajima Corp., Japan.)

Plate 3 Mechanical Design

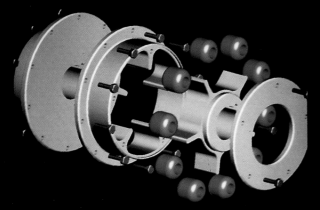

Exploded view of Mechanical Part. (Courtesy of Silicon Graphics.)

Rendering of transmission. (Image copyright Wavefront Technologies Inc., Santa Barbara, CA.)

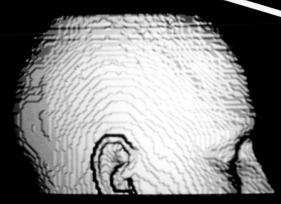

Volume element (voxel) reconstruction of skull from magnetic resonance imaging (MRI) scans. (Courtesy of Arie Kaufman—SUNY at Stony Brook—Stony Brook, NY.)

Plate 4 Medical Imaging

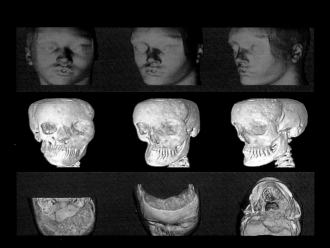

Three 3-D reconstructions of woman's face with fibrous dysplasia, from CT data. Skin rendered opaque (top), transparent (middle), translucent (bottom). (Data courtesy of Hugh Curtain, M.D. and David W. Johnson, M.D., Department of Radiology, University Health Centers of Pittsburgh, Pennsylvania. © 1987 Pixar.)

Plate 5 Flow Visualization

Visualization of subsonic flow with colors indicating pressures. (Courtesy of Douglas Aircraft Company, McDonnell Douglas Corporation.)

Navier-Stokes CFD solution of a reversed pitch fan flowfield. (Courtesy of Wayne Jones, Boeing Commercial Airplanes.)

Simulated cytotoxic anti-cancer drug-DNA crosslink. (Courtesy of Thomas C. Palmer and Frederick H. Hausheer: National Cancer Institute.)

Plate 6 Molecular Modeling

Virus molecule. (Image copyright Wavefront Technologies Inc., Santa Barbara, CA.)

Part of antibody molecule. (Illustration computed by Michael Pique, Scripps Clinic, on a Sun workstation using software by Ray-Tracing Corporation.)

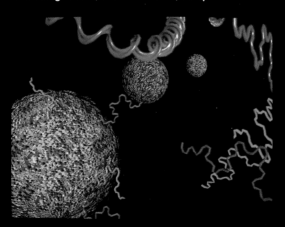

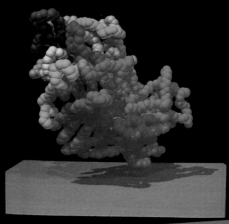

Plate 7 Circuit Design

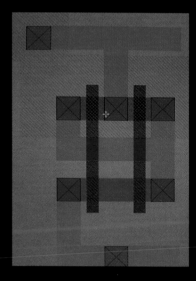

Computer-aided VLSI design for square root function. (Courtesy of Imperial College, London.)

Plate 8 Flight Simulator

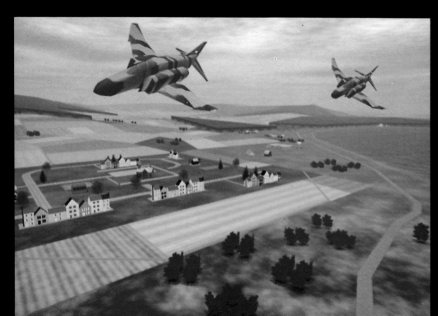

Rendered polygonal model of aircraft used in flight simulator. (Courtesy of Evans and Sutherland Computer Corporation.)

Tricycle. (Courtesy of Gary Mundell and
Andrew Pearce, Alias Research.)

Ford concept car. (Image copyright Wavefront
Technologies Inc., Santa Barbara, CA.)

Plate 9 Photorealism

Scene modeled with polygonal
terrain and quadric clouds.
(Courtesy of G. Gardener—
Grumman Data Systems.)

Plate 10 User Interface

User interface during
generation of diagram
from this book.

Plate 11 Maxwell Triangle

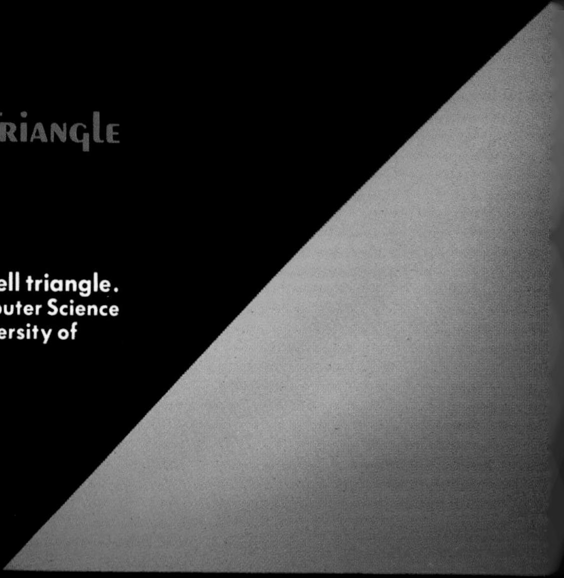

Colors on Maxwell triangle.
(Courtesy of Computer Science
Department, University of
New Mexico.)

Plate 12 Rendering

Carbon Red   Obsidian Lunar   Olive   Rust
        Rubber   Dust   Drab

Bronze Tungsten Copper   Tin   Nickel Stainless
                                           Steel

Urns rendered with different
surface properties.   (Rob Cook,
Program of Computer Graphics,
Cornell University.)

Steel Mill. Illumination using radiosity method. (Stuart I. Feldman and John B. Wallace, Program of Computer Graphics, Cornell University.)

Candle. (Image copyright Wavefront Technologies Inc., Santa Barbara, CA.)

PLATE 13 RAY TRACING

PLATE 14 RAY TRACING

Light Bulbs. Rendered using 793,900 polygons. ("Wise Guy" ©1987 James Dixon/PDI.)

Water Strider. Rendered using the equivalent of 50,000 polygons and 52 different textures. (This image was created by Daniel Langlois, using the SOFTIMAGE 4D Creative Environment software. Copyright 1988 SOFTIMAGE Inc.)

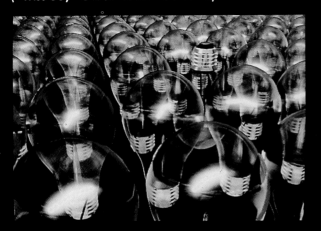

Plate 15 Solid Modeling

Solid Model of Robot. Solid primitives in foreground. (Courtesy of Purdue CADLAB.)

Plate 16 Solid Model and Mesh

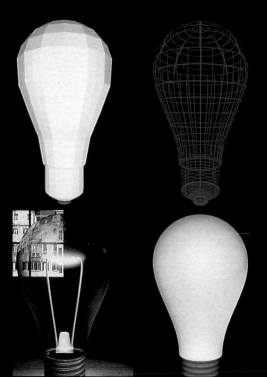

Light bulb as wire frame, rendered with simple-faceted shaded surfaces, rendered as smooth surfaced, and rendered as photorealistic. (© 1988 Pixar.)

5

Transformations and Modeling

Introduction

To a large degree, the full power of a modern graphics system rests on the system's ability to carry out transformations on graphical objects. We have used one example already in our viewing operations. Graphical objects that are defined in WC are transformed into objects in NDC, then are transformed again into objects in DC.

Transformations arise in a number of other ways. Animation involves moving graphical objects in time, normally done by transforming them from place to place. Applications such as circuit design and room layout are based on manipulating a number of objects (resistors, integrated circuits, tables, chairs) into their desired locations in the design. This positioning is accomplished through a sequence of transformations. Many architectures for computer graphics systems can be characterized by a sequence of hardware transformations that operate on graphical primitives as the latter move through the system from definition in an application program to their final display on an output device.

159

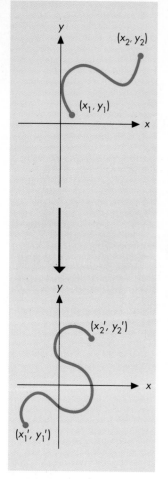

Figure 5.1
General Transformations

Our first step will be to develop the necessary mathematics for a class of line-preserving transformations known as *affine* transformations. Once we have done this, we shall develop a simple transformation package that we shall use in conjunction with our graphics system.

Next, we shall turn to the use of transformations for modeling. Until now, we have represented the world of the application in a linear way. Sophisticated models use the relationships among objects to build models of the world. For example, the wheels on a car are logically and physically related to the chassis of the car. We shall examine methods for expressing these relationships, then shall use the resulting models in our graphics system.

5.1
Affine Transformations

5.1.1 General Transformations

The primitives we use most often in graphics systems are based on lines. The reasons are multiple and include that lines occur naturally in real-world applications, are easy to generate, and, most germane to the present discussion, are easy to transform. Consider the problem of transforming or mapping a segment of a curve C between points (x_1, y_1) and (x_2, y_2) to a new segment C' by a transformation we will denote T, as shown in Figure 5.1. Using our vector representation, any point

$$\mathbf{p} = \begin{bmatrix} x \\ y \end{bmatrix},$$

on C is transformed into a new point on C'

$$\mathbf{p}' = \begin{bmatrix} x' \\ y' \end{bmatrix}.$$

We can express this relationship as

$$\mathbf{p}' = T(\mathbf{p}),$$

where the form of T describes the exact nature of the transformation.

Suppose we want to use our graphics system to display the transformed curve. In general, neither C nor C' will correspond to primitives within our graphics system. We might try something like transforming a set of points $\{\mathbf{p}_i\}$ on C into a new set points $\{\mathbf{p}'_i\}$ on C'. To produce a picture of C', we could use these transformed points to form a polyline primitive that approximates C' and could be displayed on most graphics systems. This approach, although possible, might require far too many calculations to be a useful method of displaying transformed curves.

5.1.2 Transforming Lines to Lines

As an alternative, consider one of the most appealing features of the line: It is completely defined by any two points on it. Hence, we need to store only these two points or, in the case of a line segment, the two endpoints of the segment. This is an efficient means of storage, as we can use the hardware or software to generate all other points only as needed, usually on output to the display. If a line is transformed into something other than another line, we have not solved our problem. Fortunately, however, many of the most important operations we do in the real world preserve lines. These transformations include rotation, reflection, scaling, and translation; they belong to a class of transformations known as *affine* transformations (Figure 5.2). The importance of affine transformations in computer graphics should be clear.

Suppose we have a line segment connecting points (x_1, y_1) and (x_2, y_2). If we transform these points individually by an affine transformation to (x'_1, y'_1) and (x'_2, y'_2), respectively, as in Figure 5.3, we know that all points in between are generated by the line segment connecting these two new endpoints. Since affine transformations transform line segments into line segments, any two successive affine transformations are equivalent to a single affine transformation. This fact will allow us to build up complex transformations by combining a sequence of simple transformations. The three basic transformations we will use are: rotation about the origin, translation, and scaling. In all cases, we must keep in mind that there are infinite ways to move a single point, $\mathbf{p}$, to a new point, $\mathbf{p}'$. When we consider that this point is a single point on an object and that the same operation is being applied to *all* points on the object, we see that there usually will be only a single characterization of the transformation.

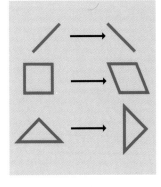

Figure 5.2
Affine Transformations

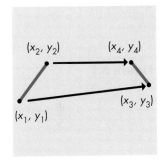

Figure 5.3
Transforming a Line Segment

5.1.3 Translation

Translation shifts all points on an object by an equal amount, as shown in Figure 5.4. We can characterize this operation by the following pair of equations:

Figure 5.4
Translation

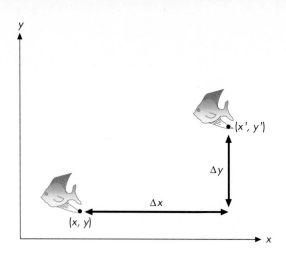

$$\begin{aligned} x' &= x + \Delta x, \\ y' &= y + \Delta y. \end{aligned}$$

In terms of our vector representation, if

$$\mathbf{p} = \begin{bmatrix} x \\ y \end{bmatrix},$$

$$\mathbf{p}' = \begin{bmatrix} x' \\ y' \end{bmatrix},$$

$$\mathbf{t} = \begin{bmatrix} \Delta x \\ \Delta y \end{bmatrix},$$

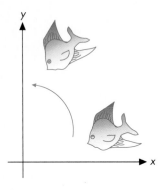

Figure 5.5
Rotation

the translation operation can be written as the vector (or column matrix) addition

$$\mathbf{p}' = \mathbf{p} + \mathbf{t}.$$

5.1.4 Rotation

Rotation about the origin by θ degrees is illustrated in Figure 5.5. We can derive the equations for rotation by noting that, as we rotate a point about the origin, that point remains a constant distance from the origin. Using polar form (Figure 5.6), we have

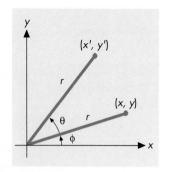

Figure 5.6
Polar Representation

$$\begin{aligned} x &= r \cos \phi, \\ y &= r \sin \phi, \end{aligned}$$

$$x' = r\cos(\theta + \phi),$$
$$y' = r\sin(\theta + \phi).$$

Using the trigonometric formulae for the cosine and sine of the sum of two angles, we find

$$
\begin{aligned}
x' &= r\cos\theta\cos\phi - r\sin\theta\sin\phi, \\
&= x\cos\theta - y\sin\theta, \\
y' &= r\cos\theta\sin\phi + r\sin\theta\cos\phi, \\
&= x\sin\theta + y\cos\theta.
\end{aligned}
$$

These equations can be expressed as a matrix-vector multiplication,

$$\mathbf{p}' = \mathbf{R}\mathbf{p},$$

where $\mathbf{R}$ is the matrix

$$\mathbf{R} = \begin{bmatrix} \cos\theta & -\sin\theta \\ \sin\theta & \cos\theta \end{bmatrix}.$$

5.1.5 Scaling

Our third basic operation, *scaling*, is illustrated in Figure 5.7. We shall allow separate scaling in the x and y directions. The scaling constants α and β determine the amount of scaling in each direction:

$$
\begin{aligned}
x' &= \alpha x, \\
y' &= \beta y.
\end{aligned}
$$

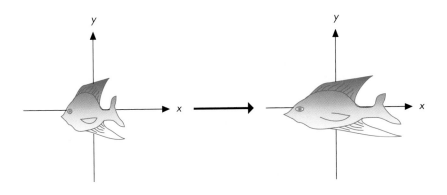

Figure 5.7
Scaling

Figure 5.8
Reflection

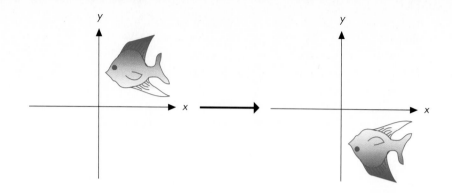

If a scaling constant is greater than 1, the size of an object is expanded in that direction. If the constant is positive but is less than 1, there is contraction along that direction.

A negative scale factor will cause reflection to take place about the corresponding axis. For example, in Figure 5.8, we have $\alpha = 1$ and $\beta = -1$. Scaling can also be expressed by the matrix-vector operation

$$\mathbf{p}' = \mathbf{Sp},$$

where

$$\mathbf{S} = \begin{bmatrix} \alpha & 0 \\ 0 & \beta \end{bmatrix}.$$

5.1.6 Shear

An additional operation, called *shear* (Figure 5.9), is also useful for forming general affine transformations. In the figure, we have illus-

Figure 5.9
x-Axis Shear

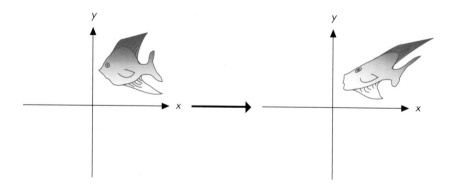

trated shearing along the x axis. The angle ϕ determines the amount of shear. A similar diagram would show y-axis shear. The equations for x-direction shear are easily found from the trigonometric considerations, shown in Figure 5.10. These equations are

$$
\begin{aligned}
x' &= x + y \cot \phi, \\
y' &= y,
\end{aligned}
$$

which leads to the x-axis shearing matrix

$$
\mathbf{H}_x = \begin{bmatrix} 1 & \cot \phi \\ 0 & 1 \end{bmatrix}.
$$

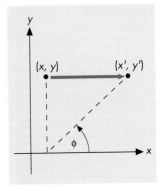

Figure 5.10
Determination of Shear Equations

The matrix for y-axis shear, $\mathbf{H}_y$, can be found in a similar manner. Although shear can be derived from the other operations, it is used so often that we will consider it one of our basic operations.

These four basic operations are not sufficient to describe all affine transformations if each is taken alone. For example, we might want to rotate an object about a point other than the origin, or to reflect an object about an arbitrary axis. We can achieve these operations by combining our basic operations.

5.2
Concatenating Transformations

Our basic transformations can be used to generate more general line-preserving transformations. If we apply two successive affine transformations to a line segment, we will still have a line segment. Hence, their combination is also an affine transformation. This process of *concatenation* is a powerful one and will yield more general transformations than we have now. Starting with a simple example, we shall find that we need to reevaluate how we represent our transformations, so that we can get an efficient method for combining them.

5.2.1 Rotating About a Fixed Point

Suppose we consider rotation about a point other than the origin, (x_f, y_f), as in Figure 5.11. This point is called the *fixed point* of the operation, since it is unchanged by the rotation. We can derive the equations for this rotation using elementary trigonometry, as we did for rotation about the origin. A more interesting approach is to derive the equations using the basic operations we already have in our repertoire.

Figure 5.11
General Rotation

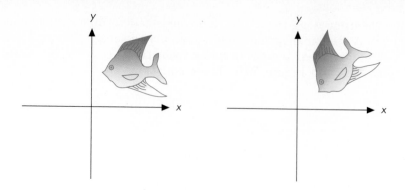

We can do the problem in three steps. We know how to rotate about the origin, so a possible strategy (and often a very good one) is to convert the problem at hand to one we have already solved. We convert this problem by first translating the fixed point to the origin. This step entails the translation of all points by $(-x_f, -y_f)$, as in Figure 5.12. An arbitrary point, (x, y), is thus transformed to a new point $(\bar{x}, \bar{y})$ by

$$
\begin{aligned}
\bar{x} &= x - x_f \\
\bar{y} &= y - y_f.
\end{aligned}
$$

Now we can rotate about the origin as before, producing the point $(\hat{x}, \hat{y})$:

$$
\begin{aligned}
\hat{x} &= \bar{x}\cos - \bar{y}\sin\theta, \\
\hat{y} &= \bar{x}\sin + \bar{y}\cos\theta.
\end{aligned}
$$

We are not yet done, since we have shifted everything by $(-x_f, -y_f)$. We can undo this shift by simply translating again by the negative of this amount, returning the fixed point to its original location. Our final point is thus (x', y'), where

$$
\begin{aligned}
x' &= \hat{x} + x_f \\
y' &= \hat{y} + y_f.
\end{aligned}
$$

This final operation is the *inverse* of our first translation. We shall often use the facts that, not only do each of our basic operations have an inverse that undoes the operation, but also the inverse operation is of the same type. As we see here, the inverse of a translation is itself a translation. By combining these equations, we now have the general rotation equations

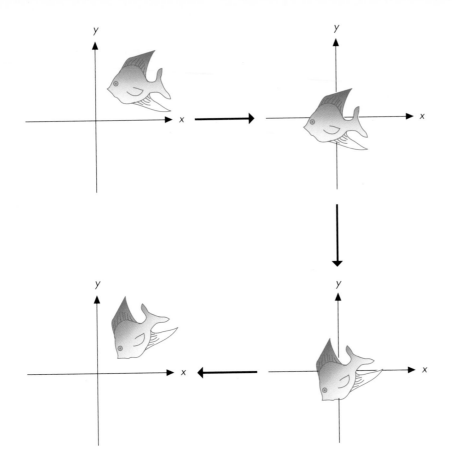

Figure 5.12
Moving the Fixed Point

$$x' = (x - x_f)\cos\theta - (y - y_f)\sin\theta + x_f,$$
$$y' = (x - x_f)\sin\theta + (y - y_f)\cos\theta + y_f.$$

5.2.2 Homogeneous Coordinates

At this point, we might wonder why we have not used the matrix and vector representations we introduced previously for our basic transformations. We could have used them, but the result would not have been particularly pleasing. The first operation—moving the fixed point to the origin—can be represented by a vector addition. Our second operation—the rotation—is a matrix-vector multiplication. Our final operation is another vector addition. The problem is how can we combine these three operations into a single form. The solution is difficult, since we cannot combine vector addition and matrix-vector multiplication into a single equivalent operation in two dimensions. We can, however, achieve a nice representation if we go to three dimensions.

Homogeneous coordinates provide a special three-dimensional representation that allows easy manipulation of two-dimensional entities. We replace the two-dimensional point

$$\mathbf{p} = \begin{bmatrix} x \\ y \end{bmatrix},$$

by the three-dimensional point

$$\mathbf{p} = \begin{bmatrix} wx \\ wy \\ w \end{bmatrix}.$$

The only restriction on w is that it must be nonzero. With this restriction we can go back and forth between a point and its homogeneous-coordinate representation by multiplying or dividing by w as necessary. In normal two-dimensional graphics, we will always be able to set w to 1, and here we shall assume that we have made this choice.

Using homogeneous coordinates, our three basic operations can be represented by matrices, as can all combinations of these operations. For example, translation of a point (x, y) with homogeneous representation

$$\mathbf{p} = \begin{bmatrix} x \\ y \\ 1 \end{bmatrix},$$

by $(\Delta x, \Delta y)$ to a new position (x', y') can be expressed as

$$\mathbf{p'} = \begin{bmatrix} x' \\ y' \\ 1 \end{bmatrix} = \mathbf{T}(\Delta x, \Delta y)\mathbf{p},$$

where $\mathbf{T}(\Delta x, \Delta y)$ is the matrix

$$\mathbf{T}(\Delta x, \Delta y) = \begin{bmatrix} 1 & 0 & \Delta x \\ 0 & 1 & \Delta y \\ 0 & 0 & 1 \end{bmatrix}.$$

By carrying out the matrix-vector multiplication, we can easily verify that we indeed get our original translation equations from the first two rows of the matrix. The third row forces w to be unchanged by the translation; thus, this matrix will be the same even if we allow values of w other than 1.

If we follow the same procedure for rotation about the origin, scaling, and x-axis shear, we get the three matrices

$$\mathbf{R}(\theta) = \begin{bmatrix} \cos\theta & -\sin\theta & 0 \\ \sin\theta & \cos\theta & 0 \\ 0 & 0 & 1 \end{bmatrix},$$

$$\mathbf{S}(\alpha, \beta) = \begin{bmatrix} \alpha & 0 & 0 \\ 0 & \beta & 0 \\ 0 & 0 & 1 \end{bmatrix},$$

$$\mathbf{H}_x(\phi) = \begin{bmatrix} 1 & \cot\phi & 0 \\ 0 & 1 & 0 \\ 0 & 0 & 1 \end{bmatrix}.$$

5.2.3 Matrix Representations

We can now see how simply we can concatenate affine transformations. Suppose we make a series of transformations with matrices $\mathbf{A}$, $\mathbf{B}$, and $\mathbf{C}$ on a point $\mathbf{p}$, where each matrix represents one of our basic operations. The transformed point will then be given by

$$\mathbf{p}' = \mathbf{C}(\mathbf{B}(\mathbf{Ap})).$$

Using the basic properties of matrices, we can rewrite this equation as

$$\mathbf{p}' = \mathbf{Mp},$$

where $\mathbf{M}$ is the matrix

$$\mathbf{M} = \mathbf{CBA}.$$

Thus, a sequence of affine transformations can be represented by a single matrix. Note that, since in general

$$\mathbf{AB} \neq \mathbf{BA},$$

we must be careful about the order of the matrices when we form a composite transformation. One additional caution is that the order operations are applied in $\mathbf{CBAp}$ is opposite the normal (left to right) reading direction in English. Many graphics books and systems replace column vectors by row vectors using the matrix transposition operation. This transposition converts our equation to the equivalent form (where the superscript T denotes matrix transposition) with row vectors,

$$\mathbf{p'}^T = \mathbf{p}^T\mathbf{A}^T\mathbf{B}^T\mathbf{C}^T = \mathbf{p}^T\mathbf{M}^T,$$

which reads in the reverse order. However, in keeping with the recent graphics systems and the physical/mathematical literature, we shall use column form.

Returning to our example of rotation about a fixed point, our three steps are

$$
\begin{aligned}
\mathbf{A} &= \mathbf{T}(-x_f, -y_f), \\
\mathbf{B} &= \mathbf{R}(\theta), \\
\mathbf{C} &= \mathbf{T}(x_f, y_f).
\end{aligned}
$$

They yield the concatenated matrix

$$\mathbf{M} = \mathbf{CBA} = \begin{bmatrix} \cos\theta & -\sin\theta & y_f\sin\theta - x_f\cos\theta + x_f \\ \sin\theta & \cos\theta & -x_f\sin\theta - y_f\cos\theta + y_f \\ 0 & 0 & 1 \end{bmatrix}.$$

5.2.4 Inverse Transformations

Before discussing how we can use transformations with our graphics system, let us consider a few more examples. One important class of operations is the inverse transformations. For instance, if we use an affine transformation A to produce a transformed point

$$\mathbf{p'} = A(\mathbf{p}),$$

the inverse operation, denoted A^{-1}, will produce

$$\mathbf{p} = A^{-1}(\mathbf{p'}).$$

Using homogeneous coordinates, A becomes the 3 by 3 matrix $\mathbf{A}$, so

$$
\begin{aligned}
\mathbf{p'} &= \mathbf{A}\mathbf{p}, \\
\mathbf{p} &= \mathbf{A}^{-1}\mathbf{p'},
\end{aligned}
$$

where $\mathbf{A}^{-1}$ is the inverse matrix. For the basic operations, these inverses always exist, unless we do something silly like using a scale factor of 0. Thus, inverses will exist for all our composite operations, since

$$(\mathbf{AB})^{-1} = \mathbf{B}^{-1}\mathbf{A}^{-1}.$$

For our basic operations, the inverse transformations are fairly obvious if we apply simply geometric arguments. For example, the inverse of rotation by θ degrees is a rotation by $-\theta$ degrees. Hence, for our basic operations of translation, rotation, and scaling, the inverse transformations are

$$
\begin{aligned}
\mathbf{T}^{-1}(\Delta x, \Delta y) &= \mathbf{T}(-\Delta x, -\Delta y), \\
\mathbf{R}^{-1}(\theta) &= \mathbf{R}(-\theta), \\
\mathbf{S}^{-1}(\alpha, \beta) &= \mathbf{S}(\frac{1}{\alpha}, \frac{1}{\beta}), \\
\mathbf{H}_x^{-1}(\phi) &= \mathbf{H}_x(-\phi).
\end{aligned}
$$

5.2.5 Concatenation Examples

Now many of our more detailed operations can be expressed in terms of our basic operations and their inverses. For example, consider scaling about a fixed point (x_f, y_f), as in Figure 5.13. As with rotation, the fixed point remains unchanged by the transformation. Our basic scaling operation had a fixed point of origin. We adopt a strategy similar to that we used for general rotation: We translate the fixed point to the origin, scale, and then move the fixed point back to its original location. The desired 3 by 3 matrix is

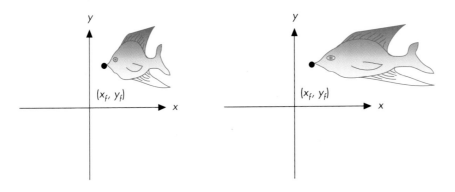

Figure 5.13
General Scaling

$$\begin{aligned}
\mathbf{A} &= \mathbf{T}(x_f, y_f)\mathbf{S}(\alpha, \beta)\mathbf{T}(-x_f, -y_f) \\
&= \begin{bmatrix} \alpha & 0 & (1-\alpha)x_f \\ 0 & \beta & (1-\beta)y_f \\ 0 & 0 & 1 \end{bmatrix}.
\end{aligned}$$

We can also note that the bottom rows in each of our transformation matrices are identical. They are the same because they are there solely to keep the "extra" variable w unchanged. For two-dimensional applications, we need to retain only the first two rows or, equivalently, a 2 by 3 matrix.

As a final example, consider the reflection of an object about an arbitrary line, as illustrated in Figure 5.14. We know that we can reflect an object about the y axis by using the scaling matrix

$$\mathbf{S}(-1, 1) = \begin{bmatrix} -1 & 0 & 0 \\ 0 & 1 & 0 \\ 0 & 0 & 1 \end{bmatrix}.$$

We will again convert the given problem into a problem that we know how to solve. Suppose the axis of reflection is the line

$$y = mx + h.$$

Starting with the slope m, we can find the angle

$$\theta = \tan^{-1} m,$$

the line makes with the x-axis. We can align the axis of rotation with

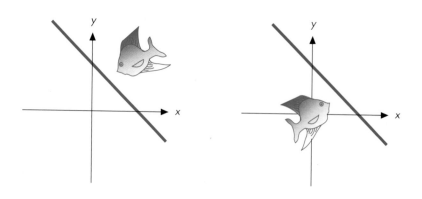

Figure 5.14
Reflection About an Axis

the y axis by a rotation of $\phi = 90 - \theta$ degrees. Note that the necessary sine and cosine are

$$\sin \phi \;=\; \frac{1}{\sqrt{1 + m^2}},$$

$$\cos \phi \;=\; \frac{m}{\sqrt{1 + m^2}}.$$

We also have to shift the rotated axis to the origin with $\mathbf{T}(0, -h)$. There are five basic transformations that we use to compose the desired transformation: a shift to the origin, a rotation to align the axis, the reflection about the y-axis, a rotation back, and a final translation back, as in Figure 5.15. The composite matrix is thus

$$\mathbf{A} = \mathbf{T}(0, h)\mathbf{R}(-\phi)\mathbf{S}(-1, 1)\mathbf{R}(\phi)\mathbf{T}(0, -h).$$

In a similar manner, we can construct arbitrary affine transformations. There are a number of ways a given transformation can be constructed. The resulting concatenated matrix should be the same, regardless of the technique used to derive it. It is also important to note that, since we often use a given affine transformation to transform hundreds or thousands of points (or even thousands of objects), the overhead incurred in deriving the transformation from a number of simpler transformations is negligible. Now we can turn to how to use transformations in graphics systems.

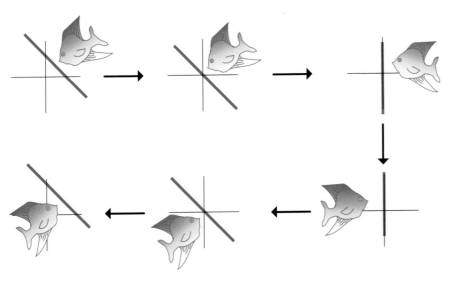

Figure 5.15
The Sequence of Transformations

5.3
Transformations in GKS

To understand the use of transformations in GKS and in many other graphics systems, we have to return to our earlier discussion of coordinate systems and the synthetic camera analogy. Primitives are defined in WC and then are transformed into NDC using the current viewing conditions. When we wish to apply a transformation, either we can apply it to the primitive in WC (i.e., before it has been transformed into NDC space) or we can apply it after the normalization transformation. These two approaches can yield very different results.

One way to see why the results vary is to reexamine the equations for the transformation from WC to NDC, which we presented in Chapter 2. We can represent this line-preserving transformation using two of our basic operations: translation and scaling. It is composed of a scaling in WC, as shown in Figure 5.16, with a fixed point of the center of the window, to the size of the viewport, followed by a translation of the lower-left corner of the window to the lower-left corner of the viewport. In Exercise 5.1, we ask you to verify that we get the same equations as in Chapter 2. Suppose we denote the matrix that defines this transformation in homogeneous coordinates $\mathbf{N}$. Now consider some affine transformation, described by a matrix $\mathbf{A}$, which we wish to apply in WC. What we find in NDC space are our original primitives, defined in WC, transformed by the composite matrix

$$\mathbf{B} = \mathbf{NA},$$

applied to each point

$$\mathbf{p}' = \mathbf{Bp}.$$

On the other hand, if we apply $\mathbf{A}$ in NDC space we are, in effect, using a composite transformation

$$\mathbf{C} = \mathbf{AN}.$$

Since matrices in general do not commute, the results of $\mathbf{B}$ and $\mathbf{C}$ applied to a primitive, in general, will be very different.

We can distinguish between these two ways we can apply transformations by referring to application of the transformation to the objects first as an *object* or *modeling* transformation. The case where the transformation is applied after the viewing operation will be called an *image* transformation. GKS and other systems such as CORE pro-

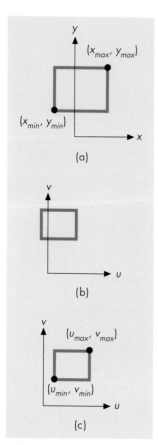

Figure 5.16
Normalization
Transformation. (a) World
Coordinates. (b) Scaled. (c)
Translated.

vide image transformations and leave object transformations to the application program.

GKS gives the user an image-transformation capability through segment transformations. A 2 by 3 transformation matrix is an attribute of each segment. As we noted before, we need to specify only the first two rows of the 3 by 3 matrix that defines an affine transformation in homogeneous coordinates. Initially, this matrix is set to the first two rows of the identity matrix

$$\mathbf{A} = \begin{bmatrix} 1 & 0 & 0 \\ 0 & 1 & 0 \end{bmatrix}.$$

This matrix can be altered by the GKS function *set segment transformation*

```
void gset_seg_tran(seg_name,tran_matrix)
Gint seg_name;
Gfloat tran_matrix[2][3];
```

The matrix **A** is set equal to `tran_matrix` and is then applied to primitives in segment `seg_name`, after they have first been transformed into NDC space. Most graphics systems also provide two utility functions, *evaluate transformation matrix* and *accumulate transformation matrix*, which allow us to set or alter the matrix `tran_matrix`. Of more interest now is to see what we can and cannot do with this facility.

Students of computer graphics often have great difficulties understanding what the differences between object and image transformations are and why GKS provides only image transformations. Recall that, in GKS, segments are associated with workstations. Conceptually, every workstation that was active when the segment was created has its own copy of its segments. So that a segment could be placed on these workstations, the viewing operation has been performed on those primitives in the segment. The segment transformation is performed after the segment is on the workstation and before the workstation transformation, as in Figure 5.17. This choice allows a physical implementation of our logical workstation to include hardware to carry out segment transformations rapidly.

One function that can be accomplished neatly using segment transformations is to zoom or pan an image. For example the matrix

$$\mathbf{A} = \begin{bmatrix} 2 & 0 & 0 \\ 0 & 2 & 0 \end{bmatrix}$$

"doubles" the size of the image of the segment, whereas the matrix

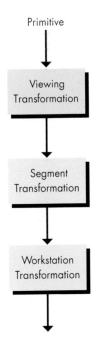

Figure 5.17
The Order of Transformations

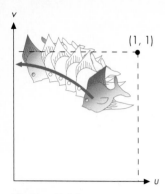

Figure 5.18
Rotation in NDC Space

$$\mathbf{A} = \begin{bmatrix} 1 & 0 & .5 \\ 0 & 1 & -.5 \end{bmatrix}$$

shifts the image of the segment down and to the right. This all seems well and good, but when we examine the problem of rotation, we encounter difficulties.

In NDC space, the origin is at the lower-left corner of the virtual screen. The application, in NDC space, of matrices of the form

$$\mathbf{A} = \begin{bmatrix} cos\ \theta & -sin\ \theta & 0 \\ sin\ \theta & cos\ \theta & 0 \end{bmatrix}$$

will result in the rotation in Figure 5.18, rather than in the usually more desirable rotation of the object about its center. At first glance, this problem might seem easy to resolve. We can use the techniques of the previous section to rotate the object in the segment about its center by using the center as a fixed point. There is, however, a major difficulty.

Since the transformation is being applied in NDC space, the fixed point is in NDC space as far as this transformation is concerned. The application programmer has no simple way of knowing what this point is, without carrying out the WC-to-NDC space transformation herself. In other words, the programmer must track the results of the viewing operation in her program, which, although possible, takes away one of the major advantages of a modern graphics system. This point is a difficult one; you may benefit by constructing simple examples that you can carry out by hand.

It is not that an image-transformation capability in GKS and many other systems is not of use. It is. However, it is intended for certain uses and not for others. If we want to zoom, pan, or construct a composite display of images, GKS segment transformations can work well. On the other hand, for applications that require the user to build and manipulate objects in WC, we will develop our own transformation capability.

5.4
A Transformation Package

If we stay with GKS (or most of the other standard programming systems), we must provide our own procedures to transform objects. The routines are all fairly simple. We need only a handful of basic procedures, and the matrices are small. We will work with 3 by 3 matrices. Although the procedures in some systems, such as GKS, use only the top two rows, we wish to be consistent with what we will do for three-dimensional graphics, where square matrices will be necessary.

The portability of our code will be increased if we add the matrix as a new data type,

```
typedef float Matrix[3][3];
```

We can substitute `Gfloat` for `float` if we are working in a GKS environment.

5.4.1 Evaluation Procedures

We can start building our transformation package with the three basic affine transformations: rotation, translation, and scaling. Our first three procedures will form or *evaluate* the matrices we have denoted $\mathbf{R}(\theta)$, $\mathbf{T}(\Delta x, \Delta y)$, and $\mathbf{S}(\alpha)$. The code for these procedures is

```
void ev_rotate(theta,result)

/* Evaluates a Rotation Matrix
for theta degrees about the origin
Note sine and cosine routines require
input in radians */

#define DEG_TO_RAD 0.01745

float theta;
Matrix result;
{
    double cos(),sin();
    result[0][0]=result[1][1]=cos(DEG_TO_RAD*theta);
    result[1][0]=sin(DEG_TO_RAD*theta);
    result[2][2]=1;
    result[0][1]=-result[1][0];
    result[2][0]=result[2][1]
            =result[0][2]=result[1][2]=0.0;
}

void ev_trans(dx,dy,result)

/* Evaluates a Translation Matrix
for translation by (dx,dy) */
```

```
float dx,dy;
Matrix result;
{
    result[0][0]=result[1][1]=result[2][2]=1.0;
    result[0][1]=result[1][0]
        =result[2][0]=result[2][1]=0.0;
    result[0][2]=dx;
    result[1][2]=dy;
}
```

```
void ev_scale(sx,sy,result)
```

```
/* Evaluates a scaling matrix with a
fixed point at the origin and scale
factors sx and sy */
```

```
float sx, sy;
Matrix result;
{
    result[0][1]=result[1][0]=result[2][0]
        =result[2][1]=result[0][2]=result[1][2]=0.0;
    result[0][0]=sx;
    result[1][1]=sy;
    result[2][2]=1.0;
}
```

5.4.2 Accumulation Procedures

We will also need procedures to combine these operations to form
the more complex operations we have already presented. One way to
do this combining is to provide a matrix-multiplication procedure, so
that we can form matrices such as **AB**. This procedure for our 3 by
3 matrices is

```
void ac_matrix(matrix_a,matrix_b,result)
```

```
/* Forms the matrix product
result=matrix_a*matrix_b */
```

```
Matrix matrix_a, matrix_b, result;
{
    int i,j,k;
    Matrix temp;
    for(i=0;i<3;i++) for(j=0;j<3;j++)
        {
```

```
        temp[i][j]=0.0;
        for(k=0;k<3;k++) temp[i][j] +=
            matrix_a[i][k]*matrix_b[k][j];
        }
    for(i=0;i<3;i++) for(j=0;j<3;j++)
        result[i][j]=temp[i][j];
}
```

In this procedure, we have created a temporary matrix `temp`, so that we can allow the product of two matrices to be placed back into either one of them at the end of the calculation.

These four procedures will allow us to create all affine transformations. For convenience, we can also add the procedure for shear. Of course, we can always create a matrix directly by simply setting all its elements. Often, we want to multiply a matrix by one of the basic matrices. We can use the preceding procedures to create such new procedures. For example, an *accumulate rotation matrix* procedure takes a matrix **A** and forms the matrix **RA**, where **R** is a rotation matrix. The C code is:

```
void ac_rotate(theta,m)
float theta;
Matrix m;
{
    Matrix temp;
    ev_rotate(theta,temp);
    ac_matrix(temp,m,m);
}
```

The procedures `ac_trans` and `ac_scale` can be defined in a similar way.

5.4.3 Applying the Transformations

Returning to a previous example, we can form the rotation matrix about a fixed point (x, y) by

```
ev_trans(-x,-y,matrix);
ac_rotate(theta,matrix);
ac_trans(x,y,matrix);
```

We handle reflection about a line

$$y = mx + h,$$

by

```
ev_trans(-h,0.0,matrix);
theta=atan(m);
ac_rotate(theta,matrix);
ac_scale(-1.,1.,matrix);
ac_rotate(-theta,matrix);
ac_trans(h,0.0,matrix);
```

We need one final procedure before we can use this group of matrix-manipulation routines; we need a procedure for actually transforming a point by one of these matrices we have formed. In other words, we need a procedure to find

$$\mathbf{p'} = \mathbf{Ap}.$$

We will call this function transform_point:

```
void transform_point(trans_matrix, old_point, new_point)

/* Computes a new point using
homogeneous coordinate transformation matrix */

Gpt *old_point, *new_point;
Matrix trans_matrix;
{
    new_point->x=matrix[0][2]+matrix[0][0]*old_point->x+
            matrix[0][1]*old_point->y;
    new_point->y=matrix[1][2]+matrix[1][0]*old_point->x+
            matrix[1][1]*old_point->y;
}
```

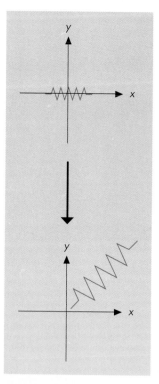

Figure 5.19
Transforming an Object

Note that, in this function, we have assumed that the third (w) component for each point remains unchanged by the transformation. If the third row of trans_matrix had been altered, we would have to change new_point by dividing both components by the proper w.

Suppose we have an object, such as a resistor in a circuit-design application, that is described by an array data of points that define a polyline. Suppose this object has been defined with its center at the origin. We can transform it to our specifications by first scaling it up (or down), then rotating it and finally moving its center. These operations result in the transformation shown in Figure 5.19. The necessary code is as follows, assuming that we want to put the transformed points into another polyline:

```
ev_scale(s,matrix);
ac_rotate(theta,matrix);
ac_trans(x,y,matrix);
for(i=0;i<npoints;i++)
    transform_point(matrix, data[i], newdata[i]);
gpolyline(npoints,newdata);
```

This sequence is a common one in modeling applications. We shall explore it in detail in the next section.

5.5 Symbols and Instances

We can now look at how we use transformations as a tool for modeling. The example in the previous section provides a hint of what we can do. Rather than defining an object where we would like it to be in the world of our application, we can define it in any convenient way and then transform it to the desired location, with the desired orientation and scale factors. There are a number of advantages to such an approach. Often, it is easier to define our objects in a simple way and to worry later about where to move them. In animation, an object may be moved many times. It is usually far easier to define it once and then to use a transformation to regenerate it when it is animated. In many applications, many objects are used over and over. For example, in a circuit-design application, certain basic shapes, such as resistors and integrated circuits, appear repeatedly in the model. In such situations, it is usually best to define each shape once and to use our transformation capability to put copies of the prototype, suitably scaled and oriented, in the model.

Until now, we have had only one way of forming a group of graphical primitives; namely, through a segment. A little thought will show that this approach is not optimal in most applications. For example, consider the design of a circuit using discrete components such as resistors, capacitors, and integrated circuits. The total design may consist of hundreds of these components. Although we can draw each of these components (the wires that connect them) using polylines, identifying each one as a segment probably does not make sense. A segment might be better used for some logically related set of circuit elements, such as those that make up an amplifier or some other sub-circuit. However, we still would like to have some way to identify elements, such as resistors, that are more complex than are our standard primitives, such as polylines. We use the term *symbol* to refer to such objects.

5.5.1 Symbols

Symbols are application dependent and user defined. We can think of symbols as being defined by functions such as

    resistor()

or

    chair()

In each function, there will be the necessary code to generate the symbol using the primitives available on the graphics system. For example, the symbol for a resistor can be defined using a single polyline. However, symbols alone are not enough to give us the desired flexibility in designing our applications. A particular symbol may appear many times in an application. Each appearance of a symbol is known as an *instance* of the symbol. To place a symbol, we must specify not only the description of the symbol, but also where to place it. This requirement leads to an immediate tie between symbols and transformations.

5.5.2 Modeling with Symbols

Many symbols will be defined most naturally in the WC system, whereas others (such as the resistor symbol or a hexagon) are shapes that may not have a particular coordinate system associated with them. To allow for this variation, we will add an additional coordinate system, called *master* or *modeling* coordinates, in which we can define a symbol. Consider as a symbol the letter "A." We can define it as centered in a master coordinate system with convenient dimensions. Such symbols are the basis of desktop publishing applications [Post85]. The symbol must be scaled to the desired size. It must also be oriented correctly by a rotation. Finally, it must be placed at the desired location by a translation. This sequence of operations, shown in Figure 5.20, yields the *instance transformation*

$$\mathbf{I} = \mathbf{TRS},$$

where $\mathbf{T}$, $\mathbf{R}$, and $\mathbf{S}$ are our translation, rotation, and scaling matrices. Note that the order in which we perform these operations is crucial. If we define symbols to be centered in master coordinates, this order is probably the best for most applications.

Returning to our earlier example of a resistor, it appears that one way to create an instance of a resistor symbol (to instance it) is

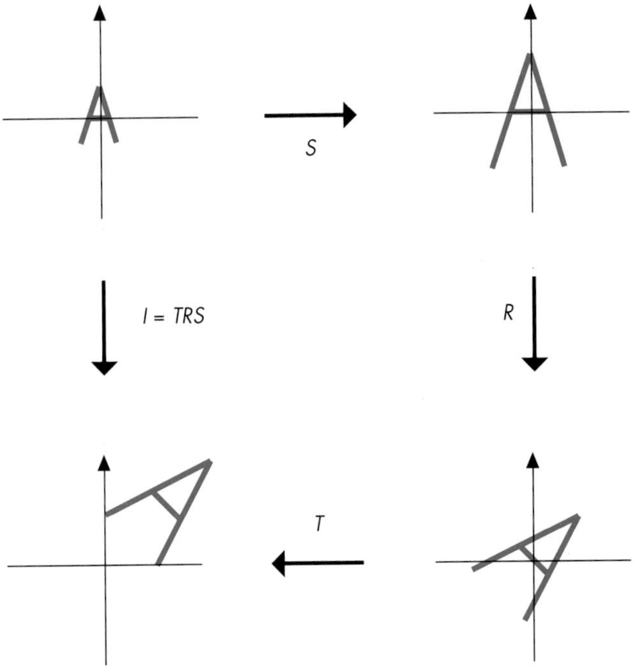

Figure 5.20
The Instance
Transformation

through a procedure such as

```
resistor(matrix)
```

where **matrix** is an instance transformation. Or we might instance the resistor by a procedure such as

```
resistor(x,y,theta,alpha,beta)
```

which gives the translation, rotation, and scaling parameters directly.

A more general and flexible mechanism might be desirable when we have a large number of symbols or we wish to add new symbols. Suppose we identify each symbol by a number. Then, we can realize all our symbols through a single procedure call

```
symbol(sym_num,instance_matrix)
```

which applies an instance transformation to the referred symbol. The procedure **symbol** can be written using some of the procedures in our transformation package. For a circuit-design application, **symbol** might, in part, look like

```
void symbol(sym_num,instance_matrix)
int sym_num;
```

```
Matrix instance_matrix;
#define RESISTOR 1
#define CAPACITOR 2
#define CHIP 3
             .
             .
             .

{
     switch(sym_num)
     {
     case RESISTOR:
         for(i=0;i<num_resist_pts;i++)
                    transform_point(........
         gpolyline(.......
         break;
     case CAPACITOR:
             .
             .
```

There are a number of alternative ways of implementing a symbol and instancing facility. We shall not dwell on these alternatives. Rather, we shall move on to address the problem of creating multilevel, or hierarchical, models.

5.6
Modeling with Relationships

So far, we have used transformations for modeling in a simple fashion—namely, by computing the transformation we wish to apply to a particular primitive or symbol. This view of modeling an application is very linear. Code to describe such a model will consist of a long list of transformation and symbol calculations, and invocations of symbol-transformation pairs. Most interesting (and complex) applications are characterized by the interconnection between their primitives and symbols.

For example, if we wish to generate a series of pictures of a car moving across a scene, as in Figure 5.21, the rate at which the wheels turn determines the speed at which the body of the car moves. From the graphics perspective, the wheels on the car may best be represented as four instances of a wheel symbol, and the chassis could then be represented separately as one or more additional symbols. If we use such as a representation, however, then the application programmer must be responsible for maintaining the link between the wheel rotatation and the forward motion of the car.

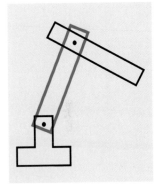

Figure 5.21
A Moving Car

In this section, we shall examine how we can use transformations to express these relationships. Our example is a simple robot arm. In the following section, we shall generalize this technique through tree-structured models.

5.6.1 A Simple Robot Arm

Consider a simple robot arm, as pictured in Figure 5.22, that can move in only two dimensions. The robot arm consists of a lower arm that is attached by a pivot to a base, and an upper arm that pivots on the lower arm. The mechanism is controlled by rotation about the pivots. Hence, once we specify the angles of rotation, the position of the arm is determined. We could use this simple arm as a model of a two-dimensional positioning device by attaching a pen or a sensor at the end of the arm, or we could make it function in three dimensions by allowing the base to rotate about the z axis.

We wish to model the arm so as to allow us to manipulate the robot easily, and possibly to change its design. We can facilitate this goal by defining the base, lower arm, and upper arm as three separate symbols, as pictured in Figure 5.23. The master coordinate system has been selected such that each symbol is centered on the vertical axis and rests on the horizontal axis. We will draw the robot by using instance transformations to place the parts in their proper positions. Note that each part in our model can be drawn with a polyline. Our problem will be how to place the parts in their correct positions relative to one another, and how to alter these positions as the arm is animated.

Figure 5.22
A Robot Arm

The equations for the robot can be derived in a number of ways. A direct approach is to picture the robot as in Figure 5.24, where the base rests on the ground with its vertical center at $(x_1, 0)$. The tip of the upper arm is at (x, y), the base pivot is located at (x_1, y_1), and the pivot between the upper and lower arms is at (x_2, y_2). We will let l_1 represent the distance between the pivot points on the lower arm, and l_2 denote the distance between the end of the upper arm and its pivot point. All these values can be represented simply from the measurements in Figure 5.24 and the values of the angles θ and ϕ.

5.6 Modeling with Relationships   185

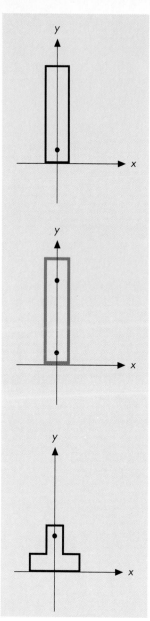

We can think of this stick figure as the skeleton of the robot; a description of its motion allows us to model easily the movement of the entire structure. The two sets of equations that describe the skeleton can be written, with simple trigonometry, as

$$
\begin{aligned}
x_2 &= x_1 - l_1 \sin(\phi), \\
y_2 &= y_1 + l_1 \cos(\phi), \\
x &= x_2 - l_2 \sin(\theta + \phi), \\
y &= y_2 + l_2 \cos(\theta + \phi).
\end{aligned}
$$

The position of the tip, (x, y), is clearly a function of both angles and thus reflects the coupling of the elements. Although correct, these equations do not relate well to our model, which separated the robot into three parts. They also do not help us to generate a sequence of images of the robot as the two angles are changed.

5.6.2 Modeling with Transformation Matrices

We can approach the problem from the perspective of transformation matrices. Let us reexamine our equations with the idea of representing all points on the robot, so that we can draw the robot with our graphics system. Both the upper and lower arms move by rotation. Suppose we think of the lower pivot point of each arm as being the origin of its own master coordinate system. Then, the motion of each arm part is a simple rotation about its own origin.

Figure 5.23
The Robot Symbols

Figure 5.24
Deriving the Robot
Equations

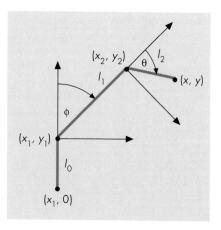

To obtain the actual position of the lower arm in WC, we must translate the origin to (x_1, y_1). If the base has a length l_0 from the bottom to the pivot, this translation matrix is

$$\mathbf{T}_1 = \begin{bmatrix} 1 & 0 & 0 \\ 0 & 1 & l_0 \\ 0 & 0 & 1 \end{bmatrix} = \mathbf{T}_1(0, l_0).$$

The lower arm rotates by a standard rotation matrix $\mathbf{R}_1(\phi)$, so the instance matrix for the lower arm is

$$\mathbf{A} = \mathbf{T}_1 \mathbf{R}_1.$$

Before we derive a similar relationship for the upper arm, consider what happens if we move the base. We could define a translation matrix $\mathbf{T}$, which could then be applied to every point defining the base. Moving the base, however, also moves both the upper and lower arms. Hence, points on these structures must also be translated by $\mathbf{T}$. For the lower arm, the instance transformation is now given by $\mathbf{TA}$. Hence, a useful interpretation of $\mathbf{A}$ is that it positions the lower arm *relative* to the base and thus incorporates the relationship between these two objects.

Continuing this argument, we can characterize the upper arm relative to the lower arm and use the relative positioning of the lower arm relative to the base to allow us to get the actual position of the upper arm. The upper arm is rotated about its origin by a rotation matrix $\mathbf{R}_2(\theta)$. Relative to the lower arm, it is initially translated by the matrix $\mathbf{T}_2(0, l_1)$. Combining these, we get the matrix

$$\mathbf{B} = \mathbf{T}_2 \mathbf{R}_2.$$

Putting together all these computations, we determine the absolute position of the upper arm by concatenating these matrices to form **TAB**.

5.6.3 Animating the Model

Suppose we wish to animate the robot by altering the positions of the upper and lower arms. We need to change only the two rotation matrices and to recalculate the positions. Here is part of the code, assuming that we have a procedure `symbol(matrix,n)` that will draw symbol n using `matrix` for the instance transformation. Our symbols are UPPER_ARM, LOWER_ARM and BASE.

```
/* Define Initial Rotation and Translation Matrices  */

static Matrix r1=
     {1.0, 0.0, 0.0, 0.0, 1.0, 0.0, 0.0, 0.0, 1.0};
static Matrix r2=
     {1.0, 0.0, 0.0, 0.0, 1.0, 0.0, 0.0, 0.0, 1.0};
static Matrix t0=
     {1.0, 0.0, X0, 0.0, 1.0, Y0, 0.0, 0.0, 1.0};
static Matrix t1=
     {1.0, 0.0, 0.0, 0.0, 1.0, L0, 0.0, 0.0, 1.0};
static Matrix t2=
     {1.0, 0.0, 0.0, 0.0, 1.0, L1, 0.0, 0.0, 1.0};


Matrix a, b, m;
int i;

/* Draw Robot Procedure */

draw_robot()
{
    symbol(t0, BASE);
    ac_matrix(t1, r1, a);
    ac_matrix(t0, a, m);
    symbol(m, LOWER_ARM);
    ac_matrix(t2, r2, b);
    ac_matrix(m, b, m);
    symbol(m, UPPER_ARM);
}


/* Draw Robot in Its Initial Position */

draw_robot();

/Increment Rotation Matrices and Redraw */

for(i=0; i<NTIMES; i++)
{
    ac_rotate(THETA, r1);
    ac_rotate(PHI, r2);
    draw_robot();
}
```

5.7
Using Hierarchy and Recursion

The model of the robot shows the dependence of one part of the model on others. We have thus far left it to the user program to express these dependencies and to send the proper instance transformations to the symbol routine. In this section, we shall explore the use of trees to represent the relationships. Programming languages such as C and Pascal allow the user to define and manipulate trees through the use of structures (or records) and recursive programming.

5.7.1 The Robot Arm as a Tree

The relationships among the parts of the robot arm can be represented as shown in Figure 5.25. This structure is a special kind of graph known as a *tree*. The tree consists of points called *nodes* or *vertices* connected by line segments called *edges*. Each node in a tree, except the top or *root* node, has exactly one *parent* node. Each node can have *child* nodes. A node with no children is called a *terminal* node. Within this structure, we have considerable flexibility in how to use the nodes and edges.

We can start by assigning a transformation matrix to each edge and a symbol to each node, as in Figure 5.25. The symbols at the nodes are the symbols we wish to draw. The matrices as defined in the previous section are those that relate the position of a primitive at one node to that of primitives at its parent node. All the information about the robot arm is in the tree. We can assign the position of the base by setting a matrix T, which we used in determining all our instance transformations in the previous section. To draw the robot arm, we have to *traverse* the tree; that is, we must trace the tree from the root node to all the children. We concatenate the matrices as we traverse the structure to obtain the correct instance transformation for each symbol we find at a node. Thus, at the root node, we have only T, which is the instance transformation for the base. At the second node, we have TA, which we apply to the lower arm. Finally, at the third node, we have TAB.

We now examine how we can do these operations from within a user program. There are two separate but related issues: How do we represent an object with a tree model; and how do we traverse this tree? We want to allow trees that are more complex than is the one for our simple robot arm. Consider, for example, the moving car. A possible tree structure is shown in Figure 5.26, where we have let each wheel be a subtree of the chassis. For a simple model of the

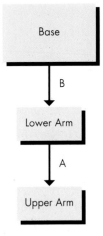

Figure 5.25
Tree of Robot Arm

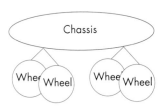

Figure 5.26
The Car

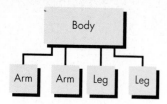

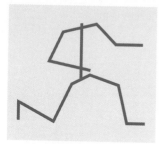

Figure 5.27
A Stick Figure

human body, we might employ the stick figure in Figure 5.27. This simple structure could easily be made more sophisticated. The point is that we need a flexible representation that will allow for an arbitrary number of children of a given node. If we note that a tree consists of a number of subtrees, each connected to their parent, we can see that recursive definitions and algorithms might be of use.

5.7.2 Representing a Tree

We will use a structure as pictured in Figure 5.28 to represent our trees. Each node on the tree will contain a pointer to a list of all children of that node, as well as the necessary information to draw a symbol associated with the node. In terms of C structures, we can define a tree node as

```
struct tnode
{
    int symbol;
    Matrix matrix;
    struct list *nodelist;
};
```

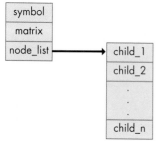

Figure 5.28
Tree Structure

Each node contains a symbol number, a pointer to a matrix, and a pointer to a linked list of nodes that are its children. The symbol is what will be drawn at that node. The matrix is a positioning matrix that positions this node relative to its parent, and this information will be accessible to all children of the node. The list of child nodes could be empty and have a NULL pointer to it. This linked-list structure can be defined as

```
struct list
{
    struct tnode *node;
    struct list *next;
};
```

Each element in the list structure is a pointer to a tree node and a pointer to the next element in the list. We require two functions, tree() and addlist(), which are necessary to allocate the necessary storage for the tree dynamically:

```
struct tnode *tree()
{
    char *calloc();
    struct tnode *p;
```

```
        p=(struct tnode *) calloc(1,sizeof(struct tnode));
        p->nodelist=NULL;
        return(p);
}
struct list *addlist()
{
        char *calloc();
        struct list *p;
        p=(struct list *) calloc(1,sizeof(struct list));
        p->next = NULL;
        p->node = NULL;
        return(p);
}
```

Here we have used the standard C utilities sizeof to return the
amount of storage needed and calloc to allocate one such structure.
These procedures get the address of the necessary free memory to add
to the tree or list and also place NULL pointers in the structure so that
the program can determine where the terminal elements are located.

Using these structures, the stick figure can be defined in a direct,
albeit ugly, manner:

```
root=tree();
root->symbol = BODY;
root->matrix = body;
root->nodelist=addlist();
root->nodelist->next=addlist();
root->nodelist->next->next=addlist();
root->nodelist->next->next->next=addlist();
root->nodelist->node = tree();
root->nodelist->next->node = tree();
root->nodelist->next->next->node = tree();
root->nodelist->next->next->next->node = tree();
root->nodelist->node->symbol = ARM;
root->nodelist->next->node->symbol = ARM;
root->nodelist->next->next->node->symbol = LEG;
root->nodelist->next->next->next->node->symbol = LEG;
root->nodelist->node->matrix = arm1;
root->nodelist->next->node->matrix = arm2;
root->nodelist->next->next->node->matrix = leg1;
root->nodelist->next->next->next->node->matrix = leg2;
```

Here BODY, ARM, and LEG are symbols that we assume have been defined in master coordinates. The matrices body, arm1, arm2, leg1,
and leg2 position these symbols relative to their parent nodes. This

code shows explicitly the paths in the tree that we use to get to each symbol, but is not pretty. We shall give a cleaner version in the next section.

5.7.3 Traversing the Model

Although our description of the stick figure is inelegant, the procedure for traversing the tree using recursion is extremely simple. We will employ the notion of the *current transformation matrix* (CTM). It is the matrix we will use at a given node to draw the symbol (if any) we find there. We draw the tree through a procedure draw_tree, which is passed a matrix pos_matrix, which positions the entire tree and a pointer to the root node of the tree. This procedure will draw whatever symbol it finds at the root node by first concatenating the matrix passed to it with the matrix it finds at that node. The result is placed in the CTM using our accumulate matrix procedure, ac_matrix. We have reserved the symbol number 0 to denote that there is no symbol to be drawn at that node. We draw symbols by passing the number of the symbol and the CTM to a symbol-drawing procedure, draw_symbol. Unless the list of child nodes is empty, we must take care of all the child nodes, which we do through a function traverselist. This procedure recursively uses draw_tree to draw all subtrees in its list. The code is

```
draw_tree(pos_matrix, root)
struct tnode *root;
Matrix pos_matrix;
{
  Matrix ctm;
  ac_matrix(pos_matrix,root->matrix,ctm);
  if(root->symbol!=0) draw_symbol(ctm,root->symbol);
  if(root->nodelist != NULL)
    traverselist(ctm,root->nodelist);
}
```

```
traverselist(pos_matrix,list_root)
Matrix pos_matrix;
struct list *list_root;
{
  draw_tree(pos_matrix,list_root->node);
  if(list_root->next != NULL)
    traverselist(pos_matrix,list_root->next);
}
```

The particular method of traversal we have employed (there are many) starts by updating the current transformation matrix that is passed in by accumulating it with the matrix at the node. If a symbol is at the node, it is drawn. If the node has any children, the linked list of child nodes has the same procedure applied to each of the tree nodes in this list.

We can follow the drawing of the robot by tracking a procedure call such as

```
draw_tree( ctm, robot);
```

where ctm points to a matrix that positions the entire structure in the world. Call this matrix **M**; initially, it might be the identity matrix. The traversal procedure first replaces **M** by **MT**, and uses the latter matrix to draw the base. There is a child of this node, and it is passed the matrix **MT**. We traverse the child subtree by first updating the CTM to **MTA**, and drawing the lower arm. This node has a child, so it is passed the CTM, which gets updated to **MTAB** before the upper arm is drawn.

5.7.4 Discussion

Our traversal procedure draws the tree from the top node down. If all our graphical elements consist ultimately of polylines or other unfilled types, the images we produce will be about the same, regardless of the traversal algorithm. If we are using filled areas, the order in which the primitives are drawn is crucial, and we might expect different traversal algorithms to produce different images. We also note that recursive tree traversal might be slow, but our focus here is on the modeling rather than on the efficiency of the final code. In practice, we can always replace the recursive tree-traversal algorithm by an iterative one.

Although this method is fairly general, there are many ways to represent hierarchical structures. In many applications, more elaborate data structures may be required. We shall examine another—the acyclic graph—later in this chapter. Tree-structured hierarchical models, however, have proved to be invaluable in modeling. Although we have used recursion and simple data structures, these need not be present in the language. Just as we constructed a set of transformation-matrix routines, we could have constructed routines to represent and manipulate trees without using these features of C. Nonetheless, these features of the language do make programming much simpler and should lead to more efficient implementations.

Finally, we note that we have looked at the modeling as being the job of the application program. It was forced on the user by the lack of certain high-level facilities in GKS. The Programmer's Hierarchical Interactive Graphics Standard (PHIGS) is a standard that incorporates many of the ideas we have just presented. In particular, the notion of the current transformation matrix is part of the system, and segments (called structures in PHIGS), are allowed to reference other segments (structures), which provides the user with a simple method for constructing hierarchical models.

5.8
Implementation of Abstract Data Types

Our previous discussion of hierarchical models emphasized the use of trees to model graphical applications. In this section, we shall emphasize the difference between the conceptual model and the implementation of that model in a particular system or programming language. As a consequence of our discussion, we shall redo our previous example in a more elegant fashion.

5.8.1 Operations on a Tree

We start with the example tree in Figure 5.29, which has three levels. We assume that each node contains the number of a symbol and a matrix that tells us how to place this symbol relative to the position of the parent node. This method is essentially the same as that we have used in previous sections to define the kinds of tree structures that are useful for graphical applications. This tree could be implemented, as in the previous section, with a linked list of children at each node. Instead, we shall take a different approach.

At this point, we have a data type, the tree. We wish to do operations on this data type. At this level of abstraction, we wish to

Figure 5.29
A Three-Level Tree

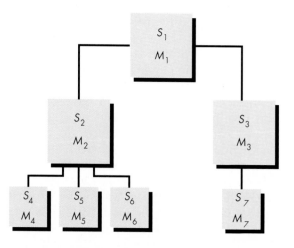

describe these operations in terms of our abstract data type, rather than in terms of its implementation. If we can describe the operations independently of any implementation, we can then write high-level programs that can leave the implementation issues to the particular realization or installation. In a sense, this separation of operations from their implementation is exactly what occurs in a graphics package. We know what the functions do, what they require as input, and what they produce as output. Application programmers do not need to pay attention to the internal workings of these procedures. For modeling applications, we wish to make the same division. Unfortunately, since hierarchical modeling is not part of GKS, we were forced to present implementation issues. However, we stress the separation of the data type from its implementation.

Returning to our example, we observe that there are two fundamental parts of our modeling with trees: the description of the tree and the drawing of the tree. The description of the tree involves adding nodes to a tree to form a more complex tree. We can describe this operation through a procedure

```
new_node(root,matrix,symbol)
```

This procedure will return a pointer to a node that is the child of the node root, with matrix and symbol stored at the new node. The code to describe our example tree will look something like

```
root = new_node(NULL,1,m1);
child1 = new_node(root,2,m2);
child2 = new_node(root,3,m3);
grandchild1 = new_node(child1,4,m4);
grandchild2 = new_node(child1,5,m5);
grandchild3 = new_node(child1,6,m6);
grandchild4 = new_node(child2,7,m7);
```

Drawing the tree requires a single procedure call,

```
draw_tree(position,root)
```

which is essentially the procedure we used before. Here, root is a pointer to a tree, and position is the matrix used to place the entire tree in the desired location.

5.8.2   Another Implementation

It should be simple to implement these two functions using the particular model of the previous section—a node structure and a linked list. To emphasize the point that the implementation is independent

Figure 5.30

Left Child-Right Sibling
Tree

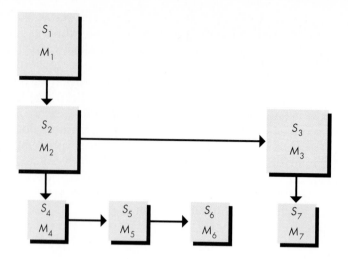

of the data type and its operations, we shall consider a somewhat different implementation. We shall use what is often called a *left child–right sibling* tree. We can implement this tree with a single data structure that has the same number of elements at each node. We can understand the structure by considering Figure 5.30. If we count null pointers, each node in this tree has exactly one sibling and one child. Careful observation should reveal that this tree contains exactly the same information as does the tree in Figure 5.28. This suggests the implementation pictured in Figure 5.31. In terms of C code, the desired structure can be described by

```
struct tnode
{
    int symbol;
    Matrix matrix;
    struct tnode *child;
    struct tnode *sibling;
}
```

Now we can use this structure to implement `new_node` and `draw_tree`. `new_node`, returns a pointer to a new node, with a desired symbol and matrix placed at that node. The first part of the necessary operation is similar to what we did before. We get the necessary memory via a memory call, such as `calloc`. We then place the desired symbol and matrix at this node, and set the left and right pointers to `NULL`. At this point, we have not related this new node to the parent node. There are two cases. If the parent node has no children, its child

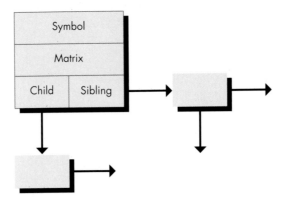

Figure 5.31
Implementing the Tree

pointer is NULL. In this case, we can simply replace the NULL pointer by the pointer to the new node. If the child pointer is not NULL, the parent node already has a child, so we must *insert* the new node. We can do this insertion, as in Figure 5.32, by moving the pointer from the parent to point to the new node and having the sibling pointer of the new node point to its sibling. There is one final complication. If the tree pointer passed to the procedure is NULL, the node we create replaces the NULL node. Here is the code:

```
struct tnode *new_node(t, s, m)
struct tnode *t;
int s;
Matrix m;
{
    struct tnode *p;
    char *calloc();
    p = (struct tnode *) calloc(1,sizeof(struct tnode));
    p->symbol=s;
```

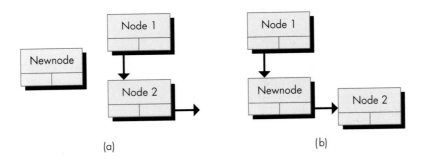

(a)   (b)

Figure 5.32
Insertion.
(a) Before.
(b) After.

5.8 Implementation of Abstract Data Types   **197**

```
            p->matrix=m;
            p->child=NULL;
            if(t==NULL)
            {
                   p->sibling=NULL;
                   t->child=p;
                   return(p);
            }
    }
```

The drawing of the tree will be similar to the method we employed
in the previous section, with one minor change—all siblings use the
same matrix passed from the parent. Our basic traversal scheme is
to draw the symbol at a node, using the procedure draw_symbol, and
then to traverse both the sibling and child trees. The code is

```
    draw_tree(m,p)
    struct tnode *p;
    Matrix m;
    {
            float ctm[2][3];
            ac_matrix(m,p->matrix,ctm);
            draw_symbol(ctm,p->symbol);
            if(p->right != NULL) draw_tree(m,p->sibling);
            if(p->left != NULL) draw_tree(ctm,p->child);
    }
```

If we use the example of the stick figure we introduced in the
previous section, this procedure will draw the tree. We assume, for
consistency, that draw_symbol interprets symbol number 0 to mean
no symbol is drawn at the node. The description of the stick figure
becomes, using the same matrices and symbols,

```
    root  = new_node(NULL,BODY,bod);
    child1 = new_node(root,ARM,arm1);
    child2 = new_node(root,ARM,arm2);
    child3 = new_node(root,LEG,leg2);
    child4 = new_node(root,LEG,leg2);
```

Once again, we note that there are many other ways to implement hierarchy. In a given application, we must always balance the
features provided by the graphics system against the features in the
programming language. In our example, we have circumvented some
of the limitations of GKS by using some of the features of C. On the
other hand, if we were using a graphics system, such as PHIGS, that

provides hierarchical structures, we could have used a FORTRAN language binding without difficulty. If we had only a FORTRAN language binding of GKS and wished to implement our tree structure, our routines for `add_node` and `draw_tree` would be very different.

5.9
From Segments to Structures

Thus far, we have concentrated on tree-structured models. Each node, whether as an abstract type or as in some implementation, has a fixed structure—for example, a matrix, a symbol number, and one or more pointers to other nodes. There is a simple reinterpretation of what we mean by a symbol that will lead us to an even more powerful modeling technique. We shall first look at how we go from a model in our user program to a segment in our graphics system.

5.9.1 Segment Contents

In our present view, modeling is part of the application program. If our program uses a system such as GKS, we shall eventually create segments that contain the primitives defined by our model. Without discussing the implementation issues covered in the next two chapters, we can make a couple of observations. First, a system that separates the modeling from the graphics system will almost definitely be less efficient than will one that ties the two together. Second, since segments are key elements in high-level applications, what goes into a segment and how a segment is formed are crucial issues.

In GKS, segments are composed of primitives. Segments are passed to the workstation in NDC. Hence, the viewing conditions are included within the segment, although indirectly. Attributes are also included indirectly. For example, individual attributes are bound to the primitive and thus are in the segment. This perspective is similar to that we employed in our discussion of metafiles in Chapter 3.

We can conclude that segments, at least in GKS-like systems, are lists of primitives that lack any structured properties of the model. Segments of this form are static entities, which allow only limited changes such as segment attributes after they have been defined. Since the traversal of the application model was done while the segment was formed, the graphics system cannot make use of the underlying model. The application of the attributes and normalization transformation as part of the segment-formation process does not lead to efficient ways of changing views or modifying the contents of the segment. This deficiency is one of the major weaknesses of GKS. One solution is to reevaluate our approach to segments and modeling.

5.9.2 Directed Acyclic Graphs

Consider the simple model of the automobile that we discussed previously. Representing it as a tree, we get the simple two-level hierarchy shown on the left of Figure 5.33. The symbol on the upper level refers to the primitives describing the chassis, whereas the symbol references in the lower level all refer to instances of the same symbol: a wheel. Suppose we include the symbols for the body and the wheel in our diagram without distinguishing between the contents of a node and the contents of a symbol. We obtain the diagram shown on the right of Figure 5.33, which is not a tree but rather a type of graph known as a *directed acyclic graph*. In a directed acyclic graph, every edge has a direction, but there are no loops. Trees are a special case of directed acyclic graphs.

5.9.3 Structures

We can now generalize our notion of a segment to allow segments to describe acyclic graphs. We call such data types *structures*, both to distinguish them from segments and to be consistent with the terminology in the PHIGS system. We replace our three building blocks (nodes, matrices, and symbols) with just two others: structures and *elements*. The structure will replace our tree. Hence, the function

```
traverse_structure(root)
```

will cause the structure pointed to by `root` to be drawn. A structure contains elements. The elements include the primitives defining our symbols. They can also include transformation matrices and attributes. An element can be thought of as simply the number or

Figure 5.33
The Automobile as (a) a Tree and (b) an Acyclic Graph

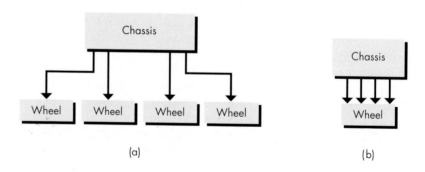

(a)

(b)

Figure 5.34
A Structure

identifier of a graphics-library function and that function's data. The
structure might be pictured as in Figure 5.34.   A simple way to create
a structure might be through the two procedures,

```
new_structure(root)
new_element(structure,element)
```

The first procedure creates a pointer to a new structure. The second
adds an element to an existing structure.

You might have detected that our structures look much like a much
simpler data structure than a tree: a list. You are right. However, we
have yet to make the structures general enough to describe directed
acyclic graphs. Because our elements correspond to procedures in
our graphics system, our model becomes fairly dynamic. Transformations and attributes do not have to be applied to the primitives
when a structure is formed. Since they are stored directly within the
structure, they can be used as necessary during the traversal of the
structure for display. This process is known as *traversal-time binding*. Such structures allow much of the work of the graphics system
to be passed to the physical workstation. In addition, they lead to
the possibility of their being altered or edited, either before they are
displayed or between successive displays.

We obtain relationships between structures by introducing a new
type of element, *execute structure*, which refers to an another structure. This element points to another structure that, during traversal,
will be traversed (executed) before we continue with the execution of
the parent (calling) structure. Entities such as transformation matrices and attributes can be passed on or inherited from the parent
structure. Structures may not contain references to themselves or to
other structures that reference them. In other words, we do not allow
cycles or loops.

It should be a simple exercise to create structures that can represent our previous examples, which used trees. In implementing structures, the difficulty lies in the traversal process. There, we must worry
about the implementation of the graphics procedures, unlike when we
used GKS-like segments, where the graphics procedures were assumed
to be organized in a simple way through matrices and the symbol
table. Now the traversal process must carry out the necessary transformations and display primitives with the correct attributes. Thus,

if we think of elements as having three fields:

```
typedef struct
{
    int type; /* element type */
    record *data; /* depends on element type */
    element *next;
} element;
```

then we can write a skeleton procedure:

```
traverse_structure(root)
{
element *pointer;
pointer=root;
while(pointer!=NULL)
    {
    execute_element(element.type,element.data);
    pointer_element.next
    }
}
```

Now the complexity has been hidden in `execute_element`, which must be able to carry out every function, including the execution of structures.

You might want to attempt to implement such a modeling system. You might also consider correcting some of the deficiencies of our simple structure. For example, the `new_element` procedure does not allow us to add elements at arbitrary points in the structure. We need such freedom if we are to modify or edit structures. We have also not addressed issues such as whether matrices (which are structure elements) should be treated locally (used only within the structure in which they are defined), or globally (carried down to all structures executed by the structure in which they are defined). We conclude this chapter with a brief discussion of PHIGS and of how some of these issues are treated there.

5.10
PHIGS

Hierarchical models are the basis of many applications that use computer graphics. Although the procedures we developed to deal with transformations and modeling are simple, we would prefer to start

Figure 5.35
Data Flow in GKS

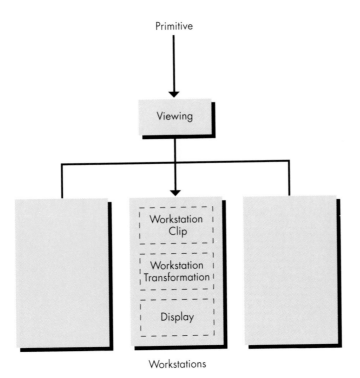

with a graphics system that contains hierarchical modeling procedures. We have reasons for desiring such software beyond simply wanting to avoid writing extra code. We want to make maximum use of the hardware (and software) capabilities of modern workstations.

PHIGS was created as an extension to the then-existing graphics standards and was motivated by the need to add modeling to those systems. Although it is not strictly compatible with GKS, its developers made it as compatible as possible without violating its design goals. We shall introduce two of its most important features: its modeling capability and its conceptual foundation of viewing a graphical database.

5.10.1 Viewing a Database

The GKS model in Figure 5.35 shows the basic data flow of primitives from specification to display. The present viewing transformation is applied to all primitives at the time each primitive is created. Although each workstation can view a different part of NDC space by having its own workstation transformation, we have only a limited ability for different viewers on different physical workstations to display the same data in different ways.

Figure 5.36
The PHIGS model

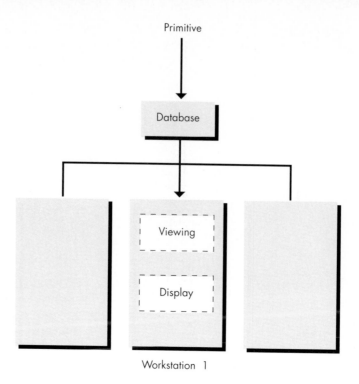

Workstation 1

A more general model, certainly appropriate to environments where many users have access to large databases through a network of computers, is the model in Figure 5.36, which is used in PHIGS. Here, primitives are placed in a central database. Each viewer can access any of the data, and the viewing operation is done by each viewer's workstation. Structures are placed in the database by user programs and may be edited and archived for later use. As we discussed in the previous section, structure elements include primitives, attributes, and transformations. Attributes are not bound to primitives until traversal of the structure for viewing. This late binding of attributes and the ability to have different workstations have different views of the data gives PHIGS a far more dynamic flavor than GKS has. In addition, since viewing is a function that is carried out by the workstation, in situations where we have multiple physical workstations sharing a common database, PHIGS can be far more efficient than GKS is.

5.10.2 Programming in PHIGS

All our previous GKS programs will be virtually identical in PHIGS. The primitives are the same, as are most of the procedures. Procedure names begin with a "p" rather than a "g." For example, the polyline procedure becomes `ppolyline`. PHIGS structures are *posted* to the workstations, a consequence of the model in Figure 5.36. A sequence of procedures such as

```
popen_struct(LINE)
ppolyline( num_pts, points);
ptext(location, string)
pclose_struct();
```

creates elements in the database, but these elements are not associated with a workstation, and no viewing operation has taken place. When the structure is posted to one or more workstations by calls such as

```
ppost_struct(wk_id, struct,priority);
```

viewing and display take place. The viewing conditions will be specified in a manner similar to that used in GKS, except that windows and viewports must be tagged with a workstation identifier. This requirement is a consequence of viewing being regarded as a workstation function; it allows each workstation to have a different view (or views) of the data. Hence, conversion of all our sample programs to PHIGS should be a simple task.

5.10.3 Modeling with PHIGS

As we have seen, in PHIGS, the structure is the basis for modeling. Unlike the GKS segment, a structure can refer to another structure by the execute structure element. This simple (to the application programmer) addition allows us to define hierarchical models easily and compactly. Consider our robot model. The structures might look like this:

```
popen_struct(ROBOT);
      .
      .
   pexecute_struct(BASE);
      .
      .
pclose_struct();
popen_struct(BASE);
      .
      .
   pexecute_struct(LOWER_ARM);
      .
```

```
        pclose_struct();
        popen_struct(LOWER_ARM);

                .

                .

            pexecute_struct(UPPER_ARM);

                .

                .

        pclose_struct();
        popen_struct(UPPER_ARM);

                .

        pclose_struct();
```

or for the stick figure

```
        popen_struct(BODY);

                .

            pexecute_struct(TORSO);

                .

            pexecute_struct(RIGHT_ARM);

                .

            pexecute_struct(LEFT_ARM);

                .

            pexecute_struct(RIGHT_LEG);

                .

            pexecute_struct(LEFT_LEG);

                .

        pclose_struct();
        popen_struct(LEFT_ARM);

                .

            pexecute_struct(UPPER_ARM);

                .

        pclose_struct();
        popen_struct(RIGHT_ARM);

                .

            pexecute_struct(UPPER_ARM);

                .

        pclose_struct();
        popen_struct(UPPER_ARM)

                .

                .

        pclose_struct();

                .

                .
```

To this code, we must add the ability to form and modify the transformation matrices that position hierarchically related elements with respect to one another. As the example indicates, two structures can refer to the same lower-level structure (UPPER_ARM in the body problem), creating an acyclic graph. If the structure execution is preceded by the correct transformation matrix, the two instances of the UPPER_ARM structure will appear in different places, with different sizes and orientations. The attributes of a structure are inherited from the parent structure, which gives the programmer even more flexibility.

5.11
Suggested Readings

The use of homogenous coordinates in computer graphics is discussed in [Reis81]. The material on modeling and instances appears in standard references such as [Foley82] and [New73]. The PHIGS system [Brown85]; [PHIGS88] has provided modeling support within the graphics system. The use of abstract data types is now part of the standard computer science curriculum [Aho83]; [Helman86].

■ Exercises

5.1 Give an expression for the normalization transformation (the WC-to-NDC mapping), in terms of a sequence of translations and scalings. Show that this sequence provides a correct matrix representation in homogeneous coordinates.

5.2 One way to determine a unique affine transformation is to identify a set of points $\{\mathbf{p}_i\}$ in both their original positions and their new positions after they have been transformed. How many such pairs of points are necessary to define a transformation?

5.3 Show that shear can be obtained through rotations, translations, and scalings.

5.4 Prove the following properties of the translation, rotation, and shearing matrices:

$$
\begin{aligned}
\mathbf{R}^{-1}(\theta) &= \mathbf{R}^T(\theta), \\
\mathbf{R}(\theta + \phi) &= \mathbf{R}(\theta)\mathbf{R}(\phi), \\
\mathbf{T}(\Delta x_1 + \Delta x_2, \Delta y_1 + \Delta y_2) &= \mathbf{T}(\Delta x_1, \Delta y_1)\mathbf{T}(\Delta x_2, \Delta y_2), \\
\mathbf{H}_x^{-1}(\theta) &= \mathbf{H}_x(-\theta).
\end{aligned}
$$

5.5 Show that you can generate all possible affine transformations by concatenating rotation, translation, and scaling matrices. Is it possible to generate any arbitrary affine transformation with only two of the basic types of transformations?

5.6 Animate an automobile by first building an appropriate model, then altering the matrices in the model.

5.7 Give an example of a design problem where hierarchical models are not appropriate or are not sufficient for building a model. What implications, if any, does your example have for graphics systems?

5.8 A square of length 2^N units can be divided into nonoverlapping square tiles, whose sides have length 2^{N-1} by bisecting the square both horizontally and vertically. Each subsquare can optionally be subdivided in a similar manner. Each of these square tiles could then be assigned a color or pattern. Describe a data structure for such a pattern.

5.9 Trees are used in computer science in a number of areas, such as in search, sorting, and data representation. Use computer graphics to display the execution of a tree-based algorithm by generating a sequence of images that show the tree at different stages of the algorithm.

5.10 In many graphics systems, the current transformation matrix (CTM) is used to build up a model. The procedures available to a user are usually a set such as

```
accumulate_ctm(matrix, ctm);
evaluate_ctm(ctm);
translate_ctm(x,y,z,ctm);
rotate_ctm(theta, ctm);
scale_ctm(sx, sy, ctm);
push_ctm(ctm, stack);
pop_ctm(ctm, stack);
```

The first five procedures allow the user to set or alter the CTM. Saving the CTM is usually done using a stack. Create all seven of the procedures and use them to implement a tree-structured model.

5.11 Implement a tree-structured modeling system without the use of recursion.

5.12 What are the advantages and disadvantages of the use of recursive techniques in computer graphics, as compared to use of a more procedural approach, such as in PHIGS?

C H A P T E R

6

Implementation

Introduction

At this point, we should be fairly adept at writing programs that use computer graphics. How the graphics actually appears on the output devices may be somewhat of a mystery. In this chapter, we shall examine how graphics primitives defined in a user program work their way from their definition in the program to eventual display.

6.1
Implementation Issues

Our starting point will once again be the graphics pipeline of Chapters 2 and 3. Our model has a user writing a graphics program in a WC system. The application program accesses the graphics through calls to a graphics library such as GKS. The graphics package takes calls to procedures and produces data that are sent to the output device. Finally, the output device generates the desired primitives.

We assume that the output device is a binary raster-display terminal. Each pixel is set to either the foreground color (on) or the background color (off). For monochromatic displays, we will consider these two colors to be black and white. When a procedure causes output to appear on the device, some pixels in the frame buffer must be set (to the foreground color), and others cleared (set to the background color).

Some of the issues we must consider are

- How are primitives mapped between coordinate systems?
- How are data communicated to the terminal?
- How do we ensure that primitives fit on the display?
- Which pixels in the frame buffer are set or cleared to generate a primitive?

The first issue arises because the programmer is working in WC. Eventually, the output data must be converted to DC for display. Within the graphics system, NDC are used. Although we have looked at these transformations previously, there are important questions regarding where these transformations should take place within the pipeline and how they can be carried out most efficiently.

Device drivers are used to convert data produced by the graphics system to the proper form to control the output device. We shall look at two simple device drivers for graphics terminals.

Primitives, as defined in a user program, may lie inside the WC window, in which case they will appear on the display device. They may also lie either fully or partially outside the window. To keep primitives within their assigned viewport, as we discussed in Chapter 3, we must clip them, so that only the parts inside the WC window ultimately will be displayed.

Finally, we need methods to scan convert the primitives produced by our graphics system. That is, we must have algorithms to select which pixels must be set and which cleared in our frame buffer to approximate a polyline, text, or any of our other primitives.

For all these problems, efficiency is extremely important. We want systems that can operate in real time with sophisticated models. Systems that can work with over 100,000 line segments in real time exist and use many of the methods we discuss here.

6.2
Following the Pipeline

In this chapter, we concentrate on our most fundamental primitive, the line segment, and follow it through the graphical pipeline. Once we understand what happens to the line segment, we can alter our procedures, as necessary, for other primitive such as fill areas, circles, and text.

The first step in specifying a line segment is to set the viewing conditions. The polyline function uses the present normalization transformation defined by a window and viewport. Our program will contain fragments such as

```
gset_win( transform_num, window_rectangle);
gset_vp( transform_num, viewport_rectangle);
    .
    .
gsel_norm_tran(transform_num);
    .
    .
gpolyline( num_points, points);
    .
    .
```

The window and viewport define a normalization transformation, as in Figure 6.1, which is used to process the line segments that comprise the polyline. In Chapter 2, we derived the equations for this transformation, which maps any point (x, y) in WC to a corresponding point (u, v) in NDC. These equations are

$$u = u_{min} + \frac{u_{max} - u_{min}}{x_{max} - x_{min}}(x - x_{min}),$$

$$v = v_{min} + \frac{v_{max} - v_{min}}{y_{max} - y_{min}}(y - y_{min}).$$

They are of the form

$$u = ax + b,$$
$$v = cy + d,$$

where the values $a, b, c,$ and d are determined by the window and viewport parameters. We can observe that, although the procedures that determine the viewing conditions cannot cause output, they set

Figure 6.1
The Normalization
Transformation

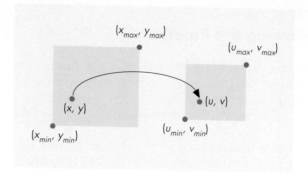

internal parameters. We can also see that we can easily write the preceding relationships using homogeneous coordinates:

$$
\begin{bmatrix} u \\ v \\ 1 \end{bmatrix} = \begin{bmatrix} a & 0 & b \\ 0 & c & d \\ 0 & 0 & 1 \end{bmatrix} \begin{bmatrix} x \\ y \\ 1 \end{bmatrix}.
$$

The specification of the viewing conditions thus defines a normalization matrix,

$$
\mathbf{V} = \begin{bmatrix} a & 0 & b \\ 0 & c & d \\ 0 & 0 & 1 \end{bmatrix}
$$

which is applied to points specified later in the polyline procedure.

The polyline procedure defines one or more line segments. Assuming we have our software clipper on, only the parts of these segments inside the world window will be transformed into NDC and may appear on the output device. Clipping will be the next topic we discuss as we follow the line segment through the pipeline.

After the line segments are (optionally) clipped, other transformations, such as segment transformations, can be applied to them. Such transformations are represented by affine transformation matrices in homogeneous coordinates. We are already familiar with this process and do not need to discuss it further.

Next, we have to consider the workstation transformation we introduced in Chapter 3. A rectangular window in NDC space is mapped to a viewport on each workstation. Of course, this transformation also has a matrix representation in homogeneous coordinates. Points in NDC space will be transformed into points in DC. Clipping is always done at this level to ensure proper display on the output. The algo-

rithms we shall develop for clipping to the world window could also
be used here, but we also have the option of doing this clipping in the
hardware.

Having the points in device coordinates is not quite enough to
make most output devices function correctly. For example, a graphics
terminal typically has two modes of operation. In its default mode,
sometimes called alpha or alphanumeric mode, it acts as a standard
character-display terminal. On receipt of a special character code, or
sequence of character codes, it changes mode and acts as a graphical
device. In graphics mode, data received by the terminal are interpreted as graphical data rather than as codes for characters to be
displayed.

To use the terminal as a graphics device, the system first must
place it into graphics mode. The device must also be told whether
the data being sent to it defines a line segment or some other primitive.
These jobs are usually the responsibility of the device driver.

Finally, we have to address the scan-conversion process. We shall
develop algorithms to set the proper pixels in the frame buffer of the
output device. In this chapter, we shall discuss lines and text, leaving
the scan conversion of other entities until we discuss raster graphics
in depth, in Chapter 7.

6.3
Clipping

The job of the *clipper* is to eliminate all parts of primitives that lie
outside the WC window. Although the portion of a primitive that is
inside the world window will be mapped to its proper viewport, the
parameters of the viewport are not necessary for the clipping process.
We will clip in WC, then map any part of the primitive remaining
inside the window to the viewport, rather than mapping primitives
into NDC space first and doing the clipping there. If we are displaying
primitives only once, this is more efficient, as it avoids the cost of the
normalization transformation for any primitives that will not appear
in the display. Even in cases where clipping is performed in some
other coordinate system, the same basic algorithms are used.

6.3.1 The Difficulty of Clipping

The difficulty of the clipping process depends on which primitive is
to be clipped. In Figure 6.2, we have three types of primitives: line
segments, curves, and characters. The curve presents the most difficult problem. To clip it properly, we must find every intersection of

Figure 6.2
Clipping

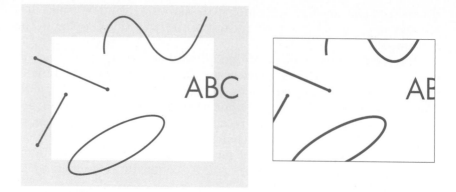

the curve with the edges of the window. Since a general curve satisfies a nonlinear equation, regardless of how we choose to represent it,
calculation of these points of intersection requires numerical methods.
For complex curves, as in Figure 6.3, we might have great difficulty in
even determining the number of intersections. Depending on the form
of the curve, the clipping problem can range from time consuming to
practically impossible.

6.3.2 Text Clipping

Depending on the precision of the text, clipping of a string of characters can be either as simple as for lines or almost as difficult as for
general curves. In Chapter 3, we saw that one of the attributes of text
is its precision, which was set by the procedure `gset_fontprec`. The
selected precision (string, character, or stroke) determines how pre-

Figure 6.3
Clipping Curves

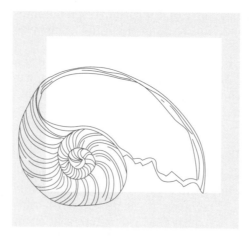

Figure 6.4
Text Precision and
Clipping. (a) Original
String. (b) String Precision.
(c) Character Precision. (d)
Stroke Precision.

cisely an implementation is requested to clip text. Figure 6.4 shows
some of the differences in clipping at the three precisions.

At the lowest level of precision, string precision, the entire string
can be clipped as a single entity. A clipping algorithm for this situation is simple. We can place a bounding rectangle about the string,
as illustrated in Figure 6.5. We determine whether this box lies inside the window. If it does, we draw the string; if not, we eliminate
the string. The same algorithm may be applied on a character-by-
character basis at the discretion of the implementor. This level of
precision is typical of systems that have only a few hardware character sets that are stored as bit patterns, such as in Figure 6.6. Such
characters cannot be altered easily, and the best we can do is either
to place them on the display or not to use them.

Even with better hardware, we may still be unable to do everything asked for by the software, such as realizing all possible character
directions or clipping individual characters in a string. However, there
are other options besides clipping out the entire string. For example,
a laser plotter may come equipped with a large number of different
fonts and character sizes, all of which are stored as bit patterns.

At the intermediate level of precision, *character precision*, strings
are treated on a character-by-character basis. Typically, the implementor will choose the best fit to the desired string from what is
available, and we might see a result like that in Figure 6.4.

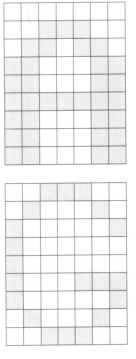

Figure 6.6
Bitmapped Characters

Figure 6.5
Character Boxes

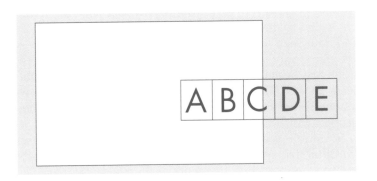

Figure 6.7
Stroke-Precision
Characters

COMPUTER

GRAPHICS

TEXT

At the highest level of precision, *stroke precision*, the characters are treated as curves. We then must clip each character using its representation by some sort of curve. In practice, characters used with stroke-precision text are stored as low-order polynomial curves. We construct each character by joining a few short polynomial segments. Clipping of each of these polynomial segments, although time consuming, is possible with low-order polynomials. Stroke characters are used in most publishing applications, as stroke text can provide almost infinite flexibility and accuracy. Figure 6.7 shows some of the possibilities.

6.4
Clipping Line Segments

In comparison with the general curve, the line segment and its extension to the polyline are easy to clip. Noting that any edge of the window is a line segment, we can use the ideas of Chapter 2 to represent and intersect any edge of the window with any line segment generated by a polyline. In fact, since our window is a rectangle whose sides are oriented parallel to the WC axes, the problem becomes even easier. The ease of the problem stems from the fact that any two nonparallel lines intersect in exactly one place. Their point of intersection can be calculated with a single floating-point division. Our aim in deriving an efficient clipping algorithm for line segments will be to minimize the number of times we must compute the point of intersection between line segments.

Let us start with a conceptual procedure for clipping line segments. The inputs to the procedure are the endpoints of a line segment, (x_1, y_1) and (x_2, y_2). The corners of the WC window, (x_{min}, y_{min}) and (x_{max}, y_{max}), are assumed to be global parameters. This procedure

```
clipper(x1,y1,x2,y2)
```

will call a second procedure

```
draw_segment(x3,y3,x4,y4)
```

if any part of the line segment between (x_1, y_1) and (x_2, y_2) is inside the window. The portion inside the window is specified by the endpoints (x_3, y_3) and (x_4, y_4) in Figure 6.8. If the entire segment lies outside the window, clipper never calls draw_segment. In Figure 6.9, we can see there are four cases of interest:

- The segment lies wholly inside the window (segment A)
- The segment lies wholly outside the window (segments B and C)
- Exactly one endpoint lies inside the window (segment D)
- Both endpoints are outside but part of the segment is inside the window (segment E)

Our conceptual procedure might consist of the following steps:

- If (x_1, y_1) and (x_2, y_2) are inside, then draw_segment(x1,y1,x2,y2)
- Else if either (x_1, y_1) or (x_2, y_2) is inside, compute the intersection point (x_3, y_3); then draw_segment(x1,y1,x3,y3) or draw_segment(x2,y2,x3,y3)

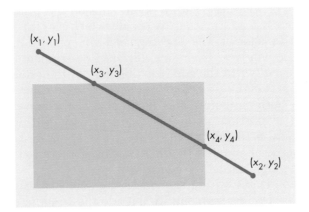

Figure 6.8
Line Clipping

Figure 6.9
Cases of Line Clipping

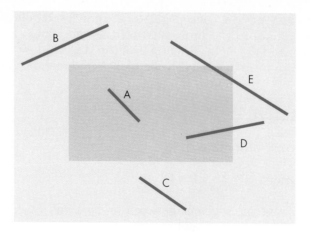

- Else if part of the line segment lies inside, compute the intersections (x_3, y_3) and (x_4, y_4); then `draw_segment(x3,y3,x4,y4)`

Our conceptual procedure requires us to be able to determine whether a given point lies inside the window. It also requires us to determine the intersection of a line segment with an edge of the window.

The first step can be accomplished by comparing the x value of the point to the right and left sides of the window, x_{min} and x_{max}, and comparing the y value to the top and bottom of the window, y_{min} and y_{max}. Thus, to determine if a line segment is fully inside the window, eight floating-point subtractions are required.

The first step in our procedure also will tell us whether we have one endpoint inside and the other outside. If we are careful in our determination of whether or not a point is inside the window, we will have the necessary information to decide which side of the window we must use to shorten the line segment when only one endpoint lies outside the window. Given an efficient line-segment intersection algorithm, we can write the code for this part of the procedure.

The final part of our procedure presents the most difficult problem. Even though both endpoints may lie outside the window, as we saw in Figure 6.9, a portion of the line segment may still be inside the window. Figure 6.10 shows the three cases of interest. Segments such as A can be eliminated by the following observation:

If both endpoints are outside the same side of the window, then the entire line segment lies outside the window.

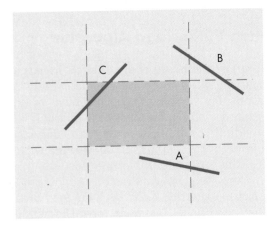

Figure 6.10
Clipping with Both
Endpoints Outside the
Window

The necessary information to determine whether this is the case is available from the first part of our procedure. Segments B and C do not have this property, but one is wholly outside the window and the other is partially inside. To distinguish between these cases, we must intersect these line segments with one or more of the lines that determine the sides of the window. This procedure is illustrated in Figure 6.11. We intersect B with the top segment. This step leaves two segments, D and E, each of which is wholly outside a window edge, so we can discard both. We intersect C with the top, creating two segments, F and G. F is above the window and can be discarded. G must be intersected with the left side of the window, creating H and I. H is outside the window, whereas I is inside and can be sent to `draw_segment`.

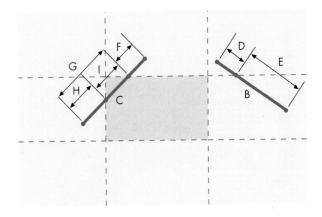

Figure 6.11
Shortening Line Segments

6.5
The Cohen-Sutherland Algorithm

Many graphical applications are characterized by large databases. In such applications, the window usually includes only a small part of the database. Consider, for example, a problem of designing a very large-scale integrated (VLSI) circuit. Such a circuit might consist of over 10,000 individual components, such as transistors. At any one time, the designer of such a system will be working with a small part of the total circuit. This situation is pictured for a mapping application in Figure 6.12. Here we display a small region of a large database (e.g. the entire city). In terms of the WC window, most primitives lie outside of at least one of the lines that form the window. Since most primitives will be eliminated in this stage by a clipping algorithm, we want to find an algorithm that does this step as efficiently as possible. The Cohen–Sutherland algorithm is one such algorithm.

Figure 6.12
Clipping a Large Database

6.5.1 Outcodes

The starting point for the algorithm is breaking up WC space into nine regions determined by the boundaries of the window, as in Figure 6.13. Each region is denoted by a 4-bit *outcode*. We compute the outcode of a point, (x, y), as follows. The most significant bit of the outcode will be set to 1 if $y > y_{max}$. The next bit will be set to 1 if $y < y_{min}$. We determine the last 2 bits by checking whether $x > x_{max}$ or $x < x_{min}$. The nine possible outcode values are indicated in Figure 6.13. By associating an outcode with a point, we know in which region the point lies. The Cohen–Sutherland algorithm uses the outcodes of the endpoints of line segments in its calculations, rather than the points themselves.

The calculation of outcodes can be done with this procedure:

1001	1000	1010
0001	0000	0010
0101	0100	0110

$y = y_{max}$

$y = y_{min}$

$x = x_{min}$ $x = x_{max}$

Figure 6.13
Outcodes for WC Space

```
#define TOP 010
#define BOTTOM 004
#define RIGHT 001
#define LEFT 001
#deine INSIDE 000
int outcode(x,y)
float x,y;
{
    extern float xmin,xmax,ymin,ymax;
    int out;
    if(y>ymax) out = TOP;
    else if(y<ymin) out = BOTTOM;
```

```
        else out=INSIDE;
        if(x>xmax) out |= RIGHT;
        else if(x<xmin) out |= LEFT;
        return(out);
}
```

We could also have used either one 4-bit field or four 1-bit fields for the outcode rather than an integer. We use `float` for points here, rather than the GKS type, `Gpt`, to emphasize that these implementation issues are being dealt with past the point where any software package definitions are important.

6.5.2 The Accept and Reject Checks

The calculation of the outcode for a given endpoint requires the same work as we did previously to check whether an endpoint was inside the window: four floating-point subtractions for each endpoint. Once the outcodes of the two endpoints are computed, we can trivially check whether the line segment is fully inside the window; it will be only if both outcodes are zero. Since we will use this check several times, we will create a macro called `accept_check`,

```
#define ACCEPT(code1,code2)  (code1|code2)
```

which is zero only if both outcodes are zero. If both outcodes are zero, the line segment will be accepted, and will be sent off to the next step in the pipeline. We also can use the outcodes to decide whether a line segment should be discarded or rejected. Checking Figure 6.13, we can observe that, whenever both endpoints of line segment are outside the same side of the window, there will be at least 1 common bit set in the two outcodes. A simple check for this is to take the bitwise logical AND operation of the two outcodes. If the result is not zero, the segment can be rejected using the macro

```
#define REJECT(code1,code2)  (code1&code2)
```

Note that, for our example of a large database, most of the line segments will by now have been either accepted or rejected. The power of this algorithm results from the fact that, once we have computed the outcodes, we process most line segments using only fast logical operations.

6.5.3 Computing Intersections

The cases we still must consider are those in Figure 6.14. For the segment with one endpoint inside and the other outside the window,

Figure 6.14
Clipping Against the Top of
the Window

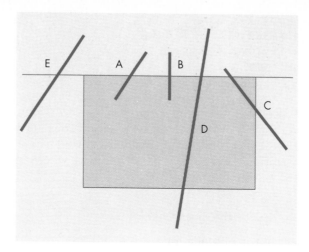

the code will be a little cleaner if we swap the points (x_1, y_1) and (x_2, y_2) if necessary to ensure that the point (x_1, y_1) is always outside the window. With (x_1, y_1) outside, we can treat all cases in the same way. Since we know that the outcode for (x_1, y_1) is not zero, we can check each bit successively until we find one that corresponds to a window edge that (x_1, y_1) is outside. Let us suppose that this edge is the top of the window, as we have done in Figure 6.14.

We start by removing the part of each of these segments that is above the window. Two of the segments (A and B) can be dispensed with by a single shortening; two others (C and D) will require further work. Once we have shortened E by removing the part above the window, we can reject the rest of E because the endpoints of the remaining segment are both outside the left side of the window. Thus, once we have shortened a line segment, we compute the outcode of the new endpoint. We then go through the algorithm again: accept if possible, reject if possible, shorten if necessary.

The removal of the part of the line segment that is above the window can be accomplished without too much difficulty. The point (x_1, y_1) is known to be above the window—that is,

$$y_1 > y_{max}.$$

So, after removal of the portion of the line that is above the window, we will have a new line segment with one old endpoint, (x_2, y_2) and one new endpoint (x_1', y_1'). Since the new endpoint will be on the line forming the top of the window,

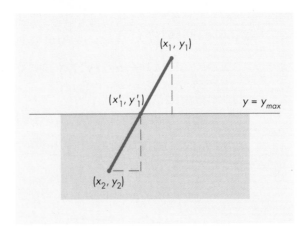

Figure 6.15
Computing the Intersection

(x_1, y_1)

(x_1', y_1')

$y = y_{max}$

(x_2, y_2)

$$y_1' = y_{max},$$

we must find the corresponding x_1'. This value can be computed via the diagram in Figure 6.15, as

$$x_1' = x_1 + (x_2 - x_1)\frac{(y_{max} - y_1)}{(y_2 - y_1)}.$$

Note that it is not possible, at this point in the algorithm, for $(y_2 - y_1)$ to be zero. A similar argument holds for the bottom, right, and left sides of the window. The code for **clipper** follows:

```
void clipper(x1,y1,x2,y2)
float x1,y1,x2,y2;
{
     extern float xmin,xmax,ymin,ymax;
     extern swap();   /* swaps two ints or floats */
     int outcode1,outcode2;
     outcode1=outcode(x1,y1);
     outcode2=outcode(x2,y2);
     if(!REJECT(outcode1,outcode2))
     {
          while((!ACCEPT(outcode1,outcode2)))
          {
               if(outcode1==INSIDE)
               {
                    swap(&x1,&x2);
                    swap(&y1,&y2);
                    swap(&outcode1,&outcode2);
```

6.5 The Cohen-Sutherland Algorithm   225

```
        }
        if(outcode1&TOP)
        {
            x1+=(x2-x1)*(ymax-y1)/(y2-y1);
            y1=ymax;
        }
        else if(outcode1&BOTTOM)
        {
            x1+=(x2-x1)*(ymin-y1)/(y2-y1);
            y1=ymin;
        }
        else if(outcode1&RIGHT)
        {
            y1+=(y2-y1)*(xmax-x1)/(x2-x1);
            x1=xmax;
        }
        else if(outcode1&LEFT)
        {
            y1+=(y2-y1)*(xmin-x1)/(x2-x1);
            x1=xmin;
        }
        outcode1=outcode(x1,y1);
    }
}
if(ACCEPT(outcode1,outcode2))
                draw_segment(x1,y1,x2,y2);
}
```

6.6
Other Clipping Methods

The Cohen–Sutherland algorithm has a long history in computer graphics. It illustrates the savings that we can accomplish by dealing with the easy cases first and replacing as many arithmetic calculations as possible with logical calculations. The Liang–Barsky algorithm [Liang84] uses the same basic logic but, because it works with the parametric representation of the line segments, is slightly more efficient.

These algorithms can be implemented either in hardware or in software. In some implementations, the same algorithm might be used in software for the clipping to the WC window and in hardware for the clipping to the NDC window that is part of the workstation

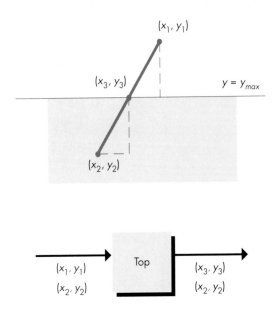

Figure 6.16
A Top Clipper

transformation. There are additional steps that we might take to make our procedures even more efficient.

6.6.1 Reentrant Clipping

First, if we look at the structure of the `clipper` procedure, we might notice possibilities for pipelining. Clipping against the four sides of the window can be looked at as four independent processes. Consider a black box that clips against the line of which the top of the window is part, as pictured in Figure 6.16. The inputs to this box are the two endpoints of a line segment that we wish to clip. Its outputs are the resulting two endpoints after the line segment has been clipped against the top of the window (or no endpoints, if the line segment is entirely above the window). Since clipping against any of the sides of the window is a similar process, we could build four virtually identical boxes and connect them in a pipeline, as in Figure 6.17. This method is known as *reentrant clipping*. Although we have more hardware than we had before, we have four times the throughput, because four line segments are being processed simultaneously. This algorithm is effective with filled primitives, such as cell arrays and fill areas (polygons), and has been built into the hardware of many display processors.

6.6.2 Using Bounding Boxes

A second way to gain efficiency is to use *extents* or *bounding boxes*. Consider a polyline with a large number of segments, as pictured in

Figure 6.17
Reentrant Clipping

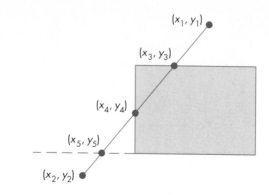

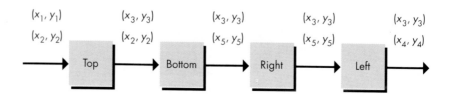

Figure 6.18
Polyline Clipping

Figure 6.19
The Bounding Box

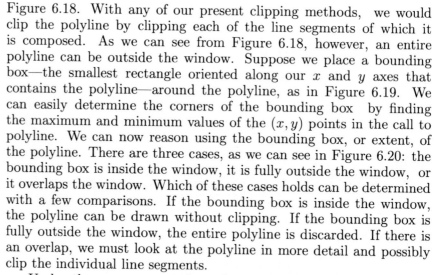

Figure 6.18. With any of our present clipping methods, we would clip the polyline by clipping each of the line segments of which it is composed. As we can see from Figure 6.18, however, an entire polyline can be outside the window. Suppose we place a bounding box—the smallest rectangle oriented along our x and y axes that contains the polyline—around the polyline, as in Figure 6.19. We can easily determine the corners of the bounding box by finding the maximum and minimum values of the (x, y) points in the call to polyline. We can now reason using the bounding box, or extent, of the polyline. There are three cases, as we can see in Figure 6.20: the bounding box is inside the window, it is fully outside the window, or it overlaps the window. Which of these cases holds can be determined with a few comparisons. If the bounding box is inside the window, the polyline can be drawn without clipping. If the bounding box is fully outside the window, the entire polyline is discarded. If there is an overlap, we must look at the polyline in more detail and possibly clip the individual line segments.

Under the same assumptions that make the Cohen–Sutherland algorithm work efficiently (large database, small window), this strategy also will work well. Bounding boxes can also be applied to other graphical entities. It should be fairly obvious that bounding boxes should work well with primitives such as text strings and cell arrays. They should also work well with programs that use modeling or segmentation. When we form a segment from a group of graphical prim-

228 Chapter 6 Implementation

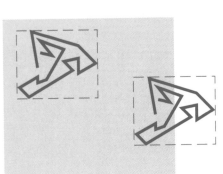

Figure 6.20
Clipping with Bounding
Boxes

itives, it might be desirable to compute automatically the bounding box for the entire group, and to store it in the segment's data structure. Then, before clipping the individual elements in the segment, we would first check whether the entire group was either inside or outside the window. Such strategies will reappear several times when we consider more advanced topics, such as hidden-surface removal.

6.7
Device Drivers

A line segment that has successfully passed through the clipper will appear on our display. If our clipper operates in WC, we will have two endpoints that must first be mapped to the specified viewport in NDC space. For each workstation, there will also be a mapping, as shown in Figure 6.21, from NDC to DC. These mappings were discussed in Chapters 2 and 3, where we derived the necessary equations. A point in WC (x, y) is transformed by the linear equations

$$
\begin{aligned}
u &= u_{min} + \frac{u_{max} - u_{min}}{x_{max} - x_{min}}(x - x_{min}), \\
v &= v_{min} + \frac{v_{max} - v_{min}}{y_{max} - y_{min}}(y - y_{min}), \\
r &= r_{min} + \frac{r_{max} - r_{min}}{u_{max} - u_{min}}(u - u_{min}),
\end{aligned}
$$

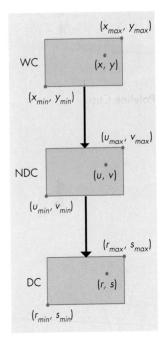

Figure 6.21
Coordinate Mappings

$$s \;=\; s_{min} + \frac{s_{max} - s_{min}}{v_{max} - v_{min}}(v - v_{min}).$$

In a typical program, the viewing conditions remain constant for relatively long periods. Hence, we can simplify these equations by writing them in terms of constants that need to change only if the viewing conditions are altered

$$
\begin{aligned}
u &= a * x + b, \\
v &= c * y + d, \\
r &= a' * u + b', \\
s &= c' * v + d'.
\end{aligned}
$$

These equations can also be represented with matrices in homogeneous coordinates, as in Section 6.2. The work required for unchanging viewing conditions is thus two multiplications and two additions for each endpoint that is produced by the clipper, and the same amount of work for each device. An alternative might be to combine these transformations into a single transformation.

Let us assume that we have a system with a single display. For a line segment that has passed through the clipper and must appear on the display, we have two endpoints, (r_1, s_1) and (r_2, s_2), which are in DC. This information will have been processed by the preceding equations. However, this information alone is not quite sufficient to cause our terminal to generate the correct output.

6.7.1 ASCII Devices

An output device such as a terminal or plotter requires two types of information: the data that are to be displayed and the control sequences to activate the necessary hardware capabilities. For example, we are assuming that our output device is a raster graphics terminal. The input to such a terminal is a sequence of ASCII (American Standard Code for Information Interchange) characters. ASCII is a 7-bit or 128-character code and is the code used by most standard terminals.[1] The characters can be numbered in decimal from 0 to 127. In the character set are the uppercase (codes 65 through 90) and lowercase (codes 97 through 122) characters, the digits 0 through 9 (codes 48 through 57), the usual punctuation marks and a number of special characters (codes 1 through 32). The special characters have names that are relics from the time these characters were used to control printers; they are available for use in controlling our graphical

---

[1] In byte-oriented computers, the eighth bit can be used for parity or to get an additional 128 characters.

devices. For example, character 13 is used as a signal to the terminal to return to the beginning of the line and is called the *carriage return* (CR) character.

In its normal or default mode, the terminal will act as a text terminal. The terminal receives sequences of coded ASCII characters from the host. ASCII codes for the uppercase and lowercase letters and for the digits 0 to 9 will cause the terminal to display bit patterns corresponding to these characters, such as the 7 by 9 patterns in Figure 6.22. The exact bit patterns depend on the terminal; they are usually stored in read-only memory (ROM) on the terminal. Reception of the ASCII code will cause the corresponding bit pattern to be placed in the terminal's frame buffer.

All the preceding discussion applies to a standard terminal with or without a graphics capability. In a graphics terminal, special characters are used as signals to leave the default mode and to commence interpreting ASCII characters as graphical data. We shall give two examples of how this interpretation can be done. The first uses unencoded sequences; the second uses encoding of the data. In each case, our device driver will take as input the endpoints of a line segment in DC, and will generate the necessary ASCII sequences to place the terminal in graphics mode, to cause it to generate the correct line segment in the frame buffer, and then to leave graphics mode.

Figure 6.22
Raster Characters

6.7.2 REGIS Drivers

Digital Equipment Corporation (DEC) terminals and their emulators use a graphics language known as REGIS. Interpreters in REGIS-compatible terminals recognize special sequences of ASCII characters in the REGIS language. These sequences are interpreted to cause the desired action, such as drawing a line segment or clearing the screen. The sequence to leave the text mode and to enter the graphics mode is the escape character (code 27), denoted ESC, followed by Pp or, in terms of their character codes: 27 80 112. Once this sequence is received, all further characters are interpreted as graphical information in REGIS form until the sequence ESC\ (codes 27 92) is received. Once this termination sequence is received, the device resumes acting like an alphanumeric terminal.

We shall consider only the sequence that has to be sent to draw a line segment. We will think of our simple device driver as a C procedure:

```
void driver(x1,y1,x2,y2)
int x1, y1, x2, y2;
```

The inputs are the endpoints of our line segment in the DC system for the particular device. For example, on many terminals the display

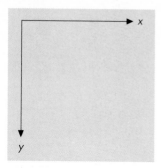

Figure 6.23
Terminal Coordinate
System

is rectangular, so the raster may be, say, 480 by 800 pixels. Since the GKS default for the workstation transformation is to use the largest square on the display, we use a raster we assume is 480 by 480 and is positioned on the left of the display.

One minor complication on these terminals is that the origin of the DC system is the upper-left corner of the display, and the positive y direction is down (Figure 6.23), which is the order in which scan lines are drawn on the device. Hence, as part of the conversion from NDC to DC, the direction of positive y must be reversed.

We will assume all coordinate transformations and clipping have been done. Values sent to the device driver through `driver` are in the DC system for this display, which corresponds to locations in the display's frame buffer. Our procedure will cause the device to put a rasterized line segment into its frame buffer.

REGIS has separate move and line commands. To define a line segment between (x_1, y_1) and (x_2, y_2), we must move to one of the points and then draw a line segment to the other. For example, to draw the line from (100,150) to (5,200), once we are in graphics mode, we move to (100,150) with a *point* (P) command followed by the co-ordinate information, then draw a line to (5,200) with the *vector* (V) command. The sequence is first to enter graphics mode by issuing an escape character followed by Pp, then to use the sequence

```
P[100,150]V[5,200]
```

and finally to issue another escape followed by \. We must be careful in writing the code, since the escape character is not a printable character, the data values are variables, and all the punctuation or delimiting characters in the sequence, such as the [, must appear as ASCII characters. Here is the full code:

```
driver(x1,y1,x2,y2)
int x1, y1, x2, y2;
{
/* DEC device driver */

/*  octal ASCII codes ESC = \033 , \ = \057 */

    printf( " \033PpP[%d,%d]V[%d,%d]\033\057 ",
            x1, y1, x2, y2 );
}
```

This strategy is particularly simple in a number of ways. A sequence of ASCII characters that is sent to such a device can easily be interpreted by the user, because sequences are readable and unencoded; for example, the point (100,200) generates the nine ASCII characters [100,200]. Once the terminal is in a mode, such as the vector (V) mode, it remains there until it receives a different mode command or is returned to alphanumeric mode. Further point information in the form $[xxx, yyy]$ is interpreted as a command to draw a line from the present position to this new point. Thus, it is simple to extend our driver to generate polylines through a single call to it.

One major weakness of this strategy is that it takes nine characters to specify a point in the frame buffer. For terminals, this requirement can be a problem, because terminals usually are connected to their host by a relatively slow serial interface. The strategy used by Tektronix devices demonstrates another approach.

6.7.3 Tektronix Drivers

Tektronix-compatible devices are designed to accept DC data accurate to 12 bits, which corresponds to a 4096 by 4096 frame buffer. Although a given device, such as a terminal, may have only a 480 by 640 frame buffer, to the host processor the device looks like a 4096 by 4096 device. The terminal is thus forced to make a coordinate transformation to its actual DC. The advantage of this approach is that all such devices can use the same device driver.

Tektronix 4010/1014 series devices and their emulators use the GS character (code 29) to enter graphics mode, and the US character (code 31) to leave graphics mode. In between, character codes are interpreted as x, y information. The first point is interpreted as a move_to command. Any following x, y data are interpreted as line_to commands. So far, this method is similar to the REGIS example. The major difference is that the x, y data are sent in encoded form.

One reason for encoding the data becomes clear when we consider the best way to represent two 12 bit numbers, an x, y pair, using ASCII code. In our first method, we simply took each digit and sent it using its ASCII code. For example, to transmit the number 1037, we sent the four ASCII codes: 49 48 51 55 (i.e., the codes for 1, 0, 3, and 7). We can achieve a more compact representation by working with the binary representation of a number. Consider an x, y pair and its binary representation

$$x = 952 = 001110111000_2,$$
$$y = 2447 = 100110001111_2.$$

Each value is broken into three parts: the highest 5 bits, the next 5 bits, and the last 2 (or *extra*) bits. The coding scheme is based on taking each 5-bit group and prefixing it with a 2-bit code to form a

7-bit number. This number is the ASCII code for a character. The first 5 bits of y get the prefix 01, the next 5 bits get the prefix 11. For x, the prefixes are 01 and 11 for the first 5 bits and second 5 bits, respectively. The 2 extra bits of y and the 2 extra bits of x are put together, and a 7-bit number is formed with the addition of the prefix 111. Thus, for our example, we form the five 7-bit numbers that follow with the ASCII characters to which these numbers correspond:

$$
\begin{aligned}
HighY &= 0110011_2 = 51_{10} = 3_{ASCII} \\
Extra &= 1111100_2 = 124_{10} = |_{ASCII} \\
LowY &= 1100011_2 = 99_{10} = c_{ASCII} \\
HighX &= 0100111_2 = 39_{10} = '_{ASCII} \\
LowX &= 1001110_2 = 78_{10} = N_{ASCII}
\end{aligned}
$$

Thus, we can accomplish a move to the point (952,2447) by sending the codes for ASCII sequence GS 3|c'N US. The general encoding scheme for an x, y point represented in binary as

$$
\begin{aligned}
x &= x_0 x_1 x_2 x_3 x_4 x_5 x_6 x_7 x_8 x_9 x_{10} x_{11}, \\
y &= y_0 y_1 y_2 y_3 y_4 y_5 y_6 y_7 y_8 y_9 y_{10} y_{11},
\end{aligned}
$$

is thus

$$
\begin{aligned}
HighY &= 01 y_0 y_1 y_2 y_3 y_4 \\
Extra &= 111 y_{10} y_{11} x_{10} x_{11} \\
LowY &= 11 y_5 y_6 y_7 y_8 y_9 \\
HighX &= 01 x_0 x_1 x_2 x_3 x_4 \\
LowX &= 10 x_5 x_6 x_7 x_8 x_9.
\end{aligned}
$$

The order in which this sequence is sent is crucial. We can see that, without knowing the order, we can confuse $Extra$ with $LowY$ and $HighY$ with $HighX$. In fact, there are well-defined rules for how to interpret sequences in which not all five characters are present. Our driver now becomes, using the binary operations in C,

```
void driver(x1,y1,x2,y2)
int x1,y1,x2,y2;
{
    putchar(\035);
    send_xy( x1, y1 );
    send_xy( x2, y2 );
    putchar(\037);
}
```

```
void send_xy( x, y )
int   x, y;
{
      int  HiY, Extra, LoY, HiX, LoX;
      HiY   = ((y&0x0F80)>>7)|(0x0020);
      Extra = (x&0x0003)|((y&0x0003)<<2)|(0x0060);
      LoY   = ((y&0x007C)>>2)|(0x0060);
      HiX   = ((x&0x0F80)>>7)|(0x0020);
      LoX   = ((x&0x007C)>>2)|(0x0040);
      printf( "%c%c%c%c%c", HiY, Extra, LoY, HiX, LoX );
}
```

Using encoding characters, we transmit five characters for an x, y pair, rather than the nine characters we used for REGIS devices. On the other hand, we must build a decoder to form the desired DC values in the device.

We have illustrated two simple drivers. We have not discussed how to generate other primitives or how to set the desired attributes. These features can be added in a manner similar to the way we sent the necessary information to draw a line segment. For each operation that we wish the device to perform, we will send one or more special characters and several data, either coded or unencoded, depending on the device. The complexity of the device driver will depend on both the capabilities of the device and the operations that are possible in the graphics system. For example, since the circle is not a primitive in GKS, although a device may have the hardware capability for generating circles, a GKS driver for that device may lack the code to use that capability.

Our discussion here has focused on a device driver for a typical raster terminal connected by a serial line to the host computer. Most serial devices operate in a similar manner. For example, a plotter might emulate a Tektronix terminal. For devices that are connected by parallel interfaces, device drivers will be more complex. However, what we are trying to do in all cases is the same. We are giving the physical device a command and the data for that command. To complete the process of display, we must consider how the device executes the command and generates a primitive on its display.

▬▬ 6.8
▬▬ Scan Converting Line Segments

We now consider the final step in the graphics pipeline: scan conversion. For our simple system with a raster terminal as our display, this process occurs in the terminal. The device driver sends the device the endpoints of a line segment in DC, and the terminal performs the scan conversion.

We shall omit issues related to how the frame buffer is read periodically and how its contents are displayed on the CRT. In a terminal, this part of the display process is handled in the electronics and is probably not under our control. For other systems, such as the graphics workstations that we shall discuss in Section 6.10, we have more options. In both cases, the scan conversion, whether done by the software or, as is becoming more common, through special-purpose graphics-processing chips, uses similar, if not identical, algorithms.

6.8.1 Setting Pixels

We shall present our algorithms as software procedures. The fundamental procedure we will need is one to set a pixel in the frame buffer. For now, we can think of our frame buffer as being binary: a pixel is either on or off. We will assume that our frame buffer is initially set to the background value or color. Hence, a call to the procedure

```
set_pixel(loc_ptr)

Rpt *loc_ptr;
```

where location is a *raster point*

```
typedef struct
{
        int x;
        int y;
} Rpt;
```

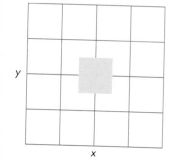

Figure 6.24
Ideal Pixel

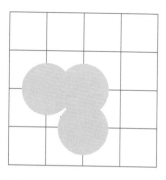

Figure 6.25
Overlapping Pixels

will set the pixel at location x, y to the foreground color. (If the frame buffer supports more than two colors, we can use a procedure set_pixel(loc_ptr, value).) The device dependence of this operation is clear when we note that both x and y are integers. It makes little sense to set a pixel except at a position in the frame buffer where a physical pixel is located. Since each frame buffer has a discrete number of pixels, we naturally seek to specify pixels' locations using integers. For now, we can think of a pixel as being centered at (x, y) and occupying a rectangular area of one unit on each side (Figure 6.24). In reality, pixels on physical devices may be round and also may overlap, as in Figure 6.25; overlap can have a large effect on the apparent brightness of groups of pixels and the readability of raster characters.

6.8.2 A Simple Algorithm

We will employ the parametric representation of a line. We have selected this form for two reasons. First, it is a natural form, since we
really want to scan convert a line segment between two given endpoints (x_1, y_1) and (x_2, y_2). Second, we must be careful not to invite
problems of axis dependence. We write these equations as

$$x = x_1 + \alpha(x_2 - x_1) = x_1 + \alpha\Delta x,$$
$$y = y_1 + \alpha(y_2 - y_1) = y_1 + \alpha\Delta y,$$

where

$$\Delta x = x_2 - x_1,$$
$$\Delta y = y_2 - y_1.$$

In Chapter 2, we saw that, as α goes from zero to one, we generate
all points on the line segment.

Both endpoints of the line segment have integer values, specified
by draw_line, that correspond to pixel locations in the frame buffer.
However, the line segment connecting these points does not need to
pass through any of the locations of pixels in the frame buffer, as we
can see from Figure 6.26. One way to deal with this problem is to use
a rounding procedure, round, which rounds its (real) argument and
returns the closest integer. Since integer values map to locations in
the frame buffer, we now have a pixel that can be set.

This algorithm is known as the DDA (digital differential analyzer)
algorithm. The DDA was an electromechanical device for generating
approximate solutions to differential equations. The position of gears

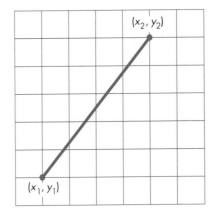

Figure 6.26
Line Segment in Frame
Buffer

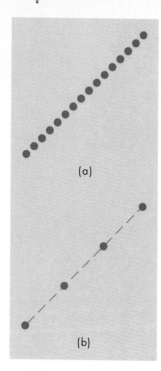

(a)

(b)

Figure 6.27
Incrementing α. (a) Large
Increments. (b) Small
Increments.

Figure 6.28
Incrementing x

in the DDA corresponds to registers in present computers. Since the line satisfies the simple differential equation

$$\frac{dy}{dx} = m,$$

its solution in the DDA is analogous to line generation by our algorithm.

The locations of the pixels that are actually set will depend on our choice of α values. If we select values of α too far apart, we will get very few pixels set in our frame buffer, as in Figure 6.27; if we make the increments in α too small, `set_pixel` will set the same pixel multiple times. The usual way to handle this problem is to increment α such that either x or y is increased by exactly one each time. Figure 6.28 shows what happens if we always increment x by one. As the slope increases, fewer pixels are set per unit length along the line. In fact, for vertical lines, this method will set only the endpoint pixels. Obviously, we prefer the situation in Figure 6.29, where we increment y by one time for lines with a large slope. The way we do this is to increment x whenever $|\Delta x| > |\Delta y|$, and to increment y otherwise. The code for a simple scan-conversion algorithm accounting for all possible slopes follows:

```
scan_convert(x1,y1,x2,y2)
int x1,y1,x2,y2;
{
    float dx, dy, x, y, increment,abs();
    Rpt location;
    int i, round();
    dx=x2-x1;
```

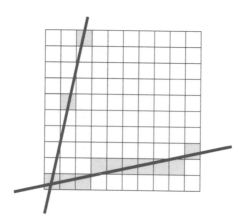

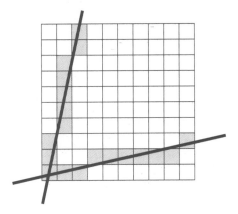

Figure 6.29
Incrementing *x* or *y*

```
dy=y2-y1;
if(abs(dx)>abs(dy))
{
    increment=dy/dx;
    for(i=x1;i<=x2;i++)
    {
        y+= increment;
        location.y = round(y);
        location.x = i;
        set_pixel(&location);
    }
}
else
{
    increment=dx/dy;
    for(i=y1;i<=y2;i++)
    {
        x+=increment;
        location.x=round(x);
        location.y=i;
        set_pixel(&location);
    }
}
}
```

Most of the work required by this method is the one floating-point addition for each pixel. Although it might not appear excessive, if we can remove this addition, we will be able to display more line segments in a real-time system. Bresenham's algorithm allows us to eliminate all floating-point operations while generating the same points as we did with our simple algorithm.

6.7 Scan Converting Line Segments 239

6.9
Bresenham's Algorithm

Bresenham's algorithm will generate the same points as the DDA algorithm. It will first check the slope to determine which of x or y should be incremented by one at each step. Since these two situations are symmetric, as is the situation for positive and negative slopes, we can focus on the case where Δx is positive and the slope of the line m satisfies

$$1 \geq m \geq 0,$$

and thus

$$\Delta x \geq \Delta y \geq 0.$$

Suppose we know we have just called `set_pixel(&location)` to set the pixel at (I, J). We use "I" and "J" to emphasize that these values are integers. We can extract some important information to help us determine what is the next pixel to be set, even without the equation of the line. Although the y coordinate of the pixel we just set is J and the x coordinate is I, this point is probably not on the actual line segment due to the rounding operation, as we can see in Figure 6.30. If y is the value of the y variable of a point on the line segment for the x value I, we know that

$$J - 0.5 \leq y \leq J + 0.5.$$

Figure 6.30
Choosing a Pixel

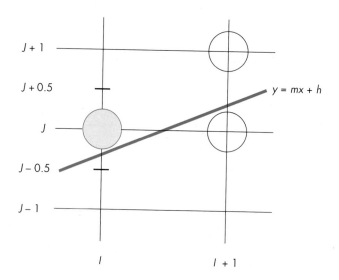

Figure 6.31
Bresenham's Algorithm

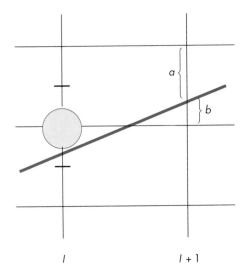

The next pixel we set will have an x coordinate of $I + 1$. Combining these two facts, we can conclude that we have only two possibilities for the location of the next pixel to be set: $(I+1, J)$ and $(I+1, J+1)$. That is, the slope of the line segment is such that we can go up at most one unit in the frame buffer as we move over one unit to the right.

Using Figure 6.31, we can convert these observations to an algorithm. Suppose we know that we have set the pixel at (I, J). We can attempt to select the next pixel to be set by looking at the distances a and b in the figure; that is,

```
location.x = I+1;
if(a-b>0) location.y=J;
else location.y = J+1;
set_pixel(&location);
```

Although it is easy to state the procedure in terms of the *decision variable* $a - b$, we must calculate these values efficiently in order to have a good algorithm. Since we are going to start with the initial x value, x_1, and increment x by one each time, we will look for an incremental algorithm, one that, instead of computing $a-b$ for each x, will look at how these quantities change as we go from I to $I+1$. We shall see in almost all our discussions of algorithms that incremental algorithms are almost always the most efficient ones.

6.9 Bresenham's Algorithm 241

Let us start with the equation of the line segment between (x_1, y_1) and (x_2, y_2), which, since we have agreed that the slope is between zero and one, can be written as

$$y = mx + h.$$

The slope m is given by

$$m = \frac{y_2 - y_1}{x_2 - x_1} = \frac{\Delta y}{\Delta x}.$$

As we go along horizontally, setting pixels in our frame buffer, I increments to $I+1$. As we move along the line segment, as x increments by one, y must increase by m to maintain the necessary slope. We can use this observation to determine how a and b change as I is incremented.

The increments in a and b will depend on whether or not we increased the vertical pixel location at the last decision. Since a is the distance between the upper candidate pixel location at $I + 1$ and the line, a will increment either by m, if only x was incremented, or by $m - 1$, if the last decision also incremented the vertical pixel location. These situations are shown in Figure 6.32. Arguing in a similar manner, we find the possible increments for b to be $-m$ and $1 - m$. Thus, our decision variable is incremented by either $2m$ or $2m - 2$.

The problem now is that the slope m is a floating-point number, even though the endpoints of the line segment are given in integer DC. If we notice that only the sign of $a - b$ is of interest, however, then we can multiply $a - b$ by any positive number and use this new quantity as our decision variable. We will use the variable

$$e = \Delta x(a - b).$$

e can be incremented by either $2m\Delta x = 2\Delta y$ or $2\Delta x(m-1) = 2(\Delta y - \Delta x)$. The heart of our algorithm consists of these steps:

```
if(e>0)
{
    e+=inc1;
    location.y=j
}
else
{
    e+=inc2;
    location.y=j+1;
```

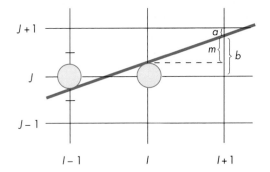

Figure 6.32
Incrementing *a* and *b*

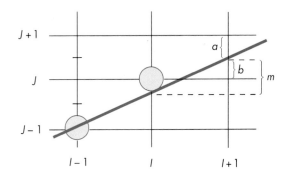

```
}
location.x=i;
set_pixel(&location);
```

where inc1 and inc2 are our two increments. Note that the work required is a comparison and an integer addition. By looking at the conditions for the initial point (x_1, y_1), we find that the initial value of e should be $2\Delta y - \Delta x$. The full algorithm, which accounts for slopes greater than one, in which case the roles of x and y are switched, and for negative slopes, which are handled by symmetry, follows:

```
void bres(x1,y1,x2,y2)
int x1,y1,x2,y2;
{
    int dx, dy, i, e;
    int incx, incy, inc1, inc2;
    int x,y;
    Rpt location;

    dx = x2 - x1;
    dy = y2 - y1;
```

6.9 Bresenham's Algorithm **243**

```
if(dx < 0) dx = -dx;
if(dy < 0) dy = -dy;
incx = 1;
if(x2 < x1) incx = -1;
incy = 1;
if(y2 < y1) incy = -1;
x=x1;
y=y1;

if(dx > dy)
{
    location.x=x;
    location.y=y;
    set_pixel(&location);
    e = 2*dy - dx;
    inc1 = 2*( dy -dx);
    inc2 = 2*dy;
    for(i = 0; i < dx; i++)
    {
        if(e >= 0)
        {
            y += incy;
            e += inc1;
        }
        else e += inc2;
        x += incx;
        location.x=x;
        location.y=y;
        set_pixel(&location);
    }
}
else
{
    location.x=x;
    location.y=y;
    set_pixel(&location);
    e = 2*dx - dy;
    inc1 = 2*( dx - dy);
    inc2 = 2*dx;
    for(i = 0; i < dy; i++)
    {
        if(e >= 0)
        {
            x += incx;
            e += inc1;
```

```
        }
        else e += inc2;
        y += incy;
        location.x=x
        location.y=y;
        set_pixel(&location);
      }
    }
  }
```

The polyline attributes can be handled as part of the scan-conversion process. The line-style and line-width attributes can be made part of the implementation of Bresenham's algorithm. The values of these attributes can be sent to the hardware, which will alter its line-drawing algorithm in a simple manner. The line-color attribute will affect the value used to set pixels. If the display is capable of color, the procedure set_pixel will set the desired color at the indicated location. We can implement this modification by either adding a color value to the procedure's parameters or using a separate command to set the present line-drawing color. Some of these variants are considered in Exercises 6.12 through 6.14.

6.10
Real-Time Processors

Although we have presented implementation for a simple terminal-like device, all the topics we have discussed must be dealt with in systems capable of performing real-time graphics. The hardware must generate primitives, clipping must be done, and all the coordinate transformations must be carried out. Of course, all these steps must be fast if we are to have a real-time system.

The fundamental speed requirement is based on the need to redraw or refresh a CRT display fast enough that the human user does not see any flicker. For the standard short-persistence phosphors used in most displays, the scan rate must be 50 to 70 scans per second. For raster displays, the technique of *interlacing*—displaying odd and even lines in the frame buffer on alternate scans—can halve this requirement by deceiving the user's visual system. However, for smooth displays on both raster and random-scan systems, the higher rate is preferable. Terminal-based systems, unfortunately, can display only static (unchanging) images at such a rate. We cannot get new information to them in real time, so we must turn to more sophisticated hardware for dynamic graphics.

Figure 6.33
Display Processor

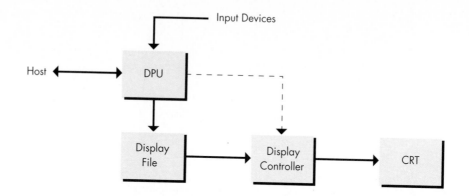

6.10.1 The Display Processor

The original solution to the problem of real-time graphics on CRT displays was to use a display processor, as shown in Figure 6.33, for a random-scan system. The display processing unit (DPU) is a special-purpose computer whose instruction set is oriented toward keeping the display refreshed. For example, it will have instructions that move the beam with the intensity either on or off. If the hardware can display text, there will be commands to place text on the display. A fragment of an assembly-language program on such a device might look like this:

```
MV 100, 200
LI 200, 200
TX Hello
END
```

The program resides in the display processor's memory, which is often called the *display file* or *display list*. The display processor executes the program in its memory repeatedly at a rate sufficient to keep the display from appearing to flicker. The generation of the primitives can be done by the display processor or, to increase speed even further, by another specialized processor called the *display controller*.

Figure 6.34
Host with Attached Display Processor

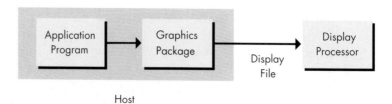

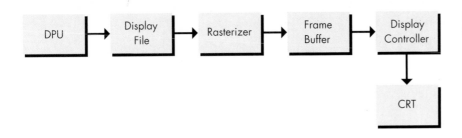

Figure 6.35
Raster Display Processor

Figure 6.34 shows the relationship between a display processor and a user program running on a host processor. The graphics package traditionally resides on the host. The host processes the user program and produces (or compiles) a display file, which is sent to the DPU to be loaded into the DPU's memory and executed. If the connection between the host and the DPU is slow, it might take a noticable amount of time to get the display on the screen; unlike in the terminal-based system, however, once the primitives are in the display file, they can be redisplayed or modified rapidly.

The configuration needs to be changed only slightly for a raster system. The necessary rasterization of the primitives is done within the display processor (Figure 6.35), using either the DPU or special hardware. Here we see a major difference between our raster terminal and a raster-display processor. The terminal takes the contents of the frame buffer and displays them over and over. Changes to the frame buffer are slow due to the slow interface between host and terminal. In the display processor, the entire display list is rerasterized every refresh cycle, which allows changes in the display list to be seen on the display almost immediately.

These configurations can been modified to permit a number of exciting possibilities. Since we can produce special-purpose hardware to carry out most of the graphics operations, the trend has been to push as much functionality as possible into the display processor. Consider the configuration in Figure 6.36. Here, the graphics package resides in the display processor. Hence, the interface between a user program in the host and the display processor consists of function calls and data in GKS form. Thus, GKS becomes the instruction set of the display processor. Operations such as clipping and coordinate transformations that are required by an application program are all carried out within the display processor.

The display file has much in common with the metafile. It describes a picture as seen by a logical workstation. Increased hardware capabilities allow present display processors to perform many operations in addition to maintaining the display. Since the display file is processed each refresh cycle, the key to real-time graphics is the ability to modify the display file.

Figure 6.36
A GKS Machine

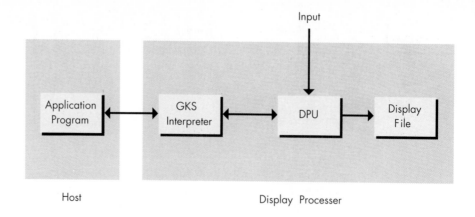

Most display-processor architectures permit segmenting of the display file. Thus, the segments that we define in our application become identifiable entities in the display processor. Consider the effect of a segmented-display file on a complex segment that contain thousands of primitives, such as we might produce in a CAD application. If we alter the appearance of this segment by changing the segment-transformation matrix, we have two distinct ways of producing a new image. Recalling that segments are associated with logical workstations, the segment may be on the host. The host can compute the new position of each primitive and send a new display list to the DPU. There are two problems with this strategy. First, the host is burdened by an additional computational load. Second, the interface between the host and the DPU will have to carry across all the transformed primitives.

The alternative is to have the transformation applied to the primitives in the segmented display file. In this case, the only communication needed between the host and the DPU is the function (*set segment transformation*) and its parameters, which consist of only the segment identifier and the coefficients of the transformation matrix. In addition, we can build fast transformation hardware as part of the display processor.

Most input functions can also be handled best by the display processor. Both locator and pick devices are often based on using timing to determine position. Since the display processor redisplays its display list at precise times, it is far easier to use the display processor to provide the timing. For example, consider a pick device such as a mouse connected to the DPU. When an interrupt from the device is generated, as when the user triggers the device, the DPU needs only to check where it is in its display file to determine the segment to which the user is pointing.

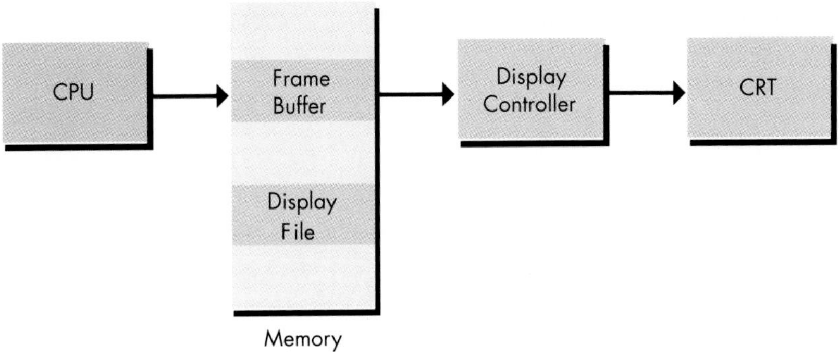

Figure 6.37
Workstation Architecture

6.10.2 Graphics Workstations

Most personal computers and graphics workstations are somewhere between the standalone display processor and a terminal-based system. Consider the architecture of a typical system, as shown in Figure 6.37. There is a single central processing unit (CPU). The frame buffer is part of the memory space of this processor. The display controller reads this part of memory and displays its contents on the CRT. The problems of communicating with a terminal are avoided, as the processor can access pixels directly.

Here, there is no display file in the sense of a special hardware memory. Such systems, however, can maintain a *pseudo–display file* in ordinary memory. We modify the display list by changing the entities in this part of memory. Usually, to reduce the computational burden, the pseudo–display file is scan converted only when a change has been made. The main limitation of such a configuration is that the single processor must perform all the processing, including both the normal processing of the application program and the processing required for displaying graphics (clipping, scan conversion).

This problem is exacerbated by the completely different types of processing that the workstation must do. The processing of the application program is usually best performed with a standard architecture, which can handle the kinds of sequential floating-point operations we have seen in our user programs. Operations such as rasterization, which are part of the display of primitives, are best performed on a completely different type of architecture. As we move toward faster workstations, we find different approaches to getting around these limitations. For the processing of the user program, we can use floating-point coprocessor chips or attached processing boards. For the display of primitives, numerous graphics coprocessor chips and boards can be added. With such additions, present workstations based on traditional architectures can offer the performance that was formerly possible on only special-purpose graphics systems. In Chapters 7 and 8, we shall see the importance of these systems for working with raster and three-dimensional graphics.

▰ 6.11
Suggested Readings

The use of outcodes for clipping was presented in [Spr68]. [Suth74] introduces reentrant clipping. Use of parametric equations for clipping is discussed in [Liang84]. Bresenham's algorithm was originally proposed for use with plotters [Bres63] and [Bres87]. The transferring of much of the implementation work to specialized VLSI chips is discussed in [Clark82]. The *geometry engine* is the basis of the Silicon Graphics workstations.

▰ Exercises

6.1 Write the code for clipping polylines using a bounding-box strategy. Assume a standard clipper, such as a Cohen–Sutherland clipper, is available.

6.2 Develop a clipping strategy for text at string precision. What kind of information might be required, possibly via inquiry procedures, to carry out your method?

6.3 Develop a clipping procedure for circles.

6.4 Develop a clipping procedure for quadratic polynomials.

6.5 An alternative clipping method, often used in raster hardware, is based on successively bisecting a line segment and checking the outcode of the middle point. Develop such an algorithm. When do you terminate the bisection process?

6.6 Suppose, for a given application, that line segments have an average length, $\bar{l}$, and are distributed in some fashion (e.g., Gaussian with a known variance σ). Also assume that you have the same information about the widow distribution. Compute the expected performance of a Cohen–Sutherland algorithm in this environment.

6.7 Write a decoder for sequences sent to a Tektronix-type graphics terminal. Your decoder should print out characters when the terminal is sent character data, and should print a line such as "POLYLINE x1, y1, x2, y2 .... " when it receives graphical information.

6.8 Repeat Exercise 6.7 for a REGIS-type sequence.

6.9 Discuss the possibility of moving all coordinate transformations into the device drivers. Which parts of our implementation pipeline would be more efficient?

6.10 Older Tektronix devices had a resolution of 10 bits. Drivers for such devices omit the *Extra* character. Discuss how you could achieve compatibility between high- and low-resolution devices; that is, explain how each device could handle data in both high- and low-resolution forms.

6.11 Show that the order of the bytes in the Tektronix encoding method is crucial. How would you handle situations where one or more of the bytes was omitted? Why might you want to omit some bytes?

6.12 Alter Bresenham's algorithm to generate lines of different types.

6.13 Alter Bresenham's algorithm to generate lines of different widths.

6.14 Suppose we could control the brightness of each pixel by setting its intensity through an additional parameter in `set_pixel`. How would you alter Bresenham's method to generate equal-brightness lines?

6.15 Emulate a frame buffer and the setting and clearing of pixels through GKS, using either the polymarker or cell-array primitives.

6.16 Suppose our physical pixels are round and have a radius r. Compute the brightness of a block of pixels as a function of r.

6.17 Investigate the effect of pixel size on the readability of characters by creating characters using either filled circles or filled squares and displaying them. Is it better to have pixels overlap or to make them distinct?

6.18 Design a pseudo-display processor. Your display processor should have a command set compatible with the GKS primitives, and should be able to implement segmentation. One approach to this problem is to build the processor around a table of segments that is altered by the addition and deletion of segments. Entries in the table can consist of segment names, pointers to where in memory the segment is stored, and segment attributes.

6.19 Explore the implementation of buffering in a display processor by using two display files, one active and one inactive.

6.20 Display processors often store the location information for primitives in relative rather than absolute form. Explain why they do so.

RASTER
GRAPHICS

Introduction

At the present time, raster displays are by far the most popular and flexible output devices. Raster output devices include most CRT terminals, both with and without a graphics capability; laser printers and plotters; and image-generation systems, such as flight simulators. Most modern graphics workstations are based on raster technology. In the early days of computer graphics, displays were random scan or stroke-oriented, but advances in solid-state memory and VLSI technology have shifted the balance toward raster systems. The additional capabilities of raster graphics make it preferable, even where cost is not an issue. This chapter will concentrate on exploiting these additional capabilities.

We have already used raster devices as a simple method of displaying output from our GKS programs. In the previous chapter, we developed Bresenham's algorithm, for implementing line drawing on a raster device. Our motivation then was to complete our discussion of the implementation of a graphics package. Our graphics systems, GKS and PHIGS, do not provide raster primitives to the user. Hence, our use of raster was only to display primitives, which also could have been displayed on random-scan (stroke) displays.

Raster displays provide a number of capabilities that are either impossible or difficult to implement on stroke systems. One is the capability to fill solid areas. Another is the ability to create realistic images by setting the color of each point on the display individually. We shall also find that processes such as hidden-surface removal, although possible on stroke systems, can be carried out far more efficiently on raster systems.

7.1
The Frame Buffer

A raster system is built around a *frame buffer*. The frame buffer contains the pixels, or picture elements. Each pixel can be displayed on the output device by a process that will differ for each device and need not concern us here. From our perspective, what we see on a raster display is a map of what is contained in the frame buffer.

The process of scan conversion determines the value that is assigned to each pixel. As we saw with the scan conversion of line segments, these values are determined in a manner that best approximates the image we are trying to display.

The frame buffer has the values of its elements changed as the program defines or changes primitives, the primitives' attributes, and the viewing conditions. From the user's perspective, his program is changing the contents of the frame buffer, whereas on the hardware side, the frame buffer is being read and displayed. A physical frame buffer is constructed using *dual-ported* memory, which can be written into and read out of by two concurrent processes. This concept allows us to separate the forming of an image in the frame buffer, our major concern, from the display of that image on a particular device.

Graphical entities such as line segments and text exist independently of any physical implementation. A point on a polyline is an abstract mathematical quantity that exists in a WC system and has no size. In contrast, it is virtually impossible to discuss a frame buffer without referring to a physical frame buffer. Points in the frame buffer are located at addresses in real memory indexed by integers. Thus, it is difficult to write device-independent code for raster systems, which in turn has made raster standards an elusive goal.

7.1.1 Conceptualizing the Frame Buffer

Although we prefer to avoid implementation issues for now, we still need a way to conceptualize a frame buffer. We will assume that our frame buffer has N rows of M pixels, and that each pixel has K bits. The K bits give the color or density of each pixel. Since K bits can be used to express any binary number between 0 and $2^K - 1$, there are 2^K possible colors we can place on the display at the location corresponding to a pixel. For example if $K = 1$, we have a single bit to determine a color, and we can have only two colors: One is considered to be the background color, and the other is the foreground color. Byte- (8-bit) oriented systems usually allow 256 $(= 2^8)$ colors.

There are two primary ways we can visualize the frame buffer, each of which has a direct realization in hardware. The first is called the *packed-pixel* representation. In this representation, we think of the pixels as arranged as either a one- or a two-dimensional list of pixels, as shown in Figure 7.1. Pixels can be viewed as lined up in memory, by rows or columns, just as we store ordinary two-dimensional arrays.

The second representation views the frame buffer as consisting of K *bit planes*, each of which is N by M, as in Figure 7.2. In this

Figure 7.1
The Packed-Pixel Representation

Figure 7.2
The Bit-Plane
Representation

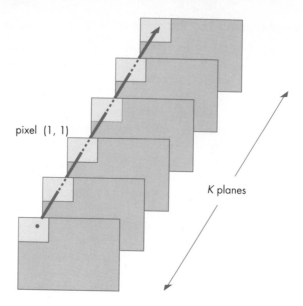

representation, the frame buffer appears three-dimensional, with all the bit planes in parallel. This representation helps us to envision the possibility of independently addressing each bit of a given pixel and of altering its value. It also leads to alternate ways of using the bit planes. For instance, K bit planes could represent K binary images, or one image with 2^K colors. Often, the choice of how to organize the bit planes is left to the user.

7.1.2 Manipulating the Frame Buffer

The basic operation necessary in using a frame buffer is one that sets a value of a given pixel. We extend our previous `set_pixel` to allow multiple-bit pixels:

```
void set_pixel(loc_ptr,value)

Rpt *loc_ptr;
int value;
```

The valid values for `value` will depend on how many bits are in the frame buffer, and the datatype `Rpt` again is a location in the frame buffer, as defined in Chapter 6.

Many algorithms for raster operations specify the value to be placed at each location in the frame buffer without regard for what value is already there. Others require us to use the value in the frame buffer to find a new value to place there. For example, fill algorithms are of both types. If the hardware allows us to inquire what is at a location in the frame buffer, we will do that through a procedure

```
int read_pixel(&location)
```

which returns the value of the pixel at `location`.

▤ 7.2
Writing in the Frame Buffer

The ability to set the value of a pixel in the frame buffer through the procedure `set_pixel` can be coupled with our ability first to determine what is in the frame buffer through `read_pixel`. This combination will generate a method of writing in a frame buffer that is more flexible and general than the one we presented in Chapter 6. In particular, we can make the value we assign to a given pixel be a function of an input value from a program and of the present value that is in the frame buffer. These more general operations are sometimes called *raster operations*.

In addition to this more general way of writing, we shall also consider the problems of doing raster operations on groups of pixels. Figure 7.3 shows a sequence of displays we might see in an interactive

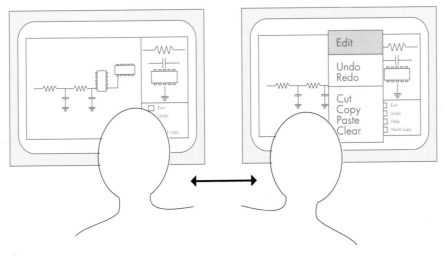

Figure 7.3
Menu Display

program that uses pull down menus. At some point, the user causes a menu to appear on the screen by an action such as clicking a mouse button. On a raster system, this menu is a rectangular block of pixels. One way to implement such an operation is to store the menu as a block of bits in memory. When the menu is required, it is copied into the frame buffer. Such operations have obvious importance in raster graphics and should be implemented as efficiently as possible both in hardware and software. They were given the name *bit-block transfer* (BitBlt) operations in the early days of raster systems.

In the ensuing discussion, we shall consider a 1-bit deep, or binary, frame buffer. There is no loss of generality in this assumption; if we envision our frame buffer as a set of parallel 1-bit planes as in Section 7.1, any operation we do on a single bit plane can be done on any other bit plane.

7.2.1 Swapping

Suppose that, as part of some application, we wish to swap two pixels. One of these pixels is in the frame buffer, and the other is somewhere in the memory of the computer. Such a problem can arise, as we described, when we wish to put a menu on the screen. Not only must we copy the menu into the frame buffer, but also we must save what was in the frame buffer where we wish to place the menu, so that we can restore it later. This situation is illustrated in Figure 7.4. Although this swapping operation appears straightforward, it can be accomplished in a number of ways. The most obvious one is to use a temporary location in memory. For example, if `value` is the pixel

Figure 7.4
Swapping. (a) Original.
(b) Step 1. (c) Step 2.
(d) Step 3.

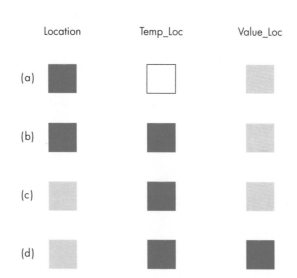

value that we wish to place in the frame buffer, we can employ the standard swapping method using temporary storage:

```
Rpt  location;
temp = read_pixel(&location);
write_pixel(&location,value);
value = temp;
```

Before considering the alternatives, we shall adopt a more general view of writing in the frame buffer. In most systems, the frame buffer is conceptually (and usually physically) part of the memory space of the processor. From this perspective, the operations of read_pixel and write_pixel are standard read and write operations. We retain the names of these procedures, but allow the location to refer to any place in memory. To be consistent in our addressing scheme, we envision all of memory as a two-dimensional array of values. In addition, we shall refer to the pixel we wish to alter in the frame buffer as the *destination pixel*, and the pixel in the memory of the computer as the *source pixel*. The source pixel may be in the part of memory that is allocated to the frame buffer. This situation is illustrated in Figure 7.5. Now we can rewrite the preceding program fragment as

```
write_pixel(temp_loc,read_pixel(&location));
write_pixel(&location,read_pixel(&value_loc));
write_pixel(&value_loc, read_pixel(&temp_loc));
```

In this example, location is the destination pixel, value_loc is the source pixel, and temp_loc is a location in memory that we use to store our temporary values.

Another possibility is to note that there is no reason to swap pixel values if they are the same. Using the unary complement operator

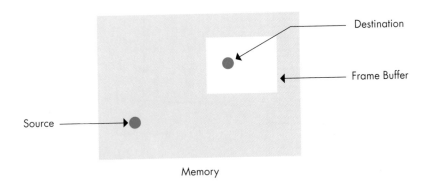

Source

Destination

Frame Buffer

Memory

Figure 7.5
Source and Destination Pixels

($\tilde{\ }$), we can perform the operations by

```
if((value = read_pixel(&location))
    != read_pixel(&value_loc));
{
    write_pixel(&location, ~value);
    write_pixel(&value_loc, value);
}
```

We have assumed that, to change a value in the frame buffer, we have to calculate it and to write it into the correct location. Suppose the hardware or software has an instruction or function that allows us to complement directly the value we find at a location in the frame buffer (or any other place in memory). Then, we could do our swapping by

```
if((read_pixel(&location)) != read_pixel(&value_loc));
{
    complement(&location);
    complement(&value_loc);
}
```

One conclusion that follows from this example is that how we do something depends heavily on what kinds of operations are available and what the cost is of each of these operations. We can also conclude that we might desire multiple ways to alter values in a frame buffer.

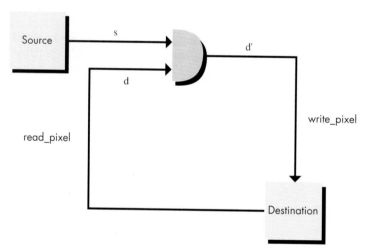

Figure 7.6
Raster-Operation Model

7.2.2 Writing Modes

In our example, we saw that what we place in the frame buffer may depend on both the source and destination pixels. Suppose we consider these values as binary inputs to a function that will determine what we place in the frame buffer as the new destination pixel. The model is shown in Figure 7.6. This function has a single binary output. For the write operation in set_pixel, we can describe the function through the table in Figure 7.7. The new destination pixel (d') is formed from the source pixel (s) and the value of the destination pixel (d) we have read. Here, we let logical one, or F, correspond to our foreground color (black for this book), and logical zero, or B, correspond to the background color (white for this book). We write by simply replacing the destination pixel's value by that of the source pixel.

Now consider the table in Figure 7.8. The table defines the new destination pixel as the logical OR of the original destination pixel and the source pixel. We can see the difference between the two writing modes in Figure 7.9. Here, we write a dashed line, which consists of a sequence of black and white pixels, that enters a black region. Which style is correct depends on what the user prefers and what the capabilities of the hardware are.

There are 16 different writing modes, which are shown in Figure 7.10. Each corresponds to a unique way of combining the source and destination pixels to form a new destination pixel. You might recognize these modes as the 16 possible logical functions of two variables. However, viewing each as a way of coloring pixels leads to interesting observations.

Suppose we number each operation by the binary number formed by the output. For example, the third column $BBFF$ is the binary representation of 3. We select the desired mode to use for write_pixel through a new procedure set_write_mode(mode), where mode refers to a column of the table. Our replacement mode is selected by set_write_mode(3), and the use of the logical OR is set by set_write_mode(7). Writing with the inverse or background color corresponds to modes 12 and 8. Mode 6 is the logical operation of exclusive OR (XOR), which has important uses we shall investigate in the next section.

7.3
Using XOR

The XOR raster operation provides interesting examples of how we can use alternate writing modes effectively. The table for XOR is shown

s	d	d'
B	B	B
B	F	B
F	B	F
F	F	F

Figure 7.7
write_pixel

s	d	d'
B	B	B
B	F	F
F	B	F
F	F	F

Figure 7.8 Writing with OR

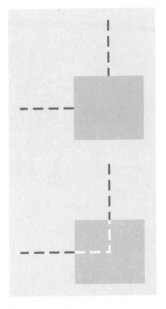

Figure 7.9
Writing Modes.
(a) Replacement. (b) OR.

Figure 7.10
Raster Operations

s	d	d'															
B	B	B	B	B	B	B	B	B	B	F	F	F	F	F	F	F	F
B	F	B	B	B	B	F	F	F	F	B	B	B	B	F	F	F	F
F	B	B	B	F	F	B	B	F	F	B	B	F	F	B	B	F	F
F	F	B	F	B	F	B	F	B	F	B	F	B	F	B	F	B	F

s	d	d'
B	B	B
B	F	F
F	B	F
F	F	B

Figure 7.11
XOR Table

in Figure 7.11; the mode number is 6. Note that XOR is 1 when exactly one of the inputs is 1. This fact gives the operation interesting properties. If a, b, and c are binary numbers and $\oplus$ denotes the XOR operation, then

$$a \oplus a = 0,$$
$$(a \oplus b) \oplus c = a \oplus (b \oplus c).$$

We can use these properties to derive methods for swapping, filling, and a number of other important operations.

7.3.1 Swapping Revisited

Suppose a and b are binary variables. Consider the following piece of C code, where ˆ is the XOR operation:

```
a ^= b;
b ^= a;
a ^= b;
```

After this sequence of operations, a contains the original value of b, and b contains the original value of a! This result can be proved with the properties of XOR from the preceding section. Using this result for writing in the frame buffer yields the code

```
set_write_mode(6);
write_pixel(destination, read_pixel(source));
write_pixel(source, read_pixel(destination));
write_pixel(destination, read_pixel(source));
```

Thus, we have swapped the pixels using three raster operations, without the use of any temporary storage. Figure 7.12 shows the sequence

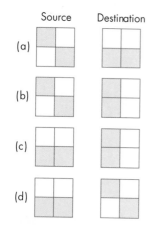

Figure 7.12
Swapping with XOR. (a) Original. (b) After first XOR. (c) After second XOR. (d) After third XOR.

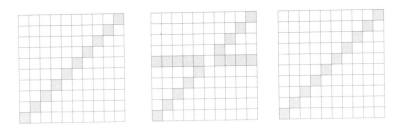

Figure 7.13
Writing and Erasing with XOR. (a) Original. (b) After First Write. (c) After Second Write.

of operations when this strategy is employed on a 2 by 2 block of pixels.

7.3.2 Erasing, Cursors, and Rubberbanding

One of the most intriguing properties of XOR is that using it twice can leave a variable unchanged, since

$$(a \oplus b) \oplus b = a.$$

In terms of writing pixels in the XOR mode, the first XOR "writes," whereas the second "erases," returning us to the original state. A little thought will show that this result is not possible using the other standard write modes. For example, Figure 7.13 shows what happens when we write a black line twice with XOR. Figure 7.14 shows what happens when we try to accomplish the same thing writing in the normal way (mode 3), and then attempting to erase by writing the line again in the background color of white. As we can see, the two methods yield the same result, except where in the frame buffer there was already a black pixel from another line segment.

Consider what happens when we put a cursor on the screen, as a prompt to a user, and change its location in response to data from a mouse or some other input device, as in Figure 7.15. As the cursor moves, we want the area of the display where the cursor has been to return to its previous state. One solution to this problem is both

Figure 7.14
Writing and Erasing with the Background Color. (a) Original. (b) Writing with Foreground Color. (c) Erasing with Background Color.

Figure 7.15
Moving a Cursor

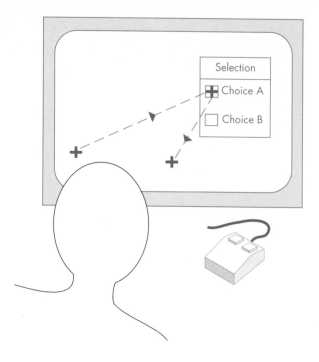

to place the cursor in the frame buffer and to remove it with the XOR writing mode. To move the cursor, we perform two writes. The first write is in the original position, which erases the previous cursor; a second write places the cursor in a new position. Note that areas "under" the cursor are always returned to the state they were in before the cursor passed over them. This method is fairly common, but it has some deficiencies. One is that the appearance of the cursor depends on what is under the cursor when it is written into the frame buffer.

The same approach can be used whenever we wish to display anything temporarily. Rubberbanding of lines was introduced as a user aid in Chapter 4. In rubberbanding, a line segment is drawn from a fixed location in the frame buffer to the location of the cursor. As the cursor moves, the line rotates and stretches to follow the cursor (Figure 7.16). The graphics system continually is erasing the last line drawn and drawing a new one to the current location of the cursor. This process presents a problem similar to that caused by drawing a cursor; namely, the contents of the frame buffer must be unaltered after the prompting is completed. Once again, we can accomplish this task by drawing pairs of line segments using the XOR mode.

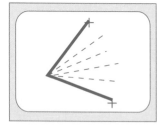

Figure 7.16
Rubberbanding

7.3.3 Simple Fill

As a final example, we can use XOR for filling closed regions, such as polygons and circles. We shall generalize this technique later in Section 7.6. Consider a single scan line, or row, in our frame buffer. This row contains M bits or pixels at successive locations in the frame buffer. Suppose there are exactly 2 bits on this row that are the foreground color. These 2 bits are at the two places where the edges of a simple shape (Figure 7.17) cross the scan line. We wish to color, or fill, all the bits between them with the foreground color, as in Figure 7.18. If we assume that there is at least one background pixel on the left of each scan line, the following code will work:

```
Rpt raster[N*M];
         .
         .
set_write_mode(6);
for(i= ROW+1; i<ROW+M ;i++)
    write_pixel(&raster[i],read_pixel(&raster[i-1]);
```

Here, `raster` is an array of the locations of the NM points in the frame buffer, and `ROW` is the index of the first pixel on a row; that is, it is an integer multiple of `M`. The XOR operation is applied to each pixel and to the one on its left, in a left-to-right order. Applying this process to every scan line will fill regions rather than single lines.

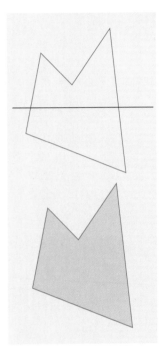

Figure 7.17
Area to be Filled

7.4
BitBlt Operations

Although the notion of a raster operation (or *RasterOp*) is of great importance in working with frame buffers, in reality we rarely do operations with a single pixel. Most of the time, we repeat the same operation on a group of pixels, as when we write a character string or display a menu. From both the hardware and software perspec-

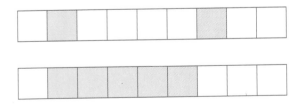

Figure 7.18
Filling with XOR

tives, we are better off if we can create raster operations in terms of rectangular blocks (bit blocks) of pixels.

7.4.1 Formulating the Operations

We can use any of our raster operations through the procedure `set_write_mode` to select a BitBlt operation on a block of pixels. Each operation involves a source block and a destination block, which will be combined bit by bit, according to the writing mode. In the simplest operations, we can assume that the source and destination blocks are the same size, say `nrow` by `ncol` bits. Thus, an operation can be invoked through a procedure such as

```
void bitblt(source, destination, nrow, ncol)
Rpt *source, *destination;
int nrow, ncol;
```

where `source` and `destination` point to blocks of pixels.

7.4.2 Clipping

If both the source and destination blocks have the same size, then the binary operation can be carried out between source and destination blocks on a pixel-by-pixel basis. When the sizes differ, we can adopt one of a number of possible strategies. One usual rule is that the BitBlt operation will apply only in regions where both the source and destination pixels are defined as in Figure 7.19. Suppose, however,

Figure 7.19
Overlapping Blocks and Clipping

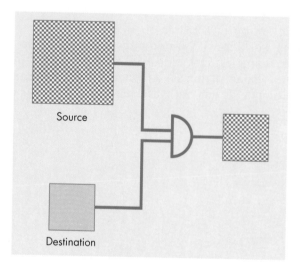

Source

Destination

that we want to apply an operation to only a part of the destination block. One example arises when the source block is a small pattern, such as a character, and the destination is the entire frame buffer. In this case, we want to alter the form of the BitBlt procedure to include a starting point in the destination block:

```
bitblt(source, destination, nrow, ncol, start)
Rpt *source, *destination, *start;
int nrow, ncol;
```

Now we assume that only the source block has **nrow** rows and **ncol** columns, and we start applying the desired operation at **start** in the destination block. We combine the first bit of the source block with the bit at **start** in the destination block. We proceed by incrementing the source and destination pixel locations as necessary to complete the operation. Clipping is done, so only bits in the destination block can be altered, as shown in Figure 7.20.

7.4.3 CharBlt

Operations involving text arise in so many applications that we might want to consider special operations for characters. We have previously noted that, in raster systems, characters are usually defined by patterns of bits. Often, multiple character sets are stored in ROM to allow characters of differing sizes and fonts to be accessed quickly. Although we could use the BitBlt operations as we defined them in

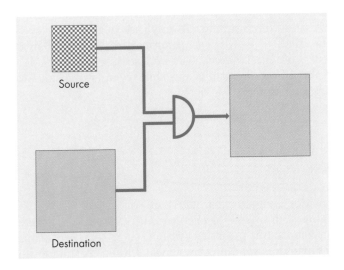

Figure 7.20
Clipping with BitBlt

the previous section to deal with characters, often we can speed up the hardware and software by adding procedures called *character-block transfer (CharBlt)* operations.

We might define one such operation as

```
charblt(destination, start, character, font)
Rpt *destination, *start;
char character;
int font;
```

Here, the character and the font determine the source block, and we can place the character at the location `start` in the destination block. Clipping can apply as for BitBlt. The writing mode will determine how the character block is combined with the destination block and is written out.

There are a number of other CharBlt operations that arise from our desire to provide flexibility with character strings in user programs. For example, we might create larger characters, as called for by our text attributes, by replicating pixels. Thus, we can create a character twice the default size by repeating each pixel twice along each row, then duplicating this row. Rotation of characters can also be done with a CharBlt operation, as can the alteration of a font to create a highlighted one.

7.5
Polygons and Raster

In computer graphics, polygons, such as generated by the GKS fill-area primitive, differ from closed polylines in that they have interiors that can be filled. Since it is impractical to perform fills on random-scan systems, polygons have become associated with raster graphics. There are three fundamental issues that we must consider with regard to polygons in graphics:

- Representation
- Clipping
- Scan conversion

As we consider each in turn, it is important to keep in mind that each polygon is an object to the graphics system. Although polylines are also objects to our graphics system, their representation, clipping, and scan conversion are almost always handled by the methods we discussed previously. Polygons, on the other hand, have many alternative representations, clipping methods, and rasterization algorithms, associated with them. The best choice depends on the application and on the particular hardware. We shall introduce just enough detail to give you some insight into the choices available.

7.5.1 Representation

In the `fill_area` primitive, a list of vertices defines the polygon. Vertices are ordered, and line segments (edges) connect successive vertices. An edge connects the last vertex in the list to the first, to close the polygon. If we use this definition to define the underlying data structure for the polygon, we use a structure like

```
typedef struct
{
    int x;
    int y;
}  Rpt;

typedef struct
{
    Rpt vertex;
    vertex_list *next;
}  vertex_list;

typedef struct
{
    int color;
    int style;
    vertex_list *vertices;
}  polygon;
```

We have included in the structure a color index that we can associate with each polygon, and a style index (e.g., solid, hatched). Each vertex is assumed to be two-dimensional, since we are working in the frame buffer. We could, however, replace our two-dimensional raster points by three-dimensional WC points to make a three-dimensional model for use in application programs.

A group of polygons, called a *mesh*, could be represented by a structure such as

```
typedef struct
{
```

```
    vertex_list *poly;
    int color;
    int style;
    polygon_list *next;
} polygon_list;
```

As in Chapter 5, we could implement procedures `draw_mesh` and `draw_polygon` that display one or all polygons. The drawing of each polygon depends on the fill-area style and the particular fill algorithm we select. An example of this structure is illustrated in Figure 7.22 for the mesh in Figure 7.21.

This structure is simple but is somewhat inefficient. Consider the mesh in Figure 7.23. Such a mesh arises from data that form two-dimensional arrays of NM two- or three-dimensional values (points). These data define $(N - 1)(M - 1)$ polygons, each with four vertices. If we use the preceding structure to define these polygons, there are two problems. First, suppose we are drawing the mesh as a group of hollow-filled polygons, so only the edges appear as in Figure 7.23. When we execute `draw_mesh`, all the edges that are shared by two polygons are drawn twice. This redrawing is a consequence of our decision to represent our mesh as a collection of individual polygons. If two polygons share an edge, then, since both polygons are drawn independently, the common edge is drawn twice.

The second problem is that the location of each vertex as a point in either two or three dimensions is repeated in the data structure each time a vertex appears in a polygon. Thus, for our mesh of four-sided polygons, all the vertices for the interior polygons appear four. times in our data structure. This use of memory is inefficient and also

Figure 7.21
A Polygonal Mesh

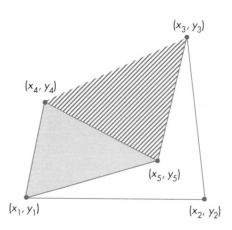

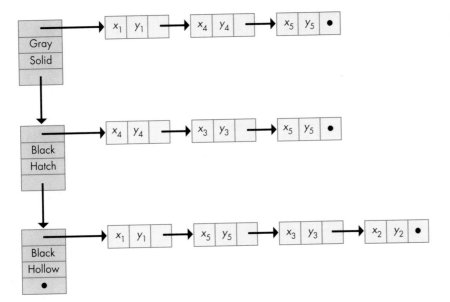

Figure 7.22
Mesh Data Structure

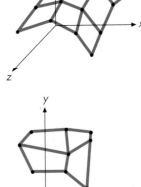

may lead to inefficient algorithms when we try to alter the mesh by relocating the position of a vertex.

The second problem can be solved quite easily by changing the `vertex_list` structure to use a pointer to the vertex:

```
typedef struct
{
    Rpt *vertex;
    vertex_list *next;
} vertex_list;
```

Figure 7.23
(a) Three-Dimensional Mesh. (b) Two-Dimensional Mesh.

Figure 7.24 shows a simple mesh with two polygons that contain four vertices and seven edges. Such a mesh cannot be represented simply as a two-dimensional array. Figure 7.25 shows this mesh stored using vertex lists. We can notice that now the locations of our vertices, or the *geometry* of the mesh, has been separated from its structure, or *topology*. Since the location of a vertex (its geometry) is stored only once, we can alter the geometry easily if the underlying topology remains unchanged.

Avoiding redrawing common edges requires a bit more work. The main idea is that, if we make a list of edges, we can go through this list to draw the mesh and each edge is drawn only once. Since an edge

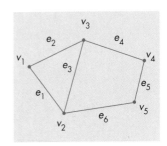

Figure 7.24
Simple Mesh Example

Figure 7.25
Mesh Structure

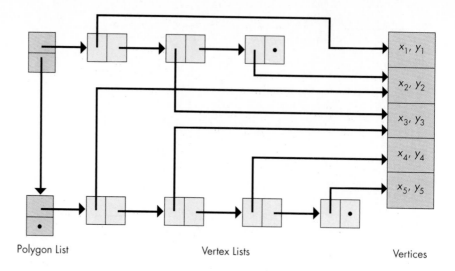

is defined by two vertices, we can create the following structure:

```
typedef struct
{
    Rpt *v1;
    Rpt *v2;
} edge;
typedef struct
{
    edge *ed;
    edge_list *next;
} edge_list;
```

For our example, this structure is shown in Figure 7.26.

Unfortunately, this new structure leaves us with other problems, the major one being that we now have nothing in this structure that identifies an individual polygon. The edge list works for a mesh of hollow-filled polygons but, without modification, it cannot easily be used to fill a polygon with a color or pattern. There are a number of possible solutions to this problem. Most involve creating a more elaborate data structure or even maintaining more than one representation of the mesh.

7.5.2 Clipping

In a sense, clipping of polygons is conceptually no more difficult than is clipping of line segments. Since the edges of the polygon are determined by line segments, the mathematics of intersecting a polygon

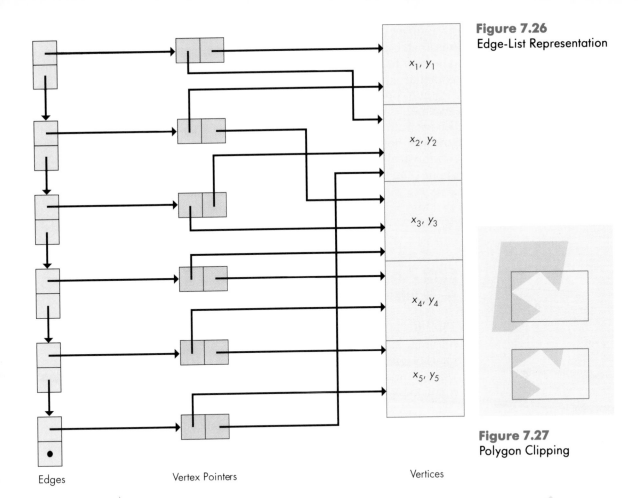

Figure 7.26
Edge-List Representation

Edges   Vertex Pointers   Vertices

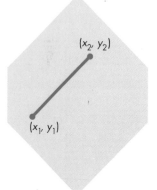

Figure 7.27
Polygon Clipping

with a window is the same as for intersecting line segments from a polyline with the window. We must keep in mind, however, that the object being clipped is a polygon and that the result of clipping is zero, one, or more polygons, as in Figure 7.27. Thus, clipping a polygon may yield more than a single like entity, which can pose some messy implementation problems.

This problem can be avoided by the use of *convex* polygons. A convex object (Figure 7.28) is one for which, if we connect any two points in it by a line segment, all points along this segment lie inside it. Spheres, parallelograms, and triangles are convex objects. Restricting ourselves to convex objects makes it far easier to implement many operations. For example, clipping any convex object either clips out the entire object or leaves a single convex object. Hence, we often use

Figure 7.28
Convex Object

Figure 7.29
Triangular Mesh

triangular polygonal meshes (as in Figure 7.29) rather than general mesh structures. If we are using three dimensions, triangular meshes are even more important, as each polygon in three dimensions defines a planar surface.

For convex polygons, it is easy to implement a reentrant clipping scheme, as described in Chapter 6. The input to each clipping box in Figure 7.30 will be a vertex list (or other data structure for a polygon), and the output will be a similar structure. For nonconvex polygons, we must allow the clipper to create multiple structures representing more than one polygon. The use of bounding boxes to avoid detailed clipping is as important with polygons as it is with polylines, and it often behooves us to store the bounding box in the polygon data structure.

≡ 7.6
≡ Fill

The idea of filling a region, such as the interior of a polygon or a GKS fill area, is deceptively simple. Suppose we start with the boundary on the left in Figure 7.31. A filled version of the area defined by this boundary is shown on the right. A simple conceptual algorithm might be

> Determine whether a point is inside the polygon. If it is, color it with the fill color.

To apply this directive to a region algorithmically, we need a method of distinguishing inside from outside. The boundary in Figure 7.32 shows that this problem is not necessarily simple, and there are mul-

Figure 7.30
Reentrant Clipping

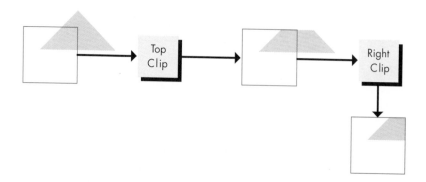

tiple ways to define *inside* and *outside*. Most standard systems have adopted definitions that work in raster systems.

There are a number of additional problems in implementing a fill algorithm on a raster system. These problems are caused by the discrete nature of the frame buffer. One is how to determine where the boundary lies after that boundary has been rasterized, as shown in Figure 7.33. Algorithms based on tracing a boundary in the frame buffer must be written with extreme care or they will be unable to proceed from one boundary pixel to the next.

7.6.1 GKS Fill Areas

In GKS, the fill area procedure defines a polygon by a vertex list. Within the implementation, we might use a different data structure to represent the polygon, but the importance of the vertex list is that we know exactly where the boundary of the polygon lies, a crucial aid in distinguishing inside from outside. Figures 7.31 and 7.32 make a polygon appear to have three parts: an inside, an outside, and a boundary that separates them. In GKS, the boundary is considered to be part of the inside and is not displayed for solid, hatched, or pattern-filled polygons. If we wish to display a red solid polygon with a green border, we must use a solid filled red polygon and then draw a green polyline on top of it.

In most graphics systems, distinguishing the inside from the outside of a region is done by scan-line crossings. This method is especially appropriate for raster systems, where we would like to fill a region in the frame buffer line by line, preferably in real time. Figure 7.34 illustrates a region defined by a boundary with two scan lines shown. As we go across a scan line from left to right, we will assume that we always start outside any polygon we might encounter. Hence,

Figure 7.31
Fill

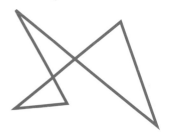

Figure 7.32
A Nonsimple Boundary

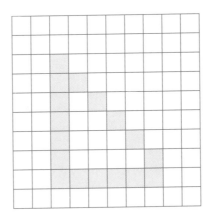

Figure 7.33
Rasterized Boundary

Figure 7.34
Scan-Line Crossings

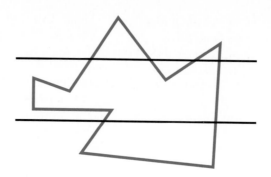

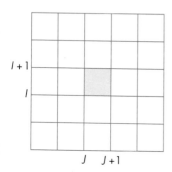

Figure 7.35
Pixel in the Frame Buffer

the first edge or boundary we cross is a transition from outside the polygon to inside. Then, the second crossing of an edge must return us to the outside of the polygon. Repeating the argument allows us to make the simple assertion that, after crossing an odd number of edges along a scan line, we are inside the polygon; after crossing an even number, we are outside.

With this definition, we can revise our earlier conceptual algorithm. The idea of *scan-line coherence* is that we can find groups of points on each scan line that are either all inside or all outside a polygon. We can also observe that *fill is a sorting problem.* Since we know (or can find) where all the intersections of scan lines with edges lie, we can sort these intersections first by scan line and then by distance along the scan line. Then, for any scan line we alternate between filling and not filling as we go through our sorted intersections. This algorithm is still not complete, as we must decide how to determine these intersections and how to do the sort.

7.6.2 Where Are the Intersections?

So far, fill may seem simple. Unfortunately, we are working in the frame buffer, where pixels are located at points on a rectangular lattice. This fact forces us to look at the consequences of using limited-precision integer arithmetic. Suppose we consider a frame buffer in which each pixel is a square that fills the area to the next pixel, as in Figure 7.35. We will let the location (i, j) refer to the lower-left corner of the pixel. This notation is a departure from that of the previous chapter, but will avoid certain potential problems in fill. Consider the two situations pictured in Figure 7.36. In each case, we have a polygon vertex that lies on a scan line. If we try to apply our odd–even definition to these situations, we conclude that in one case we must count the vertex as an even number of crossings (either none or two),

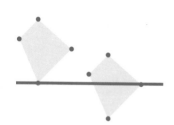

Figure 7.36
Singularities

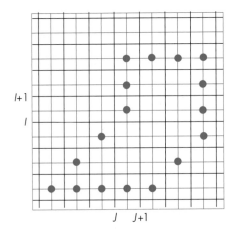

Figure 7.37
Rasterized Polygon Without
Singularities

and in the other case as a single crossing. Such situations are known as *singularities* as they arise when certain precise conditions, such as the vertex lying exactly on the scan line, are met.

Although we could construct algorithms that check for vertices lying on scan lines, in most situations, to do so proves to be inefficient. An alternative is to ensure that vertices never lie on scan lines. One way to accomplish this restriction is to force all vertices to be located midway between scan lines. We can do that by moving a vertex at (i, j) to $(i + \frac{1}{2}, j)$ or, equivalently, moving the scan lines between integers. Now neither of the singularities can arise, although we have made a slight distortion to the geometry.

If we consider a polygon such as that in Figure 7.37 we can observe that many potential problems in a fill algorithm have been avoided. Along every scan line, there is an even number of crossings of edges. Problems with horizontal edges are avoided, as a horizontal edge cannot lie on a scan line. There is still a potential problem for nonsimple polygons, such as in Figure 7.32, if two edges intersect on a scan line. We shall consider only simple polygons.

7.6.3 Edge-Flag Methods

In Section 7.4, we used the XOR operation as a method of filling a simple region. Such an algorithm is one of a number of algorithms based on being able to use the frame buffer directly. That is, we can write to it in one or more modes, and can read the values in it before deciding how to alter them. If we can ensure that no singularities appear along a scan line, these methods usually apply to more general regions than polygons.

Figure 7.38
Scan Converting the Edges

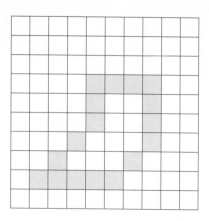

Suppose we have a single polygon we wish to fill. We start by scan converting its edges directly into the frame buffer, as in Figure 7.38, by a method such as Bresenham's algorithm. Note that, not only will this procedure be efficient, requiring only integer adds and compares, but also it will not have any problems with either horizontal or vertical lines. By placing the vertices at the center of pixels, we also ensure that there will be an even number of pixels colored with the edge or foreground color on each line.

We need only to apply the idea of scan-line coherence to each scan line to obtain a filled region. One way is through the use of our previous algorithm using the XOR writing mode. Another, perhaps more general, approach is to change a binary flag at each crossing of an edge. The flag indicates whether we are inside or outside the region. Thus, along each scan line as we proceed from pixel to pixel, we do something like

```
if(read_pixel(&location) == edge_color) flag = !flag;
if(flag) write_pixel(&location, inside_color);
```

Here, we assume a standard write operation, although what we are doing is equivalent to using the XOR method.

7.6.4 Priority Methods

Extending these ideas to situations with overlapping polygons such as in Figure 7.39 is possible, although there are a few complications. One possibility is to fill each polygon somewhere else in memory, then to copy the result into the frame buffer. Another approach, when there is more than a single bit per pixel, is to use for the edge a

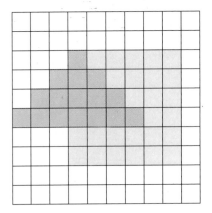

Figure 7.39
Overlapping Polygons

special color that cannot be confused with the interior color of any region.

The major issue with overlapping polygons is the order in which they are filled. Implicitly or explicitly, the polygons have a priority ordering. Most of the fill algorithms extend to *painting* algorithms, in which the polygons are filled in reverse-priority order. Each polygon paints over any polygon of lesser priority. These are called *painter's* algorithms, as they mimic what an artist will do while painting a picture. Alternate methods are based on the idea of *tiling,* where only the visible parts of polygons are filled, and on working on one scan line at a time. We shall see some of these variations in Chapter 9, as they are often part of hidden-surface–removal algorithms.

7.6.5 Recursive Methods

A different conceptual approach to fill is to use recursive techniques. Suppose we have drawn the boundary of our polygon or other region in the frame buffer and that we know one point, called a *seed*, inside the region. Furthermore, we assume that the rasterized boundary has an even number of edge points on every row and column.

We assumed the original seed is inside, which means that, if it is colored with the foreground color, it is an edge. If we cannot ensure that the original seed is inside, we can apply an odd–even test. If the seed is the background color, we color it with the foreground color and repeat the algorithm at the four surrounding points. If the seed is colored with the foreground color, we exit the procedure. This method is known as *flood fill* as the interior is flooded with the inside color. The code is straightforward:

```
Rpt raster[N*M]
```

```
                       .
                     .
                   .
         flood_fill(&raster[i])
                     .
                   .
                 .
         flood_fill(seed)
         Rpt *seed;
         {
             if(read_pixel(seed) == BACKGROUND_COLOR)
             {
                 write_pixel(seed,FOREGROUND_COLOR);
                 flood_fill(seed+1);
                 flood_fill(seed-1);
                 flood_fill(seed+M);
                 flood_fill(seed-M);
             }
         }
```

seed is a pointer to the seed point. If we have M points per scan line,
then seed+1 is a pointer to the pixel to the right of seed in the frame
buffer, and seed+M is a pointer to the point below seed in the frame
buffer. Generalizing to multiple-bit pixels is a simple exercise.

Figure 7.40 shows a simple region and the order in which the pixels
are filled. Although it is not difficult to establish that this algorithm
works under our conditions, the simplicity with which we can state
the algorithm masks many of the associated problems. Note that
individual pixels can be visited multiple times, even though they have
already been filled. In addition, for large regions, we can face serious
memory problems, as the number of unfinished procedures can place
large memory demands on the system stack.

Figure 7.40
Flood Fill

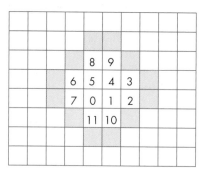

7.6.6 Sorting Methods

The two methods we have considered so far are fairly general in that they can be extended to regions more general than polygons and can be implemented in either hardware or software. There are a number of methods that are particular to polygons and are important since polygons are the principal elements in many modeling systems. In such systems, polygons are not only displayed on the screen as filled objects but are also fundamental objects in hidden-surface–removal and rendering algorithms. In such systems, which we consider in Chapters 9 and 10, the filling of polygons is part of other algorithms, and the efficiency of the fill algorithm should be judged within the context of the total package. It is in these cases that sorting methods, which usually involve the creation of a moderately sophisticated data structure, may best apply.

We have already observed that, if we have all the intersections of scan lines with edges of the polygon, our fill algorithm can be looked at as a problem of sorting these intersections in the proper order. Unfortunately, if we have k objects, the best sorting algorithms require time proportional to $k \log k$. This number can be very large. For example, if the raster is 1000 by 1000, a polygon which is one-half of the height of the display must have at least 1000 intersections with scan lines.

Fortunately, there are numerous clever methods available. Consider the simple polygon in Figure 7.41. Suppose the polygon is stored as a list of vertices. A simple method of obtaining the desired intersections of edges with scan lines is to start with the first vertex (A) and to go around the polygon clockwise, computing intersections until we return to vertex A.

Note that, once we are on an edge, successive intersections can be computed easily. Suppose the slope of the edge is nonzero. If (x_1, y_1)

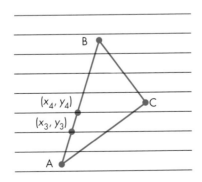

Figure 7.41
A Simple Polygon

and (x_2, y_2) are any two points on the same edge (such as the two vertices), then

$$m = \frac{y_2 - y_1}{x_2 - x_1} = \frac{\Delta y}{\Delta x}.$$

If (x_3, y_3) is an intersection of a scan line and an edge, then, as we move up (or down) to the next scan line, $\Delta y = 1$; thus, the next intersection is at

$$(x_4, y_4) = (x_3 + \frac{1}{m}, y_3 + 1),$$

a calculation that requires a single addition, assuming that $\frac{1}{m}$ has been computed and is stored in our data structure.

If we pursue this strategy in a direct manner, we will be left with a large sort, as we have not computed the intersections in the order we need them if we are to fill in scan-line order. One possibility is to compute a linked list of sorted intersection as we compute each intersection; that is, as we find an intersection, we insert it into the list. Another is to maintain a separate list of intersections for each scan line, which also will allow us easily to insert each intersection as it is computed.

A different approach is often necessary for generating real-time displays. Here, we want the intersections available scan line by scan line, so that we can do the fill on the fly. If polygons are stored in vertex lists, we might have to expend quite a bit of effort, since, for each scan line, we must determine which, if any, edges it crosses. In *scan-line* methods, a data structure organized by scan lines is pre-calculated. This data structure is somewhat more complex than are the others we have discussed, and it needs a number of accompanying procedures to manipulate it as polygons are altered in the database. Once the structure is computed, however, the fill can be done quickly. In Chapter 9, we shall examine a scan-line method for hidden-surface removal that will include fill within it.

7.7
Color

Thus far, we have used, without question, a simple model of color; namely, that a color is specified by an index and that the index points to a triplet of values: red, green, and blue. To exploit a raster system fully and to understand the architecture of most color graphics devices and systems, we shall find some additional information helpful.

Not only does color provide us with many new techniques for our graphics applications, but also the study of color is extremely interesting in its own right. The foundation of color graphics combines elements of anatomy, physiology, psychology, and physics. Here, we shall build up a model that will be adequate for most graphics applications. You should be aware that the use of color, since it involves human perception, is impossible to present completely in a short space. Also, it is not possible to guarantee that any two individuals will perceive colors in exactly the same way.

Light can be thought of as a region in the electromagnetic spectrum that excites the human visual system. Most references consider this part of the spectrum to be that with wave lengths in the range of 350 to 750 nanometers (nm). If we look at each individual frequency in this range by passing the light through either a prism or a filter, we interpret the individual frequencies as having color. A wavelength of 400 nm is blue, one of 600 nm is green, and one of 750 nm is red.

A distribution of intensities from a source such as in Figure 7.42, however, defies simple description. We perceive the light, since it falls within our visual bandwidth, but it is not clear what color name we associate with such a distribution. In computer graphics, we are concerned with both understanding what this color is to the viewer and producing the color on a display.

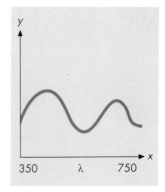

Figure 7.42
A Color

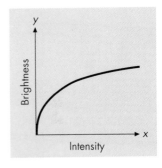

Figure 7.43
Brightness versus Intensity

7.7.1 Brightness and Intensity

When she is viewing a monochromatic display, a user perceives light arriving at her eye. This light can be described by a pattern as in Figure 7.42. As we vary the intensity of the display, we do not change the distribution of frequencies. We perceive the intensity of the display as *brightness*. The relationship between brightness, a perceptual quantity, and intensity, a measurable physical quantity, is approximately logarithmic (Figure 7.43). This nonlinear effect applies to all frequencies and can be compensated for separately. Hence we will not consider it further. This omission will allow us to discuss color using a simple linear model.

We do not perceive all frequencies within the visible part of the spectrum equally. The relationship in Figure 7.44 is known as the *C.I.E.* (Commission Internationale de L'Eclairage) *Standard Observer* curve. This curve shows that humans are rather imperfect filters of the electromagnetic spectrum; near the edges of our visual range, we have greatly decreased sensitivity. Thus, we must make blue or red much more intense for a viewer to perceive them as having a brightness equal to that of green. If our source in Figure 7.42 has a distribution of intensities as a function of frequency characterized by a function

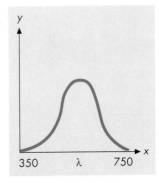

Figure 7.44
The C.I.E. Standard
Observer Curve

$C(\lambda)$, and the observer curve is described by a function $S(\lambda)$, the perceived brightness of the source is given by the integral

$$Y = \int C(\lambda)S(\lambda)d\lambda,$$

where we integrate over the visible frequencies.

7.7.2 Three-Color Theory

The curve in Figure 7.44 might lead us to conclude that the human visual system is primarily a green sensor. The curve shows that our brightness measure is based mostly on green light, with minor contributions from the red and blue. In fact, the eye has three types of sensors: one green, one blue, and one green-yellow. Each sensor has its own relative sensitivity curve. The crucial issue is that we have three types of sensors, not what the exact form of their sensitivity curves is. Most physical devices, such as film and vidicons, have red, green, and blue sensors. To incorporate all these devices in a common model, we shall refer to the sensors as red, green, and blue. Their sensitivity curves, $R(\lambda), G(\lambda)$, and $B(\lambda)$, might appear as in Figure 7.45. These curves will differ across humans, different types of film, and color vidicons.

Following what we did previously, given a color distribution $C(\lambda)$ that impinges on the eye, we "see" three *tristimulus* values,

$$
\begin{aligned}
T_1 &= \int C(\lambda)R(\lambda)d\lambda, \\
T_2 &= \int C(\lambda)G(\lambda)d\lambda, \\
T_3 &= \int C(\lambda)B(\lambda)d\lambda.
\end{aligned}
$$

Since only this triplet of values, (T_1, T_2, T_3), is communicated to the brain, we reach the following conclusion:

Figure 7.45
Three Color Sensors

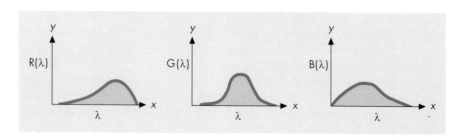

Any two colors that produce the same tristimulus values are indistinguishable to the human visual system.

Thus, we may have two colors with very different distributions as a function of frequency that cannot be distinguished from each other visually. In addition, this three-color theory is linear. If two colors produce tristimulus values (T_1, T_2, T_3) and (T_1', T_2', T_3'), then the sum of the colors will produce the vector sum of the tristimulus values.

7.7.3 The Color Solid

Although the equations make mathematical sense for any tristimulus values, positive or negative, we must take into account that the eye and other sensors perceive intensity or energy that is nonnegative. All sensors have limits on the maximum intensity they can sense.

If we consider the production of light through a CRT or any other device, the same considerations apply. Such devices produce nonnegative intensities up to a maximum value determined by their limitations.

We can normalize this maximum to be 1, and can restrict tristimulus values to satisfy

$$1 \geq T_i \geq 0, i = 1, 2, 3.$$

We can now represent a color $\mathbf{C}$ by its tristimulus value or as a point in a three-dimensional color space:

$$\mathbf{C} = (T_1, T_2, T_3).$$

This point must lie in a unit cube, as in Figure 7.46, called the *color solid*. Using the unit vectors, $\mathbf{R}$, $\mathbf{G}$, and $\mathbf{B}$, we can express a color as a three-dimensional vector,

$$\mathbf{C} = T_1\mathbf{R} + T_2\mathbf{G} + T_3\mathbf{B}.$$

The triangle connecting the $\mathbf{R}$, $\mathbf{G}$, and $\mathbf{B}$ axes is known as the *Maxwell triangle* and shows all colors whose tristimulus values satisfy

$$T_1 + T_2 + T_3 = 1.$$

The expression of a color as a vector in a three-dimensional color space is the first part of understanding how we use color in graphics systems. We have to combine this knowledge with that of how we produce output on our displays.

Figure 7.46
The Color Solid with
Maxwell Triangle

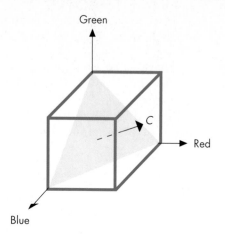

7.7.4 Producing Color

Since we sense only the tristimulus values, we should be able to produce colors with three primaries, adjusting their intensities to match the tristimulus values of any desired color. Colors can be produced in either an additive or subtractive manner. Both systems are based on three color primaries, and the two systems are complimentary.

We form *additive color* by adding together light sources, each of which produces light with its own distribution of frequencies. Such is the situation with the color CRT. Triads of red, green, and blue phosphors, as in Figure 7.47, are distributed on the surface of the tube.

Figure 7.47
Color Triads

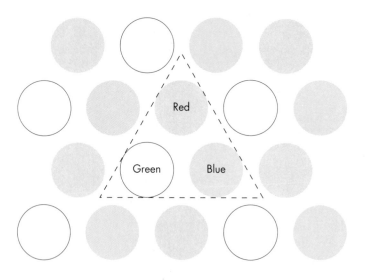

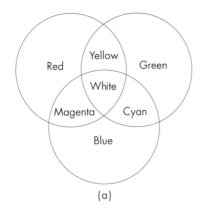
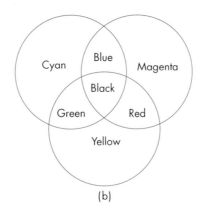

Figure 7.48
(a) Additive Color.
(b) Subtractive Color.

One or more electron beams is used to excite these phosphors. In the area of a triad, we have three primaries, each with its own intensity, forming a local color. A similar situation applies to forming a color by projecting three primary colors onto a white screen (Figure 7.48a). Suppose that, in this figure, each of the primaries is fully on. If we consider the areas of overlap, we find that we have eight basic "colors." The background where there is no color is black. Each of the three primaries—red, green, and blue—appears. Where two colors overlap, we obtain the complementary colors yellow, magenta, and cyan. Where all three overlap, we have white.

If we can adjust the intensities of each color, we obtain more colors. For example suppose we can adjust any of the primaries to a resolution of k bits. We will then have 2^k values for each primary, and 2^{3k} possible colors.

There is an alternate way to interpret and produce color. If we start with a source such as white light (which contains all the visible frequencies), we can remove colors by filters. This method of producing colors, called *subtractive color,* is the way colors are produced by natural phenomena. For example, grass is green because it absorbs other frequencies but reflects frequencies in the green range. In subtractive systems, the *complementary* colors of cyan, magenta, and yellow are usually considered to be the primaries, and the diagram in Figure 7.48b is usually employed. Where two primaries, such as magenta and yellow, overlap, only the colors they share, in this case red, pass through the filter. Additive and subtractive color allow us the same capabilities, so, with no loss of generality, we shall consider only additive color for the present.

Both the colors we perceive and the colors we can produce are characterized through the color solid. Since we are using additive color, we produce nonnegative intensities, which must be limited by the maximum output level of the given technology. For example, the color solid for a CRT display is based on the maximum intensities producible with its phosphors. Color Plate 11 shows all the colors on a standard CRT which lie on the Maxwell triangle.

7.7.5 Color Matching and Color Systems

The spectral sensitivity curves of the human visual system do not match those of a typical CRT display or of any other system. Hence, when we use the unit cube to describe both systems, we must realize that the representation of a given color is in terms of the tristimulus values within a particular system. A given color might be represented as

$$\mathbf{C} = T_1\mathbf{R} + T_2\mathbf{G} + T_3\mathbf{B},$$

in the human visual (**RGB**) system but as

$$\mathbf{C} = T_1'\mathbf{R}' + T_2'\mathbf{G}' + T_3'\mathbf{B}',$$

in the CRT (**R'G'B'**) system. It follows that a color that can be perceived by a human must also lie in the CRT's color cube, for us to be able to match it on the display. We can obtain the relationship between the representations of a color in two systems by using simple linear algebra.

Each of the three primaries for the CRT system can be represented as a color in the human visual system. For example,

$$\mathbf{R}' = r_r\mathbf{R} + r_g\mathbf{G} + r_b\mathbf{B},$$

where (r_r, r_g, r_b) are the tristimulus values in the human system. Likewise,

$$\begin{aligned}
\mathbf{G}' &= g_r\mathbf{R} + g_g\mathbf{G} + g_b\mathbf{B}, \\
\mathbf{B}' &= b_r\mathbf{R} + b_g\mathbf{G} + b_b\mathbf{B}.
\end{aligned}$$

These equations can be written in matrix form as

$$\begin{bmatrix} T_1' \\ T_2' \\ T_3' \end{bmatrix} = \begin{bmatrix} r_r & r_g & r_b \\ g_r & g_g & g_b \\ b_r & b_r & b_b \end{bmatrix} \begin{bmatrix} T_1 \\ T_2 \\ T_3 \end{bmatrix} = \mathbf{M} \begin{bmatrix} T_1 \\ T_2 \\ T_3 \end{bmatrix}.$$

The 3 by 3 matrix **M** enables us to convert tristimulus values in one system to tristimulus values in the other. For every pair of color systems, there will be such a matrix. To convert a color representation from one system to another, we apply $\mathbf{M}$ to its tristimulus values. If the transformed values lie inside the unit cube, the color can be produced in the second system.

There are at least three color systems of concern to the users of graphics systems. Certainly, one must be the human visual system. A second corresponds to the physical phosphors in a CRT. This RGB system has been specified by the National Television Systems Committee (NTSC), which sets the color standards for television in the United States. The primaries corresponding to the color dyes in film are also important. The literature uses colors in the XYZ system, which is a theoretical system and does not correspond to any physical primaries. It was created by C.I.E. to allow unambiguous specification of any physically producible color. Once a color is specified in XYZ space, we can transform it to any other space, using the proper matrix $\mathbf{M}$, to determine whether it can be produced.

In our graphics software, we specify a color by a color index. This index specifies a point in a unit cube that was selected by the *set color representation* procedure. Given the properties of a physical device, such as the number of bits available for each color, a system such as GKS does a best fit to this triplet of real numbers. What is not specified is which color primaries are being used. Hence, the user must be aware of what system is employed in a given implementation or device. To guarantee that two colors will appear the same on two devices, such as a CRT and a printer, the user may have to find the correct matrix $\mathbf{M}$ to adjust the values used in setting a color on the two different workstations.

7.7.6 Perceptual Color

Although RGB systems correspond to the physical primaries that are used either to sense or to display color information, perceptually we think of color in a different way. When we see a color, we assign to it a name, or *hue*, such as *red* or *yellow*. We also perceive how bright it appears to be, or notice its *lightness*. In addition, we can distinguish a hue that is very pure from a color of the same hue to which white light has been added. This third attribute is known as the *saturation* or color *purity*.

We now have a new color system called *HLS*. This system can be pictured as in Figure 7.49. The principal diagonal of the color solid contains equal amounts of red, green, and blue, and thus represents only the shades of gray. The least saturated colors are near this diagonal. The length of the color vector represents the color's lightness. The orientation of the color vector as it circles the principal diagonal determines the color's hue. This system can be interpreted as a polar-

Figure 7.49
The *HLS* System

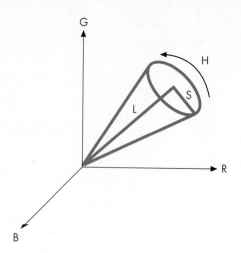

coordinate representation of a color. It is often displayed as a double cone, as in Figure 7.50. Colors in HLS space are usually specified such that

$$1 \geq L \geq 0,$$
$$1 \geq S \geq 0,$$
$$360 \geq H \geq 0.$$

Figure 7.50
HLS Double Cone

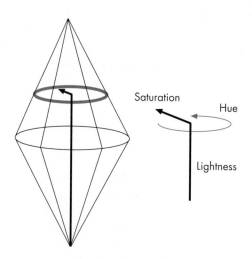

7.8
Using Multiple-Bit Pixels

Throughout this chapter, we have worked with a single-bit-per-pixel frame buffer. In this final section, we shall examine the consequences of having multiple bits for each pixel. Operations involving multiple-bit pixels can be obtained as extensions of our raster operations. For example, any of the logical operations between a source bit and a destination bit can be done in parallel to all the bits in both pixels. A more general approach is to allow any arithmetic operation between source and destination pixels.

7.8.1 Lookup Tables

Suppose we have k bits allocated for each pixel in our frame buffer, and we have a color display with separate red, green, and blue inputs. Suppose we send each k-bit pixel, as in Figure 7.51, processed through the digital-to-analog converters and the rest of the necessary electronics, to all three color inputs. We will have a *gray-scale* image, since we will always have the same amount of red, green, and blue at every point on the display. In this case, we can generate 2^k possible levels or shades of gray, since we can view each k-bit pixel value as a level between black (0) and white ($2^k - 1$).

Now, suppose each pixel has $3m$ bits and we send a separate group of m bits to each input, as in Figure 7.52. In many graphics systems, k and m are 8, and we can produce any of 16M colors (M=1024^2). Such a display is often called a *true color* display since, with so many colors available, we can generate an excellent approximation to any desired color. However, the required memory (24 bits per pixel) may seem excessive when we can observe that a 1024 by 1024 display could show only 1M colors at a single time. Color lookup tables provide an interesting alternative that allows the display of a wide variety of colors with a limited number of bits per pixel.

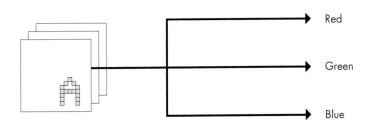

Figure 7.51
Gray-Scale Display

Red

Green

Blue

Figure 7.52
True Color Display

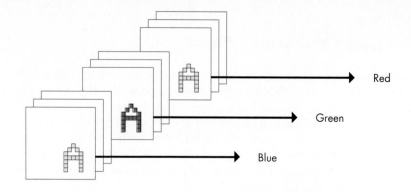

Consider a color display that can display 2^m shades of each of red, green, and blue. We need $3m$ bits to specify a unique color on this display. Suppose the frame buffer has only k bits per pixel, where $k < 3m$. We will put a table of 2^k rows of m-bit entries between the frame buffer and each of the color inputs, as in Figure 7.53. The three tables can be visualized as a single table, as in Figure 7.54. With this configuration, we can interpret each k-bit pixel as an index or pointer into this *color lookup* table. A k-bit–deep frame buffer gives us 2^k indices and allows us to use 2^k colors at any time. Since we can select from 2^m reds, 2^m greens, and 2^m blues, we have a color *palette* of 2^{3m} colors from which to choose the 2^k we shall use on our display.

This configuration often provides an ideal combination, minimizing the amount of memory required while still allowing great flexibility in color selection. For example, with $k = m = 8$, we can select any 256 out of 16M colors. We can also use these tables to do color corrections, as may be required when more than one color system is used, such as when we wish to produce the same image on both a CRT and film. If each device has its own color lookup tables, each could interpret the color index as necessary for its own color system.

Figure 7.53
Lookup-Table Architecture

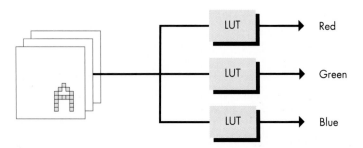

Input		Red	Green	Blue
0 1 . . . $2^k - 1$				

|← *m* bits →|← *m* bits →|← *m* bits →|

Figure 7.54
Lookup Table

An additional important factor in the use of color tables is that colors we see on the display can be changed without altering the data in the frame buffer. Rather than change the value of a pixel, we instead alter entries in the lookup tables. This technique not only is fast, since the color tables comprise a very small amount of memory, but also prevents destruction of the data during such changes to the display.

Although we have looked at color tables as part of the hardware implementation of a graphics systems, GKS color attributes use the same idea. Color attributes are set by indices through procedures that, for example, set the polyline color index (`gset_line_colr_ind`). The color indices are set on each workstation through the *set colour representation* procedure (`gset_colr_rep`).

7.8.2 Antialiasing

Multiple-bit pixels can also enable us to smooth out some of the jagged edges on rasterized primitives. Figure 7.55 shows an ideal line and the same line after it has been scan converted into a 1-bit-per-pixel frame buffer. This jagged display illustrates a problem called *aliasing*. The problem arises because, given the physical constraints of a real frame buffer, we cannot produce the line we want. As we know, pixels can be placed only at integer locations in the frame buffer. If we consider a number of possible lines close to the line in Figure 7.55, all may be scan converted into the same set of pixels. We can say that each of these lines belongs to one of a class of lines that are *aliased* by this sequence of pixels. The converse of this assertion is that, given a set of pixels in a frame buffer, we cannot tell which line segment produced this pattern of pixels. Such problems occur in all digital or discrete systems, since we can only approximate continuous phenomena, except under special conditions.

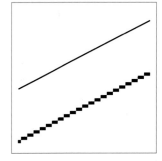

Figure 7.55
Aliased Line

One solution to aliasing problems is to use a higher-resolution frame buffer. Unfortunately, such frame buffers may not exist. Even if they did, we must remember that, every time we double the size of a frame buffer, we quadruple the number of pixels with which we must work. At some point, any increase in the resolution of a frame buffer will be a mixed blessing.

With a single-bit-per-pixel frame buffer, there is not much we can do to correct the aliasing problem, since each pixel is either on or off. With multiple bits per pixel, however, we can attempt to smooth the jaggedness of the rasterized line by a process called *antialiasing*, in which we alter the color, or gray level, of the pixels.

Although there are a number of approaches to antialiasing, the ones used most often in graphics are based on *area averaging*. Suppose we argue that a line segment in a frame buffer, unlike its mathematical representation, has a width, and this width should be one pixel wide. Such a line can be drawn over the frame buffer, as in Figure 7.56.

This raster line partially covers more than a single pixel for each scan line or column in the frame buffer. For each pixel in the frame buffer, we use the area of a pixel covered by this line to set its intensity. The calculation is straightforward, as each pixel box clips the line into trapezoids. The area of the each trapezoid can be computed from the endpoints of the line segment.

We can also take care of an additional problem as part of antialiasing. Consider the two scan-converted lines in Figure 7.57. After scan conversion, they may appear to have unequal brightness, since the number of pixels per unit length of line is inversely proportional to the slope of the line. Scan-conversion algorithms partially correct for this problem by incrementing y instead of x when the magnitude of the slope exceeds one. However, we can do better by adjusting the intensity of pixels as the slope changes. Both antialiasing and slope correction were used on the lines in Figure 7.58. Note that the antialiased line is smoother than the aliased line; it is also wider.

Antialiasing can be applied to other primitives. Polygons may be smaller than a pixel, and multiple polygons may intersect a single pixel, such as in Figure 7.59. The method we developed for lines can easily be extended to polygons. Our antialiasing method can be viewed as replacing an ideal line by a polygon of the proper width and then clipping this polygon with the pixel boxes. For antialiasing of polygons, we can assign a color to a pixel based on the portion of the pixel occupied by any polygons that intersect it. The assigned color will be a blend of the colors of each polygon, weighted by the area that the polygon occupies and the background color.

For realistic scenes, such as we might construct using the hidden-surface–removal and rendering techniques we shall discuss in Chapter 9, antialiasing is necessary to provide a high-quality image. Due to

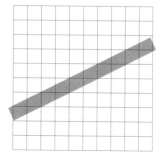

Figure 7.56
One Pixel Wide Line

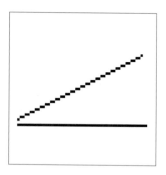

Figure 7.57
Unequal Brightness Lines

the work involved, antialiasing is usually the last step in the creation of the image, and is done only when only a final picture is required. The large number of calculations in antialiasing often leads us to perform this step on a large number-crunching machine. Alternately, there are a number of approximations that can be used to speed up the process.

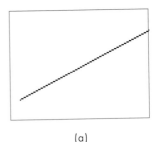

(a)

7.9
Suggested Readings

Details of many scan-conversion algorithms can be found in [Rog85], [Dun83], [Pav82]. Raster operations and BitBlt are part of the *Smalltalk* 80 system. [Gold83] and [Smith82] are discussed in [Guib82], [Ing81], and [Pike84]. Further information on color and human perception is presented in [Corn70], and [Pratt78]. Antialiasing methods are discussed in [Rog85], [Cat78], and [Crow81].

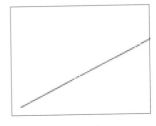

(b)

Exercises

7.1 Menus presented to a user as part of an interactive program can either be stored as bit patterns and moved into the frame buffer as needed, or regenerated each time they are needed. Which option is preferable? Describe the assumptions that influenced your choice.

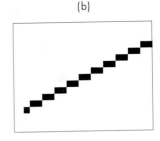

(c)

7.2 Most card games (such as the various solitaire games, poker, and bridge) use a deck of 52 cards. Each card has one of four symbols (club, diamond, heart, spade) and a denomination (2, 3, 4, 5, 6, 7, 8, 9, 10, J, Q, K, A). Design a deck of cards as bit patterns. Then implement an interactive game such as any solitaire variant using these patterns and BitBlt operations.

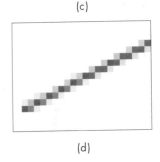

(d)

7.3 One option for extending bit operations in multiple-bit pixels is to perform the same operation between source and destination pixels to each corresponding pair of bits in the two pixels. Another option is to regard each multiple-bit pixel as containing a value and to extend the possible operations to arithmetic operations between source and destination pixels. Which arithmetic operations might be meaningful? What would this additional capability require from the hardware and software?

Figure 7.58
Antialiasing Lines.
(a) Aliased Line.
(b) Antialiased of (a).
(c) Magnifications of (a).
(d) Magnifications of (b).

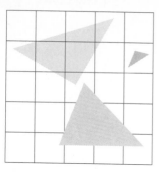

Figure 7.59
Aliasing and Polygons

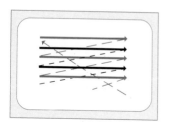

Figure 7.60
Interlaced Display

Figure 7.61
Overlapping Rectangles

7.4 Use BitBlt operations to implement zooming and panning operations.

7.5 Find an algorithm that uses BitBlt operations to achieve 90-degree rotations of bit patterns.

7.6 Suppose a set of characters is available as bit patterns of the same size. Using BitBlt operations, implement the GKS text procedures, including text attributes.

7.7 In a typical raster system, the CRT is redisplayed in an interlaced manner: All the odd lines are displayed on one frame, and all the even lines are displayed on the next frame (Figure 7.60). This process repeats 30 times per second. Approximately 10 percent of the time it takes to scan a line is allowed to bring the beam back from right to left, and about 10 percent of the total time is allowed to bring the beam back from the bottom to the top. Assume that you want to design a 480 by 640 display. How much time is available to get one pixel out of the frame buffer, perhaps to alter it in some way, and to put it up on the display? How much time would be available in a high-resolution (1200 by 1000) display? How do your answers change if you eliminate interlacing?

7.8 Create a data structure for polygons that stores them by scan lines. For each polygon, you should be able to determine which scan lines it crosses and where. Discuss the efficiency (time and space) of your structure in comparison to the representations discussed in this chapter.

7.9 Using the data structure in Exercise 7.8, implement a fill algorithm for polygons that fills in scan-line order.

7.10 You can implement thick lines either by modifying Bresenham's line-drawing algorithm or by considering thick lines as filled polygons. Why might you prefer to use the second approach?

7.11 Consider the overlapping filled rectangles in Figure 7.61. Painting methods produce the image by filling the entire area of each, the foreground rectangle being painted over, or filled after, the background rectangle. In tiling methods, we avoid the extra fills by breaking up a rectangle into subrectangles that either appear or are subsequently covered over by other filled rectangles. Only the rectangles that ultimately appear are filled on the display. Produce a tiling program for rectangles. How can you extend tiling to other filled objects, such as circles or polygons? Under what circumstances might tiling be a strategy better than is painting?

7.12 Digitized pictures are arrays of pixels, where the value of each pixel represents a gray level or density. Halftoning can be used to display such an image using a binary frame buffer. Consider an 8-bit (256-level) image. A rectangular array of values, the *halftone mask,* (Figure 7.62) is subtracted from successive blocks of pixels in the image. A positive result causes a white (1) bit to be placed at that location in the frame buffer, a negative result leads to a black (0) bit. Implement halftoning with our binary raster operations. What properties of the halftone mask are necessary to make your strategy work?

10	50	140	120	20
70	170	210	190	60
130	240	250	230	160
90	200	220	180	100
30	110	150	80	40

Figure 7.62
Halftone Mask

7.13 Many video games use small blocks of pixels, sometimes called *sprites,* to represent objects used in the game (e.g., rocket ships, daemons, obstacles). The flow of the game can be represented in terms of operations on these sprites. For example, if two sprites overlap, they have collided, which causes a specified action to take place. Design a sprite-manipulation library and use it to design a simple interactive game.

7.14 If you do not have a frame buffer available, you can use GKS to emulate a frame buffer through polymarkers or cell arrays. Construct such a software frame buffer, then write the fundamental software procedures: `set_pixel`, `read_pixel`, and `set_write_mode`.

7.15 We can extend the notion of raster operations to *display-list operations.* For example, with such operations, we could read something from the display list, then replace it by some other item. Define such a set of operations and use them to implement a pseudo display processor.

7.16 Implement cursor motion without an XOR writing mode.

7.17 Suppose each pixel has K bits and we interpret each K bits as a density or gray level value. How do we extend the XOR write mode to this situation?

7.18 Derive a procedure for entering polygons interactively using rubberband lines as prompts.

7.19 Use BitBlt operations to create a painting program that employs multiple brushes that can be represented by bit patterns. Use the various writing modes to control how paint is applied to the raster canvas.

7.20 Given a representation of a polygonal mesh, convert it into a mesh of triangular polygons.

7.21 Often, when working with polygons, we have to do consistency checks on the topology of our data structures to ensure that we do not have a degenerate case caused by the particular geometry. Find a method of testing a triangular mesh to ensure that the vertices of any triangle do not lie on the same line.

7.22 In a mesh of three-dimensional polygons, it is often left to the application to ensure that the individual polygons are planar. Devise such a test using one of the representations for a mesh.

7.23 Consider the polygon in Figure 7.63, where two edges cross. How can you alter our fill algorithms to allow for the case where this intersection falls on a scan line?

7.24 Construct an algorithm for converting between the RGB and *HLS* color systems.

7.25 Write a program that will allow users to select colors from a palette. The colors should be displayed and the user should be able to mix a color using one or more of the color systems.

7.26 Humans perceive light intensity as brightness. This relationship is logarithmic: $B \sim \log(I)$. Show how to use the lookup tables to ensure that equal increments in pixel values appear as equal increments in brightness.

Figure 7.63
Intersecting Edges

7.27 Describe how the area of a polygon is affected by the scan-conversion process.

7.28 Implement a fill algorithm for multiple-bit pixels.

7.29 Derive a fill algorithm for polygons with a distinct (visible) edge and a different inside (fill) color.

7.30 A certain color terminal is advertised to allow the display of four of 64 colors. What does this claim tell you about the terminal?

8

Three-Dimensional Graphics

Introduction

In many ways, three-dimensional graphics is a natural extension of two-dimensional graphics. The viewing model we introduced through the synthetic camera analogy is equally valid in two and three dimensions. We expect to maintain the separation between viewer and objects in modern three-dimensional graphics systems. We shall find that our three-dimensional object-specification procedures will be direct extensions of those we used for two dimensions. The specification of the viewing conditions will be more complex, due to the extra dimension. We shall also find direct extensions of two-dimensional transformations and modeling techniques to three dimensions.

There are two primary differences between two- and three-dimensional graphics. First, since the image produced on our output device is two-dimensional, whereas both the objects and the viewer are in a three-dimensional world, an additional step called *projection* is necessary. Second, we will have to be more careful in the implementation, as the additional dimension will force us to do more work, which makes efficiency issues even more important than before.

In this chapter, we shall start with the extension of our object specifications from two to three dimensions. This extension will consist of two parts: the extension of our two-dimensional primitives, such as polylines, to three dimensions, and the extension of our transformations to three dimensions. Once we are able to describe our three-dimensional world, we shall discuss how to view it. We shall see that viewing in computer graphics is a natural extension of the classical viewing process used in art, architecture, and drafting. Finally, we shall address some of the implementation issues.

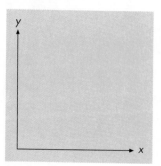

Figure 8.1
Two-Dimensional
Coordinates

8.1
Three-Dimensional Representations

In two-dimensional graphics, there is general acceptance of the coordinate system shown in Figure 8.1. As we go to three dimensions, the decision where to place the third dimension, z, is not so uniformly agreed on. If we start by accepting this two-dimensional system for the plane of the figure (or the page), we have two options for the positive z direction: into the page or out of the page. These options are known as the *left-handed* and *right-handed coordinate systems,* and are pictured in Figure 8.2. The figure shows one way of remembering the direction. If the hand is wrapped around the z axis with the fingers curling from the positive x to positive y direction, the thumb points in the positive z direction. We could also use three fingers on one hand to form a coordinate system, with the thumb for the x axis,

Figure 8.2
Left-and Right-Handed
Coordinate Systems

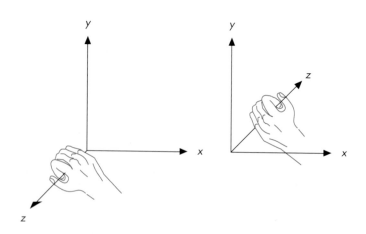

the index finger for the y, and the middle finger for z. In one sense the distinction is trivial, as we can convert from one system to the other by simply changing the sign of the z variables. The problem arises when we are not sure which coordinate system our graphics system is using, and we are in danger of going off in the wrong direction. Many graphics systems use both systems, usually using right-handed coordinates for object specifications and left-handed ones for viewing, or right for WC and left for NDC. We shall avoid this confusion by always using right-handed systems.

There is another possible source of confusion that we overlooked in two dimensions: the direction of a positive rotation. A positive rotation about an axis will be counterclockwise when we look toward the origin from the positive side of the axis, as in Figure 8.3.

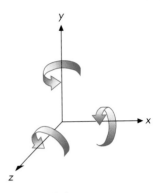

Figure 8.3
Positive Rotation

8.1.1 Three-Dimensional Curves and Surfaces

The mathematics necessary to work in three dimensions is a direct extension of our two-dimensional mathematics. For example, a point (x, y, z) in three dimensions will be represented as the vector, or column matrix,

$$\mathbf{p} = \begin{bmatrix} x \\ y \\ z \end{bmatrix}.$$

We obtain parametric representations of curves by simply adding a third parametric equation,

$$\begin{aligned} x &= x(\alpha), \\ y &= y(\alpha), \\ z &= z(\alpha). \end{aligned}$$

For example, the line connecting (x_1, y_1, z_1) and (x_2, y_2, z_2) has the parametric representation

$$\begin{aligned} x(\alpha) &= (1 - \alpha)x_1 + \alpha x_2, \\ y(\alpha) &= (1 - \alpha)y_1 + \alpha y_2, \\ z(\alpha) &= (1 - \alpha)z_1 + \alpha z_2. \end{aligned}$$

The explicit and implicit forms we used for two-dimensional curves do not extend to three dimensions. The explicit equation

$$z = f(x, y)$$

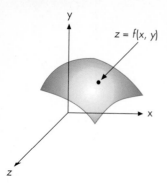

Figure 8.4
Explicit Surface

represents a surface, as in Figure 8.4, as does the implicit form

$$g(x, y, z) = 0.$$

Curves in three dimensions can be obtained by the intersection of two surfaces, as in Figure 8.5.

8.1.2 Planes

Of particular importance in computer graphics is the extension of the implicit equation for the line in two dimensions,

$$ax + by + d = 0,$$

to the three-dimensional equation

$$ax + by + cz + d = 0.$$

This is the equation of a plane.

We can obtain the interpretation of the parameters in the equation for the plane by following a similar argument to that we used for the implicitly defined line in Chapter 2. It will yield important insights. As long as $d \neq 0$, we can divide the equation by d and not change the plane. This fact implies that there are really only three unique parameters in the equation. Hence, any three noncolinear points will determine a plane. One convenient normalization is to multiply the equation by a constant so that, in the resulting equation,

$$a^2 + b^2 + c^2 = 1.$$

Figure 8.5
Intersecting Surfaces

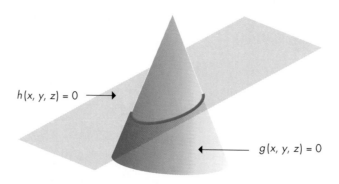

$h(x, y, z) = 0$

$g(x, y, z) = 0$

In this case, d will be the distance from the origin to the plane. In addition, all planes with the same a, b, and c are parallel to one another.

If we consider a plane with $d = 0$, we get one further insight. This plane,

$$ax + by + cz = 0,$$

must pass through the origin. The point (x, y, z) is an arbitrary point on the plane and can be represented as

$$\mathbf{p} = \begin{bmatrix} x \\ y \\ z \end{bmatrix}.$$

The line or vector from the origin to (x, y, z) lies in the plane. We can also take the triplet (a, b, c), which is a point in three dimensions, and write it as

$$\mathbf{n} = \begin{bmatrix} a \\ b \\ c \end{bmatrix}.$$

Figure 8.6
Intersecting Planes

Using the *dot product* of two vectors, we can now write the equation of the plane through the origin as

$$\mathbf{p} \cdot \mathbf{n} = 0.$$

Recalling that the dot product of two vectors is zero if and only if the vectors are perpendicular or orthogonal, we conclude that $\mathbf{n}$ is orthogonal to *all* vectors in the plane and hence must be a *normal* to the entire plane. If we have done our normalization, $\mathbf{n}$ is the *unit normal* to the plane. Since d affects only the distance from the plane to the origin, a, b, and c always define a normal vector to the plane

$$ax + by + cz + d = 0.$$

These relationships are illustrated in Figure 8.7. The characterization of a plane in terms of its normal is often helpful for conceptual purposes, as $\mathbf{n}$ controls the orientation of the plane in three-dimensional space. We shall use planes extensively both to form three-dimensional primitives and, in viewing, to represent the view surface.

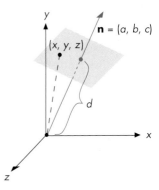

Figure 8.7
The Plane

8.2
Three-Dimensional Primitives

In a three-dimensional world, we can think of many new objects we might want to have available in our graphics systems. We certainly want to extend primitives such as the polyline to three dimensions, and we have the potential of adding completely new objects, such as planes and more general surfaces. We might also want to add three-dimensional objects, such as spheres or cones. We shall start with a simple set of primitives based on the idea that all our two-dimensional primitives should have extensions to three dimensions, and that our two-dimensional programs should run in a three-dimensional system.

8.2.1 The Polyline

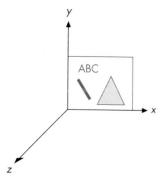

Figure 8.8
Two-Dimensional Primitives in Three Dimensions

We start with the polyline. Since we demand that our two-dimensional programs run in three dimensions, the procedure **gpolyline** will still refer to the two-dimensional polyline. The points that determine this polyline are specified as x, y pairs. Our three-dimensional system will interpret them as x, y, z points, where the z value has been set to zero. In other words, the polyline and all our two-dimensional primitives will be interpreted as lying in the plane $z = 0$, as we see in Figure 8.8.

We saw in the previous section that there was no problem in extending the definition of a line segment from two to three dimensions. A natural structure for us to use is a point in three dimensions:

```
typedef struct{
    Gfloat x;
    Gfloat y;
    Gfloat z;
} Gpt_3;
```

We can use **num_pt** three-dimensional points to define a three-dimensional polyline procedure,

```
void gpolyline_3( num_pt, points)

Gint num_pt;
Gpt_3 *points;
```

Since each line segment in **gpolyline_3** exists, the three-dimensional polyline always exists as a three-dimensional object. The two-dimensional polyline attributes (line width, line style, and line color) extend without difficulty to **gpolyline_3**.

8.2.2 Extending the GKS Primitives

The other two-dimensional primitives can be extended but require some changes. Primitives such as text and fill areas are planar; that is, the entire primitive is assumed to be in a plane, which can be defined anywhere in our three-dimensional WC system. For three-dimensional text, we want to be able to start the text at any point in three dimensions and to have it lie in an arbitrary plane, as illustrated in Figure 8.9. From our earlier discussion of planes, we can specify an arbitrary plane in a variety of ways. One way is through one point and two direction vectors that can be thought of as emerging from the point, as in Figure 8.10. Text starts at the point and exists in the plane determined by it and the two vectors. Once the plane is specified, all the two-dimensional text attributes—such as path, font, and color—can be applied. The procedure is called by

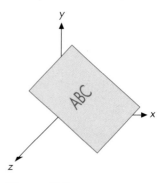

Figure 8.9
Text in Three Dimensions

```
void gtext_3(start,vectors,string)

Gpt_3 *start, *vectors;
Gchar *string;
```

where `vectors` is an array of two three-dimensional points. Each of these points determines a vector from the origin to the point. The origin and these two points determine a plane.

Extending cell arrays to three dimensions (`gcellarray_3`) also requires the specification of an appropriate plane in three dimensions. Markers and fill areas are defined by the following procedures:

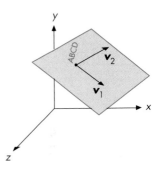

Figure 8.10
Specifying the Text Plane

```
void gfillarea_3(num_pt,points)
void gpolymarker_3(num_pt, points)

Gint n;
Gpt_3 *points;
```

The individual three-dimensional points in the array `points` are assumed to lie in the same plane by the system, and it is the user's responsibility to force this assumption to be valid. If we use points that do not lie in the same plane, we cannot guarantee what will happen to our program during execution. Often, this problem will not be too serious, as all primitives are eventually projected onto a planar view surface for output. There can be serious problems, however, in hidden-surface removal, where we might use the first three points to calculate the parameters of the plane in which all points are assumed to lie.

8.3
Transformations

As with two-dimensional graphics, affine transformations are the basis for both modeling and viewing. We can extend our basic transformations (translation, scaling, rotation, and shear) to three dimensions without too much difficulty. The extra dimension will mean we have to work with larger matrices and vectors, and we will also use a larger number of matrices to form an arbitrary affine transformation.

8.3.1 Homogeneous Coordinates

Once again, we shall use homogeneous coordinates, which will now be in four dimensions. A point (x, y, z) will be represented as

$$\mathbf{p} = \begin{bmatrix} wx \\ wy \\ wz \\ w \end{bmatrix},$$

where again the only restriction is that $w \neq 0$.

When using a three-dimensional homogeneous coordinate representation of a point in two dimensions, we were always able to set $w = 1$ and to maintain this value after a transformation. Recovery of the two-dimensional point from its homogeneous coordinate representation was almost trivial. Unfortunately, this strategy will not always be possible in three dimensions. The problem will arise later in perspective viewing. In this section, where we are concerned with setting up our basic transformations, we will be able to maintain a given value of w.

We will write a point as

$$\mathbf{p} = \begin{bmatrix} x \\ y \\ z \\ w \end{bmatrix},$$

where at least initially we can take $w = 1$. If $\mathbf{p}$ is transformed to $\mathbf{p}'$ by an affine transformation, $\mathbf{p}'$ can be represented by

$$\mathbf{p}' = \begin{bmatrix} x' \\ y' \\ z' \\ w' \end{bmatrix}.$$

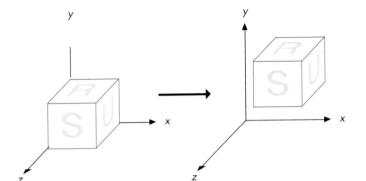

Figure 8.11
Translation

8.3.2 Translation

In three dimensions, translation involves displacements in all three variables, as shown in Figure 8.11. The coordinates of the transformed point are given by

$$\begin{aligned} x' &= x + \Delta x, \\ y' &= y + \Delta y, \\ z' &= z + \Delta z, \\ w' &= w. \end{aligned}$$

In homogeneous coordinates,

$$\mathbf{p}' = \mathbf{T}(\Delta x, \Delta y, \Delta z)\mathbf{p},$$

where $\mathbf{T}(\Delta x, \Delta y, \Delta z)$ is the matrix

$$\mathbf{T}(\Delta x, \Delta y, \Delta z) = \begin{bmatrix} 1 & 0 & 0 & \Delta x \\ 0 & 1 & 0 & \Delta y \\ 0 & 0 & 1 & \Delta z \\ 0 & 0 & 0 & 1 \end{bmatrix}.$$

8.3.3 Scaling and Shear

We will allow independent scaling in all three dimensions, as shown in Figure 8.12. The representation is obtained as in two dimensions,

$$\mathbf{p}' = \mathbf{S}(\alpha, \beta, \gamma)\mathbf{p},$$

8.3 Transformations **307**

Figure 8.12
Scaling

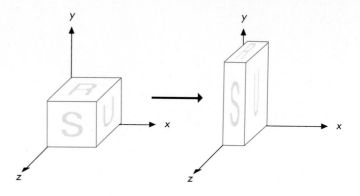

where $\mathbf{S}(\alpha, \beta, \gamma)$ is the matrix

$$\mathbf{S}(\alpha, \beta, \gamma) = \begin{bmatrix} \alpha & 0 & 0 & 0 \\ 0 & \beta & 0 & 0 \\ 0 & 0 & \gamma & 0 \\ 0 & 0 & 0 & 1 \end{bmatrix}.$$

An object can be sheared in six independent ways. Shearing along the x axis is shown in Figure 8.13. It leaves the y and z values unchanged. The amount of shear depends on two independent parameters. The equations are

$$\begin{aligned} x' &= x + y \cot \theta + z \cot \phi, \\ y' &= y, \\ z' &= z. \end{aligned}$$

Figure 8.13
x Direction Shear

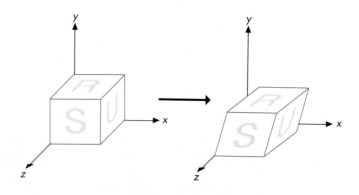

In homogeneous coordinates,

$$\mathbf{p}' = \mathbf{H_x}(\theta)\mathbf{p},$$

where $\mathbf{H}_x(\theta, \phi)$ is the matrix

$$\mathbf{H}_x(\theta, \phi) = \begin{bmatrix} 1 & \cot\theta & \cot\phi & 0 \\ 0 & 1 & 0 & 0 \\ 0 & 0 & 1 & 0 \\ 0 & 0 & 0 & 1 \end{bmatrix}.$$

Matrices $\mathbf{H}_y$ and $\mathbf{H}_z$, for y and z shear, follow in a similar manner. Note that each of these matrices can be decomposed into two simpler matrices. For example,

$$\begin{aligned} \mathbf{H}_x(\theta, \phi) &= \mathbf{H}_x(\theta, 0)\mathbf{H}_x(0, \phi) \\ &= \mathbf{H}_{xy}(\theta)\mathbf{H}_{xz}(\phi) \end{aligned}$$

These matrices show the two independent components of the x direction shear.

8.3.4 Rotation

In three dimensions, there are independent rotations about all three axes. Consider a rotation about the z axis, as shown in Figure 8.14. Once again, our definition of the operation of rotation is rotation about the origin of our coordinate system. From the figure, we can notice that, when we rotate a point about the z axis, its z value is unchanged. This observation allows us to reduce the problem to a

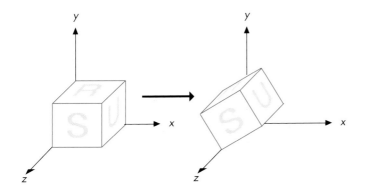

Figure 8.14
Rotation about the z Axis

two-dimensional x, y rotation in a fixed z plane. These equations are the ones we developed in Chapter 5:

$$\begin{aligned} x' &= x\cos\theta - y\sin\theta, \\ y' &= x\sin\theta + y\cos\theta. \end{aligned}$$

When we couple these equations with the equations

$$\begin{aligned} z' &= z, \\ w' &= w, \end{aligned}$$

we can express rotation about the x axis in matrix-vector form as

$$\mathbf{p}' = \mathbf{R}_z(\theta)\mathbf{p},$$

where $\mathbf{R}_z(\theta)$ is the matrix

$$\mathbf{R}_z(\theta) = \begin{bmatrix} \cos\theta & -\sin\theta & 0 & 0 \\ \sin\theta & \cos\theta & 0 & 0 \\ 0 & 0 & 1 & 0 \\ 0 & 0 & 0 & 1 \end{bmatrix}.$$

Rotations about the x and y axes are shown in Figure 8.15. Rotation about the x axis leaves x values unchanged; likewise, rotation about the y axis leaves y values unchanged. Thus, the homogeneous coordinate matrix representations $\mathbf{R}_x$ and $\mathbf{R}_y$ can be derived as for rotation about the z axis. These matrices are

$$\mathbf{R}_x(\theta) = \begin{bmatrix} 1 & 0 & 0 & 0 \\ 0 & \cos\theta & -\sin\theta & 0 \\ 0 & \sin\theta & \cos\theta & 0 \\ 0 & 0 & 0 & 1 \end{bmatrix},$$

$$\mathbf{R}_y(\theta) = \begin{bmatrix} \cos\theta & 0 & \sin\theta & 0 \\ 0 & 1 & 0 & 0 \\ -\sin\theta & 0 & \cos\theta & 0 \\ 0 & 0 & 0 & 1 \end{bmatrix}.$$

We can obtain the inverses of these matrices either by carrying out the inversion or, as we did in Chapter 5, by recognizing what the inverses must be by what each matrix does. The inverses are

$$\mathbf{T}^{-1}(\Delta x, \Delta y, \Delta z) = \mathbf{T}(-\Delta x, -\Delta y, -\Delta z),$$

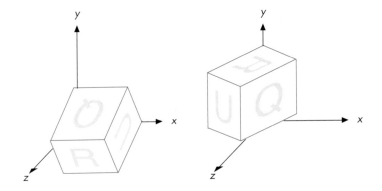

Figure 8.15
Rotations about the x and y
Axes

$$\mathbf{S}^{-1}(\alpha, \beta, \gamma) = \mathbf{S}(\frac{1}{\alpha}, \frac{1}{\beta}, \frac{1}{\gamma}),$$
$$\mathbf{H}_x^{-1}(\theta, \phi) = \mathbf{H}_x(-\theta, -\phi),$$
$$\mathbf{R}_x^{-1}(0) = \mathbf{R}_x(-\theta) = \mathbf{R}_x^T(\theta).$$

8.3.5 A Three-Dimensional Transformation Package

We can build up a three-dimensional transformation package analogous to our two-dimensional package. Our package will use 4 by 4 matrices. We will use the data type

```
typedef Gfloat[4][4] Matrix_3;
```

much as we used `Matrix` in Chapter 5. A translation matrix m can be formed through a procedure such as

```
ev_trans_3(dx,dy,dz,m)
float dx, dy, dz;
Matrix_3 m;
```

We will also want to alter an existing matrix by an accumulation procedure,

```
ac_trans_3(dx,dy,dz,m)
float dx, dy, dz;
Matrix_3 m;
```

In this way, we add our rotation, scaling, and shear transformations:

```
ev_scale(alpha,beta,gamma,m)
ac_scale(alpha,beta,gamma,m)
```

8.3 Transformations   311

```
ev_shear_3x(theta,phi,m)
ac_shear_3x(theta,phi,m)
ev_shear_3y(theta,phi,m)
ac_shear_3y(theta,phi,m)
ev_shear_3z(theta,phi,m)
ac_shear_3z(theta,phi,m)
ev_rot_3x(theta,m)
ac_rot_3x(theta,m)
ev_rot_3y(theta,m)
ac_rot_3y(theta,m)
ev_rot_3z(theta,m)
ac_rot_3z(theta,m)
```

Of course, as in two dimensions, we also want to concatenate two transformations and to be able to apply a given transformation to some x, y, z points. Analogous to the procedures in Chapter 5, we define

```
ac_matrix_3(m1,m2,m3)
transform_point_3(m,old_point,new_point)
```

Applying these procedures to a given problem will be a bit more difficult than it was in Chapter 5. The principal problem will be in defining a general rotation. We shall examine this problem within the context of instancing in the next section.

8.4
An Example

The tools we developed in Chapter 5, such as the instance transformation and hierarchical models, can be used in three dimensions; as we shall see, however, they require more work. We shall follow through one example. Consider the right parallelepiped in Figure 8.16. It is located with its center at a point (x_0, y_0, z_0) and has sides of lengths A, B, and C. It has an orientation in space that we shall describe. We can view this object as the result of manipulating a prototype, such as a cube, with our transformations to get the desired object in the specified position and orientation. In this case, we are constructing a three-dimensional instance transformation that we will use on a three-dimensional symbol: a unit cube.

8.4.1 Instancing a Cube

We start with the unit cube in Figure 8.17, which is centered at the origin. If we scale it by A, B, and C units along its axes, it will have

Figure 8.16
A Right Parallelepiped

y

A

B

C

(x_0, y_0, z_0)

x

z

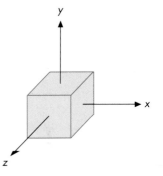

Figure 8.17
The Unit Cube

y

x

z

the dimensions of our parallelepiped. We can also translate it to be centered at (x_0, y_0, z_0). In fact, if we add shearing, we can convert the cube to an arbitrary, rather than right, parallelepiped. We now have two parts of an instance (scale-rotate-translate) transformation,

$$\mathbf{I} = \mathbf{TRS},$$

that we can use to instance parallelepipeds.

The rotation matrix will govern the orientation of the resulting parallelepiped. It will be applied to the scaled cube before we translate it to have its center at (x_0, y_0, z_0). We will construct the desired rotation matrix $\mathbf{R}$ out of independent rotations about the x, y, and z axes; that is,

$$\mathbf{R} = \mathbf{R}_x\mathbf{R}_y\mathbf{R}_z.$$

Remember that, since matrices do not commute, we must be careful about this order. In fact, there will be alternate orders for computing $\mathbf{R}$ (see Exercise 8.7), and the amount of rotation about each axis will vary depending on the order. In the end, however, we will arrive at the same matrix $\mathbf{R}$, so we can pick any order that works.

To understand this particular order, we consider a vector from the origin to a point on the z axis and what happens to it as we apply the three rotations in Figure 8.18. The first, $\mathbf{R}_z$, is a twist about the z axis; it leaves this vector unmoved but rotates the pointer (the letter "A") on its tip. The rotation about the y axis keeps this vector in the plane $y = 0$. Then, the rotation about the x axis raises the vector to its final position. With a little thought, you should be able

Figure 8.18
The Three Rotations

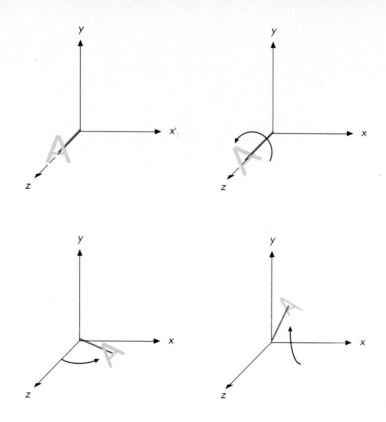

to convince yourself that any orientation of the vector can be obtained in this way.

Next, we will find the individual rotation matrices. They will be a bit easier to determine if we solve the problem backward. We start with a unit vector from origin in an arbitrary orientation with an associated twist. We can put this vector into the x, z plane by a rotation about the x axis, determining a matrix $\mathbf{R}'_x$. We can then rotate it about the y axis to align it with the z axis, determining $\mathbf{R}'_y$. Finally, we can undo the twist, determining $\mathbf{R}'_z$, leaving us with the vector we started with at the top of Figure 8.18. This combined matrix

$$\mathbf{R}' = \mathbf{R}'_z \mathbf{R}'_y \mathbf{R}'_x$$

is the inverse of the matrix we set out to find. Hence,

$$\mathbf{R} = \mathbf{R}'^{-1} = \mathbf{R}'^{-1}_x \mathbf{R}'^{-1}_y \mathbf{R}'^{-1}_z = \mathbf{R}_x \mathbf{R}_y \mathbf{R}_y,$$

314   Chapter 8   Three-Dimensional Graphics

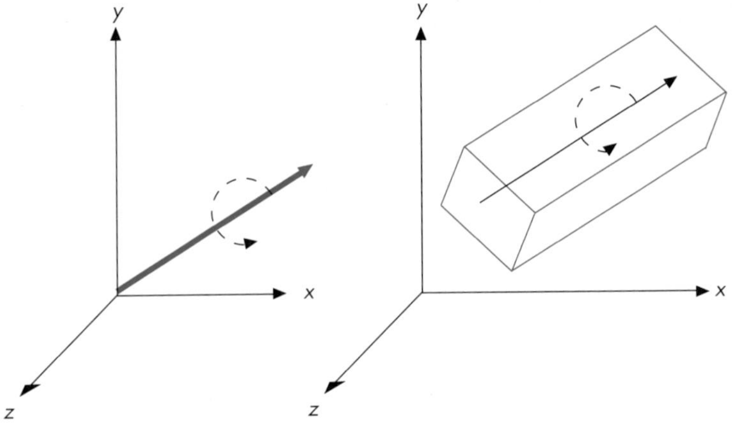

Figure 8.19
Specifying an Orientation

an expression that is even simpler when we use the fact that, for any of the individual rotation matrices, the inverses are given simply; for example,

$$\mathbf{R}_x^{-1}(\theta) = \mathbf{R}_x(-\theta) = \mathbf{R}_x^T(\theta).$$

8.4.2 Direction Cosines

Unfortunately, we are rarely given the individual angles of rotation to compute our rotation matrices, as this information is not the most natural way for most applications to specify an orientation. More commonly, we are given the *direction cosines*, which we use to find the individual angles of rotation. We will take this approach. Exercises 8.10 and 8.11 suggest alternatives.

Returning to Figure 8.16, we can describe the orientation of the parallelepiped by specifying an orientation vector $\mathbf{v}$ and a rotation or twist of θ degrees about this axis, as in Figure 8.19. Since our orientation vector specifies only a direction, we can let it be a unit vector,

$$\mathbf{v} = \begin{bmatrix} a \\ b \\ c \end{bmatrix},$$

$$a^2 + b^2 + c^2 = 1.$$

Note that the vector $\mathbf{v}$ and each of the axes form a plane. Let α, β, and γ denote the angles $\mathbf{v}$ makes with the x, y, and z axes, respectively.

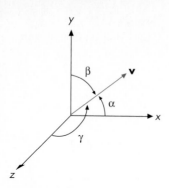

Figure 8.20
Direction Angles

These are the *direction angles* shown in Figure 8.20. Since **v** is a unit vector, it is easy to verify that

$$\cos \alpha = a,$$
$$\cos \beta = b,$$
$$\cos \gamma = c,$$

giving a, b, and c the name *direction cosines*. Note that, since their squares sum to one, only two direction cosines are necessary to specify the orientation vector. The rotation by θ about this vector gives us the third parameter we will use to determine **R**.

Suppose we are given, or can compute, θ and the direction cosines. We will find $\mathbf{R}'_x$, $\mathbf{R}'_y$, and $\mathbf{R}'_z$ by concatenating a matrix that will align the vector **v** with the z axis, with one that rotates by θ about the z axis. The rotation by θ determines $\mathbf{R}'_z$:

$$\mathbf{R}'_z(\theta) = \begin{bmatrix} \cos\theta & -\sin\theta & 0 & 0 \\ \sin\theta & \cos\theta & 0 & 0 \\ 0 & 0 & 1 & 0 \\ 0 & 0 & 0 & 1 \end{bmatrix}.$$

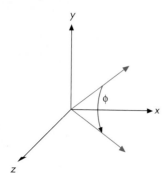

Figure 8.21
Determining $\mathbf{R}'_x$

As we saw, the alignment problem has two parts: a rotation of **v** so that it lies in the x, z plane that determines $\mathbf{R}'_x$, as in Figure 8.21 and a rotation about the y axis, as in Figure 8.22, which aligns **v** with the z axis. Since we are doing the inverse of the problem that we really want to solve, we will use the inverses of these matrices to determine $\mathbf{R}_x$, $\mathbf{R}_y$, and $\mathbf{R}_z$.

The desired angle of rotation about the x axis, ϕ, can be determined from Figure 8.23. We can find this angle of rotation by using the projection of **v** onto the y, z plane forming the vector **w**. This step preserves the angle ϕ. We can envision the projection operation by shining a parallel beam of light on **v**; the vector **w** is the shadow of **v** on the y, z plane. We now have the sine and cosine of ϕ,

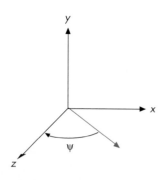

Figure 8.22
Determining $\mathbf{R}'_y$

$$\cos \phi = \frac{b}{\sqrt{b^2 + c^2}},$$

$$\sin \phi = \frac{c}{\sqrt{b^2 + c^2}},$$

which yield

$$\mathbf{R}'_x(\phi) = \begin{bmatrix} 1 & 0 & 0 & 0 \\ 0 & \cos\phi & -\sin\phi & 0 \\ 0 & \sin\phi & \cos\phi & 0 \\ 0 & 0 & 0 & 1 \end{bmatrix}.$$

The rotation ψ about the y axis can be determined from Figure 8.24:

$$\begin{aligned} \cos\psi &= \sqrt{b^2 + c^2}, \\ \sin\psi &= a, \end{aligned}$$

and thus

$$\mathbf{R}'_y(\psi) = \begin{bmatrix} \cos\psi & 0 & -\sin\psi & 0 \\ 0 & 1 & 0 & 0 \\ \sin\psi & 0 & \cos\psi & 0 \\ 0 & 0 & 0 & 1 \end{bmatrix}.$$

Remembering to use the negatives of these angles, we obtain the composite rotation matrix,

$$\mathbf{R} = \mathbf{R}'_z(-\phi)\mathbf{R}'_y(-\psi)\mathbf{R}'_x(-\theta).$$

This example has a couple of important interpretations and extensions. We can use a similar process to describe the general rotation of an object about an axis, as shown in Figure 8.25. Without deter-

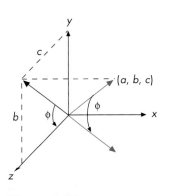

Figure 8.23
Determining ϕ

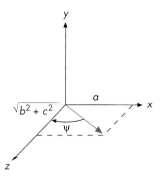

Figure 8.24
Determining ψ

Figure 8.25
General Rotation

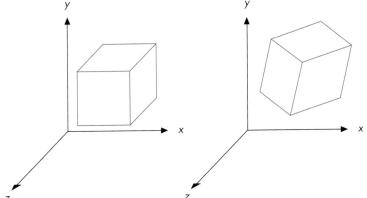

mining the individual matrices, we can argue that this problem can be shifted to the origin by a translation, the desired axis of rotation aligned with any axis by the procedure we have used, and the desired rotation carried out about this new axis. Now, however, the rotations to align the axes and the translation must be undone. In this way, we can compose a general rotation matrix through seven simpler matrices:

$$\mathbf{R} = \mathbf{T}^{-1}\mathbf{R}_x^{-1}\mathbf{R}_y^{-1}\mathbf{R}_z\mathbf{R}_y\mathbf{R}_x\mathbf{T}.$$

We can also note from this example that the instance transformation is equivalent to a change of variables between two orthogonal coordinate systems. An object starts in its own coordinate system and is instanced into the WC system. Later, we shall use just such a sequence as part of the implementation of the viewing transformation. This observation allows us to use a simple coordinate system, knowing that we can change coordinate systems as necessary, following the sequence we just developed.

8.5
Projections and Normalization

We start our discussion of projections by returning to a picture from Chapter 2, which we repeat in Figure 8.26. We see that there are three entities of interest: one or more objects, a projection plane, and projectors. A two-dimensional image of our three-dimensional objects is formed on the projection plane by the viewing process. This im-

Figure 8.26
Projection

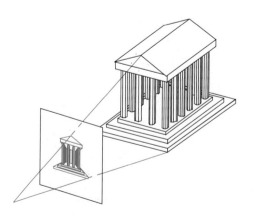

age is what we see on our display. The viewing process uses lines called *projectors*. For each point on the object, there is a projector that passes through it. Where this projector intersects the projection plane is the location of the image of this object point. The relationships between the projection plane, projectors, and objects determine the image and the particular type of view—for example, perspective, isometric, or oblique. These relationships will be discussed in the next section. In this section, we consider three-dimensional viewing from the perspective of the application program.

Since we expect the graphics system to do all the necessary calculations to produce the image, the task of the application programmer is to describe the required entities to construct an image by invoking the necessary functions from within his program. We accomplished the first part of the task by extending our two-dimensional objects to three dimensions. The description of projectors and of the projection plane are part of the three-dimensional viewing process.

We shall take the pipeline approach to viewing used in GKS-3D (the three-dimensional extension of GKS [GKS86]) and other systems such as PHIGS. Viewing consists of a number of successive transformations and clipping operations (Figure 8.27) that are performed on primitives. Each transformation corresponds to a change of coordinate systems so, just as with two-dimensional viewing, we start with a primitive in WC and wind up with the primitive, properly clipped, in DC.

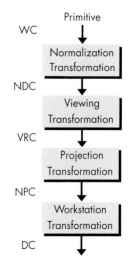

Figure 8.27
Coordinate Transformation Pipeline

8.5.1 The Normalization Transformation

The first step in the viewing pipeline is to convert from WC to NDC through a normalization transformation. As in two-dimensional GKS, we allow multiple normalization transformations and use the procedure `gsel_norm_tran` to choose which one to employ. When we go to three dimensions, we have the opportunity to specify a three-dimensional window in WC through this procedure:

```
void gset_win_3(tran_num,window3)

Gint tran_num;
Glim_3 *window3;

typedef struct
{
  Gfloat xmin;
  Gfloat xmax;
  Gfloat ymin;
  Gfloat ymax;
```

```
        Gfloat zmin;
        Gfloat zmax;
    } Glim_3;
```

Here, we specify the normalization-transformation index and a structure Glim_3, which consists of the minimum and maximums in the x, y, and z variables, which yields a right clipping parallelepiped in WC.

The NDC region is an extension of the unit square in two dimensions to a unit cube in three dimensions. The three-dimensional viewport function

```
    void gset_vp_3(tran_num,viewport)

    Gint tran_num;
    Glim_3 *viewport;
```

specifies a right parallelepiped within the unit cube. The normalization transformation is shown in Figure 8.28. As in two dimensions, objects are (optionally) clipped to the WC window and transformed to NDC space in the corresponding viewport. The normalization transformation precedes projection, as its fundamental job is to allow the user to collect objects that may have been specified in many different WC systems into a single space using NDC space.

PHIGS takes an approach slightly different from that of GKS-3D. In GKS and GKS-3D, models are built in WC, then are mapped to NDC. In PHIGS, there is no NDC space. Models are built in *modeling*

Figure 8.28
The Normalization
Transformation

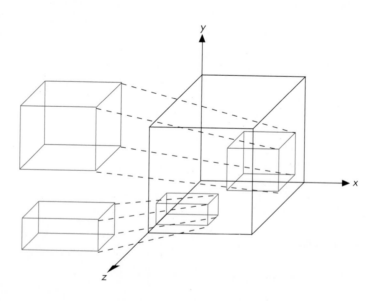

coordinates and mapped to WC. At this point, both systems move on to viewing coordinates.

8.5.2 Specifying a Projection Plane

We can now turn to the viewing operation. Our first step will be to find a way to describe the projection plane. The specification of its position involves the use of the equations of the plane. We can assume that the plane is specified in NDC space, although this choice is not crucial to the viewing process.

Consider again the equation of the plane

$$ax + by + cz + d = 0.$$

We know that the triplet (a, b, c) determines a vector $\mathbf{n}$ normal to the plane. The orientation of the plane is fixed by the view-plane normal, and the procedure

```
void gset_view_plane_normal(normal)

Gpt_3 normal;
```

can be one of our viewing procedures. We know that all the planes with the same normal are parallel, and the parameter d determines the distance from the origin to the plane. However, the value of d is not necessarily a parameter that is natural to specify in a user problem since it involves the calculation of a distance. An alternative is to be given any point on the plane, since, given that point and the normal, the graphics system can solve for d. This point is called the *view reference point* and can be set by a procedure,

```
void set_view_reference_point(point)

Gpt_3 point;
```

8.5.3 Viewing Coordinates

Although we have specified a projection plane, only part of it can be displayed on an output device. We must therefore specify a window in the projection plane, as pictured in Figure 8.29. This figure illustrates why we might want to introduce another coordinate system. The projection plane can be oriented in an arbitrary fashion with respect to the NDC system. If we work in NDC, it is a nasty but necessary trigonometric problem to specify this rectangular window in the plane. Suppose we reorient the picture in Figure 8.29 by viewing

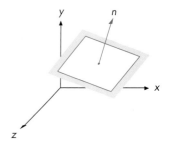

Figure 8.29
Windowing

Figure 8.30
Reorienting

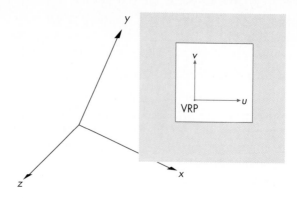

the plane from along the view-plane normal, as in Figure 8.30. The window now seems easy to describe, as it appears to be in a simple two-dimensional plane. This observation strongly suggests that we consider a coordinate system specified in terms of the orientation of the view plane.

Remembering that the projection plane is the view plane and that we will see what is projected onto this plane as our image, we now describe a coordinate system in this plane, called the *viewing reference coordinate system* (VRC). The view reference point is the origin of this coordinate system. The view-plane normal determines one of the three principal directions (n). The other two directions, u and v, lie in the view plane, thus making them normal to n. The v or *up* direction is specified by the procedure

```
void gset_view_up(up)

Gpt_3 up;
```

This vector is specified in NDC and thus may not lie in the plane. Since it may be difficult for the user to specify a vector in the plane, we get the up direction by letting the system project the view up vector onto the plane, which gives the second (v) direction. We pick the u direction by rotating -90 degrees from v. These relationships are shown in Figure 8.31. We now have two different coordinates systems in our figure, the x, y, z system of NDC and the new u, v, n system. Objects in NDC are transformed into objects in this new system. In other words, there is a matrix $\mathbf{V}$, called the *view orientation matrix*, which corresponds to this transformation. This transformation is affine; we can construct it from our specifications by concatenating a sequence of rotations and translations. GKS-3D provides a utility function, `evaluate_view_orientation_matrix_3`, for this purpose.

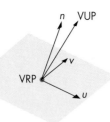

Figure 8.31
Specifying Viewing
Reference Coordinates

This procedure will also check that the specifications are valid. For example, a view up vector that is parallel to the view-plane normal has a projection of zero length and will be detected as an error. We shall derive this matrix in Section 8.7.

8.5.4 Projection

We can now address the problem of projection in the convenient u, v, n coordinate system. We assume that our viewer is located at a point called the *projection reference point* (PRP). In Figure 8.32, we see our view plane, points on an object, and projectors. All coordinate values are in the u, v, n system.

This type of projection, where all projectors emanate from a common point called the *center of projection*, is known as a *perspective projection*. It is the type of projection that is present in most physical image-formation processes, such as the one used by the eye or the camera. If we let the projection reference point move to infinity, the projectors become parallel to one another and define a *direction of projection*. This type of projection is naturally called a *parallel projection* and has properties that are important in many applications. These will be discussed in the next section.

One difficulty in implementing three-dimensional viewing in a graphics system is that, although the parallel projection is mathematically the limiting case of perspective projection, we can more easily carry out its specification and implementation by treating it

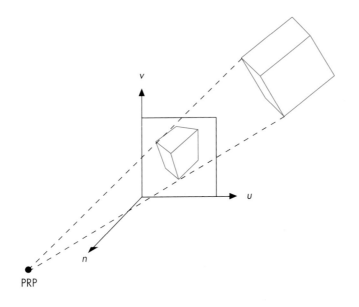

Figure 8.32
Perspective Projection

Figure 8.33
Parallel Projection

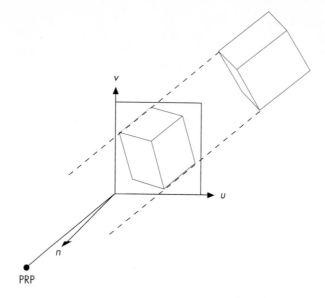

separately, rather than by attempting to take limits in the hardware or software. For parallel viewing, we will use Figure 8.33. The direction of projection is characterized by a vector from the view reference point, the origin in the u, v, n system, to the projection reference point.

8.5.5 Clipping

The necessary information to carry out a projection is contained in the projection reference point and a flag that indicates which type of projection is desired. Additional capabilities can be useful. In particular, we often want to clip against a volume in u, v, n space. All objects within this volume will appear on workstations (if they are also in the workstation window). The volumes will be somewhat different for parallel and perspective projections, so we shall consider the two cases separately, starting with the parallel clipping volume.

We specify a rectangular window in the projection plane by two points in u, v coordinates: (u_{min}, v_{min}) and (u_{max}, v_{max}). We may also want to specify front and back clipping planes, often called the *hither* and *yon* planes, which are parallel to the projection plane and are specified by their distances from the origin measured along the view-plane normal in Figure 8.34. We can now determine a clipping volume by drawing four lines through the corners of the window in the direction of projection. These lines intersect the front and back clipping planes, determining a clipping parallelepiped. Note that this need not be a right parallelepiped since the sides are parallel to the direction of projection, not the view plane normal.

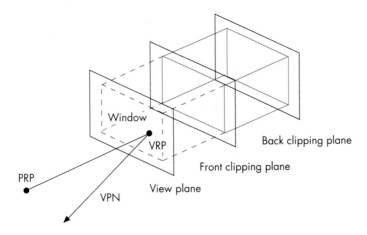

Figure 8.34
Parallel Clipping Volume

For perspective projections, we proceed in a similar manner. The window in the projection plane and front and back clipping planes are specified as in Figure 8.35. The volume is determined by lines or projectors from the center of projection, the projection reference point, through the corners of the window. The resulting volume is a truncated pyramid, or *frucstrum*.

From the application programmer's point of view, the clipping limits, perhaps a flag to allow clipping to be disabled, and the type of projection desired can be combined with our previous viewing procedures to determine a projected and clipped image. These parameters are specified to the system through the *set view mapping* procedure.

We still require a final specification: a workstation transformation that allows us to send selected parts of our projections to specific areas

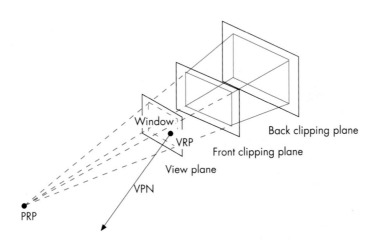

Figure 8.35
Perspective Clipping Volume

8.5 Projections and Normalization   **325**

on individual workstations. This specification is a direct extension of what we did in two dimensions. The workstation transformation is also three-dimensional and can be set by the functions

```
void gset_ws_win_3(ws_id, window);
void gset_ws_vp_3(ws_id, viewport);

Gint ws_id;
Glim_3 *window;
Glim_3 *viewport;
```

These procedures allow the possibility that many of the required operations to implement three-dimensional viewing can be carried out by the individual workstations.

These issues will be clearer after we develop the mathematics of parallel and perspective projections as part of the implementation in Section 8.7. At this point, we should be able to specify a unique three-dimensional view within a three-dimensional graphics system, and to write three-dimensional application programs.

▰ 8.6
▰ Classical and Computer Graphics

Many of the jobs that were formerly done by hand drawing, such as architectural rendering, drafting, and mechanical-parts design, are now done routinely with the aid of computer graphics. At this point, it might help us to examine the relationships between the classical and computer approaches to producing images of a three-dimensional world.

The basic elements in both cases are the same. We have objects and a viewer. Both classical and computer graphics allow the viewer to be an infinite distance from the objects and include both parallel and perspective viewing. Most physical systems have approximately planar view surfaces and their projectors are lines. Thus, what is done in physical terms by a viewing system such as a camera or the human visual system is accomplished mathematically within our three-dimensional computer graphics system.

8.6.1 Classical Viewing

Looking back at our three-dimensional viewing procedures, we see that there are only two fundamental types of viewing: parallel and perspective. On the other hand, classical graphics appears to have a host of different views, ranging from multiview orthographic projections to one-, two-, and three-point perspectives. This seeming discrepancy arises in classical graphics due to the desire to show a specific relationship among an object, the viewer, and the projection plane, as opposed to the computer-graphics approach of complete independence of all specifications.

For example, when we draw an image of a building, we know which side we wish to display and thus where we should place the viewer in relationship to the building. Each classical view is determined by one such relationship; in computer graphics we usually have no coupling between the parameters to the functions that determine such a view.

In classical viewing, there is the underlying notion of a principal face. The types of objects viewed in real-world applications, such as architecture, tend to be composed of a number of planar faces, each of which can be thought of as a principal face. For a rectangular object, such as a building, there is natural notion of the front, back, top, bottom, right, and left faces. In addition, since in many real-world objects the faces meet at right angles, such objects often have three orthogonal directions associated with them.

Figure 8.36 shows the main types of views. We shall start with the most restrictive view for each of the parallel and perspective types, and shall move to the less restrictive conditions.

8.6.2 Orthographic Projections

Our first classical view is the *orthographic projection* shown in Figure 8.37. In all orthographic (or orthogonal) views, the projectors are perpendicular to the projection plane. In a *multiview orthographic projection*, the projection plane is parallel to one of the principal faces of the object. Usually, we display at least three views—such as the front, top, and right—to display the object. The reason that we produce multiple views should be clear from Figure 8.38. For a boxlike object, only the faces parallel to the projection plane appears in the image. A viewer usually needs more than two views to visualize what an object looks like from its multiview orthographic projections. Visualization from these images can take some skill on the part of the viewer. The importance of this type of view is that it preserves both distances and angles. Since there is no distortion of either distance or shape, multiview orthographic projections are well suited for working drawings.

8.6.3 Axonometric Projections

If we want to see more principal faces of our boxlike object in a single view, we must remove one of our restrictions. In *axonometric*

Figure 8.36
Classical Views

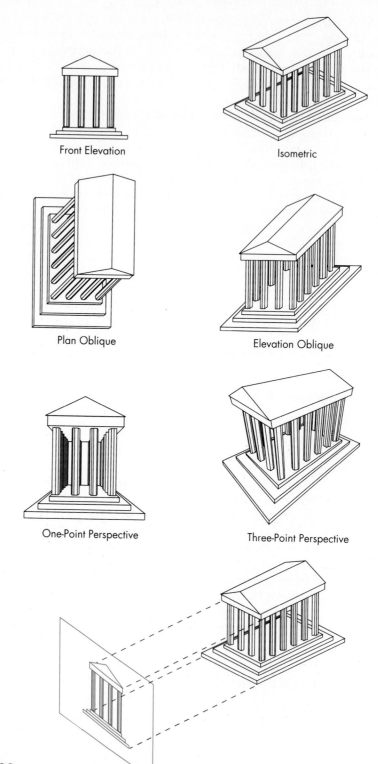

Front Elevation

Isometric

Plan Oblique

Elevation Oblique

One-Point Perspective

Three-Point Perspective

Figure 8.37
Orthographic Projection

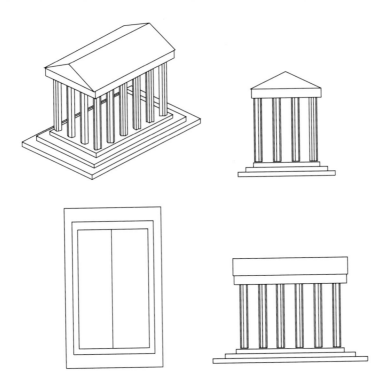

views, the projectors are still orthogonal to the projection plane, as in Figure 8.39, but the projection plane can have any orientation with respect to the object. If the projection plane is placed symmetrically with respect to the three principal faces that meet at a corner of our rectangular object, we have an *isometric* view. If the projection plane is placed symmetrically with respect to two of the principal faces, the view is *dimetric*. The general case is a *trimetric* view. These views are shown in Figure 8.40. Note that, in an isometric view, the foreshortening of distances in the three principal directions is the same, which allows us to make some distance measurements. In the dimetric view, however, there are two different foreshortening ratios; in the trimetric view, there are three. We can also see that, although lines are preserved in the image, which allows us to consider projections as a type of affine transformation, angles are not. A circle will be projected into an ellipse. This distortion is the price we pay for the ability to see more principal faces in a view that can be produced fairly easily either by hand or by computer. Axonometric views are used extensively in architecture and mechanical design.

8.6   Classical and Computer Graphics   329

Figure 8.39
Constructing an
Axonometric Projection

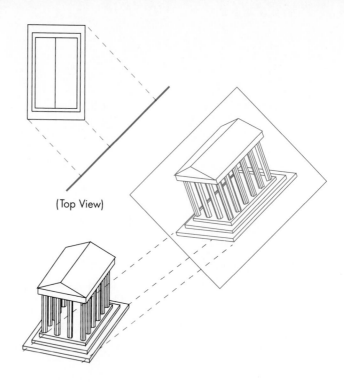

(Top View)

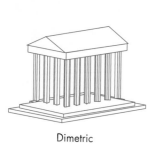

Dimetric

Trimetric

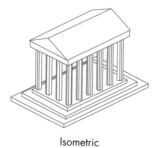

Isometric

Figure 8.40
Axonometric Projections

8.6.4 Oblique Projections

The *oblique* views are the most general parallel views. We allow the projectors to make an arbitrary angle with the projection plane, as shown in Figure 8.41. In an oblique projection, angles in planes parallel to the projection plane are preserved. A circle in a plane parallel to the projection plane will be projected into a circle and, we will still be able to see more than one principal face of the object. Oblique views are the most difficult to construct by hand. They are also somewhat unnatural, as most physical viewing devices produce perspective views, which, if the viewer is far from the object, are approximately orthogonal.

As we have already noted, there is no real difference, from the application programmer's point of view, between the different parallel views. The problem for the application programmer is how to specify the parameters in the viewing procedures so as best to view an object or to produce a specific classical view.

8.6.5 Perspective Viewing

All perspective views are characterized by dimuition of size. When objects are moved farther from the viewer, their images become smaller.

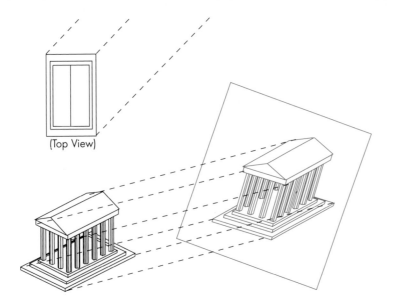

Figure 8.41
Constructing an Oblique
View

(Top View)

This size change gives perspective views their natural appearance but, since the amount by which a line is foreshortened depends on how far the line is from the viewer, we cannot make measurements from a perspective view. Hence, the major use of perspective views is in applications such as architecture and animation, where it is important to achieve real-looking images.

In the classical perspective views, the viewer is located symmetrically with respect to the projection plane, as shown in Figure 8.42. Thus, the pyramid determined by the window in the projection plane and the center of projection is a symmetric or right pyramid. This symmetry is caused by the fixed relationship between the back of the

Figure 8.42
Perspective Viewing

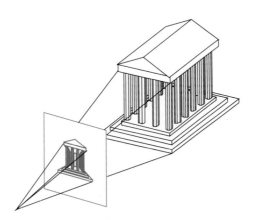

8.6 Classical and Computer Graphics   331

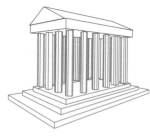

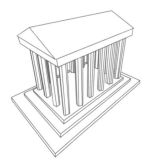

Figure 8.43
One, Two, and Three Point
Perspective Views

eye and its lens for human viewing, the back of a camera and its lens for standard cameras, and similar fixed relationships in most physical situations. Some cameras have movable film backs and can produce general perspective views. The model used in computer graphics includes this general case.

The classical perspective views are usually known as one-, two-, and three-point perspectives. The difference among the three cases is based on how many of the three principal directions in the object are parallel to the projection plane. Consider the three perspective projections of the building in Figure 8.43. Any corner of the building includes the three principal directions. In the most general case, the three-point perspective, parallel lines in all three principal directions converge at three *vanishing points*. If we allow one of the principal directions to become parallel to the projection plane, we have a two-point projection, in which lines in only two of the principal directions converge. Finally, in the one-point perspective, two of the principal directions are parallel to the projection plane, and we have only a single vanishing point. It should be apparent that, just as with parallel viewing, from the programmer's point of view, the three situations are merely special cases of general perspective viewing, which we shall implement in the next section.

8.7 Implementation

In this final section, we shall look at some of the issues involved in implementing three-dimensional graphics. If we follow a primitive as defined by a user program, it must go through the same operations that a two-dimensional primitive encountered in Chapter 6. There may be a number of transformations as part of the modeling process. There will be a normalization transformation, a viewing transformation, and a workstation transformation. Clipping must be done one or more times. Since our view surface is two-dimensional, there will be a projection of our three-dimensional primitive onto this surface. Finally the primitive must be displayed by the hardware. This pipeline is pictured in Figure 8.44.

Operations such as the final display of the primitives are exactly the same in both two- and three-dimensional graphics, since, once we have carried out the projection operation, we are working with two-dimensional primitives in both cases. We have already seen that transformations for three-dimensional graphics are similar to those for two-dimensional graphics, and we have introduced four-dimensional homogeneous coordinates to deal with these transformations. There are two operations that require a detailed look: clipping and viewing (including projection). Clipping must be extended to three dimensions, and projection is a new operation.

8.7.1 Orthogonal Viewing

We shall start by following the simplest view, an orthogonal projection, through the process. Since we have already examined three-dimensional modeling, we begin this discussion with the normalization process. Objects in a three-dimensional WC window are clipped and mapped to a viewport, as shown in Figure 8.45. Suppose our primitive is a line segment between (x_1, y_1, z_1) and (x_2, y_2, z_2). The world window is the right parallelepiped determined by

$$
\begin{aligned}
x_{min} &\leq x \leq x_{max}, \\
y_{min} &\leq y \leq y_{max}, \\
z_{min} &\leq z \leq z_{max}.
\end{aligned}
$$

Using the parametric form of our line segment,

$$
\begin{aligned}
x(\alpha) &= (1 - \alpha)x_1 + \alpha x_2, \\
y(\alpha) &= (1 - \alpha)y_1 + \alpha y_2, \\
z(\alpha) &= (1 - \alpha)z_1 + \alpha z_2,
\end{aligned}
$$

we can easily compute the intersection of the segment with any side of the clipping volume. For example, if $x = x_{min}$, we can use the value x_{min} in the equation for x to determine the corresponding α.

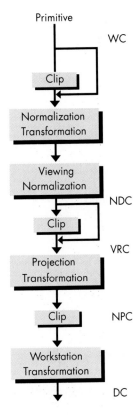

Figure 8.44
The Three-Dimensional Pipeline

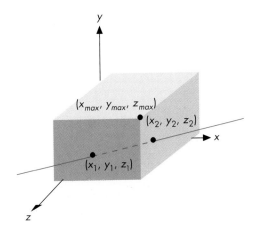

Figure 8.45
Clipping in Three Dimensions

Figure 8.46
Three-Dimensional
Outcodes

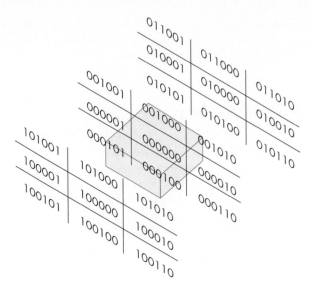

This α allows us to find the appropriate (y, z) using the parametric equations.

The methods used for clipping are direct extensions of the standard two-dimensional clippers, such as the Cohen–Sutherland algorithm. The sides of the clipping volume divide space into 27 regions, as in Figure 8.46. We can assign a 6-bit outcode to a point determined by the region in which the point lies; that is, by a procedure similar to the one we used in Chapter 6:

```
#define BACK 040
#define FRONT 020
#define ABOVE 010
#define BELOW 004
#define RIGHT 002
#define LEFT 001
#define INSIDE 000

int outcode(point)
Gpt_3 point;
{
    extern float xmin, xmax, ymin, ymax, zmin, zmax;
    int out;
    if(point.z>zmax) out=BACK;
        else if(point.z<zmin) out=FRONT;
            else out=INSIDE;
    if(point.y>ymax) out|=ABOVE;
        else if(point.y<ymin) out|=BELOW;
    if(point.x>xmax) out|=RIGHT;
```

```
        else if(point.x<xmin) out|=LEFT;
    return(out);
}
```

The procedures for deciding whether a segment is accepted or rejected are direct extensions of the procedures in Chapter 6 and are left to you to determine.

Clipping is also required after the normalization transformation, since we can specify another clipping volume in projection coordinates. A final clip to the workstation window is also necessary. For orthogonal projections, these procedures will be similar to the one we just discussed. We will have to make some adjustments for oblique and perspective viewing.

8.7.2 Computing the View-Orientation Transformation

After normalization, our objects are in NDC space. We next apply the viewing transformation to the u, v, n or viewing reference coordinates, then apply another clipping. The function of this coordinate change is to represent everything in a coordinate system in which viewing is simplified.

The *view-orientation transformation* is an affine transformation that converts a point represented in the x, y, z NDC system to one in the u, v, n system. With homogeneous coordinates, we can represent this transformation with a 4 by 4 matrix $\mathbf{V}$. The information to find $\mathbf{V}$ is specified by the parameters of the three procedures

```
set_view_plane_normal(n);
set_view_reference_point(r);
set_view_up(p);
```

As we see from Figure 8.47, in NDC space, $\mathbf{p}$ and $\mathbf{n}$ are vectors giving the directions

$$\mathbf{p} = \begin{bmatrix} p_x \\ p_y \\ p_z \end{bmatrix}, \quad \mathbf{n} = \begin{bmatrix} n_x \\ n_y \\ n_z \end{bmatrix},$$

and

$$\mathbf{r} = \begin{bmatrix} r_x \\ r_y \\ r_z \end{bmatrix}$$

is a point on the projection plane.

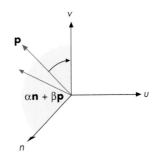

Figure 8.47
Shifting the Problem to the Origin

The 4 by 4 homogeneous coordinate matrix $\mathbf{V}$ can be composed of rotation, translation, and scaling matrices:

$$\mathbf{V} = \mathbf{TRS}.$$

Since the conversion from x, y, z to u, v, n will not change the size of any entity, the scaling matrix must be the identity matrix $\mathbf{I}$. The translation matrix makes the view reference point the origin of the u, v, n system, so it is given by

$$\mathbf{T} = \mathbf{T}(-r_x, -r_y, -r_z).$$

We will derive the rotation matrix $\mathbf{R}$ in two stages. First, we will use $\mathbf{n}$ and $\mathbf{p}$ to find $\mathbf{u}$ and $\mathbf{v}$. Then, we will use $\mathbf{u}$, $\mathbf{v}$, and $\mathbf{n}$ to form $\mathbf{R}$. It will be a bit easier to derive $\mathbf{R}$ if we work in the original three-dimensional space, rather than in homogeneous coordinates. The resulting 3 by 3 rotation matrix can be embedded in a 4 by 4 matrix at the end of the process.

The vector $\mathbf{v}$ is the projection of $\mathbf{p}$ onto the plane

$$n_x x + n_y y + n_z z = 0.$$

From Figure 8.47, we see that the projection $\mathbf{v}$ must lie in this plane. Thus, $\mathbf{v}$ is orthogonal to $\mathbf{n}$,

$$\mathbf{n} \cdot \mathbf{v} = 0.$$

In addition, $\mathbf{v}$ must also lie in the plane formed by $\mathbf{n}$ and $\mathbf{p}$. All vectors in this plane can be described by the two-parameter family of vectors

$$\mathbf{v} = \alpha \mathbf{n} + \beta \mathbf{p}.$$

For now, however, we are interested only in the direction of $\mathbf{v}$, and not in $\mathbf{v}$'s magnitude, so we can set β to one. Taking the dot product of this equation with $\mathbf{n}$, we find

$$\alpha = -\frac{\mathbf{p} \cdot \mathbf{n}}{\mathbf{n} \cdot \mathbf{n}},$$

and

$$\mathbf{v} = \mathbf{p} - \frac{\mathbf{p} \cdot \mathbf{n}}{\mathbf{n} \cdot \mathbf{n}} \mathbf{n}.$$

We obtain the vector **u** by noting that it must be orthogonal to both **p** and **n** and thus is given by their *cross-product*

$$\mathbf{u} = \mathbf{p} \times \mathbf{n} = \begin{bmatrix} p_y n_z - p_z n_y \\ p_z n_x - p_x n_z \\ p_x n_y - p_y n_z \end{bmatrix}.$$

We now have three orthogonal vectors but, since they do not have unit magnitude, there will be a scaling induced. We solve this problem by replacing these vectors with unit vectors in the same directions. Thus, for **n**,

$$\mathbf{n}' = \frac{\mathbf{n}}{|\mathbf{n}|},$$

where

$$|\mathbf{n}| = \sqrt{n_x^2 + n_y^2 + n_z^2}.$$

We find **u**' and **v**' in the same way. These three vectors form a *unit basis* for u, v, n.

We now have two orthogonal coordinate systems, x, y, z and u, v, n, where the unit basis vectors in u, v, n—**u**',**v**', and **n**'—have been expressed in terms of the unit basis vectors in the x, y, z system. What we really want is a way to express a point or vector in the original x, y, z system in the new u, v, n system. Suppose that we write the unit basis vectors in x, y, z as

$$\mathbf{e}_x = \begin{bmatrix} 1 \\ 0 \\ 0 \end{bmatrix},$$

$$\mathbf{e}_y = \begin{bmatrix} 0 \\ 1 \\ 0 \end{bmatrix},$$

$$\mathbf{e}_z = \begin{bmatrix} 0 \\ 0 \\ 1 \end{bmatrix}.$$

An arbitrary vector $\mathbf{q}$ can be expressed in the x, y, z system as

$$\mathbf{q} = \begin{bmatrix} q_x \\ q_y \\ q_z \end{bmatrix} = q_x \mathbf{e}_x + q_y \mathbf{e}_y + q_z \mathbf{e}_z,$$

and in u, v, n as

$$\mathbf{q} = s_u \mathbf{u}' + s_v \mathbf{v}' + s_n \mathbf{n}'.$$

We can obtain the necessary equations for converting between the two systems by expressing the unit basis vectors in x, y, z in terms of the basis vectors in u, v, n :

$$
\begin{aligned}
\mathbf{e}_x &= c_{xu}\mathbf{u}' + c_{xv}\mathbf{v}' + c_{xn}\mathbf{n}', \\
\mathbf{e}_y &= c_{yu}\mathbf{u}' + c_{yv}\mathbf{v}' + c_{yn}\mathbf{n}', \\
\mathbf{e}_z &= c_{zu}\mathbf{u}' + c_{zv}\mathbf{v}' + c_{zn}\mathbf{n}'.
\end{aligned}
$$

We must now find the coefficients in this equation. In matrix form, these relationships become

$$\begin{bmatrix} \mathbf{e}_x & \mathbf{e}_y & \mathbf{e}_z \end{bmatrix} = \begin{bmatrix} 1 & 0 & 0 \\ 0 & 1 & 0 \\ 0 & 0 & 1 \end{bmatrix} = \mathbf{I},$$

$$\mathbf{C} = \begin{bmatrix} c_{xu} & c_{xv} & c_{xn} \\ c_{yu} & c_{yv} & c_{yn} \\ c_{zu} & c_{zv} & c_{zn} \end{bmatrix},$$

$$\begin{bmatrix} \mathbf{u}' & \mathbf{v}' & \mathbf{n}' \end{bmatrix} = \begin{bmatrix} u_x & v_x & n_x \\ u_y & v_y & n_y \\ u_z & v_z & n_z \end{bmatrix} = \mathbf{U}.$$

Using these definitions in the above equations, we have

$$\mathbf{CU} = \mathbf{I},$$

which implies that

$$\mathbf{C} = \mathbf{U}^{-1} = \begin{bmatrix} \mathbf{u}' & \mathbf{v}' & \mathbf{n}' \end{bmatrix}^{-1}.$$

Since $\mathbf{U}$ must be a rotation matrix, its inverse is its transpose; hence,

$$\mathbf{C} = \mathbf{U}^T.$$

The matrix $\mathbf{C}$ allows us to rewrite any vector $\mathbf{q}$ expressed in the original x, y, z system in terms of the unit vectors of the u, v, n system; that is,

$$\mathbf{q} = s_u \mathbf{u}' + s_v \mathbf{v}' + s_n \mathbf{n}' = \mathbf{Us}.$$

Although we have derived a three-dimensional rotation matrix, we obtain the equivalent homogeneous coordinate matrix $\mathbf{R}$ by

$$\mathbf{R} = \begin{bmatrix} c_{xu} & c_{yu} & c_{zu} & 0 \\ c_{xv} & c_{yv} & c_{zv} & 0 \\ c_{xn} & c_{yn} & c_{zn} & 0 \\ 0 & 0 & 0 & 1 \end{bmatrix}$$

and the desired view-orientation matrix $\mathbf{V}$, which includes the original translation, by

$$\mathbf{V} = \mathbf{TR} = \begin{bmatrix} c_{xu} & c_{yu} & c_{zu} & -r_x \\ c_{xv} & c_{yv} & c_{zv} & -r_y \\ c_{xn} & c_{yn} & c_{zn} & -r_z \\ 0 & 0 & 0 & 1 \end{bmatrix}.$$

8.7.3 An Example

Let us consider a simple example of an isometric projection of a cube, as in Figure 8.48. We can take for a view-plane normal

$$\mathbf{n} = \begin{bmatrix} 1 \\ 1 \\ 1 \end{bmatrix}.$$

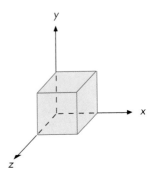

Figure 8.48
Isometric of Cube

The equal magnitudes of the three components ensure an isometric view of any right parallelepiped aligned with the x, y, z axes. We will take the view up to be the original y direction,

$$\mathbf{p} = \begin{bmatrix} 0 \\ 1 \\ 0 \end{bmatrix},$$

and let the view reference point be the x, y, z origin. Inserting these vectors into our formulae, we find

$$\mathbf{v} = \mathbf{p} - \frac{\mathbf{p} \cdot \mathbf{n}}{\mathbf{n} \cdot \mathbf{n}} \mathbf{n} = \begin{bmatrix} 1 \\ 0 \\ 0 \end{bmatrix} - \frac{1}{3} \begin{bmatrix} 1 \\ 1 \\ 1 \end{bmatrix} = \begin{bmatrix} 2/3 \\ -1/3 \\ -1/3 \end{bmatrix},$$

and

$$\mathbf{u} = \mathbf{p} \times \mathbf{n} = \begin{bmatrix} 0 \\ 1 \\ -1 \end{bmatrix}.$$

After normalization of the lengths, we have

$$\mathbf{u}' = \frac{1}{\sqrt{2}} \begin{bmatrix} 0 \\ 1 \\ 1 \end{bmatrix}, \quad \mathbf{v}' = \frac{1}{\sqrt{6}} \begin{bmatrix} 2 \\ -1 \\ -1 \end{bmatrix}, \quad \mathbf{n}' = \frac{1}{\sqrt{3}} \begin{bmatrix} 1 \\ 1 \\ 1 \end{bmatrix}.$$

Finally, we can put these entries into $\mathbf{V}$:

$$\mathbf{V} = \begin{bmatrix} 0 & \frac{1}{\sqrt{2}} & \frac{1}{\sqrt{2}} & 0 \\ \frac{2}{\sqrt{6}} & \frac{-1}{\sqrt{6}} & \frac{-1}{\sqrt{6}} & 0 \\ \frac{1}{\sqrt{3}} & \frac{1}{\sqrt{3}} & \frac{1}{\sqrt{3}} & 0 \\ 0 & 0 & 0 & 1 \end{bmatrix}.$$

For the unit cube in Figure 8.48, we see that it is easy to use $\mathbf{V}$ to obtain the u, v, n representation of any points on it. For example, the point on the principle diagonal, $(1, 1, 1)$ in x, y, z coordinates, maps to $(0, 0, \sqrt{3})$, and is at the same distance from the origin in both spaces and is along the normal direction.

8.7.4 Projection

In the u, v, n system,[1] the projection plane is the plane

$$z = 0.$$

Although it appears that the view-orientation transformation is adding an extra level of transformation and the additional floating-point operations to carry it out, this is not the case. The work is recovered by the simplicity of the projection, and we even save work as subsequent clipping steps are simplified.

[1] We will express points in view reference coordinates as (x, y, z) where x is the distance along the u axis, y along v and z along n.

We are now ready to do the projection. In this coordinate system, an orthogonal projection is simple, as we can see from Figure 8.49. In normalized projection coordinates, since the projection plane is the plane $n = 0$, the projectors, being orthogonal to this plane, are lines of constant u and v. If the operation of projection takes a point (x, y, z) and projects it into the point (x_p, y_p, z_p) in the projection plane, then, for our orthogonal projection,

$$x_p = x,$$
$$y_p = y,$$
$$z_p = 0.$$

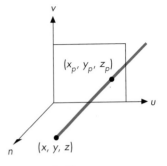

Figure 8.49
Orthogonal Projection

These equations can be expressed using homogeneous coordinates. If **p** is the homogeneous coordinate representation of (x, y, z) and **p'** is its projection, then

$$\mathbf{p'} = \mathbf{M}_o \mathbf{p},$$

where $\mathbf{M}_o$ is the *orthogonal projection matrix*

$$\mathbf{M}_o = \begin{bmatrix} 1 & 0 & 0 & 0 \\ 0 & 1 & 0 & 0 \\ 0 & 0 & 0 & 0 \\ 0 & 0 & 0 & 1 \end{bmatrix}.$$

This matrix allows us to view the act of projection as another transformation. If clipping were unnecessary, we could concatenate this matrix with the other matrices in our pipeline. For the first time, we have a matrix that is not invertible. This nonsingularity results from the fact that all points on a projector project (i.e., points with the same z) to the same point.

8.7.5 Oblique Viewing

For oblique viewing, the process will be the same as for orthogonal viewing until we get to the projection step. Now we have the general case of a parallel projection, as in Figure 8.50. The direction of projection and the view-plane normal no longer point in the same direction, which makes both the projection and clipping operations more difficult. Suppose we describe the intersection of a projector with the projection plane by the two angles in Figure 8.50. The angle α is the angle the projectors makes with the projection plane when viewed from the top, whereas β is the angle we see from the side.

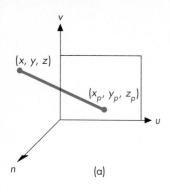

(a)

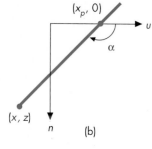

(b)

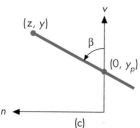

(c)

Figure 8.50
(a) Oblique Projection. (b) Topview. (c) Sideview.

Since the projection plane is the plane $n = 0$, the projection of any point (x, y, z) will have

$$z_p = 0.$$

We can derive one of the other equations by considering the top view in Figure 8.50. We see the u, n plane in this view, and our projector from (x, z) intersects the projection plane at $(x_p, 0)$. Using a little trigonometry, we find

$$x_p = x - z \cot \alpha,$$

and, in a similar manner, from the side view,

$$y_p = y - z \cot \beta.$$

These relationships can be expressed in homogeneous coordinates as

$$\mathbf{p}' = \mathbf{M}_{ob}\mathbf{p},$$

where $\mathbf{M}_{ob}$ is the oblique projection matrix

$$\mathbf{M}_{ob} = \begin{bmatrix} 1 & 0 & -\cot \alpha & 0 \\ 0 & 1 & -\cot \beta & 0 \\ 0 & 0 & 0 & 0 \\ 0 & 0 & 0 & 1 \end{bmatrix}.$$

Clipping for oblique projections is more difficult, as we can see from Figure 8.34. Since the sides of the clipping volume do not meet at right angles, calculating the intersection of a line segment with one of these sides will require more arithmetic than for orthographics projections.

Some of the additional calculation can be avoided by another type of normalization involving the *shearing transformation*. We can write $\mathbf{M}_{ob}$ as the product

$$\mathbf{M}_{ob} = \mathbf{M}_o \mathbf{M}_{sh},$$

where $\mathbf{M}_o$ is our orthogonal projection matrix and $\mathbf{M}_{sh}$ is the shearing matrix

$$\mathbf{M}_{sh} = \begin{bmatrix} 1 & 0 & -\cot \alpha & 0 \\ 0 & 1 & -\cot \beta & 0 \\ 0 & 0 & 1 & 0 \\ 0 & 0 & 0 & 1 \end{bmatrix}.$$

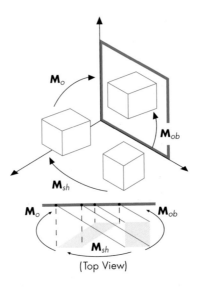

Figure 8.51
The Shearing
Transformation

M_o

M_{ob}

M_{sh}

M_o

M_{ob}

M_{sh}

(Top View)

This matrix is nonsingular and distorts an object, as shown in Figure 8.51, so its orthogonal projection is equivalent to an oblique projection of the original object. The advantage of this transformation is that it also converts the clipping volume to a right parallelepiped. Hence, if we shear first, we can use our simple clipping algorithm, then apply an orthogonal projection.

Three-dimensional graphics systems such as GKS-3D and PHIGS use the shearing transformation as the projection transformation in the pipeline. Objects in projection reference coordinates are converted into objects in normalized projection coordinates (NPC) by the projection transformation. The three-dimensional workstation transformation is then carried out before the final simple orthogonal projection. The reasons for this seemingly convoluted order have to do with making the best use of available hardware. By keeping in three dimensions as long as possible, we can invert operations and, if any clipper is disabled, concatenate the transformations on either side of it into a single transformation. All clipping operations clip against right parallelepipeds, which not only simplies the clipping operations, but also allows us to use the same or similar hardware and software for each clipper.

8.7.6 Implementing Perspective Viewing

We can employ similar arguments with perspective viewing. First, the view-orientation matrix will place the projection plane at $n = 0$. Then, we can convert any perspective view to an orthogonal view

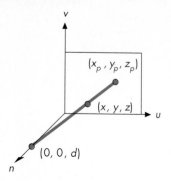

Figure 8.52
Perspective Projection

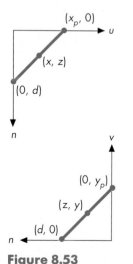

Figure 8.53
Top and Side Views of
Perspective Projection

by distorting the objects by a *perspective transformation*. We shall consider only the simple case, where the center of projection forms a right pyramid with the projection plane. Not only does this case correspond to most real-world viewing, but also, if we can solve this problem, we can solve the general case without much difficulty.

Since the first steps are identical in parallel and perspective viewing, we can start in viewing reference coordinates. The viewing transformation places the projection plane at $n = 0$ and, for the simple perspective view, the center of projection is at $(0, 0, d)$, where $d > 0$. A projector connects this point with a point (x, y, z) on the object. These relationships are shown in Figure 8.52. We can derive the equations of projection by considering the top and side views in Figure 8.53. Solving for the projection point $(x_p, y_p, 0)$, we find

$$x_p = \frac{x}{1 - z/d},$$
$$y_p = \frac{y}{1 - z/d}.$$

The appearance of z in the denominator shows why objects farther from the viewer are smaller in perspective projections and also shows the nonlinearity of perspective viewing. It is surprising that we can also express this relationship using homogeneous coordinates. Consider the equation

$$\mathbf{p}' = \mathbf{M}_p\mathbf{p},$$

where $\mathbf{M}_p$ is the perspective matrix

$$\mathbf{M}_P = \begin{bmatrix} 1 & 0 & 0 & 0 \\ 0 & 1 & 0 & 0 \\ 0 & 0 & 0 & 0 \\ 0 & 0 & -\frac{1}{d} & 1 \end{bmatrix}.$$

These equations are deceptively simple. Suppose we write out both $\mathbf{p}$ and $\mathbf{p}'$ as

$$\mathbf{p} = \begin{bmatrix} x \\ y \\ z \\ w \end{bmatrix},$$

$$\mathbf{p}' = \begin{bmatrix} x' \\ y' \\ z' \\ w' \end{bmatrix}.$$

These equations give us

$$\begin{aligned} x' &= x, \\ y' &= y, \\ z' &= 0, \\ w' &= w - \frac{z}{d}. \end{aligned}$$

For the first time, we have a homogeneous coordinate transformation that alters w. We get the standard perspective equations when we divide x', y' and z' by w'. Although this operation is implicit in all our homogeneous coordinate representations, until now we have been able to avoid explicitly carrying out this division by forcing $w' = 1$. In perspective viewing, we cannot require that $w' = 1$, and the division becomes necessary. This division can significantly slow down a graphics system and should not be looked at as a trivial additional amount of work.

Clipping for perspective views is more complex than that for parallel viewing; we can see from Figure 8.35 that we must clip against a truncated pyramid. Although all the sides are planes and we can derive a Cohen–Sutherland algorithm, there will be considerably more work than for the simple case of an orthogonal projection. We can adopt a technique similar to the one we employed with oblique views. It is a direct exercise to show that the perspective projection matrix can be written as the product of a *perspective normalization matrix* and an orthogonal projection matrix. The perspective normalization transformation will distort the objects and the clipping volume. The distorted objects will be projected orthogonally into their correct positions, whereas the clipped volume will be distorted into a rectangular parallelepiped.

The perspective normalization matrix is the projection transformation for parallel viewing and thus is the major addition we must make to implement perspective viewing. If we can afford the required division operations, then parallel and perspective viewing can be implemented in a single pipeline process consisting of four-dimensional homogeneous coordinate transformations and clippers.

8.8
Suggested Readings

Both [New73] and [Foley82] discuss three-dimensional viewing and transformations, but they use the older CORE system, which uses both right- and left-handed coordinate systems. The relationships between classical and computer graphics are explored in [Carl78].

The slight but incompatible differences between viewing in PHIGS and in GKS-3D arise because GKS-3D includes GKS as a subset and therefore must run all GKS programs. See [GKS86] and [PHIGS86].

■ Exercises

8.1 Using the simple robot in Chapter 5 as a basis, design a three-dimensional robot where motion in the third dimension is obtained by rotation about the base. Write a program that can show the robot moving between two positions.

8.2 Starting with the equation for the plane

$$ax + by + cz + d = 0,$$

find the distance between the plane and the origin.

8.3 Given three points, not in a line, derive the equation for the plane they determine.

8.4 How would you test whether three points lie in the same line?

8.5 In two dimensions, a unique affine transformation is determined by the locations of three points before and after they have been transformed. How many such transformation pairs are required to determine a unique three-dimensional affine transformation?

8.6 Write a three-dimensional transformation package that includes all the necessary accumulation and evaluation procedures.

8.7 In Section 8.4, we showed that an arbitrary rotation matrix could be written as a product of rotation matrices about the x, y, and z axes. Show that the same matrix can be obtained as a rotation about the x axis, followed by a rotation about the y axis, then by another rotation about the x axis.

8.8 Given two points (x_1, y_1, z_1) and (x_2, y_2, z_2), find the direction cosines of the line they determine.

8.9 Determine, in terms of the direction cosines, the matrix that aligns a vector with the z axis.

8.10 Suppose we have two orthogonal coordinate systems x, y, z and x', y', z' that share the same origin. Hence, there is a rotation matrix that converts points represented in one system to their representation in the other. Let $\cos_{xx'}$ be the cosine of the angle between the x axis and the x' axis. In a like manner, we could denote the eight other cosines of the angles between axes in one system and axes in the other. Derive the rotation matrix in terms of these cosines.

8.11 In a flight simulator, we model an airplane as being oriented in its own coordinate system, as shown in Figure 8.54, where, rather than the direction cosines, we use the *yaw, pitch,* and *roll* angles. Relate these angles to the angles that determine the direction cosines.

8.12 A three-dimensional graphics system must check for errors in the viewing conditions. Give a list of the errors for which each of our procedures must check. How do any errors get reflected in the viewing matrix?

8.13 In random-scan systems, it is often difficult to view an image consisting of lines on the screen and to perceive the necessary depth relationships. The process of *depth cueing* makes lines farther from the viewer less bright, which often helps the viewer to interpret the image. How would you implement such a technique?

8.14 The extension of the two-dimensional primitives to three dimensions yields a restrictive group of three-dimensional primitives. Give a set of primitives you would use to build up a three-dimensional graphics system. Discuss the difficulties of implementing each primitive.

8.15 The intersection of a line segment with a plane was a crucial part of clipping. Design a procedure that tests whether such a point exists and, if it does, finds the point.

8.16 It has been proposed to use spherical clipping volumes as an alternative to clipping against parallelepipeds. Derive an algorithm for clipping lines against spheres.

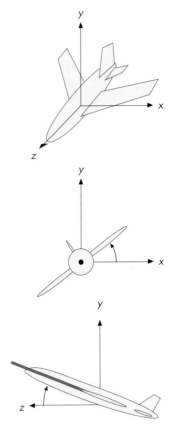

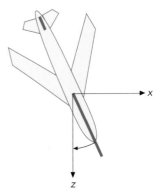

Figure 8.54
Aircraft Coordinate System

8.17 In architecture, specification of a perspective view is usually done in terms of the viewer's location (the *station point*) and of her line of sight. How would you convert such specifications to the viewing specifications we have used?

8.18 A major problem in interactive three-dimensional graphics is the user interface. Consider the problem of entering three-dimensional data such as line segments using the two-dimensional display on a CRT and a two-dimensional input device such as a mouse. What would you display on the CRT to enable the user to describe accurately a position in three dimensions?

8.19 Given that $\mathbf{p}_0$ is a point and $\mathbf{n}$ is a vector, show that the equation

$$(\mathbf{p} - \mathbf{p}_0) \cdot \mathbf{n} = 0$$

determines a plane. Interpret this form graphically.

8.20 In Section 8.2, we specified a text plane through two points that defined vectors $\mathbf{v}_1$ and $\mathbf{v}_2$. Give the equation of the plane in terms of these points.

8.21 How would you check whether a group of points all lie in the same plane?

8.22 Prove the inverse relationships for the following transformation matrices:

$$
\begin{aligned}
\mathbf{T}^{-1}(\Delta x, \Delta y, \Delta z) &= \mathbf{T}(-\Delta x, -\Delta y, -\Delta z), \\
\mathbf{S}^{-1}(\alpha, \beta, \gamma) &= \mathbf{S}(\frac{1}{\alpha}, \frac{1}{\beta}, \frac{1}{\gamma}), \\
\mathbf{H}_\mathbf{x}^{-1}(\theta) &= \mathbf{H}_\mathbf{x}(-\theta), \\
\mathbf{R}_\mathbf{x}^{-1} &= \mathbf{R}_\mathbf{x}(-\theta).
\end{aligned}
$$

8.23 Write a procedure that will take the view reference point, view-plane normal, and view up, and compute the view-orientation matrix.

8.24 Some graphics systems allow the near clipping plane to be behind the viewer. What happens to objects behind the viewer? What happens to a line segment where one endpoint is behind the viewer and the other is in front of him?

8.25 Consider the problem of developing a user interface that will allow you to produce the classical views through a computer graphics system such as GKS-3D. Your interface should allow the user to enter the necessary information on the desired view and to generate calls to the graphics package. How do you describe the objects and their principal faces?

8.26 Write a three-dimensional clipping program for parallel viewing. Extend it to include perspective viewing.

8.27 Derive the equations governing a general perspective view in which the projection plane is $z = 0$ but the viewer can be located anywhere except in this plane.

8.28 Find the equations for an orthogonal projection into an arbitrary plane. Show that these equations are equivalent to a viewing transformation followed by an orthogonal projection in the z direction.

8.29 Consider the design of a three-dimensional display processor. Give a set of instructions you would include. How would you choose the number of bits required for data representation and the number of bits for instruction representation.

CHAPTER

C H A P T E R

9

Working with Polygons

Introduction

Polygons are the basic elements that are used to construct models of three-dimensional objects. The use of polygons, rather than of more general forms such as curved surfaces, is dictated by a number of convenient properties. Polygons can be represented and manipulated in a flexible manner by both the hardware and software. They can be processed rapidly by modern raster hardware. Where curved surfaces are required, we can usually approximate them as accurately as necessary by meshes of polygons.

9.1
Polygons and Realism

When we start working with a three-dimensional-object, we usually display a *wire-frame* model of it, as in Figure 9.1. The name comes

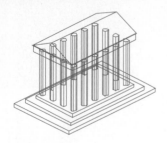

Figure 9.1
Wire-Frame Image

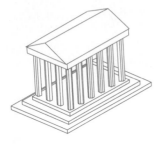

Figure 9.2
Hidden Surfaces Removed

from the observation that the sides have no solidity and the object appears to be constructed from thin lines or wires. The advantage of the wire-frame image is that it can be displayed easily through one-dimensional primitives, such as polylines, on virtually all output devices. From the point of view of the application programmer building a model, however, polylines are usually too low level to be useful for modeling.

The issue of what primitives a user should employ for modeling is still one of great debate. Consider the problem of representing an object as simple as a cube. If we use polylines, the cube is represented by 12 line segments; if we use polygons, only six are required. On the other hand, a solid-modeling system might regard a cube as a single primitive.

If we consider an object such as a sphere, we can see that use of a sphere primitive, as might be the case in a solid-modeling system, is not without problems. For example, since the sphere has no edges and edges are what graphics systems can display with ease, a sphere primitive may be difficult for the graphics system to display. A polygonal approximation to a sphere will avoid this problem. Although a simple representation might be available and desirable at the user's level, polygons often are necessary for the graphical part of the design process.

If the objects are solid or are comprised of opaque surfaces, at some point in an application we would like to display or *render* them as they might appear in the real world. The first step in creating a realistic image is to find which surfaces are visible to the viewer. For our example, this step results in an image such as that in Figure 9.2, where only the visible surfaces are displayed. We shall find that there exist efficient methods for constructing hidden-surface–removed images when the model is based on polygons.

The next step in rendering is usually to illuminate the model with light sources, and to consider the surface properties of the object, such as its color and its reflectivity. The result will be an image such as in

Figure 9.3
Rendered Image

Figure 9.3, which is based on a simple model of the surface properties of the object and a single light source. Once again, efficient algorithms exist for polygonal models.

▦ 9.2
▦ Representing Polygons in Three Dimensions

In most graphics systems, polygons are required to be planar objects; that is, the vertices of each polygon are required to lie in the same plane. We shall assume that it is the responsibility of the user to ensure that polygons are indeed planar objects. In addition, we shall assume that there are no degenerate polygons, such as those for which all vertices lie on the same line.

As we have already seen in Chapter 7, a polygon can be represented by its vertices, by its edges, or by both. We will use vertex representations for now. Since we will be working with the model in the user program, a simple representation using WC might be

```
typedef struct
{
    Gpt_3 vertex;
    vertex_list *next;
} vertex_list;

typedef struct
{
    vertex_list *vertices;
} polygon;
```

9.2.1 Polygons and Normals

Many of the manipulations we will do with polygons will depend on the orientation of the planes in which the polygons lie. The implicit representation of a plane,

$$ax + by + cz + d = 0,$$

contains the necessary information. We have already observed that only three of the parameters are independent. This observation yields two important results. First, any three noncolinear points determine a unique plane. Second, we can choose one additional condition on the parameters $a, b, c,$ and d. We will impose the normalization

$$a^2 + b^2 + c^2 = 1,$$

which forces the normal to the plane

$$\mathbf{n} = \begin{bmatrix} a \\ b \\ c \end{bmatrix},$$

to be a unit normal. Since this normal will be so important to us, we will add it to the data structure rather than being forced to recalculate it whenever it is needed:

```
typedef struct
{
    Gpt_3 normal;
    vertex_list *vertices;
} polygon;
```

9.2.2 Computing the Normal

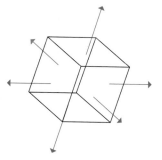

Figure 9.4
Cube with Normals

The normal can be computed by the user program or by the graphics system using the first three vertices in the vertex list. The normal must be computed carefully, so that we can distinguish between the inward-pointing and outward-pointing normal, which differ only in sign. Figure 9.4 shows a cube with all the outward-pointing normals. If we are consistent, we can use the normal to tell us whether we have a front- (towards the viewer) or back-pointing face from the information in the representation.

A standard way to calculate a normal is to use three vertices of the polygon in the equation of the plane:

$$\begin{aligned} ax_1 + by_1 + cz_1 + d &= 0, \\ ax_2 + by_2 + cz_2 + d &= 0, \\ ax_3 + by_3 + cz_3 + d &= 0. \end{aligned}$$

We assume that d can be set arbitrarily, which is possible as long as the plane does not pass through the origin. If it does pass through the origin, then $d = 0$. It is a simple exercise to show that these equations have a unique solution if the three points do not lie on the same line. We obtain the unit normal by scaling (a, b, c) to have unit length and rewriting the equation as

$$a'x + b'y + c'z + d' = 0.$$

The scaling constant is simply the length of $\mathbf{n}$,

$$s = \sqrt{a^2 + b^2 + c^2},$$

and thus

$$a' = \frac{a}{s},$$
$$b' = \frac{b}{s},$$
$$c' = \frac{c}{s},$$
$$d' = \frac{d}{s}.$$

Noting that any two vectors $\mathbf{n}$ and $-\mathbf{n}$ have the same length but point in opposite directions, we can force the unit normal to point outward by using the vertices in a consistent manner. In a right-handed system, if we order the vertices in a clockwise order when we look at the outside surface, this method will generate the outward-pointing normal.

An equivalent method is to note that the determinant of the matrix

$$\mathbf{D} = \begin{bmatrix} x & y & z & 1 \\ x_1 & y_1 & z_1 & 1 \\ x_2 & y_2 & z_2 & 1 \\ x_3 & y_3 & z_3 & 1 \end{bmatrix}$$

yields a linear equation in x, y, and z. Since this determinant is zero whenever (x, y, z) is replaced by any of the other three points in the matrix, this equation is that of the plane determined by these three points. For example, consider the top face of the cube in Figure 9.5, which is a polygon with vertices, in clockwise order, of $(0, 1, 0), (0, 1, 1), (1, 1, 1)$, and $(1, 1, 0)$. The determinant yields

$$\begin{vmatrix} x & y & z & 1 \\ 0 & 1 & 0 & 1 \\ 0 & 1 & 1 & 1 \\ 1 & 1 & 1 & 1 \end{vmatrix} = y - 1 = 0,$$

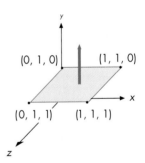

Figure 9.5
Normal to a Cube

and thus the normal is

$$\mathbf{n} = \begin{bmatrix} 0 \\ 1 \\ 0 \end{bmatrix}.$$

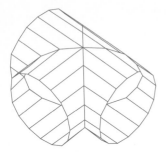

Figure 9.6
Object Modeling with a
Mesh

Likewise the bottom face yields the equation

$$-y - 1 = 0,$$

and the normal is

$$\mathbf{n} = \begin{bmatrix} 0 \\ -1 \\ 0 \end{bmatrix}.$$

You should verify that these results will be the same no matter which three vertices are selected, as long as the vertices are used in clockwise order.

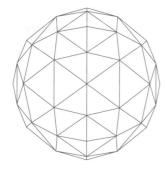

Figure 9.7
Mesh Approximation to a
Sphere

9.3
Polygonal Meshes

Groups of polygons or meshes are the basis of many three-dimensional modeling techniques. Such models can be used to form objects in user programs, such as in Figure 9.6; to approximate curved solid objects within either a user program or a graphics package, as in Figure 9.7; and to display data, as in Figure 9.8. In this section, we shall examine ways to define and use meshes in three dimensions.

Figure 9.8
Mesh Surface Representing
Data

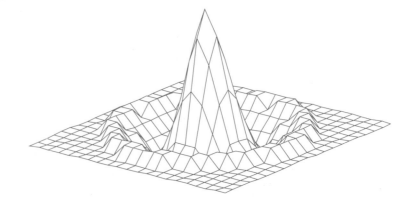

9.3.1 Edges, Surfaces, and Volumes

We have already seen that we have a number of ways to represent a single polygon. As a result, we have many options for representing a mesh of polygons. Suppose that our mesh represents a single object, such as a cube. Figure 9.9 shows two different renderings of the cube, as a wire frame with all edges shown, and with the lines and surfaces that could not be seen by a viewer if the sides were opaque (or the object were solid) removed. In terms of an underlying representation, for the wire-frame image, a model that uses either vertices or edges might be perfectly sufficient; for the hidden-surface–removed image, however, we usually need a representation that uses surfaces. In many design applications, both types of displays might be required at different points in the process. We seek representations that will allow both types of displays.

Suppose we consider a representation based on our use of edge lists in Chapter 7. Then, a polygonal surface can be modeled as an ordered list of edges. We might construct a model of a solid object as a set of such surfaces. A pictorial representation of a possible structure might be as in Figure 9.10, and the C code would consist of structures like

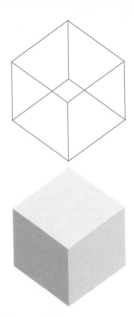

Figure 9.9
Wire-Frame and Hidden-
Surface–Removed Images

```
typedef struct
  {
     Gpt_3 *vertex1;
     Gpt_3 *vertex2;
  } edge;

typedef struct
  {
     edge *ed;
     edge_list *next;
  } edge_list;

typedef struct
  {
     edge_list *surface
     surface_list *next;
  } surface_list;

typdef  surface_list *3D_object;
```

In this representation, a three-dimensional object is a pointer to a list of surfaces. Surfaces are lists of edges, and edges are pairs of vertices or three-dimensional points.

Figure 9.10
Representing a Cube

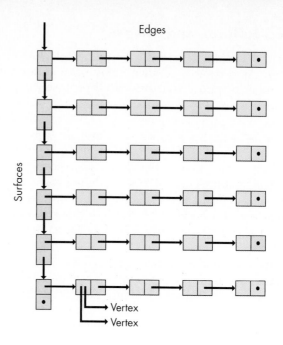

Using such a structure, we use only the edge and vertex data when a wire-frame image is to be constructed. We use the surfaces when we want to do hidden-surface removal. Such a structure is also somewhat flexible in that it can model a variety of different objects composed of or approximated by polygons. In many problems, we generate special sets of polygons that can be modeled more efficiently with simpler data structures. The remainder of this section presents two examples of how meshes can be used.

9.3.2 Quadrilateral and Triangular Meshes

Data are often generated as a set of y values for a set of values of x and z; that is, we generate the set of values $\{y(x_i, z_j)\}, i = 1, ..., N, j = 1, ..., M$. For example, if we measure a set of two-dimensional curves, $y = f(x)$, at different times, the data will be of this form where z is the time variable. One way to display such data is by forming a set of three-dimensional polygons from the four adjacent points $(x_i, y(x_i, z_j), z_j)$, $(x_{i+1}, y(x_{i+1}, z_j), z_j), (x_{i+1}, y(x_{i+1}, z_{j+1}), z_{j+1})$, and $(x_i, y(x_i, z_{j+1}), z_{j+1})$, and displaying this mesh of polygons as in Figure 9.11. Here, we have displayed a mesh for which hidden-surface removal is not necessary, as all outward-pointing surfaces are completely visible. We shall discuss hidden-surface removal in Section 9.4.

Figure 9.11
Quadrilateral Mesh

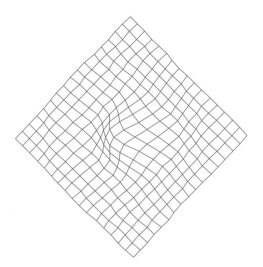

It is also important to notice that each polygon has exactly four sides and each vertex is determined by a data point. If the data are generated at equal spacings of x and z, the N by M array

$$\mathbf{Y} = [y_{ij}],$$

where

$$y_{ij} = y(x_i, z_j),$$

completely describes the mesh and is a valid data structure for representing it. This array of vertices can be used far more efficiently than can a more general mesh data structure.

If we display the mesh as a wire frame, we need not be concerned with the shape of the surface defined by each set of four vertices. However, if we decide to fill each polygon or to display a hidden-surface–removed image, we may encounter serious problems if the four vertices do not lie in the same plane. Since any three noncolinear points determine a unique plane, a mesh composed of triangles may avoid many potential problems. Each quadrilateral polygon can be decomposed into two triangular polygons, using $y(x_i, z_j), y(x_i, z_{j+1})$ and $y(x_{i+1}, z_j)$ for one, and $y(x_i, z_{j+1}), y(x_{i+1}, z_{j+1})$ and $y(x_i, z_{j+1})$ for the second. Such a mesh is displayed in Figure 9.12, using the same data that generated Figure 9.11.

Figure 9.12
Triangular Mesh

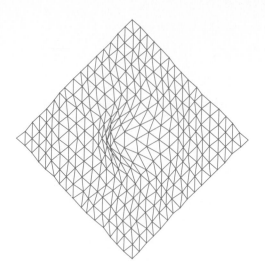

9.3.3 Approximating Spheres

As a final example, we shall consider the deceptively simple problem of displaying a sphere in a graphics system. Systems that work with three-dimensional objects often have spheres as primitives, since a sphere has a simple mathematical characterization and provides an object with nonzero curvature. Unfortunately, as we noted before, graphics systems can have difficulty displaying spheres. One way to get around this problem is to use a polygonal approximation to the sphere. The application program can work in terms of the sphere, while the display process will draw the approximating surface. Spheres and other solid objects or closed surfaces can be approximated with closed polygonal meshes, or *polyhedra*.

Creating a polyhedron which approximates a sphere can be accomplished in a number of different ways. In many applications, we would like to approximate an object with a set of identical polygons. Such a polyhedron is known as a *regular* polyhedron. A unit cube is a regular polyhedron. A tetrahedron can also be made regular, but unfortunately neither the cube nor the tetrahedron has enough sides to provide a good approximation to an object such as a sphere. One possibility is to start with a regular tetrahedron and to subdivide each face recursively into finer and finer meshes composed of triangles, as shown in Figure 9.13. This approach is outlined in Exercises 9.5 and 9.6.

Another possibility is based on *surfaces of revolution*. If we start with a N identical circles, we can place each successive circle $180/N$ degrees offset from the previous one, creating circles of constant longi-

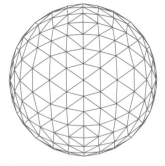

Figure 9.13
Sphere Approximated by
Triangular Mesh

tude on the sphere. Next, we can create M circles of constant latitude by dividing any of our circles into M equal divisions, producing the mesh as shown in Figure 9.14. This mesh consists of all quadrilateral polygons except at the poles where we have triangular polygons. We could of course convert all the polygons in the mesh to triangles, but that would not leave us with a regular polyhedron. Both approaches provide interesting challenges in choosing an appropriate data structure for representation.

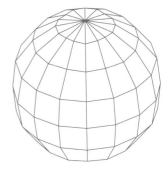

Figure 9.14
Approximating a Sphere
by Longitude and Latitude

9.4
Hidden-Surface Removal

The problem of removing hidden lines and surfaces arises whenever we want to display a realistic-looking image of three-dimensional objects. The particular combination of the modeling system used to represent the objects and the graphics system can make the problem anywhere from a simple additional step in the viewing pipeline to an extra extremely intensive computation. Although we shall start by posing the problem in a fairly general way, we shall find that most algorithms are computationaly feasible only with objects constructed from polygons.

Hidden-line and hidden-surface removal are two conceptually different ways of generating similar images. Hidden-line–removal methods assume that objects are modeled with lines. They look at these lines and determine which will appear in the image. The argument behind hidden-surface–removal algorithms is that lines are created where surfaces such as planes meet. If only the visible surfaces are drawn, the invisible lines will automatically have been eliminated. For example, in Figure 9.15, surfaces A, B, and C are visible. Line segment e would be determined to be invisible by a hidden-line–removal algorithm, whereas d would be found to be visible. If we used a hidden-surface–removal algorithm, d would appear, because A and B would be found to be visible and thus would be scan converted. Line segment e would not appear, because the two surfaces that form it both would be hidden and would not be scan converted. Hidden-surface–removal algorithms are also more general, as they can deal with objects composed of surfaces and no lines, such as ellipsoids, and with shading of surfaces. In raster systems, the hidden-surface–removal algorithms, usually based on polygonal models, are far more efficient; we shall consider them exclusively.

Even for polygonal models, there are a number of approaches to the problem. Multiple approaches are important, since the characteristics of the particular problem will determine which algorithm is best in a given situation. It is important to look for special characteristics

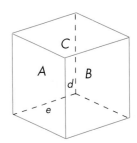

Figure 9.15
Hidden-Line versus
Hidden-Surface Removal

Figure 9.16
Hidden-Surface Removal

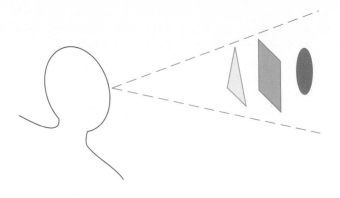

of a problem, as the most general algorithms will be the slowest in practice.

9.4.1 Hidden-Surface Removal and Sorting

The conceptual basis for hidden-surface removal starts with our viewing model, which we have redrawn in Figure 9.16 to show a viewer and a few surfaces. Since we will work on a surface-by-surface basis, we will regard each surface as a distinct object in this discussion. Each surface is considered to be opaque and has a color that we can specify by a color index. If we look along any projector, as in Figure 9.17, from either the center of projection or where the projector intersects the projection plane, we might encounter one or more of our surfaces. The color we see along that projector is the color of the closest surface. This observation leads to a generic hidden-surface–removal algorithm:

Figure 9.17
Moving Along a Projector

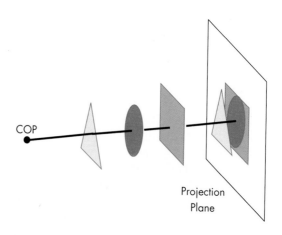

COP

Projection
Plane

Compute the intersections of all the surfaces with all projectors. Sort these intersections by distance along each projector. For each projector, use the color of the surface that generated the intersection closest to the viewer to color the pixel through which the projector passes.

Such a conceptual algorithm leaves much to be determined, but indicates some of the problems in hidden-surface removal. First, by looking at hidden-surface removal as a sorting problem, we face many of the same issues we considered in our discussion of fill algorithms. In particular, we must be careful in how we organize our sorts, or we might be left with an extremely large number of intersections to sort. The relationship between fill and hidden-surface removal is a strong one and will be exploited in some of our algorithms.

A second problem arises in the part of the procedure necessary to compute intersections of projectors with our objects. The difficulty of this problem depends on the types of surfaces we allow in our system. If we use polygons, this intersection problem is simple to solve, which is one of the principal reasons polygonal modeling techniques are so prevalent.

9.4.2 Object-Space versus Image-Space Approaches

Before discussing any algorithms in detail, we can get a rough idea of the work required in hidden-surface removal by examining two fundamental approaches to the problem. The first approach is based on working with the objects in the model; algorithms based on this idea have been called *object-space* methods. These approaches are appropriate whenever we can determine that each object has a simple relationship to other objects in the scene. For example, consider the three polygons in Figure 9.18. Since polygon A is in front of polygon B, and B is in front C, once we have determined these relationships, we can deal with each polygon individually. In this example, we can paint or fill C, then paint B, and finally paint A onto the display.

The basic approach, if we have K objects, is to take one of the objects and to determine its relationship to each of the other $K - 1$ objects. At this point, we will be finished with this object. It will be either discarded, painted, or partially painted, depending on its relationship to the other objects. We now repeat this procedure recursively, starting with any of the remaining $K - 1$ objects, until we have a single pair of objects that we can compare with each other. Thus, our fundamental operation is to compare pairs of objects to determine the relationship between them. We do this operation $(K - 1) + (K - 2) + ...2 + 1 = K(K - 1)/2$ times. Regardless of the particular method of doing the pairwise comparison of objects, we

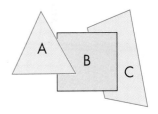

Figure 9.18
Object-Space Sorting

Figure 9.19
Image-Space Approach

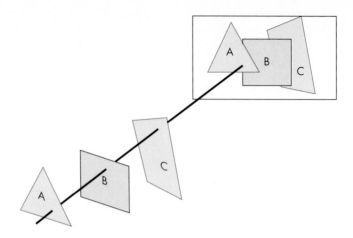

see that such methods have a worst-case complexity of $O(K^2)$. Hence, they may not be appropriate for scenes with many objects.

The *image-space* methods work with the projectors. Suppose we redraw the three polygons in Figure 9.18 with the image plane included, as shown in Figure 9.19. If we follow any projector, we can intersect it with each of the surfaces determined by the objects, and then find which surface is closest to the viewer. Such an approach should have a worst-case complexity of $O(K)$, rather than the $O(K^2)$ we found for the object-space approaches. We also note that, for a raster display, we need (at least) one projector for each pixel. If we double the resolution of a display, we should expect an algorithm to require four times the work. These calculations yield upper bounds, and we can hope to do better with individual algorithms. The object-space methods are best for images with a small number of objects or other special properties; image-space algorithms provide more constant performance over a broad class of problems.

9.5
Object-Space Algorithms

Object-space approaches to hidden-surface removal work directly with the surfaces as individual objects. We will assume that each object is a planar polygon. We shall start with a special but commonly occurring case, and shall work our way up to a more general algorithm.

9.5.1 Removing Back-Facing Polygons

Figure 9.20 shows a simple convex polygonal object, a tetrahedron, with hidden-surfaces removed. Each polygonal face in our object has a normal, which is shown in Figure 9.21. We can observe that, in the hidden-surface–removed image, polygons are either fully in the image or do not appear at all, and those polygons that do appear have their normals facing toward the viewer (i.e., out of the page). This simple observation applies to all closed convex polygonal models. We can derive a simple algorithm based on testing polygon normals for forward-facing polygons. Figure 9.22 shows the vectors that govern the situation. A polygon is front facing when θ, the angle between the viewer and the normal to the polygon, lies between -90 and +90 degrees, or, equivalently, when

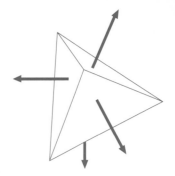

Figure 9.20
Convex Object

$$\cos \theta \geq 0.$$

Rather than computing either θ or its cosine directly, we can test the sign of the dot product,

$$\mathbf{v} \cdot \mathbf{n} = |\mathbf{v}||\mathbf{n}| \cos \theta,$$

since both magnitudes are positive.

This test is easy to perform and will be even easier if we have carried out the transformation into normalized projection coordinates that we discussed in Chapter 8. This normalization transformed all views to equivalent parallel projections in the direction of the view plane normal. In this u, v, n space, the projection plane is the plane

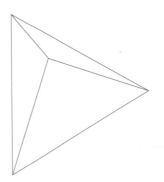

Figure 9.21
Object with Normals

$$z = 0,$$

Figure 9.22
Viewing a Polygon

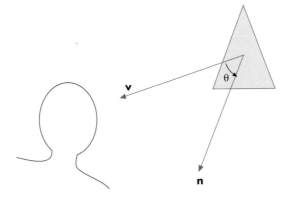

and the direction of projection is along the n axis. If a polygon has a normal

$$\mathbf{n} = \begin{bmatrix} a \\ b \\ c \end{bmatrix},$$

the vector in the direction of the viewer is simply

$$\mathbf{v} = \begin{bmatrix} 0 \\ 0 \\ 1 \end{bmatrix},$$

and our test becomes a sign check of

$$\mathbf{n} \cdot \mathbf{v} = c.$$

Although most models are not convex, and scenes composed of a collection of convex parts cannot have this algorithm applied to them, this method can be used in conjunction with others. For example, if we know that back-facing polygons are not visible, we can reduce the problem to one that the other algorithms can handle. Alternately, we might be able to apply this algorithm to each convex subpart of a scene within the framework of another algorithm.

9.5.2 Depth Sort

Consider the mesh in Figure 9.23. If the mesh is to be viewed as a thin sheet rather than as a solid, some back-facing polygons—namely, those polygons that have no other polygons in front of them—will be

Figure 9.23
Hidden-Surface Removal
on a Mesh

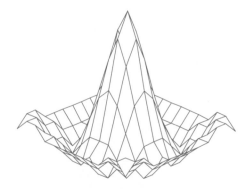

Figure 9.24
Sorting the Faces

visible. In addition, the mesh does not form a convex model. There is still considerable structure in the mesh, however, which indicates that we may not have to do hidden-surface removal by the most general of methods.

There are two observations we can use to build an algorithm. First, the structure of the mesh is such that we know the spatial relationship among the individual polygons in the mesh. Second, polygons in the mesh do not intersect one another. If we sort the polygons back to front, we can scan convert each one individually. Polygons that lie in front of other polygons will be painted in an order that will obscure the polygons behind them—this is the idea behind *depth-sort* algorithms.

The mesh example usually avoids the sorting problem, since the data usually are generated and stored in the mesh data structure in sorted order. On the other hand, for a scene such as that in Figure 9.24, we will have to do a sort of the polygons, which increases the complexity of the method. The simplest sort in this situation is to sort only on the range of distance from the viewer that a given polygon occupies. If we have normalized the problem, this calculation is almost trivial. In normalized projection coordinates, distances from the projection plane are simply the z values. Thus, by finding z_{max} and z_{min} for each set of vertices, we know the z extent of each polygon. It is this step that gives this algorithm the name *depth sort*.

9.5.3 The General Case

In simple problems, the depth sort may be sufficient to determine the order in which to paint the polygons. Consider the situations in Figure 9.25. In each case, the polygons overlap in depth, but we can create the hidden-surface–removed image by painting the polygons in

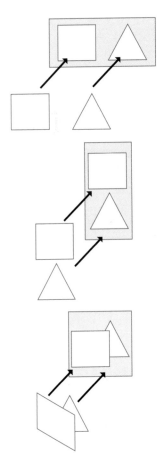

Figure 9.25
Overlaps in Depth

Figure 9.26
Cyclic Overlap

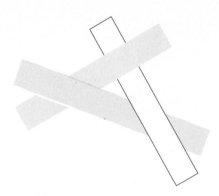

the correct order. General depth-sort algorithms go through a set of increasingly more complex tests to attempt to find an order in which to paint the polygons. The performance of the general algorithm will depend on the likelihood of these more difficult situations arising.

The simplest test is based on the observations that, even if two polygons overlap in depth (z), they must also overlap in both x and y if they are to intersect each other. It is easy for a program to check whether this condition exists by looking through the vertices of the two polygons or by storing this information in the data structure for the polygons.

Even if two polygons overlap in all three of their dimensions, it is still possible that one can be painted before the other. These situations arise as when one polygon is either in front of or behind the plane determined by the other, as depicted on the bottom of Figure 9.25. This test involves more work than did the previous tests, since we must use the equations of the plane determined by each polygon with the vertices of the other to determine whether one polygon is in front of the other.

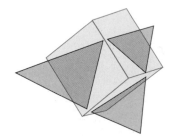

Figure 9.27
Intersecting Polygons

Two situations can arise that, although possible to resolve, may lead us to try another approach. The first is illustrated in Figure 9.26, which shows a cyclic overlap. We cannot create a hidden-surface–removed image by scan converting the polygons in some order. If one of the polygons is split in two, however, the four polygons thus created can be painted back to front. A similar solution is necessary for the case where two or more polygons intersect, as in Figure 9.27. We can resolve this situation by breaking up one or more of the polygons. The difficulty here is the time required to compute the intersections between polygons. Carrying out such calculations may be worse than turning to another method. There are many classes of problems where we know from the structure of the problem that neither of these situations can possibly arise. For example, suppose we are working with solid objects. Although the model might use polygonal surfaces, the solidity of the actual objects dictates that no polygons can intersect, and a depth sort might work well.

9.6 Image-Space Algorithms

Image-space approaches to hidden-surface removal are very general and can be implemented in both software and hardware. These methods tend to have consistent performance over a wide range of problems. In addition, these algorithms work well with the graphics-pipeline approach to implementing three-dimensional viewing, since they require a limited amount of additional work to go from a wire-frame image to a hidden-surface–removed image.

9.6.1 The z-Buffer Algorithm

The z-buffer algorithm is direct implementation of the image-space view of hidden-surface removal. In the most versions of the algorithm, we build the image one polygon at a time directly in the frame buffer. The major difference between simply scan converting each polygon and producing a true hidden-surface–removed image is that we keep track of depths along each projector as we do the scan conversion. To store this information, the algorithm requires a z, or depth, buffer. This depth buffer has the spatial resolution of the display and at each location must have a number of bits consistent with the depth resolution required. In practice, this number of bits usually is at least 16. The low cost and high density of available memory has led to the incorporation of a hardware depth buffer in many high-end graphics systems.

Once more, we will assume that we have done our conversion into normalized projection coordinates. If we have not, the adjustments required in the algorithm will be equivalent to performing this normalization. In the normalized view, all projections are parallel with the projectors orthogonal to the projection plane. The z direction is the depth direction, and the depth of a point on any object is that point's z value. Suppose that we use a projector for each pixel, as illustrated in Figure 9.28.

Initially, the frame buffer is filled with the background color and the z-buffer is filled with values corresponding to the farthest distance from the projection plane ($z = 0$). The algorithm is based on scan converting each polygon. Although each polygon lies in an arbitrary plane in three dimensions, the projection of the polygon onto

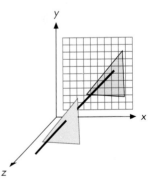

Figure 9.28
z-Buffer Distances

Figure 9.29
z-Buffer Algorithm

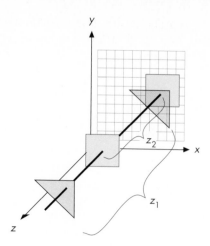

the plane $z = 0$ allows the algorithm to fill two-dimensional polygons using one of our standard polygon-fill algorithms. As each point on a two-dimensional polygon is encountered by the fill process, the depth of the point on the corresponding three-dimensional polygon is checked, using the equation of the three-dimensional plane, against the distance already in the depth buffer. These relationships are shown in Figure 9.29. If the depth of the given point is less than the depth already at that point in the z-buffer, we have already placed in the frame buffer a color of a point in front of the point under consideration, and the present point can be discarded. If the depth of the point being considered is less than that in the frame buffer, we place the color of this point in the frame buffer, and we place the point's depth in the z-buffer.

The amount of calculation depends on the particular polygon-fill algorithm used. In most variants, each polygon is filled one scan line at a time. In the normalized problem, the projectors are lines of constant x and y. Hence, the point (x, y, z) projects into $(x, y, 0)$. For any plane in three dimensions,

$$ax + by + cz + d = 0,$$

the differences in x, y, and z between any two points in the plane satisfy the incremental equation

$$a\Delta x + b\Delta y + c\Delta z = 0.$$

As we move along a scan line in the projection plane,

$$\Delta x = 1,$$
$$\Delta y = 0,$$

370 **Chapter 9 Working with Polygons**

and the change in depth of the unprojected polygon is

$$\Delta z = -\frac{a}{c}.$$

Since normalization, projection, and fill are part of our standard viewing operations, regardless of whether or not hidden-surface removal is desired, this step represents most of the additional work for hidden-surface removal.

Although, in our initial discussion, we indicated that the work required for hidden-surface removal using an image-space algorithm should increase linearly with the number of objects in the scene, this assertion is not true in most implementations of the z-buffer algorithm. The two views in Figure 9.30 are of the same objects, but the viewer is closer to the objects in one view. In the image produced with the viewer closer to the objects, there are fewer objects visible, but the image of each object is larger. Since the z-buffer algorithm works in image-space, the most important factor is the area to be filled in an image by the scan conversion of polygons. This area remains approximately constant as the viewer moves in and out. Consequently, the work for hidden-surface removal tends to be independent of the number of objects, which gives the algorithm fairly constant performance.

Figure 9.30
Zoomed Image

9.6.2 The Scan-Line Algorithm

The main disadvantage of the z-buffer algorithm is the necessity of maintaining a large z-buffer. If this memory is unavailable, we can seek variants that work one scan line at a time. Such algorithms have the potential of allowing us to generate the display in real time, line by line. The scan-line algorithm has the additional advantage that it can avoid many of the depth calculations in the basic z-buffer algorithm.

Consider the three scan lines in Figure 9.31. The upper scan line passes through only one of the two polygons. If this information is

Figure 9.31
Scan-Line Algorithm

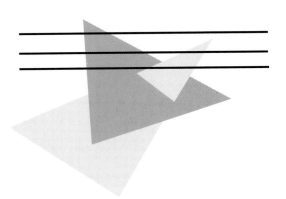

known, no depth calculations need to be done and the pixels along this scan line can be set by a standard fill algorithm. The middle scan line passes through two polygons, but, if we proceed from left to right along the scan line, we are inside at most one of the polygons at a time, so once again no depth calculations are necessary. Along part of the lower scan line, we are simultaneously in both polygons and, to determine which color to place at these points, we must perform depth calculations.

Our reasoning seems to imply that we can construct an algorithm that not only requires less calculation than does the z-buffer algorithm, but also requires less memory. Unfortunately, implementation of these ideas is not simple and involves the careful construction of a few interesting data structures. Without going into the details of the implementation, we can examine some of the necessary elements.

Since we are working one scan line at a time, we need a depth buffer of only one line. The main difficulty in implementing the algorithm is how we organize the information about the polygons. As we proceed along a scan line, we encounter the edges of various polygons. Since the filling of a polygon begins when we enter it at an edge and ends when we leave it at another edge, an ordered list of the intersections of edges with scan lines will contain most of the necessary information. If we start with a standard representation of polygons, such as a list of polygons each of which is a list of vertices, then we might have a problem computing which edges are encountered along each scan line. Usually, we compute a new data structure containing this information at the beginning of the process. Such a structure might be a list of which edges will be encountered or active on each scan line. For each scan line, the active edges are sorted by x. If this structure is simply a list of edges, it can be very large, as one edge can cross many scan lines. The usual structure employed contains the information about the edges—such as their slopes, and initial and final scan lines. Each edge needs to appear only once, yet the ordered edge–scan line intersections are still easily available to the program. In addition, since in most applications we will be changing the scene by adding or removing polygons or moving existing polygons, our data structure may be constantly changing and hence we must also create the necessary utilities to modify it.

9.7 Rendering

Although hidden-surface removal provides an image that is far more realistic than is a wire-frame image, much more computation is required if we want to create an image comparable in realism to a photograph. There are two important aspects of imaging that we have left out thus far, and that we must include if we want truly realistic images. First, we have not considered the effects of light sources. Hidden-surface removal requires only knowledge of the location of the objects and the viewer, but if there are no light sources, there will be no light to illuminate the objects. Different types of lighting produce different images, just as a photograph taken at noon on a sunny day will differ from one taken of the same scene at dusk on a cloudy day.

We must also consider the surface-reflectivity properties of our objects. An object may absorb light and appear black. It may absorb some frequencies of light and reflect other frequencies, giving it color. An object might scatter light striking it or it might reflect incident light along a very narrow angle, as does a polished surface. Color Plate 12 shows multiple copies of the same object illuminated with two light sources. Each object shows different surface-reflectivity properties. If only hidden-surface removal was done, all the objects would appear identical in the image.

We will build up a simple model of lighting and surface reflectivity that can be used with objects that are more general than those based on polygons. As a practical matter, rendering of nonpolygonal objects is extremely computationally intensive. With the exception of the low-order polynomial surfaces of the type we shall consider in the next chapter, rendering is usually applied to only polygonal models. Although we focus our algorithms on polygonal objects, the surface-model and ray-tracing ideas we shall present here can be applied to any type of model.

9.7.1 Ray Tracing

Rendering of graphical objects is in large part an attempt to simulate the optical phenomena we study in physics. Suppose we start with a point source of light, as in Figure 9.32, and use geometrical optics to follow rays of light from the source. Some rays go off into space and are of no particular interest to us. Others may strike various objects in the scene, causing some light to be absorbed and some to be reflected. Other rays enter our eyes directly from the source. Of all possible rays, whether they come directly from the source or are reflected, only those rays that enter the eye of the viewer contribute to the image she "sees."

Considering this situation incorporating the projection plane in Figure 9.33, we note that all rays that pass through the projection plane contribute to the image. Since the projection plane is mapped to the frame buffer, each pixel corresponds to an area on this plane. All rays passing through this area contribute to the color assigned to the pixel. We might construct an algorithm by following all rays

Figure 9.32
Ray Tracing

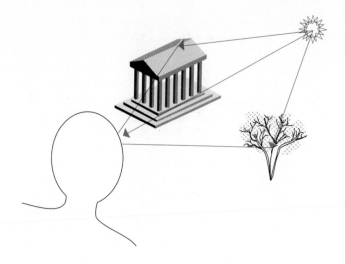

Figure 9.33
Tracing Rays through the
Projection Plan

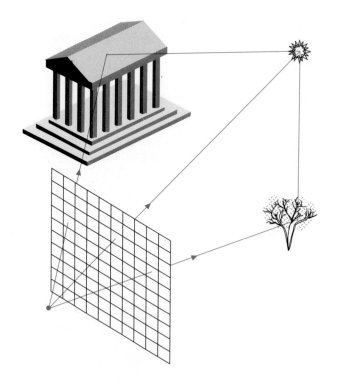

and modeling the physics that occur when a ray is absorbed by or reflected from an object in the scene. The tracing of a ray will stop when the ray passes through a pixel, is completely absorbed, or goes off to infinity.

Unfortunately, this approach leads to a computationally infeasible algorithm. Most of the rays coming from a source will not intersect a pixel and will make no contribution to the image. The effort expended is tracing such rays is wasted. The solution to this problem used in computer graphics is to reverse this process and to *cast* rays.

9.7.2 Ray Casting

Suppose we start a ray at the center of projection or in the normalized space along any of the parallel rays, and pass it through a pixel, as in Figure 9.34. This ray must make a contribution to the image. If this cast ray goes off to infinity, the pixel will be colored black or some background color. If the ray hits the light source, its intensity and color, and the distance between the viewer and the source, will determine the coloring of the pixel. If the ray strikes an object, then we must consider what happens at the point of intersection. This case will depend on the surface-reflectivity properties of the object and on whether the object is illuminated by any light sources.

Note that this argument is the same in normalized projection coordinates. The only change will be that the cast rays will all be parallel to one another. We shall use the perspective model in our discussion because it corresponds to a human viewer looking at a scene and may be conceptually easier to grasp.

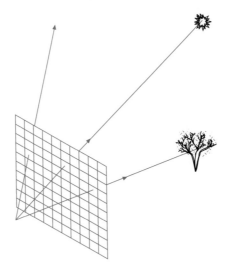

Figure 9.34
Cast Rays

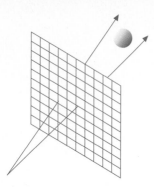

Figure 9.35
Aliasing in Ray Tracing

9.7.3 Aliasing and Rendering

The advantage of ray casting is that we have an algorithm in which every ray contributes to the image. Although we must cast at least one ray for each pixel, a single ray per pixel can lead to an aliasing problem. Consider the situation in Figure 9.35, where two rays cast through adjacent pixels miss intersecting a small object in the world. In the rendering of this scene, this object will not appear. This omission can be a serious problem, especially where the rendering is of one frame in an animation. The object may be in motion and thus may be struck by cast rays in one frame and not in others. In such a case, the object will actually appear and disappear in successive frames of a sequence of images. This problem will also be present in hidden-surface–removal algorithms, as we can note by observing the similarities between ray casting and the z-buffer algorithm.

The solutions to this problem come at a high price. We can construct a model of the world that does not allow very small objects. More often, we sample the world more closely by casting multiple rays through each pixel. Such a solution will of course require far more work, as the computation required in rendering is proportional to the number of rays cast.

9.7.4 Shadow Rays

Returning to a cast ray that intersects a surface, we must determine if any light strikes this point. Light can illuminate a point on an object in a multitude of ways. The simplest, and the only one we will consider, is that the light strikes the point directly from one or more sources. Contributions are also possible, however, from light reflected from other objects in the world.

If we consider only light striking an object directly from a source, we can look at this problem as one of hidden surfaces. A viewer, standing at the point on an object intersected by a cast ray, will sense light only if a source is visible. Thus, if we construct rays called *shadow rays* from the point to each source, we must determine whether these rays pass through any opaque objects that might block the light. In the general case, this calculation can be more complicated if we allow surfaces that are transparent or refract light, possibly causing multiple shadow rays that must be traced. If we allow reflected light, other objects can act as light sources. If our surfaces are opaque, we have a hidden-surface problem, where there is a "viewer" at each light source. A large part of the work in ray casting is the solution of multiple hidden-surface–removal problems of this type. The use of light sources more general than point sources quickly leads to computations requiring a supercomputer.

Figure 9.36
Shadow Rays

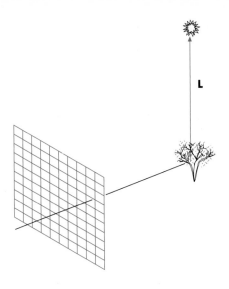

Once we have determined that a point of intersection on an object is illuminated, we have to determine how the incident illumination is seen by a viewer. We can consider the light incident on this point from a single source to have an intensity I and to strike the point at an angle that can be described by a vector $\mathbf{L}$ from the point to the source, as in Figure 9.36. The contributions from multiple sources are added together.

The model we have built up so far is monochromatic. We can extend it to color through the three-color model from Chapter 7. The appropriate model for surfaces uses subtractive color, since surfaces are filters that remove certain frequencies from the light that is incident on them. We can model our light source as having three independent primary components. Thus, a source is described by the three intensities, I_R, I_G, and I_B, and there will be cyan, magenta, and yellow models of the surface properties of our objects.

9.7.5 Rendering Without Ray Tracing

Ray tracing is a powerful technique for producing realistic images. However, it can require a tremendous amount of calculation, especially in situations where objects may be in shadow or where there are important contributions from reflected light. Often, we wish to have a more realistic image than can be produced by hidden-surface removal, but are unwilling to do a complete rendering. If we ignore multiple interactions between light and objects and instead assume that all the light from a source strikes any surface facing it, we can avoid most ray-tracing calculations.

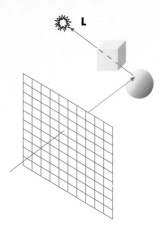

Figure 9.37
Avoiding Ray Tracing

We can obtain an efficient algorithm for this case by using the relationship between ray casting and hidden-surface removal by image-space methods. Casting a ray and finding which surface it intersects first is exactly what we do in hidden-surface removal by an image space method. If we assume light from any sources strikes such surfaces directly, we need not compute shadow rays. This is the situation shown in Figure 9.37. Here we see a shadow ray that a full ray-tracing algorithm would find is blocked from the source. The corresponding point on the object would not be illuminated. In the simplified algorithm, we use this light and do not see a shadow in the resulting image. If we are willing to accept the missing shadows, then, since we carry out a hidden-surface removal anyway as part of the imaging process, we have not yet made any additional calculations. Additional calculations are necessary to incorporate the surface properties of the object.

9.8
Shading Models

To complete the ray-tracing process, we must consider what happens to the incident light when it strikes a surface. What happens depends on the orientation of the surface, the angle between the source and the surface normal, and the surface properties of the object. This calculation can be done point by point in the image plane or frame buffer, and thus combines nicely with hidden-surface removal in both hardware and software.

Once we have cast a ray and followed it to where it intersects a surface, we must calculate a color to place at the point in the frame buffer corresponding to the cast ray. Looking at the surface in Figure 9.38, we find three vectors or directions of importance for a single light source. The surface is struck by the cast ray **V**. Appealing to

Figure 9.38
Vector Model

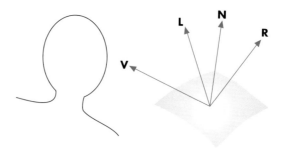

our synthetic camera analogy, we can view this cast ray as a projector from the surface to the viewer. The orientation of the surface is determined by the normal vector $\mathbf{N}$ at each point. Finally, we have the vector $\mathbf{L}$ from the point on the object to the light source. It will simplify subsequent calculations if we scale each of these vectors to have unit length,

$$|\mathbf{N}| = |\mathbf{L}| = |\mathbf{V}| = 1.$$

It will be helpful to add a fourth vector to our model, that of a perfect reflection of the light source. Since the angle of incidence is equal to the angle of reflection, this vector $\mathbf{R}$ is determined from $\mathbf{L}$ and $\mathbf{N}$. Noting that $\mathbf{L}$, $\mathbf{N}$, and $\mathbf{R}$ lie in the same plane, it is a simple exercise (Exercise 9.16) to show that the unit length vector with this property is

$$\mathbf{R} = 2(\mathbf{L} \cdot \mathbf{N})\mathbf{N} - \mathbf{L}.$$

These vectors are sufficient to build a simple model of light reflecting from a surface.

When light strikes a surface, some of it is absorbed, and the rest of it is reflected. Whereas an ideal mirror reflects an incident ray in a single direction, a *diffuse* surface reflects an incident ray in all directions. Most real surfaces are somewhere in the middle: They tend to reflect more light in certain directions than others. Using the vectors we introduced, the three major types of scatterers are as shown in Figure 9.39. For each type of scattering, we need a method of computing the intensity to place at the point where a cast ray intersects the surface. The intensity of this point determines its color or *shading* as seen by the viewer.

Figure 9.39
Scatterers. (a) Perfect Reflector. (b) Forward Scatterer. (c) Diffuse Reflector.

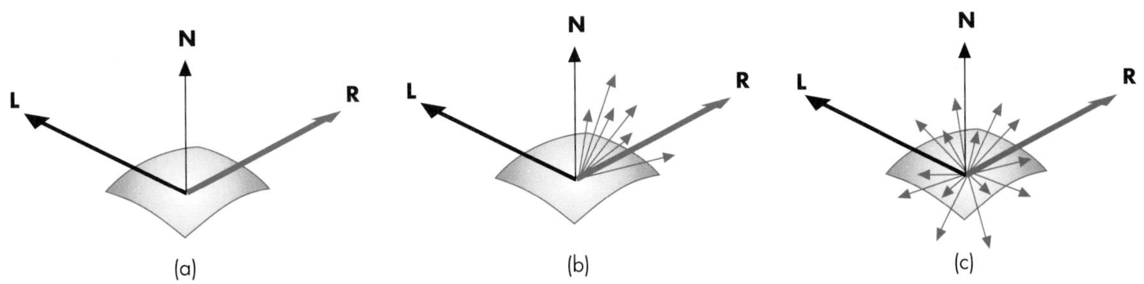

(a) (b) (c)

9.8.1 Diffuse Reflections

Light that is reflected from a perfectly diffuse surface is scattered equally in all directions. Such a surface appears the same to all viewers, and the vector $\mathbf{V}$ does not enter into the calculation. However, the incident intensity, I_s, is foreshortened according to Lambert's law, which states that the diffuse component is the projection of the incoming light onto the surface. This component is proportional to $\cos\theta$, where θ is the angle between $\mathbf{L}$ and $\mathbf{N}$. Assuming that $\mathbf{L}$ and $\mathbf{N}$ are unit vectors,

$$\cos\theta = \mathbf{L} \cdot \mathbf{N}.$$

Of the incident light, only a fraction k_d will be diffusely reflected; the rest will be absorbed. This constant must satisfy

$$1 \geq k_d \geq 0,$$

and is a property of the surface. Hence, for a single monochromatic source, the reflected intensity is

$$I = I_s k_d \cos\theta = I_s k_d \mathbf{L} \cdot \mathbf{N}.$$

For color, we will use the model three times with three different absorption constants and three different source intensities. For multiple sources, we add a like term for each source.

The model does not include the effects of the distance d from the source to the surface. This distance effect can be important if objects are at significantly different distances from a source. Although the light seen by the viewer should be proportional to $1/d^2$, where d is the distance between the surface and the viewer, in practice a term of the form $1/(d + d_0)$, for a suitably chosen constant d_0, is usually used. Thus, each diffuse term is of the form

$$I = \frac{I_s k_d \mathbf{L} \cdot \mathbf{N}}{d + d_0}.$$

9.8.2 Ambient Light

One of the major problems in rendering is to provide lighting effects that appear natural without requiring excessive calculation. Our model for diffuse sources should be applied for every possible incident light source. For a few point sources, this process presents no particular difficulty. Unfortunately, point sources can produce harsh images that are poor models of the real world. If we attempt to model real light sources, which are distributed, we usually need so many point sources that such a method is impractical.

An alternative is to use an ambient light level with intensity I_a to model the effect of many distributed sources and the contribution of light bouncing from surface to surface. This light will be partially absorbed at a point on the surface, so the contribution will be of the form

$$I = I_a k_a.$$

9.8.3 Specular Reflections

The surface-reflectivity properties of an object are dependent on the local smoothness of the surface. The smoother a surface is, the more like a mirror it will act; the rougher it is, the more like a diffuse reflector it will act. If a surface is smooth enough, we can notice *specular highlights* in an image, which are caused by a significant amount of the incident light being reflected at angles near that of a perfect reflector. These highlights are often seen as the bright spots of reflected light we see on polished surfaces. Modeling such reflections can be based on physical principles, but such an approach leads to complex models requiring considerable calculation. The Phong model [Phong75] requires a limited amount of calculation and provides a good approximation to real specular reflectors.

A viewer in the direction $\mathbf{V}$ will see more specular highlights the closer $\mathbf{V}$ is to $\mathbf{R}$. In the Phong model, we use $\mathbf{V} \cdot \mathbf{R} = \cos \psi$ where ψ is the angle between the vectors as our fundamental variable. The cosine has the property that, as the magnitude of ψ increases, the magnitude of $\mathbf{V} \cdot \mathbf{R}$ decreases toward zero. We can increase the concentration of specular highlights near $\mathbf{R}$ by using $\cos^\alpha \psi$, rather than $\cos \psi$. The value of α characterizes the material; higher values of α correspond to more highly polished surfaces. The intensity of the specular reflection will depend on an absorption constant, k_s, dependent on the material. More complex models will include the dependence of θ on k_s. We might also incorporate a distance term. A basic model with a single point source incorporating ambient, diffuse, and specular terms is of the form

$$I = \frac{I_s}{d + d_0}(k_d \mathbf{L} \cdot \mathbf{N} + k_s (\mathbf{R} \cdot \mathbf{V})^\alpha) + I_a k_a.$$

Individual terms in this expression can be eliminated if they are not necessary for a particular application.

9.9
Polygonal Shading

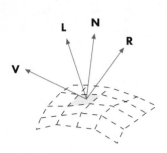

Figure 9.40
Polygonal Shading

The shape of a surface at any point is described by the normal at this point. If we are willing to compute the normal at every point on a surface, we will have all the components of our surface model at every point. Everything we have presented about ray tracing and rendering will apply to such a surface. Such an approach presents a number of computational difficulties. Not only must we determine a normal at each point on the surface, but also we must then apply the appropriate shading at each point. The use of polygons simplifies the calculations enormously and fits in well with the efficient hidden-surface–removal algorithms we have discussed for polygonal models.

Figure 9.40 shows one polygon that is part of a three-dimensional mesh, and our four vectors $\mathbf{N}, \mathbf{V}, \mathbf{L}$, and $\mathbf{R}$. For a polygon, $\mathbf{N}$ is the same at every point. Suppose that we consider only ambient and diffuse reflections and that the light source is sufficiently far away that it can be regarded as parallel, so $\mathbf{L}$ will be the same at every point on the polygon. In this case, our shading calculation will be the same at every point on the polygon and will need to be done only once for each polygon. If specular reflections are important and either the polygon is small or the viewer is far away, we also might be able to assume that $\mathbf{V}$ is constant over the polygon. Then we still might be able to use a single shading computation for the entire polygon. This method is known as *constant shading* and is a fast one for rendering polygonal meshes.

9.9.1 Gouraud and Phong Shading

The difficulty with constant shading is that the human visual system is sensitive to changes between two shades of gray or two colors and may perceive this transition at the boundary between two polygons. If this happens, the viewer may not perceive the rendered mesh as a curved surface, as is usually intended, but may instead see the underlying mesh of filled polygons. The Gouraud and Phong models smooth out the differences at edges while still avoiding the point-by-point calculations required to shade a curved surface.

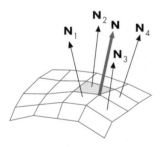

Figure 9.41
Approximating Normals

In a mathematical sense, normals do not exist at the edges or vertices of a polygon. We can obtain approximate edge and vertex normals by averaging. Consider the vertex in Figure 9.41. Four polygons meet at this vertex. By averaging them, we can obtain an approximate vertex normal

$$\mathbf{N} = \frac{\mathbf{N}_1 + \mathbf{N}_2 + \mathbf{N}_3 + \mathbf{N}_4}{4}.$$

We perform similar calculations at each vertex in the mesh, yielding a set of vertex normals for each polygon.

In *Gouraud shading* [Gour71], intensities over the surface of the polygon are obtained by a bilinear interpolation using the vertex intensities. This computation is usually done on a scan line basis, which fits in well with the other steps in forming a rendered image. Consider the example in Figure 9.42, where the four approximate vertex intensities are $I_a, I_b, I_c,$ and I_d. Consider a scan line that intersects edges AB and BD at E and F, respectively. The intensities at the E and F are obtained by the two linear interpolations

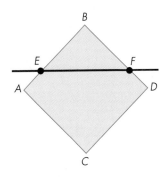

Figure 9.42
Gouraud Shading

$$I_E = (1 - \alpha)I_A + \alpha I_B,$$
$$I_F = (1 - \beta)I_B + \beta I_D,$$

where α and β are determined by the distances along the edges to the scan-line intersections. The intensities along the scan line between E and F are obtained by a second linear interpolation between I_E and I_F using

$$I(\gamma) = (1 - \gamma)I_E + \gamma I_F.$$

As γ goes from 0 to 1, we color all the pixels between E and F.

Gouraud shading can be carried out fairly efficiently, but the image may suffer from some of the defects of constant shading if the polygons are large or if there are significant specular reflections. In these cases, the additional work of *Phong shading* [Phong75] may be necessary. Phong shading starts off in a similar manner to Gouraud shading by calculating approximate vertex normals. These vertex normals are now used as the basis of a bilinear interpolation of normals across the polygon. For our example, we would obtain normals at E and F by the interpolation

(a)

$$\mathbf{N}_E = (1 - \alpha)\mathbf{N}_A + \alpha\mathbf{N}_B,$$
$$\mathbf{N}_F = (1 - \beta)\mathbf{N}_B + \beta\mathbf{N}_D.$$

Now normals could be interpolated across the scan line using $\mathbf{N}_E$ and $\mathbf{N}_F$. These normals must be scaled to have unit length so that they can be used in the final step—the application of the shading model at every point along the scan line. This work represents a considerable increase over that required by Gouraud shading. Figure 9.43 shows the variation of intensity over a single rectangular polygon obtained using the Gouraud and Phong modes. Color Plates 13 and 14 show the realism that can be achieved with polygonal models.

(b)

Figure 9.43
(a) Gouraud Shaded Polygon. (b) Phong Shaded Polygon

9.10
Suggested Readings

The book by Rogers [Rog85] includes many variants of the algorithms we have discussed here. Many of the original papers are reprinted in [Joy88]. The paper [Suth74b] is still of interest. The z-buffer algorithm was proposed by Catmul [Cat75b]. The original scan-line and depth-sort algorithms have gone through numerous modifications, which are described in [Rog85].

The lighting model we have used [Gour71][Phong75] can be replaced by more complex models; see [Cook82], [Hall83], and [Whit80], for example. Aliasing in ray tracing is discussed in [Crow77], [Crow81], and [Cat75]. Much of the pioneering work on ray tracing can be found in [Joy88]; recent work is discussed in [Mag87] and [Rog87]. Hardware aspects of rendering polygonal models are discussed in [Akel88].

Exercises

9.1 Design a data structure for a polygonal mesh that will allow us to keep track of the direction (clockwise or counterclockwise) in which the vertices are traversed.

9.2 Design a depth-sort algorithm for three-dimensional convex solids.

9.3 Write an algorithm for displaying a function $y = f(x, z)$ as a mesh of polygons.

9.4 Find four points on a sphere that are equidistant. These points determine a regular tetrahedron.

9.5 You can obtain an approximation to a sphere by recursively subdividing the tetrahedron. Write a program to find this approximation by subdividing a triangle by the bisectors of each side. Ensure that the radius is unchanged after each subdivision.

9.6 An alternate to the method described in Exercise 9.5 is to subdivide triangles by bisecting each angle. Is this approach better? Explain your answer.

9.7 Approximate ellipsoids using ellipses of constant longitude and latitude.

9.8 Write a procedure that will intersect two planar polygons. First solve the problem for convex polygons, then attempt to generalize your solution.

9.9 An alternate method to display data generated by samples of a function $y = f(x, z)$ is to plot a series of polylines corresponding to the data for a constant z. As opposed to the polygon-mesh algorithms, which process the data back to front, these algorithms proceed front to back. Starting with the idea that any curve can be obscured only by the data in front of it, write such a procedure.

9.10 Suppose that we have objects in a space that has not been normalized. Hence, the projection plane and viewer can be located anywhere. Investigate the additional work required in our hidden-surface–removal algorithms.

9.11 Write a procedure for determining whether a polygon is completely in front of another polygon when viewed from an arbitrary location.

9.12 Where in the process of creating a realistic image can parallelism in the hardware help? Explain your answer.

9.13 Consider the problem of making a sequence of realistic images. Which parts of the image generation have to be repeated for successive frames if a light source is moved? Which have to be repeated if an object is moved? Which have to be repeated if there is viewer motion?

9.14 How do we modify our ray-casting algorithms if surfaces both reflect and transmit light, as in Figure 9.44?

9.15 Why is rendering made easier if there is only a single light source at the eye of the viewer?

9.16 Given a unit surface normal $\mathbf{N}$ and light incident from a source in the direction $\mathbf{L}$, show that a vector in the direction of a perfect reflector is given by $2(\mathbf{L} \cdot \mathbf{N})\mathbf{N} - \mathbf{L}$.

9.17 Write a rendering program for a class of simple objects, such as all convex polygons or all spheres.

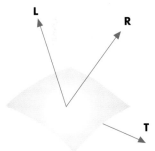

Figure 9.44
Partially Transmitting Surface

10

CURVES AND SURFACES

Introduction

As we consider more sophisticated applications of computer graphics, the limitations placed on us by our use of linear objects such as lines and planes becomes a serious problem. Although we have modeled complex shapes with linear approximations, such as using a mesh of planar polygons to model a sphere, eventually the large number of approximating objects can become a problem. The alternative is to use more sophisticated primitives, such as curves and surfaces. Although, from the application user's point of view, this solution might appear to be the obvious one, we must be careful to make sure that the graphics system can handle such objects.

We shall argue that polynomials provide the proper mixture of flexibility and ease of evaluation. After we examine using various types of polynomial curves—principally cubics—we shall extend our arguments to polynomial surfaces. Much of what we present here has its basis in approximation theory and numerical analysis. However, the special requirements of applications in computer graphics have made certain forms more important than others are. It is on these important forms that we shall focus.

▬ 10.1
▬ Explicit, Implicit, and Parametric Curves

In Chapter 2, we introduced three different ways (explicit, implicit, and parametric) of representing curves in two dimensions. There, we were interested in these forms primarily as a way of representing and manipulating lines and line segments. Each form can describe more general curves in both two and three dimensions, and can be extended to describe surfaces.

10.1.1 Explicit Form

In two dimensions, the explicit representation of a curve can be of the form

$$y = f(x),$$

or

$$x = g(y).$$

In three dimensions, we require two equations, such as

$$y = f(x),$$
$$z = g(x).$$

Of course, we have the possibility of using y (or z) as the independent variable, and of writing two equations for x and z (or x and y). If this form exists for a given curve, it has two obvious advantages. First, for a given range of values of x, it leads directly to a way of obtaining points on the curve by simply evaluating the function(s) for a set of x values. This gives us the second advantage, which is that we automatically have a scan-conversion algorithm of the form

```
Rpt location;
int x, value;
float f()
        .

        .
```

```
for(x=FIRST;x<=LAST;x++)
{
    location.x=x;
    location.y=f(x)+.5; /* rounds y to closest int */
    set_pixel(&location, value);
}
```

This is a simple generalization of the DDA algorithm for scan converting line segments; it simply says "for each x in the frame buffer, set the pixel at the closest y."

The disadvantages of the form are many. The principal one is that the form may not exist even when the object does. This drawback exists for even our most basic primitives. The usual explicit representation of the line,

$$y = mx + h,$$

fails because the slope m is infinite for vertical lines. Since the circle has two y values for each x value, there can be no explicit representation valid for the entire circle.

In general, choosing to represent y as a function of x (or vice versa) leads to problems of *axis dependency*. Although we could switch to representing curves as functions of y rather than of x when the magnitude of the slope is greater than one, as we did in our scan conversion algorithms for lines, such a tactic requires too much calculation for general curves.

10.1.2 Implicit Form

The implicit form of a two-dimensional curve is described by a single equation,

$$g(x, y) = 0.$$

In three dimensions, the corresponding equation,

$$g(x, y, z) = 0,$$

describes a surface. An implicit curve can be obtained by the intersection of two implicitly defined surfaces,

$$g(x, y, z) = 0,$$
$$h(x, y, z) = 0,$$

if these surfaces do indeed intersect.

The advantage of the implicit form is that many curves and surfaces can be expressed simply. Planes, spheres, and other quadric surfaces are usually expressed implicitly. However, the form cannot be used directly to generate points on a line or surface; rather, it is used as a test to determine whether a given point is indeed on a certain curve or surface. This difficulty makes the form of limited usefulness in computer graphics. The implicit form is most useful when it is used in conjunction with either of the other forms, particularly in rendering.

10.1.3 Parametric Form

Parametric form provides the curve and surface representations of choice for most graphics applications. Each variable is given by an explicit equation whose independent variable is a parameter t. In two dimensions, we have

$$x = x(t),$$
$$y = y(t).$$

In three dimensions, we simply add an additional equation,

$$z = z(t).$$

Since each variable is governed by its own equation, the form is far more general and axis independent than is the explicit form. The separate equations also make it easier to generate scan-conversion algorithms.

10.1.4 Example

Consider a circle of radius r centered at the origin as we did in Chapter 2. The usual way we learn to describe such a circle is by the equation

$$x^2 + y^2 = r^2,$$

which is really an implicit representation, where

$$g(x, y) = x^2 + y^2 - r^2 = 0.$$

We often incorrectly write an "explicit" representation,

$$y = \pm\sqrt{r^2 - x^2}.$$

This representation is not an equation at all. What is meant is that the circle can comprise the two semicircles

$$y = \sqrt{r^2 - x^2},$$
$$y = -\sqrt{r^2 - x^2},$$

each of which can be expressed explicitly. There are a couple of additional problems lurking here. Neither form leads to an efficient scan-conversion algorithm for circles. Imbedded within these representations is the understanding that

$$r \geq x, y \geq -r.$$

Neglecting to ensure that this condition is true will cause major difficulties in the use of this representation within a graphics system. Although these conditions are obvious for the circle, they do take time to enforce, and equivalent requirements might not be easy to determine for more general curves. Such problems do not arise with the parametric form

$$x = r \cos t,$$
$$y = r \sin t.$$

For any value of t, we have a point on the circle (although we might complain about having to evaluate trigonometric functions).

Some of the axis-dependency problems can also be illustrated with the circle. The slope of the curve will not exist at all points, since dy/dx is infinite for $x = \pm 1$. As Figure 10.1 should make clear, however, the curvature of the circle is constant everywhere. Any form that fails for a specific value of x or y is manifesting some axis dependency. The ordinary derivative dy/dx has this problem, and its use should be avoided. From the figure, we see that the tangent to the curve exists at every point on the circle, even where the slope goes to infinity. The parametric form allows us to work with the derivatives of x and y with respect to the parameter t:

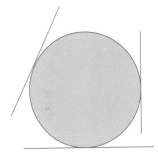

Figure 10.1
Circle and Tangent Lines

$$x'(t) = \frac{dx}{dt},$$
$$y'(t) = \frac{dy}{dt}.$$

The tangent vector is given by

$$\mathbf{t} = \begin{bmatrix} dy/dt \\ dx/dt \end{bmatrix}.$$

The ordinary derivative,

$$\frac{dy}{dx} = \frac{y'(t)}{x'(t)},$$

can be computed from the parametric form whenever $x'(t) \neq 0$. Although problems of axis dependency are minimized by the use of parametric form, the problems cannot be completely solved without a coordinate-system–free representation. Such a representation uses curvature, normals, and tangents as its basic variables. These issues are discussed in the literature on geometric modeling.

10.2 Polynomial Curves

Polynomial curves provide a balance between our desire to control the shape of a curve to meet design criteria and the ease with which it can be evaluated. Polynomial curves are important in all three forms. For example, in explicit form, we have expressions such as these for a three-dimensional curve:

$$y = f(x) = 5x^2 + 3x - 5,$$
$$z = g(x) = 10x^4 + 3.$$

Using two-dimensional implicit form, the two variable polynomial

$$g(x, y) = x^2 + y^2 - 1 = 0$$

describes a circle. Note that the ability to represent the curve using an implicit polynomial does not guarantee a polynomial explicit form. Since, in three dimensions, an implicit polynomial describes a surface, we can describe an implicit curve by intersecting two polynomial surfaces. The equations

$$f(x, y, z) = 2x - 5y + z - 2 = 0,$$
$$g(x, y, z) = x^2 + y^2 + z^2 - 3 = 0$$

describe a plane and a sphere. Their intersection is a circle. Applying the parametric form in three dimensions, we have three polynomials in the parameter t, as in the example

$$x(t) = 5t^3 + 2,$$
$$y(t) = 3t - 1,$$
$$z(t) = t^2,$$

which describe a curve.

For the reasons that we discussed in the previous section, we shall be concerned primarily with explicit and parametric forms. In both these cases, we have polynomials of a single variable of degree N, which can be written as

$$p(t) = \sum_{i=0}^{N} c_i t^i.$$

The independent variable t can be the independent variable in the parametric form, or we can substitute x for t when we want to work with an explicit form. The dependent variable p can represent x, y, or z if we are discussing the parametric form, or can represent y in the explicit form $y = p(x)$.

Since the $N + 1$ coefficients $\{c_i\}$ define a polynomial of degree N, any set of $N + 1$ independent conditions will allow us to find these coefficients and will specify a unique polynomial. Different forms of curves and surfaces will be determined by which kinds of conditions we impose.

10.2.1 Cubic Polynomials

Although polynomials are usually simple functions to manipulate and evaluate, polynomials of high degree can present significant practical problems. Regardless of the method of evaluation, the higher the degree of the polynomial, the more calculation is required to evaluate a point on it. In addition, the higher the degree of the polynomial, the larger the effect will be of small numerical errors such as roundoff.

On the other hand, if the degree is too low, there will be little flexibility to control the shape of the curve, as we will have few coefficients to adjust. We can achieve a balance between these problems by using a number of low-order polynomials, each defined over a short range. These curve segments are usually joined at their endpoints, as in Figure 10.2. Each curve segment is determined locally by both the data at the *control points*, and any conditions we need to satisfy any continuity requirements at the knots.

Figure 10.2
Curve Segments

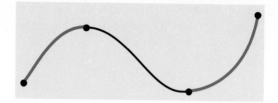

In computer graphics and in other fields that use polynomials for geometric modeling, cubic polynomials are often used to provide a good balance between ease of use and ability to model a desired shape. Cubic polynomials can be used for explicit forms as

$$y(x) = ax^3 + bx^2 + cx + d,$$

or in general parametric equations for a curve:

$$x(t) = a_x t^3 + b_x t^2 + c_x t + d_x,$$
$$y(t) = a_y t^3 + b_y t^2 + c_y t + d_y,$$
$$z(t) = a_z t^3 + b_z t^2 + c_z t + d_z.$$

They can also be used to generate implicitly defined curves and surfaces. For example, a two-dimensional curve can be described by the bicubic polynomial

$$g(x,y) = \sum_{i=0}^{3}\sum_{i=0}^{3} a_{ij} x^i y^j = 0,$$

which is specified by the 16 coefficients $\{a_{ij}\}$.

In the parametric formulation, points on a curve in three dimensional space can be described by a vector curve of the form

$$\mathbf{p}(t) = \begin{bmatrix} x(t) \\ y(t) \\ z(t) \end{bmatrix}.$$

Since the form of the three polynomials in this vector is the same, rather than repeating our equations for each case, we will use the single representation

$$p(t) = at^3 + bt^2 + ct + d,$$

where p can be x, y, or z. If we want to consider an explicit form, we will substitute x for t and y for p, leaving us with usual explicit form,

$$y = p(x).$$

For each scalar polynomial, $p(t)$, we will have to determine four coefficients, which means that we can satisfy four independent conditions. For example, if we wish to form an *interpolating* cubic polynomial—one that passes through the control points—we expect to use four points to determine such a polynomial. In the case of the explicit form of a two-dimensional curve, $y(x)$, these data points will be the values of y at four values of x: $y(x_0)$, $y(x_1)$, $y(x_2)$, and $y(x_3)$. For the parametric form, we will have our parametric curve pass through the points

$$\mathbf{p}(t_0) = \begin{bmatrix} x(t_0) \\ y(t_0) \\ z(t_0) \end{bmatrix}, \qquad \mathbf{p}(t_1) = \begin{bmatrix} x(t_1) \\ y(t_1) \\ z(t_1) \end{bmatrix},$$

$$\mathbf{p}(t_2) = \begin{bmatrix} x(t_2) \\ y(t_2) \\ z(t_2) \end{bmatrix}, \qquad \mathbf{p}(t_3) = \begin{bmatrix} x(t_3) \\ y(t_3) \\ z(t_3) \end{bmatrix}.$$

Although there are three cubic polynomials to be determined here, and thus 12 coefficients, each polynomial is independent of the other two. Hence, we really have three identical problems of determining the coefficients of a scalar cubic polynomial, $p(t)$. Only the data will differ in each case.

10.3
Interpolating Form

The interpolating form is not used often in computer graphics, since interpolating polynomials do not have the smoothness desired in most applications. However, the steps required to derive an interpolating polynomial are common to many of the other polynomial types. These steps will be easy to demonstrate for the interpolating polynomial, so we will derive this form and will use it as a basis for the others. Although we could derive the general forms for each type of polynomial, we will be content to derive the specific results for cubics in recognition of their particular importance in computer graphics.

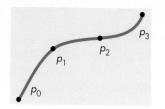

Figure 10.3
Cubic Interpolating
Polynomial

10.3.1 The Cubic Interpolating Polynomial

Suppose we have a sequence of control points $p_i = p(t_i), i = 0, 1, ...$ Since we are working with cubic polynomials, the first four points determine a polynomial (Figure 10.3) of the form

$$p(t) = at^3 + bt^2 + ct + d,$$

which passes through them. We can derive the values of $a, b, c,$ and d by writing the equation of the polynomial at each of the control points:

$$p_0 = at_0^3 + bt_0^2 + ct_0 + d,$$
$$p_1 = at_1^3 + bt_1^2 + ct_1 + d,$$
$$p_2 = at_2^3 + bt_2^2 + ct_2 + d,$$
$$p_3 = at_3^3 + bt_3^2 + ct_3 + d,$$

or, in matrix form

$$\begin{bmatrix} p_0 \\ p_1 \\ p_2 \\ p_3 \end{bmatrix} = \mathbf{A}_I \begin{bmatrix} a \\ b \\ c \\ d \end{bmatrix},$$

where $\mathbf{A}_I$ is the matrix

$$\mathbf{A}_I = \begin{bmatrix} t_0^3 & t_0^2 & t_0 & 1 \\ t_1^3 & t_1^2 & t_1 & 1 \\ t_2^3 & t_2^2 & t_2 & 1 \\ t_3^3 & t_3^2 & t_3 & 1 \end{bmatrix}.$$

As long as the values t_i are distinct, it is easy to show that $\mathbf{A}_I$ is nonsingular, so the equations can be solved for the desired parameters

$$\begin{bmatrix} a \\ b \\ c \\ d \end{bmatrix} = \mathbf{A}_I^{-1} \begin{bmatrix} p_0 \\ p_1 \\ p_2 \\ p_3 \end{bmatrix} = \mathbf{M}_I \begin{bmatrix} p_0 \\ p_1 \\ p_2 \\ p_3 \end{bmatrix}.$$

The matrix $\mathbf{M}_I$ is known as the the *interpolating geometry matrix* and is determined by only the locations of the independent variable, not by the values being interpolated.

Consider the use of this form to determine interpolating polynomials for three-dimensional curves. Using parametric form, we have to do the interpolation for each of x, y, and z. Suppose that we define our parametric polynomial over the range 0 to 1, which, as we shall see, entails no loss of generality. We usually assume that the data are given at equally spaced points in parameter space; that is, $p(0), p(1/3), p(2/3),$ and $p(1)$. Thus, $\mathbf{A}_I$ becomes the matrix

$$\mathbf{A}_I = \begin{bmatrix} 0 & 0 & 0 & 1 \\ (\frac{1}{3})^3 & (\frac{1}{3})^2 & \frac{1}{3} & 1 \\ (\frac{2}{3})^3 & (\frac{2}{3})^2 & \frac{2}{3} & 1 \\ 1 & 1 & 1 & 1 \end{bmatrix},$$

which has the inverse

$$\mathbf{M}_I = \begin{bmatrix} -4.5 & 13.5 & -13.5 & 4.5 \\ 9 & -22.5 & 18 & -4.5 \\ -5.5 & 9 & -4.5 & 1 \\ 1 & 0 & 0 & 0 \end{bmatrix}.$$

We use this same matrix in our calculations for x, y, and z, and thus we need to calculate it or to look it up only once. Each set of values we calculate for a, b, c, and d will, of course, be different, since the values of the control points will be different for x, y, and z.

10.3.2 Joining Curve Segments

Suppose we have now constructed our interpolating polynomial through the first four control points p_0, p_1, p_2, and p_3, and we wish to construct another polynomial using the next group of control points. We virtually always want to enforce some degree of continuity between the interpolating curves we construct. At a minimum, we want the end of one curve segment to be the beginning of the next. We can achieve this continuity by having the second curve segment interpolate the control points p_3, p_4, p_5, and p_6, as shown in Figure 10.4. With the interpolating form, we get continuity at p_3, since both polynomials interpolate p_3, but the first three derivatives (the higher ones are all zero) will not be continuous there. This lack of derivative continuity is a major weakness of the interpolating form.

If we are working with parametric polynomials, it might seem that the logical path would be to work through our equations again using values of t of 1, 4/3, 5/3, and 2. This computation would generate a new interpolating matrix $\mathbf{M}_I$. A more efficient procedure might be to

Figure 10.4
Interpolating Polynomials

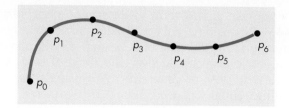

shift the new problem back to the original interval, 0 to 1. Consider the polynomial

$$p(t) = at^3 + bt^2 + ct + d.$$

Suppose we make the change of variables

$$t' = t - 1.$$

Our polynomial becomes

$$p(t') = a(t' + 1)^3 + b(t' + 1)^2 + c(t' + 1) + d,$$
$$= a't'^3 + b't'^2 + c't' + d',$$

where

$$
\begin{bmatrix} a' \\ b' \\ c' \\ d' \end{bmatrix}
=
\begin{bmatrix}
1 & 0 & 0 & 0 \\
-3 & 1 & 0 & 0 \\
3 & -2 & 1 & 0 \\
-1 & 1 & -1 & 1
\end{bmatrix}
\begin{bmatrix} a \\ b \\ c \\ d \end{bmatrix}.
$$

Thus, by a simple transformation we can convert the problem over the interval 1 to 2 to one over 0 to 1, with the idea that we could easily adjust the coefficients later to shift back to the interval starting at 1. This shifting tells us that we do not have to calculate a new $\mathbf{M}_I$. Instead, we calculate

$$
\begin{bmatrix} a' \\ b' \\ c' \\ d' \end{bmatrix}
= \mathbf{M_I}
\begin{bmatrix} p_3 \\ p_4 \\ p_5 \\ p_6 \end{bmatrix},
$$

We either transform these values to the desired $a, b, c,$ and d or, equivalently, transform t to be over the desired range. As we use the same matrix repeatedly, the labeling of $\mathbf{M}_I$ as *the* interpolating geometry matrix is appropriate.

10.3.3 Blending Polynomials

Returning to the original polynomial

$$p(t) = at^3 + bt^2 + ct + d,$$

we can, for the control points p_0, p_1, p_2, and p_3, insert our solution for a, b, c, and d, which allows us, after some manipulation, to rewrite the polynomial in the form

$$p(t) = \sum_{i=0}^{3} b_i(t) p_i,$$

where each function $b_i(t)$ is a cubic polynomial. These *blending polynomials* are given by

$$b_0(t) = -\frac{1}{2}(3t - 1)(3t - 2)(t - 1),$$

$$b_1(t) = \frac{9}{2}t(3t - 2)(t - 1),$$

$$b_2(t) = -\frac{9}{5}t(3t - 1)(t - 1),$$

$$b_3(t) = \frac{1}{2}t(3t - 1)(3t - 2).$$

These polynomials are shown in Figure 10.5. In this form, we can see the contribution that each data point makes to the final polynomial. The blending functions have all their zeros in the interval 0 to 1. This property causes them to vary considerably over the very interval over which we wish to use them. The effect is that interpolating polynomials, although they are forced to pass through the control points, are not very smooth and can be unsuitable for modeling in many applications. An additional consequence of this lack of smoothness is that, if a control point is moved slightly, say as part of an interactive design process, we might see a large change in the interpolating polynomial. This instability is especially noticeable when we are using higher-degree polynomials.

Figure 10.5
Blending Polynomials

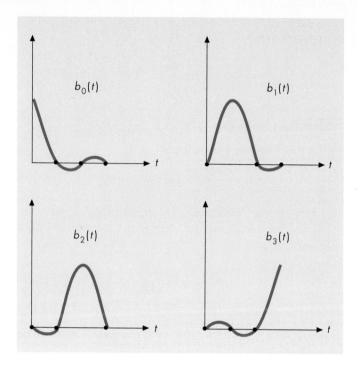

10.3.4 Approximating a Circle

Before moving on to the smoother polynomial forms, we shall derive the interpolating polynomial for a problem of interest to us—the
generation of circles. We shall resolve this problem later using other
polynomial forms. Circles are important modeling objects; they also
are entities we often want to display. While we can work with the implicit representation of a circle for modeling, eventually we will want
to display the circle. Although there is an extension of Bresenham's
algorithm line-drawing algorithm to circles, many systems approximate circles with polynomial curves.

Most techniques for circle display use the eight-fold symmetry of
the circle, which we see in Figure 10.6 for a circle centered at the
origin. The symmetry in the equation of the circle shows us that, if
we know one point on a circle, we in fact know seven others. Thus, we
need only to generate a 45-degree sector of a circle by any rasterization
algorithm. The rest of the curve is obtained by symmetry. We will
generate an interpolating polynomial for the wedge of a unit circle
from $(0, -1)$ to $(\sqrt{2}/2, -\sqrt{2}/2)$. The slope of the circle starts at 0
and goes to 1 along this wedge.

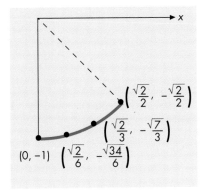

Figure 10.6
Eight-Fold Symmetry

Suppose we desire an explicit representation,

$$y = ax^3 + bx^2 + cx + d.$$

If the data points are equally spaced in x at $x = 0, \sqrt{2}/6, \sqrt{2}/3, \sqrt{2}/2$, then the corresponding values of y are $-1, -\sqrt{34}/6, -\sqrt{7}/3, -\sqrt{2}/2$ (Figure 10.7). These four x values are used as t_0, t_1, t_2, and t_3 in the matrix

$$\mathbf{A}_I = \begin{bmatrix} t_0^3 & t_0^2 & t_0 & 1 \\ t_1^3 & t_1^2 & t_1 & 1 \\ t_2^3 & t_2^2 & t_2 & 1 \\ t_3^3 & t_3^2 & t_3 & 1 \end{bmatrix}.$$

and its inverse, $\mathbf{M}_I$, is computed. We then multiply this matrix times the vector of the y values to find the coefficients of the polynomial.

Figure 10.7
Wedge of Circle

The resulting polynomial is

$$y = 0.295x^3 + 0.347x^2 + 0.021x - 1.0.$$

Alternatively, we can use the parametric form to derive two cubic polynomials:

$$x = p_x(t) = a_x t^3 + b_x t^2 + c_x t + d,$$
$$y = p_y(t) = a_y t^3 + b_y t^2 + c_y t + d.$$

Suppose we let the first interpolate the x values at $t = 0, \frac{1}{3}, \frac{2}{3}, 1$, and the second interpolates the y values for the same values of t. We can now use same matrix $\mathbf{M}_I$ to find

$$
\begin{bmatrix} a_x \\ b_x \\ c_x \\ d_x \end{bmatrix}
=
\begin{bmatrix}
-4.5 & 13.5 & -13.5 & 4.5 \\
9 & -22.5 & 18 & -4.5 \\
-5.5 & 9 & -4.5 & 1 \\
1 & 0 & 0 & 0
\end{bmatrix}
\begin{bmatrix} 0 \\ \frac{\sqrt{2}}{6} \\ \frac{\sqrt{2}}{3} \\ \frac{\sqrt{2}}{2} \end{bmatrix}
=
\begin{bmatrix} 0.0 \\ 0.0 \\ 0.707 \\ 0.0 \end{bmatrix}.
$$

In the same way, we find the coefficients for the second polynomial

$$
\begin{bmatrix} a_y \\ b_y \\ c_y \\ d_y \end{bmatrix}
=
\begin{bmatrix}
-4.5 & 13.5 & -13.5 & 4.5 \\
9 & -22.5 & 18 & -4.5 \\
-5.5 & 9 & -4.5 & 1 \\
1 & 0 & 0 & 0
\end{bmatrix}
\begin{bmatrix} -1 \\ \frac{-\sqrt{34}}{6} \\ -\frac{\sqrt{7}}{3} \\ \frac{\sqrt{2}}{2} \end{bmatrix}
=
\begin{bmatrix} 0.104 \\ 0.174 \\ 0.015 \\ -1.0 \end{bmatrix}.
$$

The polynomial for x is the simple linear equation,

$$x(t) = \frac{\sqrt{2}}{2} t,$$

and, when substituted into the equation for $y(t)$, will yield the explicit interpolating form we derived previously. This result, although expected, shows a subtle axis-dependent effect we can avoid by a slight change in our use of the parametric form. We chose our values to interpolate to be equally spaced in x. Suppose that we instead choose our values to be equally spaced along the circle, as in Figure 10.8. Now the control points are at $(0, -1)$, $(\sin(15), -\cos(15))$,

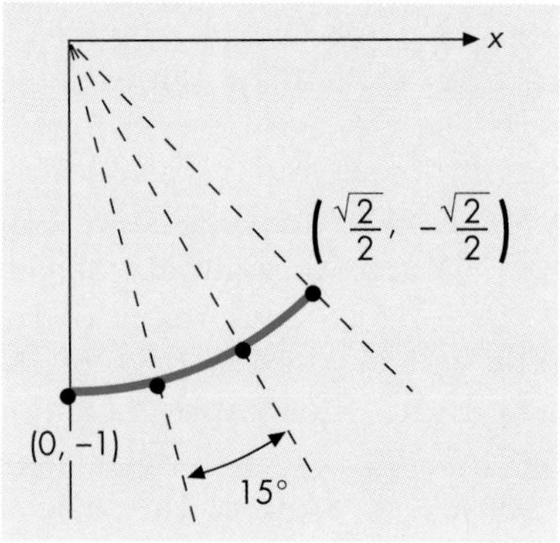

Figure 10.8
Equally Spaced Control
Points

$(\sin(30), -\cos(30))$, and $(\sin(45), -\cos(45))$. Resolving the problem with these data yields

$$
\begin{bmatrix} a_x \\ b_x \\ c_x \\ d_x \end{bmatrix} = \begin{bmatrix} -4.5 & 13.5 & -13.5 & 4.5 \\ 9 & -22.5 & 18 & -4.5 \\ -5.5 & 9 & -4.5 & 1 \\ 1 & 0 & 0 & 0 \end{bmatrix} \begin{bmatrix} 0 \\ \sqrt{\frac{1-\frac{\sqrt{3}}{2}}{2}} \\ 0.5 \\ \frac{\sqrt{2}}{2} \end{bmatrix} = \begin{bmatrix} -0.074 \\ -0.005 \\ -0.786 \\ 0.0 \end{bmatrix},
$$

$$
\begin{bmatrix} a_y \\ b_y \\ c_y \\ d_y \end{bmatrix} = \begin{bmatrix} -4.5 & 13.5 & -13.5 & 4.5 \\ 9 & -22.5 & 18 & -4.5 \\ -5.5 & 9 & -4.5 & 1 \\ 1 & 0 & 0 & 0 \end{bmatrix} \begin{bmatrix} -1 \\ \sqrt{\frac{1+\frac{\sqrt{3}}{2}}{2}} \\ -\frac{\sqrt{3}}{2} \\ \frac{\sqrt{2}}{2} \end{bmatrix} = \begin{bmatrix} -0.031 \\ 0.327 \\ -0.003 \\ -1.0 \end{bmatrix}.
$$

This parametric form provides a better approximation to the circle and cannot be reduced to a simple explicit representation.

The circle and its polynomial approximation are so close that it is difficult to see the difference without magnification. Although the approximations are close, we can notice one important defect. The derivative of the circle at $x = 0$ is zero. For our explicit approximation,

$$
\frac{dy}{dx}(0) = 0.021.
$$

For the parametric approximation,

$$
\frac{dy}{dx}(0) = \frac{\frac{dp_y}{dt}(0)}{\frac{dp_x}{dt}(0)} = \frac{c_y}{c_x} = 0.004.
$$

We can see that the value for the parametric form is closer to the correct value of zero than is that for the explicit curve. This disparity should be expected as the parametric form, by virtue of its use of separate polynomials for x and y, provides a better approximation. In both cases, the approximating curve leaves the point $(0, -1)$ with a positive slope. When we generate the approximation to the circle on the left of $(0, -1)$, the symmetry of the circle tells us that the slope at any point will be the negative of the slope at the corresponding point on the right. Hence, we have created a discontinuity in the first derivative at the $(0, -1)$. This discontinuity may make this approximation useless, in spite of the fact that the interpolating polynomial is close to the circle. Smoothing polynomials can provide approximations without this problem.

10.4
Smoothing Polynomials

When we joined two curve segments at a joint, we found the interpolating form gave us continuity between the two segments but did not give us continuity of the first derivative. As we can see from Figure 10.9 and our example in the last section, this lack of smoothness is usually unacceptable when we are modeling with real data or designing a shape. For example, if our approximating curves represent the shape of the body of an automobile or airplane, we could not (nor would we want to) manufacture such a shape if there were such discontinuities.

Where the smoothness of the approximating function and the continuity of derivatives at the joints is important, we cannot use interpolating polynomials. Instead, we generate different classes of polynomials by altering the conditions that define the polynomial. For cubic polynomials, although we have only four conditions with which to work, we can generate much smoother approximations and even get continuity of both the first and second derivatives at the endpoints.

Figure 10.9
Continuity at the Endpoint

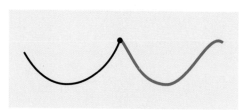

10.4.1 Hermite Polynomials

A cubic Hermite polynomial shows that it is possible to get first-derivative continuity at the joints. Consider the polynomial

$$p(t) = at^3 + bt^2 + ct + d,$$

over the interval

$$0 \le t \le 1.$$

Suppose that the four conditions we use to determine $p(t)$ are now the values of the polynomial at the endpoints, $p(0)$ and $p(1)$, and the first derivatives at the endpoints, $p'(0)$ and $p'(1)$. Since we can differentiate the polynomial, these four conditions give us the four equations

$$p(0) = d,$$
$$p(1) = a + b + c + d,$$
$$p'(0) = c,$$
$$p'(1) = 3a + 2b + c,$$

which can be solved for the coefficients of our polynomial. The solution is

$$
\begin{bmatrix} a \\ b \\ c \\ d \end{bmatrix}
=
\begin{bmatrix} 2 & -2 & 1 & 1 \\ -3 & 3 & -2 & -1 \\ 0 & 0 & 1 & 0 \\ 1 & 0 & 0 & 0 \end{bmatrix}
\begin{bmatrix} p(0) \\ p(1) \\ p'(0) \\ p'(1) \end{bmatrix}
= \mathbf{M}_H
\begin{bmatrix} p(0) \\ p(1) \\ p'(0) \\ p'(1) \end{bmatrix}.
$$

The matrix $\mathbf{M}_H$ is known as the *Hermite geometry matrix*. Figure 10.10 shows the continuity we can expect at the joint, as the same values and first derivatives are used at both sides of it; that is, these data are shared between the polynomials on the left and on the right of the endpoints. Note that we could obtain more continuity at

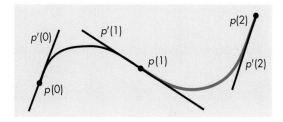

Figure 10.10
Hermite Polynomial

the endpoints by going to higher-degree polynomials. A Hermite polynomial of degree $2N + 1$ will have continuity of the first N derivatives at the joints.

Hermite polynomials have much more smoothness than do the interpolating forms. It is simple to verify this assertion by examining the blending functions. Hermite polynomials, however, suffer from one major defect: the values of the coefficients depend on having derivative information at the endpoints. In most applications, data are given as values at control points, rather than as derivatives, which precludes the direct use of the Hermite polynomials.

10.4.2 Bezier Polynomials

Bezier polynomials use the same control-point data as do the interpolating polynomials; they use these data to approximate the derivatives in the Hermite form. Suppose we have the four control points p_0, p_1, p_2, and p_3, which are the same points we used in the last section to determine an interpolating polynomial. The first and last points can be used to determine the values at the endpoints:

$$p(0) = p_0,$$
$$p(1) = p_3.$$

The first two points can be used to *approximate* the derivative at the left joint:

$$p'(0) \approx \frac{p_1 - p_0}{\frac{1}{3}} = 3(p_1 - p_0).$$

Likewise, at the right joint,

$$p'(1) \approx 3(p_3 - p_2).$$

In matrix form, we have

$$\begin{bmatrix} p(0) \\ p(1) \\ p'(0) \\ p'(1) \end{bmatrix} = \begin{bmatrix} 1 & 0 & 0 & 0 \\ 0 & 0 & 0 & 1 \\ -3 & 3 & 0 & 0 \\ 0 & 0 & -3 & 3 \end{bmatrix} \begin{bmatrix} p_0 \\ p_1 \\ p_2 \\ p_3 \end{bmatrix},$$

an expression that can be substituted into the Hermite form to obtain a solution for the coefficients of the desired polynomial,

$$
\begin{bmatrix} a \\ b \\ c \\ d \end{bmatrix} = \mathbf{M}_B \begin{bmatrix} p_0 \\ p_1 \\ p_2 \\ p_3 \end{bmatrix},
$$

where $\mathbf{M}_B$ is the *Bezier geometry matrix*

$$
\mathbf{M}_B = \begin{bmatrix} -1 & 3 & -3 & 1 \\ 3 & -6 & 3 & 0 \\ -3 & 3 & 0 & 0 \\ 1 & 0 & 0 & 0 \end{bmatrix}.
$$

The resulting curve is as in Figure 10.11. The Bezier polynomial has a simple expression in terms of four blending functions:

$$
p(t) = t^3 p_0 + 3t^2(1-t)p_1 + 3t(1-t)^2 p_2 + (1-t)^3 p_3.
$$

Since each blending polynomial has its zeros at the ends of the unit interval, the function is fairly smooth for t between zero and one. In addition, since $p(t)$ is a linear combination of the data values with coefficients between zero and one, $p(t)$ must lie in the *convex hull* of the points p_0, p_1, p_2, and p_3, as shown in Figure 10.12. As we can see, we construct the convex hull by joining the data points with line segments. Hence, a curve that is constrained to lie in the convex hull must be close to its control points, although it may pass through none of them. In this case, the Bezier curve does not pass through either p_1 or p_2, as does an interpolating curve.

We can achieve some additional flexibility in the Bezier curve by making a number of small changes. For example, if we force the next point on the right of p_4 to lie on the line defined by p_2 and p_3, we will have continuity of the first derivative at p_4. We can also allow nonuniform spacing of control points. Thus, if we assume that

$$
p_1 = p(h),
$$

where $0 < h < 1$, then we can rederive the Bezier polynomial using

$$
p'(0) = \frac{1}{h}(p_1 - p_0),
$$

and a similar expression for $p'(1)$. This technique is often done inter-

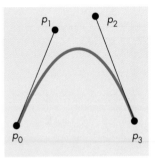

Figure 10.11
Bezier Polynomial

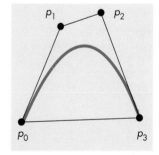

Figure 10.12
Convex Hull of Data

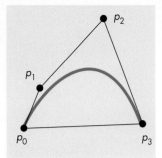

Figure 10.13
Nonuniform Spacing of
Control Points

actively in drawing applications by allowing the user to move p_1 along a constant-slope line from p_0. The effect of such an action is shown in Figure 10.13. When p_1 is moved closer to p_0, the effect of p_1 on the slope at p_0 is much more local.

Another important aspect is the additional flexibility gained by use of the parametric form. At any point where the derivative exists,

$$\frac{dy}{dx}(t) = \frac{(dy/dt)(t)}{(dx/dt)(t)}.$$

Thus, any α can be used in the approximation

$$
\begin{aligned}
x'(0) &\approx \alpha(x_1 - y_0), \\
y'(0) &\approx \alpha(y_1 - y_0),
\end{aligned}
$$

in our defining equations. Geometrically, this approximation states that any point (x_1, y_1) on the tangent line from (x_0, y_0) can be used in the Bezier form. The distance between (x_0, y_0) and (x_1, y_1) will affect how locally this approximation to the slope applies. The same argument can be applied to the parametric form of the Hermite polynomial and to the spline curves we discuss next.

10.4.3 Splines

The Bezier polynomial does not have first-derivative continuity at its endpoints, since we used an approximation in the Hermite form that is different on the left and right sides of an endpoint (Figure 10.14).

Figure 10.14
Joint of Bezier Polynomial

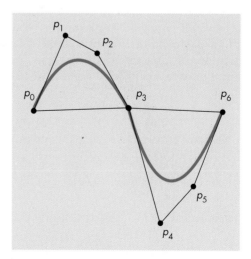

For the first curve segment, we use p_2 and p_3 to approximate $p'(1)$, whereas for the next segment, we use p_3 and p_4 for its derivative on the left side. Unless the control-point data are fairly smooth, we can notice this defect in the resulting polynomials.

One possibility is to move to higher-degree approximating polynomials, where each might be used over a larger range. Such a strategy would give us more flexibility, since we would have more coefficients that we could adjust. In computer graphics, we avoid this more global approach to determining curves in favor of using our low-degree polynomials. The advantages of staying with low-order polynomials include the reduced computational requirements, the greater stability of the low-order polynomials, and the local control of shape.

This last advantage is probably the key one. When we are working interactively with shapes, we do not want a situation where a change in one part of the curve will alter that curve's shape everywhere. With both interpolating cubic polynomials and cubic Bezier polynomials, a change in the data at a control point can affect at most two curve segments.

A better solution to the continuity problem is to use the same approximation for the derivative on both sides of an endpoint. To accomplish this new type of approximation while still having each curve segment determined by only local control point data, however, we will ultimately have to do more work. Our presentation is informal and is meant only to demonstrate what is possible with splines.

Suppose we use the four points p_0, p_1, p_2, and p_3 to determine a cubic polynomial, $p(t)$, that we will use only between p_1 and p_2. If this polynomial must interpolate p_1 and p_2, we get the two conditions, assuming t goes from 0 to 1 between them,

$$p(0) = p_1 = d,$$
$$p(1) = p_2 = a + b + c + d.$$

We will use an approximation to the derivative that makes use of data *outside* the unit interval over which the polynomial is to be used. This trick enables us to use the same data in the determination of adjacent polynomials. On the left side of the interval, we use the symmetric approximation to the derivative,

$$p'(0) \approx \frac{p_2 - p_0}{2} = c,$$

as shown in Figure 10.15; we use a similar approximation at the right end of the interval,

$$p'(1) \approx \frac{p_3 - p_1}{2} = 3a + 2b + c.$$

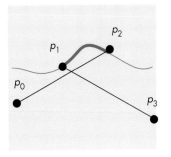

Figure 10.15
Approximating Derivatives

Solving yields polynomial coefficients:

$$
\begin{bmatrix} a \\ b \\ c \\ d \end{bmatrix} = \frac{1}{2} \begin{bmatrix} 3 & -5 & -7 & -1 \\ -1 & -3 & 4 & 1 \\ -1 & 0 & 1 & 0 \\ 0 & 1 & 0 & 0 \end{bmatrix} \begin{bmatrix} p_0 \\ p_1 \\ p_2 \\ p_3 \end{bmatrix}.
$$

This polynomial will be used between p_1 and p_2.

The general case will define the coefficients of a cubic polynomial with the preceding matrix. This polynomial will interpolate p_k and p_{k+1}, have as its derivative at the left end be $(p_{k+1} - p_{k-1})/2$, and have $(p_{k+2} - p_k)/2$ as the derivative on the right. These polynomials achieve the desired first-derivative continuity at the endpoints but as we can see from Figure 10.15 do not satisfy a convex hull property.

Getting started and terminating require a slight modification of the general case. The initial control point is p_0. Between p_0 and p_1, we can find a cubic polynomial that interpolates these two points, uses $(p_3 - p_1)/2$ to approximate the derivative at p_2, and uses $p_1 - p_0$ to approximate the derivative at the left. Termination uses the final four control points in a similar manner.

Although this polynomial might seem a great advantage over our previous polynomials, we are doing three times as much work. Each time we add a control point, we determine a new polynomial valid only between two control points, as opposed to in the Bezier polynomial, where each three additional control points determined a new polynomial.

If we are willing to do this additional work, however, we can add even more continuity at the endpoints through the use of spline curves. We will derive a simple uniform cubic B-spline from the same four control points, p_0, p_1, p_2, and p_3. We know that, to determine a unique cubic polynomial, we must specify four independent conditions. Suppose that we define four conditions at the endpoints that are in terms of approximations to the first two derivatives at the endpoints, and that we do not worry about interpolating any control points. For example, we can use the preceding approximation for the two first derivatives at the endpoints. Two additional conditions can be obtained from symmetric approximations of the second derivative at the endpoints:

$$
\begin{aligned}
p''(0) &\approx p_2 - 2p_1 + p_0 = 2b, \\
p''(1) &\approx p_3 - 2p_2 + p_1 = 6a + 2b.
\end{aligned}
$$

These four equations do not involve the variable d. They are dependent, but any three can be solved for a, b, and c. We can apply another independent condition to determine d. If we set d via the symmetric equation (about the left endpoint)

$$p(0) \approx \frac{p_0 + 4p_1 + p_2}{6} = d,$$

then we can solve for a polynomial determined by the coefficients

$$\begin{bmatrix} a \\ b \\ c \\ d \end{bmatrix} = \frac{1}{6} \begin{bmatrix} -1 & 3 & -3 & 1 \\ 3 & -6 & 3 & 0 \\ -3 & 0 & 3 & 0 \\ 1 & 4 & 1 & 0 \end{bmatrix} \begin{bmatrix} p_0 \\ p_1 \\ p_2 \\ p_3 \end{bmatrix} = \mathbf{M}_S \begin{bmatrix} p_0 \\ p_1 \\ p_2 \\ p_3 \end{bmatrix}.$$

This particular choice of d yields, evaluating $p(1)$,

$$p(1) = \frac{p_1 + 4p_2 + p_3}{6}.$$

Although we could have chosen d in another manner, this particular choice gives us symmetric conditions at the endpoints.

This matrix can be used to generate a cubic polynomial between each pair of control points, p_k and p_{k+1}, using p_{k-1}, p_k, p_{k+1}, and p_{k+2}. At the endpoints, there will be continuity of the approximating polynomials and of their first two derivatives. Although, in general, the spline passes through none of the control points, the convex-hull property ensures that the curve will not lie far from the control points. In applications where a great deal of smoothness is necessary, splines may be needed, even though they will require three times as much calculation as would a Bezier curve using the same control points.

All our forms can be generalized to higher-degree polynomials, and the mathematics provides much insight into the geometry of approximating polynomials. Later in this chapter, we shall see how all forms can be extended to generate polynomial surfaces.

10.4.4 Example

All these forms can be used to approximate the 45-degree wedge of the circle. All should provide better approximations than our previous cubic interpolating polynomial. We shall show each polynomial for the explicit form, although we could just as well derive the two parametric polynomials of each type. We will use the same data from the previous section at the equally spaced, in x, points: $(0, -1)$, $(\frac{\sqrt{2}}{6}, -\frac{\sqrt{34}}{6}), (\frac{\sqrt{2}}{3}, -\frac{\sqrt{7}}{3}), (\frac{\sqrt{2}}{2}, -\frac{\sqrt{2}}{2})$. We use our formulae with the parameter t, with p representing y. Once we have derived $p(t)$, the transformation

$$x = \frac{\sqrt{2}}{2}t$$

will convert the unit interval in t to the desired range of x; that is, 0 to $\sqrt{(2)}/2$.

The conditions for the Hermite form are

$$p_0 = -1.0,$$
$$p_1 = -\frac{\sqrt{2}}{2},$$
$$p'(0) = 0.0,$$
$$p'(1) = 1.0.$$

The resulting polynomial, transformed to the correct range of x, is

$$y = 0.851x^3 - 0.196x^2 - 1.0.$$

Both the Bezier and spline curves use the y data at the four equally spaced control points. The resulting polynomials, again transformed to the correct range of x, are, for the Bezier curve,

$$y = 0.048x^3 + 0.299x^2 + 0.107x - 1.0,$$

and, for the uniform B-spline,

$$y = 0.341x^3 + 050x^2 + 0.075x - 0.962.$$

It is important to remember that this spline is valid only for x between $\frac{\sqrt{2}}{6}$ and $\frac{\sqrt{2}}{3}$. For the range 0 to $\frac{\sqrt{2}}{6}$, we must use the y values at x values of $-\frac{\sqrt{2}}{6}$, 0, $\frac{\sqrt{2}}{6}$, and $\frac{\sqrt{2}}{3}$ to generate another spline. A third spline must be defined for x between $\frac{\sqrt{2}}{3}$ and $\frac{\sqrt{2}}{2}$.

▬ 10.5
▬ Scan Converting Polynomials

Before moving on to surfaces, we pause to consider the problem of generating a polynomial on a raster display. Although we have a number of ways to generate equations for polynomials, ultimately we must set or clear pixels in our frame buffer to display polynomials. Just as we developed Bresenham's algorithm to scan convert line segments, we need efficient algorithms to generate pixels as close as possible to points on a polynomial curve segment.

Suppose we start with a cubic polynomial,

$$y = p(x) = ax^3 + bx^2 + cx + d,$$

where we can assume that the units are the device coordinates of our frame buffer. We can compute values of $p(x)$ for x_0, $x_0 + 1$, $x_0 + 2$, ... Since these y values may not be integers, we can round them to the closest integer to obtain a simple scan-conversion algorithm (Figure 10.16):

```
int x, round(), value;
float p();
void set_pixel();
Rpt location;
        .
        .
        .
for(x=FIRST;x<=LAST, x++)
{
    location.x=x;
    location.y=round(p(x));
    set_pixel(value, location);
}
```

We can economize on the number of operations required in this algorithm by a couple of methods. The function that calculates $p(x)$ can calculate a y value with three multiplications by rewriting the polynomial as

$$p(t) = d + t(c + t(b + at)).$$

If the successive values of t are equidistant from each other, we can eliminate all multiplications by the use of forward differences.

10.5.1 Forward Differences

The use of *forward differences* allows us to generate points on a polynomial using only additions. Suppose we consider our polynomial at equally spaced values of its independent variable,

$$t_i = t_0 + ih, i = 0, 1, ...,$$

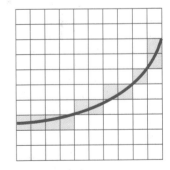

Figure 10.16
Scan Converting a
Polynomial

where h is the spacing between successive values. The corresponding values of p will be denoted by

$$p_i = p(t_i).$$

The first forward difference is a function that we obtain by taking the difference of the values of p for values of t separated by h:

$$\Delta p(t) = p(t+h) - p(t).$$

For our cubic polynomial, we can evaluate this function analytically as the quadratic polynomial

$$\Delta p(t) = (3ah)t^2 + (3ah^2 + 2bh)t + (ah^3 + bh^2 + ch).$$

We can apply this definition recursively, each time yielding a polynomial of degree one less than before, until we have a constant. The second and third difference polynomials for a cubic are

$$\Delta^{(2)}p(t) = \Delta(\Delta p(t)) = (6ah^2)t + (6ah^3 + 2bh^2),$$
$$\Delta^{(3)}p(t) = \Delta(\Delta^{(2)}p(t)) = 6ah^3.$$

Since we are interested in values of p only at t_i, we can generate an algorithm if we rewrite these relationships in the reverse order. If we let Δp_i denote $\Delta p(t_i)$, our equations are

$$\Delta^{(3)}p_{i+1} = 6ah^3,$$
$$\Delta^{(2)}p_{i+1} = \Delta^{(3)}p_{i+1} + \Delta^{(2)}p_i = 6ah^3 + \Delta^{(2)}p_i,$$
$$\Delta p_{i+1} = \Delta^{(2)}p_{i+1} + \Delta p_i,$$
$$p_{i+1} = \Delta p_{i+1} + p_i.$$

These relationships show that, if we have values for p_i, Δp_i, and $\Delta^{(2)}p_i$, we can move forward and compute p_{i+1}, Δp_{i+1}, and $\Delta^{(2)}p_{i+1}$ with three additions. This observation is the basis of the forward-difference method.

To initialize the algorithm, we could either use a, b, c, and d as before or, equivalently, compute the first four values p_0, p_1, p_2, and p_3 directly and use them. Either way, the starting conditions are

$$\Delta^{(3)}p_3 = 6ah^3 = p_3 - 3p_2 + 3p_1 - p_0,$$
$$\Delta^{(2)}p_3 = p_3 - 2p_2 + p_1,$$
$$\Delta p_3 = p_3 - p_2.$$

t	0	1	2	3	4	5
p	1	7	23	55	109	191
Δp	6	16	32	54	82	
$\Delta^{(2)} p$	10	16	22	28		
$\Delta^{(3)} p$	6	6	6			

Figure 10.17
Forward-Difference Table

Note that, if we were simply given four values, p_0, p_1, p_2, and p_3, assumed to be on the curve, we could compute $\Delta^{(3)}p_3$, $\Delta^{(2)}p_3$, and Δp_3 by simply taking the difference of the data, as in our original definition.

Forward differencing is the essence of most polynomial scan-conversion methods and can be extended to surfaces and to higher-order polynomials. It is not free from limitations. Build up of numerical errors can be significant for higher-order polynomials or when many points are generated. However, if we use low-order polynomials, such as cubics in short segments, the use of forward differences should generate a suitable algorithm.

10.5.2 Example

Consider the polynomial

$$p(t) = t^3 + 2t^2 + 3t + 1,$$

which we wish to scan convert for $t = 0, 1, \ldots$. The forward differences are shown in Figure 10.17, where the arrows indicate the flow of the calculation. Since the polynomial is cubic, the first four entries in the first row completely determine the polynomial and the values below them in the table (Figure 10.18). We can generate the rest of the table using our formulae, where the flow is indicated by the arrows in Figure 10.19. Each successive entry involves an addition in each of the first three rows of the table.

t	0	1	2	3
p	1	7	23	55
Δp	6	16	32	
$\Delta^{(2)} p$	10	16		
$\Delta^{(3)} p$	6			

Figure 10.18
Initial Table

10.5.3 Scan Conversion by Subdivision

An alternative method is to compute a set of points on the polynomial $\{(p(x_i), x_i)\}$ and to connect them with an interpolating polyline. The scan-conversion algorithm is then of the form

```
for(i=0; i<num_pts, i++)
{
```

Figure 10.19
Generating Values of a Polynomial

t	0	1	2	3	4	5
P	1	7	23	55 →→ 109 →→ 191		
ΔP	6	16	32 →→ 54 →→ 82			
$\Delta^{(2)} P$	10	16 →→ 22 →→ 28				
$\Delta^{(3)} P$	6 →→ 6 →→ 6					

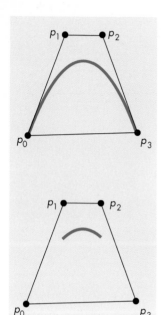

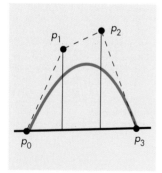

Figure 10.20
Convex Hulls. (a) Bezier. (b) B-spline.

```
        points[i].x=x[i];
        points[i].y=p(x[i]);
    }
gpolyline(num_pts, points);
```

In this variant, we are working in WC and the actual scan conversion is done to lines in the frame buffer.

The main difficulty with such an approach is that the polynomial changes slope with x, and a polyline based on equally spaced values of x may provide a poor appoximation where the slope is steep. Decreasing the spacing between successive values of x will be inefficient, many polyline segments will be used for shallow parts of the curve where only a few would suffice.

Recursive-subdivision methods can adapt to the local slope of a curve and achieve any desired accuracy of the approximating polyline. Consider the Bezier and B-spline forms. For each polynomial segment, we know that the polynomial must lie within the convex hull formed by the control points (Figure 10.20). If we connect a line segment from $p(0)$ to $p(1)$, we can compute the distance from the vertices of the convex hull to this line, as in Figure 10.21. The maximum of these distances is an upper bound on the approximation error of the line. If this error exceeds a threshold, the polynomial can be subdivided into two polynomials of the same type as in Figure 10.22. The subdivision process for a Bezier polynomial is sketched in Exercises 10.11 and 10.12. Subdivision can be repeated recursively until the desired accuracy is achieved. Although this process can also be used on forms such as the interpolating polynomial, the lack of a convex-hull property can leave us with an approximation that does not meet the error criterion at every point.

Although the recursion may make the algorithm slower than it would be with a forward-difference method, it may be a better al-

Figure 10.21
Error in Approximating Bezier Curve with a Line

gorithm if the equations are in parametric form. In the parametric form,

$$x = a_x t^3 + b_x t^2 + c_x t + d_x,$$
$$y = a_y t^3 + b_y t^3 + c_y t + d_y,$$

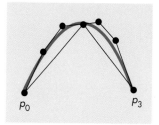

the problem is altered a bit, since equally spaced values of t do not correspond to equally spaced values of either x or y in the frame buffer. Thus, with forward differences we may have difficulty determining an appropriate step size for a given error criteria, whereas with the subdivision method we can always enforce an error bound.

Figure 10.22
Subdividing a Polynomial

10.6 Parametric Surfaces

A surface in x, y, z space can be modeled with three parametric equations, each with two independent variables:

$$x = x(s, t),$$
$$y = y(s, t),$$
$$z = z(s, t).$$

We shall describe a surface in terms of *surface patches* (Figure 10.23), each of which correspond to restricting s and t to have a limited range. We can assume, with no loss of generality, that s and t are defined over the unit square

$$1 \geq s, t \geq 0.$$

Figure 10.23
A Surface Patch

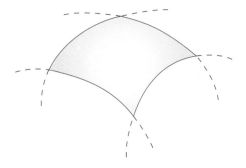

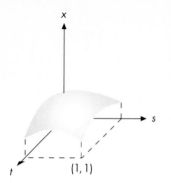

x

s

t

(1, 1)

Figure 10.24
Parametric Surface

We can convince ourselves that we are indeed describing a surface by noting that, for a constant value $s = s_0$, $x(s_0, t)$ is a curve. If we consider a family of closely spaced curves for $s = s_0 + i\delta, i = 0, 1, ...$, where δ is small, each value of i will generate a new curve that, as long as x is a reasonable function, will be close to the previous curve. As we let δ get smaller and take more curves, this family of curves blends together, forming a surface $x(s, t)$ in parameter (x, s, t) space, as in Figure 10.24. Likewise, $y(s, t)$ and $z(s, t)$ are surfaces in y, s, t and z, s, t spaces, respectively.

Points in parametric vector form,

$$\mathbf{p}(s, t) = \begin{bmatrix} x(s, t) \\ y(s, t) \\ z(s, t) \end{bmatrix},$$

describe a surface in our normal x, y, z system. The fact that each of the three functions x, y, and z is itself a surface (in parameter space) often causes some confusion.

10.6.1 The Plane and the Sphere

Two simple examples of parametric surfaces are the plane and the sphere. A set of parametric equations for a plane determined by the points (x_0, y_0, z_0), (x_1, y_1, z_1), and (x_2, y_2, z_2) are

$$x(s, t) = x_0 + (x_2 - x_0)t + (x_1 - x_2)st,$$
$$y(s, t) = y_0 + (y_2 - y_0)t + (y_1 - y_2)st,$$
$$z(s, t) = z_0 + (z_2 - z_0)t + (z_1 - z_2)st.$$

As s and t vary over the rectangle $0 \leq s, t \leq 1$, the surface patch in x, y, z space is the triangle determined by the three defining points. Similar triangles are described in x, s, t, y, s, t, and z, s, t spaces (Figure 10.25). For values of s and t outside the unit square, we obtain points on the plane outside the triangle.

For a sphere centered at the origin, one parametric representation is given by

$$x(s, t) = r \sin(2\pi s),$$
$$y(s, t) = r \cos(2\pi s) \sin(\pi t),$$
$$z(s, t) = r \cos(2\pi s) \cos(\pi t).$$

As s and t vary over the unit square, we generate all points on the sphere. In this case, the surface in x, y, z space is very different from

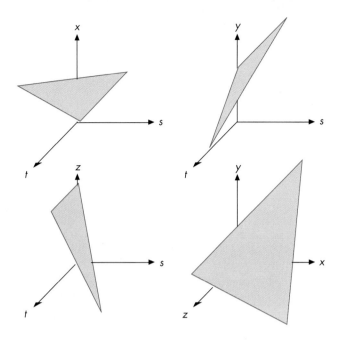

Figure 10.25
Parametric Plane

any of the three parametric surfaces in Figure 10.26, and, if we allow s and t to be outside the unit square, we still obtain points on the sphere.

10.6.2 Bicubic Polynomials

We shall work with x, y, and z in forming parametric surface patches, just as we did with parametric curves. We will use the single form

$$p = p(s, t),$$

substituting x, y, or z for p as necessary.

The properties that made polynomials useful for generating curves extend to surfaces. A two-dimensional polynomial of degree N in s and M in t can be written as

$$p(s, t) = \sum_{i=0}^{N} \sum_{j=0}^{M} c_{ij} s^i t^j,$$

which requires us to determine $(N+1)(M+1)$ coefficients c_{ij} to define a particular polynomial. It is often convenient to be able to write the

Figure 10.26
Parametric Sphere

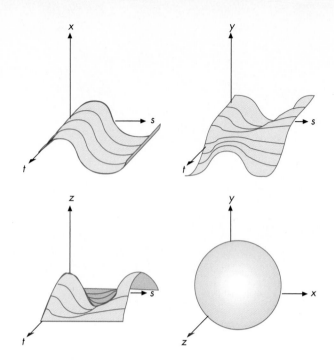

polynomial in matrix-vector form as

$$p(s,t) = \begin{bmatrix} 1 & s & \cdots & s^N \end{bmatrix} \mathbf{C} \begin{bmatrix} 1 \\ t \\ \cdot \\ \cdot \\ \cdot \\ t^M \end{bmatrix},$$

where $\mathbf{C}$ is the $N+1$ by $M+1$ matrix

$$\mathbf{C} = \begin{bmatrix} c_{00} & c_{01} & \cdots & c_{0M} \\ c_{10} & c_{11} & \cdots & c_{0N} \\ \cdot & \cdot & \cdots & \cdot \\ \cdot & \cdot & \cdots & \cdot \\ \cdot & \cdot & \cdots & \cdot \\ c_{N0} & c_{N1} & \cdots & c_{NM} \end{bmatrix}.$$

The extension of cubic polynomial curves to bicubic surfaces requires the determination of a 4 by 4 matrix $\mathbf{C}$ for each of x, y, and z.

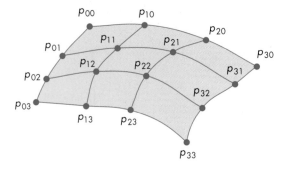

Figure 10.27
Interpolating Surface

10.6.3 Interpolation

Interpolating surface patches, although not as smooth as Bezier or spline patches, illustrate how we can extend our techniques for specifying curves to surfaces. Suppose we have the 16 data points $p_{ij}, i, j = 0, ..., 3$. These points can be assumed to lie in parameter space at the equally spaced values

$$s = 0, \frac{1}{3}, \frac{2}{3}, 1,$$

$$t = 0, \frac{1}{3}, \frac{2}{3}, 1,$$

as in Figure 10.27. Since the bicubic patch must interpolate each of these points, we have 16 independent equations for the coefficients of the matrix $\mathbf{C}$.

Rather than going through the exercise of finding $\mathbf{C}$, from 16 linear equations in 16 unknowns, we can use our results for the interpolating cubic polynomial curve to solve the problem. Consider the curve for $t = 0$:

$$p(s, 0) = \begin{bmatrix} 1 & s & s^2 & s^3 \end{bmatrix} \mathbf{C} \begin{bmatrix} 1 \\ 0 \\ 0 \\ 0 \end{bmatrix}.$$

This curve must interpolate p_{00}, p_{10}, p_{20}, and p_{30}. Using the interpolating geometry matrix $\mathbf{M}_I$, $p(s, 0)$ is given as

$$p(s, 0) = \begin{bmatrix} 1 & s & s^2 & s^3 \end{bmatrix} \mathbf{M}_I \begin{bmatrix} p_{00} \\ p_{10} \\ p_{20} \\ p_{30} \end{bmatrix}.$$

In a similar manner, we know that $p(s, \frac{1}{3})$ must be the interpolating curve given by

$$p(s, \frac{1}{3}) = \begin{bmatrix} 1 & s & s^2 & s^3 \end{bmatrix} \mathbf{C} \begin{bmatrix} 1 \\ \frac{1}{3} \\ (\frac{1}{3})^2 \\ (\frac{1}{3})^3 \end{bmatrix},$$

$$= \begin{bmatrix} 1 & s & s^2 & s^3 \end{bmatrix} \mathbf{M}_I \begin{bmatrix} p_{11} \\ p_{11} \\ p_{21} \\ p_{31} \end{bmatrix}.$$

We can write similar equations for $p(s, \frac{2}{3})$ and $p(s, 1)$. These 16 equations can be put together as

$$\begin{bmatrix} 1 & s & s^2 & s^3 \end{bmatrix} \mathbf{M}_I \mathbf{P} = \begin{bmatrix} 1 & s & s^2 & s^3 \end{bmatrix} \mathbf{C} \mathbf{A}_I^T,$$

where $\mathbf{P}$ is a matrix composed of the data at the control points,

$$\mathbf{P} = \begin{bmatrix} p_{00} & p_{01} & p_{02} & p_{03} \\ p_{10} & p_{11} & p_{12} & p_{13} \\ p_{20} & p_{21} & p_{22} & p_{23} \\ p_{30} & p_{31} & p_{32} & p_{33} \end{bmatrix},$$

and $\mathbf{A}_I$ again is the matrix

$$\mathbf{A}_I = \begin{bmatrix} 0 & 0 & 0 & 1 \\ (\frac{1}{3})^3 & (\frac{1}{3})^2 & \frac{1}{3} & 1 \\ (\frac{2}{3})^3 & (\frac{2}{3})^2 & \frac{2}{3} & 1 \\ 1 & 1 & 1 & 1 \end{bmatrix}.$$

Since $\mathbf{M}_I$ is the inverse of $\mathbf{A}_I$, we are left with the simple relationship

$$\mathbf{C} = \mathbf{M}_I \mathbf{P} \mathbf{M}_I^T.$$

We can gain further insight by using the four interpolating blending functions, $b_i(t)$, that we derived previously. Since an interpolating curve through p_0, p_1, p_2, and p_3 is of the form

$$p(t) = \sum_{i=0}^{3} b_i(t) p_i,$$

these cubic polynomials must have the property

$$b_i(t_j) = \begin{cases} 0, & i \neq j, \\ 1, & i = j. \end{cases}$$

Using this argument for an interpolating surface, we can write our cubic surface patch using the same blending functions as

$$p(s,t) = \sum_{i=0}^{3} \sum_{j=0}^{3} b_i(s) b_j(t) p_{ij}.$$

Once we have the result in this form, it should be clear that the properties of the interpolating form of curves, both good and bad, extend to the interpolating surface patch. Fortunately, the methods we have established here can be used to generate other fitting surfaces from our knowledge of smoothing curves.

10.6.4 Bezier Patches

Interpolating surfaces suffer from the same shortcomings as do the interpolating curves—principally, they lack smoothness. Bezier patches use the same data and require about the same amount of effort to calculate, but they are smoother. Although splines give even more smoothness, the additional work required to compute splines usually makes Bezier patches more appealing in practice (at least as a first approximation).

We could approach the Bezier surface by applying four suitable conditions at the corners of the patch to determine a matrix $\mathbf{C}$, as before. Instead, however, we shall use our second approach, which will be to use the blending functions of the Bezier curve to define a Bezier surface. The four blending functions,

$$b_0(t) = (1 - t)^3,$$
$$b_1(t) = 3t(1 - t)^2,$$
$$b_2(t) = 3t^2(1 - t),$$
$$b_3(t) = t^3,$$

can be combined to form a bicubic polynomial

$$p(s,t) = \sum_{i=0}^{3} \sum_{j=0}^{3} b_i(s) b_j(t) p_{ij},$$

which blends the data at our 16 control points. This expression is precisely the form for the interpolating surface; only the blending functions have been changed. We should expect then that the properties of the Bezier curves will carry over to the Bezier surface, as is indeed the case. For example, the surface lies within the convex hull of the 16 control points and therefore is always close to the data.

We can look at the corners of the patch to determine the continuity conditions. The symmetry of form allows us to look at any of the corners and to extrapolate the results to the other three. At $t = 0$, $s = 0$, we find

$$p(0,0) = p_{00},$$

$$\frac{\partial p(0,0)}{\partial s} = 3(p_{10} - p_{00}),$$

$$\frac{\partial p(0,0)}{\partial t} = 3(p_{01} - p_{00}),$$

$$\frac{\partial^2 p(0,0)}{\partial s \partial t} = 3(p_{11} - p_{00}).$$

Thus, the Bezier surface interpolates the four corner points, as in Figure 10.28, and uses the four data points at the corners to approximate the two first partial derivatives and the first mixed partial derivative at the corner.

An expression for the Bezier surface patch in terms of the coefficients of a bicubic polynomial

$$p(s,t) = \begin{bmatrix} 1 & s & s^2 & s^3 \end{bmatrix} \mathbf{C}_B \begin{bmatrix} 1 \\ t \\ t^2 \\ t^3 \end{bmatrix}$$

Figure 10.28
A Bezier Surface Patch

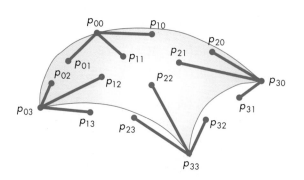

can also be obtained following our procedure for the interpolating surface. The Bezier surface matrix, $\mathbf{C}_B$, is given as

$$\mathbf{C}_B = \mathbf{M}_B \mathbf{P} \mathbf{M}_B^T,$$

where $\mathbf{M}_B$ is the Bezier geometry matrix.

Our methods can be applied to splines, and we will find similar forms for both the blending-form representation and a representation based on the spline matrix $\mathbf{M}_S$. The resulting cubic-spline surface, based on the data at our 16 control points, will be valid only over the region

$$\frac{1}{3} \leq s, t \leq \frac{2}{3}.$$

Consequently, the patch is valid over one-ninth of the area of a Bezier patch using the same data. Hence, although spline surfaces provide great smoothness between adjacent patches, this smoothness comes at a high price.

10.7 Realism

In principle, most of the methods we discussed in Chapter 9 could be applied to our curved surfaces. Unfortunately, the computational aspects can make many of those techniques impractical. We will examine hidden-surface removal and ray tracing briefly to see where the problems arise.

10.7.1 Hidden Surface Removal

Hidden-surface removal with curved surfaces can be attempted with object space methods, but the resulting equations are often of too high a degree to lead to practical methods. Consider the intersection of two parametric surfaces, as shown in Figure 10.29. They can be described by six equations using two sets of parameters:

$$x = x(s, t),$$
$$y = y(s, t),$$
$$z = z(s, t),$$
$$\hat{x} = \hat{x}(\alpha, \beta),$$
$$\hat{y} = \hat{y}(\alpha, \beta),$$
$$\hat{z} = \hat{z}(\alpha, \beta).$$

Figure 10.29
Intersecting Curved
Surfaces

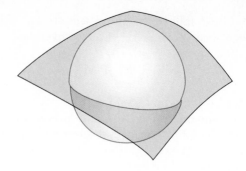

At any point common to the two surfaces, we must have

$$x = \hat{x}, y = \hat{y}, z = \hat{z}.$$

These relationships determine a curve of intersection. If we assume that we can "solve" these equations, we can use two of them to find a representation of one set of parameters in terms of the other:

$$\alpha = f_1(s, t),$$
$$\beta = f_2(s, t).$$

We can use these functions in the third equation to determine an implicit relationship

$$g(s, t) = 0,$$

which describes a curve in the (s, t) parameter space. Any point on this curve will generate a point $(x(s, t), y(s, t), z(s, t))$ on the curve of intersection between our original two surfaces.

We cannot solve these equations analytically for any but the simplest of surfaces, such as intersecting planes. For parametric polynomial surfaces, the problem can be reduced to the determination of the roots of a polynomial, which must be solved for numerically. Other methods are based on finding a set of points on the curve of intersection, then attempting to follow the path of the curve. Still, the degree of the equations, even for bicubic patches, is high enough that image-space algorithms are usually more practical.

The appeal of the image-space approach is we can reduce the problem to one of intersecting lines (the projectors) with the surfaces, rather than one of intersecting surfaces with surfaces. Consider the

z-buffer algorithm illustrated in Figure 10.30. Each projector has a parametric representation of the form

$$x(s) = x_0 + \alpha d_x,$$
$$y(s) = y_0 + \alpha d_y,$$
$$z(s) = z_0 + \alpha d_z,$$

where (x_0, y_0, z_0) is any point on the projector and the vector $\mathbf{d} = (d_x, d_y, d_z)$ describes the projector's direction. Suppose we have an implicit representation for our surface,

$$g(x, y, z) = 0.$$

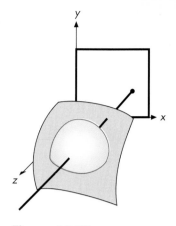

Figure 10.30
Surfaces and Projectors

Substitution of the parametric form of the line yields a single non-linear equation in α that, using numerical methods, can be solved for points of intersection on the surface. Once these intersections are determined, the z-buffer algorithm proceeds as before.

The difficulty of this approach depends on the complexity of implicit representation. If we start with a bicubic parametric surface patch, it is possible to find an implicit representation as a polynomial. Finding the intersection of this polynomial with a line reduces to finding the roots of a polynomial of degree 18. This calculation is possible, but does require a large amount of calculation and must be repeated for each projector. On the other hand, many modeling systems are based on simpler objects. Quadric surfaces allow us to model with spheres, cones, and cylinders, and the intersections with projectors are solvable problems since they can be reduced to quadratic equations. You can develop this special case on your own to build up a simple surface modeling system.

10.7.2 Rendering

Rendering curved surfaces is based on virtually the same process that we used in rendering polygons. If we employ a ray-tracing approach, we must intersect lines (rays) with our surfaces. As we just discussed, the difficulty of this problem depends on the type of surface representation and the degree of polynomials we use. A surface described by an implicit cubic polynomial will be far easier to work with than will one described by a bicubic parametric form. We can use the same model as that we developed in Chapter 9 to model lighting and surface properties. The major problem is that, on a curved surface, the normal changes at every point, which is precisely why the surface is curved. The implication is that we must recalculate the terms in our reflection model at every point on a surface.

If we are working with parametric form, we can obtain the normal at any point on the surface by taking the two partial derivatives

$$\mathbf{t}_s = \begin{bmatrix} \partial x/\partial s \\ \partial y/\partial s \\ \partial z/\partial s \end{bmatrix},$$

$$\mathbf{t}_t = \begin{bmatrix} \partial x/\partial t \\ \partial y/\partial t \\ \partial z/\partial t \end{bmatrix}.$$

These vectors both lie in the tangent plane at this point, as illustrated in Figure 10.31. Since the cross-product of two vectors is perpendicular to them both, the normal is given by

$$\mathbf{n} = \mathbf{t}_s \times \mathbf{t}_t.$$

Thus, we have a situation where we can obtain the necessary information, but the computation required may increase our appreciation of polygonal models and polygonal shading methods.

An alternative to doing all the calculations for rendering surfaces is to use polygons to approximate the surfaces. Consider a Bezier patch, as in Figure 10.32, with corners $\mathbf{p}_{00}$, $\mathbf{p}_{03}$, $\mathbf{p}_{30}$ and $\mathbf{p}_{33}$. By connecting $\mathbf{p}_{00}$ to $\mathbf{p}_{33}$ with a line segment, we create two planar polygons that approximate the patch. We can use these two triangles instead of the curved patch for hidden-surface removal and rendering. Since we are using curved surfaces because they provide a better approximation to some object we wish to model, we do not want to replace them with polygons unless the surfaces are fairly flat. This information can be determined in a number of ways. We could use the convex-hull property of the Bezier surface. Or we could calculate the distance from a point in the middle of the patch to the approximating polygon. If this distance is too great, the patch can be subdivided. The subdivision process can be repeated recursively until the resulting polygons provide a suitable fit.

Figure 10.31
Tangent Plane to Surface

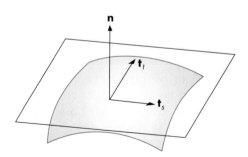

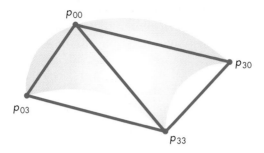

Figure 10.32
Subdividing a Patch

p_{00}

p_{30}

p_{03}

p_{33}

10.7.3 Scan Conversion

Both recursive subdivision and forward differencing can be used to scan convert parametric surfaces. For example, suppose we represent the surface through cubic blending polynomials as

$$x(s,t) = \sum_{i=0}^{3}\sum_{j=0}^{3} b_i(s)b_j(t)x_{ij},$$

$$y(s,t) = \sum_{i=0}^{3}\sum_{j=0}^{3} b_i(s)b_j(t)y_{ij},$$

$$z(s,t) = \sum_{i=0}^{3}\sum_{j=0}^{3} b_i(s)b_j(t)z_{ij}.$$

We can apply a forward-differencing technique in both s and t to generate points on the surface.

This work must be compared to the work required to subdivide the surfaces into planar polygons and to scan convert the simple flat polygons. The advantage of this approach is that many systems have extremely efficient polygon algorithms built into the hardware and software; the major disadvantage is that the overhead of the subdivision process is high.

10.8
Solid Modeling

Our approach to modeling three-dimensional objects has been to describe their surfaces. A cube was modeled as six polygons. More complex objects were modeled with polynomial surface patches. Throughout, our major concern has been the relationship between the form of the model and the image's display on a graphics system. However,

Figure 10.33
Box with Cylinder Removed

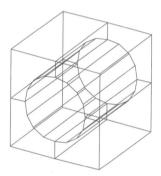

Figure 10.34
Wire Frame of Box and
Cylinder

from the perspective of someone such as a mechanical-parts designer or an architect, our approach places too much emphasis on a part of the problem—image display—that may be of secondary importance to the designer.

For someone working with a design application, a major weakness of our approach is that our primitives may be too limited for many three-dimensional applications. Primitives such as parallelepipeds or polygonal meshes, which are based on the ease with which we can use them both mathematically and within the graphics system, can model even the simplest of curved surfaces only through approximations.

A further limitation in our approach is that our surface-based models cannot easily represent volumetric properties of the object, such as density or center of mass. Consider the simple object in Figure 10.33, which consists of a box with a cylindrical rod removed. With our present primitives, we would model this object as set of surfaces, the curved surfaces being modeled by a number of simple polygons. Since we are working with surfaces, we may not be able to distinguish this solid object with a hole in it from a solid object with a cylinder of a different material through its center, or from a solid cylinder enclosed within a thin-walled box. All three of these cases could have the same wire-frame image as in Figure 10.34. If we were interested only in simple displays of the object, we might not be overly concerned with these distinctions. If, however, we wish to use our model to build the object, then we have a serious deficiency within our modeling system. The designer needs a system that can provide such entities as the weight of the object and the materials needed to manufacture it, and even information on how the object can be manufactured.

Going from two-dimensional (surface-based) representations to solid or volumetric representations introduces other difficulties that we have only touched on previously. An object that might possess a simple conceptual representation, such as a sphere, and that might be desirable to a designer, may require a complex internal representation if our graphics system is to be able to work efficiently.

10.8.1 Object Classes

Previously, we defined a set of three-dimensional primitives by taking the natural extension of our two-dimensional objects, such as polylines and polygons, to three dimensions. We eliminated some of the limitations of these primitives, such as their lack of curvature, by extending our primitives to include simple curved surfaces. Unfortunately, we still might require a large number of such objects to represent nontrivial three-dimensional objects.

One of the basic problems in selecting a set of three-dimensional primitives is that there are far more possibilities for three-dimensional primitives than there were for two-dimensional primitives. Practical considerations, such as that ultimately we will produce displays on two-dimensional devices, yield restrictions that force us to consider specialized classes of three-dimensional primitives. One such class consists of objects that are usually referred to as *two-and-one-half-dimensional*. We obtain this class by extending any available two-dimensional primitive to a three-dimensional solid by one of a number of simple techniques.

Extrusion starts with any two-dimensional object that lies in a plane, and obtains a three-dimensional object by replicating the object along an axis, usually orthogonal to the plane, as in Figure 10.35. Thus, rectangles extrude to parallelepipeds, and circles to cylinders. A planar polygon will produce a generalization of a cylinder. Another technique starts with any arbitrary object in the plane and rotates it, either about its own center or about some other point, to generate a three-dimensional *object of revolution*, as in Figure 10.36. With this technique, a circle can generate either a sphere or a torus, depending on where we place the center of rotation.

We can obtain more general classes of objects by starting with primitives that are simple three-dimensional volumes. Figure 10.37 shows a possible set of primitive volumes. Many of the restrictions we place on these objects are due to the problems we encounter in putting together and rendering objects. For example, when we assemble a more complex object from these simple shapes, there will

Figure 10.35
Extruded Objects

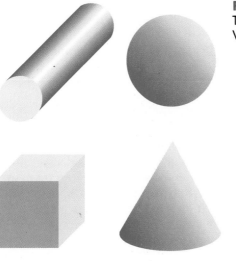

Figure 10.37
Three-Dimensional
Volumes

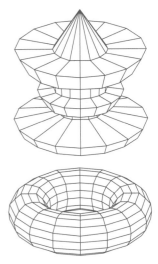

Figure 10.36
Objects of Revolution

10.8 Solid Modeling   431

Figure 10.38
Symbol Table

Symbol	Attributes
sphere	radius, skew
parallelepiped	height, width, length, skew
cone	height, radius, skew
cylinder	length, radius, skew

be intersections between the simple components. As we saw in the previous section, finding the curve of intersection between two curved surfaces is a difficult problem that can involve many numerical calculations. In many systems, quadric shapes such as spheres, cylinders, and cones, in addition to objects composed of polygons, provide enough flexibility to model an application.

10.8.2 Constructive Solid Geometry

Suppose that we have selected a set of volumes as our primitives. Assembling a model from these primitives has much in common with our use of symbols and instances from Chapter 5. We can regard the shape and any volumetric properties, such as density, as attributes of the shape. A modeling system that used parallelepipeds, cones, cylinders, and spheres might have the symbol attributes shown in Figure 10.38.

We now need a way of assembling our primitives into more complex objects. Hierarchical models again will be our fundamental tool, but the new possibilities in working with volumes, such as removing one volume from another volume, lead us to an approach slightly different from that of Chapter 5.

The approach taken in *constructive solid geometry* (CSG) is to use set algebra to describe the interconnection of three-dimensional objects. The basic operations are union ($\cup$), intersection ($\cap$) and subtraction ($-$).

Hence, we can form a "dumbell" by considering $(A \cup B) \cup B$, or remove a cylindrical hole from a cube by considering $A - C$, as in Figure 10.39. More complex shapes are represented by more complex algebraic expressions. Color Plate 15 shows an object built up from simple primitives. The attributes of each solid primitive, such as the size and position, are found within the symbol-instance data structure. The CSG approach is obviously attractive to the modeler.

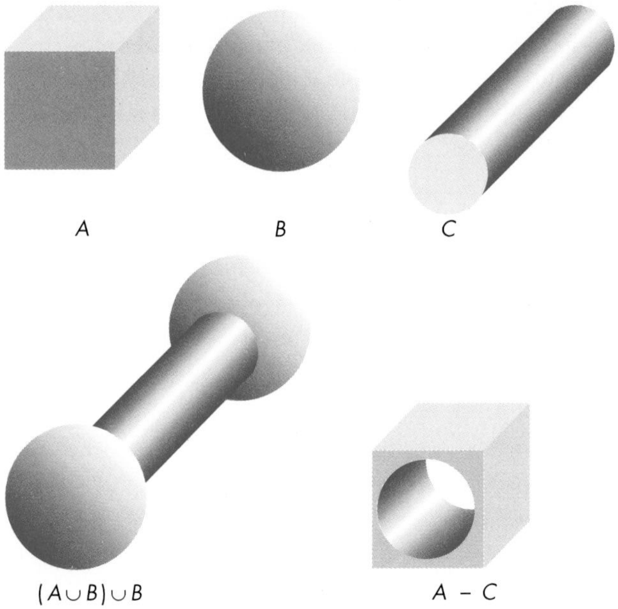

Figure 10.39
Constructive Solid
Geometry

A   B   C

$(A \cup B) \cup B$ $A - C$

10.8.3 Boundary Representations

The use of curved solids can present significant implementation problems on the graphics side. Virtually all our methods have been based on displaying the edges or surfaces of our primitives. Thus, if our solid-modeling system included a sphere as a primitive, we might have no simple direct way of displaying that sphere, since a sphere lacks edges. Producing images of curved objects often requires a computationally expensive approach, such as ray tracing.

From the graphics point of view, we usually prefer objects that are represented by their boundaries or are approximated by polygonal meshes, as in Figure 10.34. Now we have gone almost full circle. We argued that the usual graphics primitives were not necessarily what a designer would like to use, and then we argued that simple volume primitives are not those for which the graphics system is best suited. We face a serious dilemma.

The power of modern computers provides a possible solution to some of these difficulties. Many systems use complex internal data structures that possess multiple representations of our objects. The user might work with a system based on CSG at the user-interface level. However, the underlying data structure might include both a volume representation and a boundary representation. The boundary representation is used by the graphics part of the system, but will be transparent to the user. Color Plate 16 shows a rendering of an object

10.8 Solid Modeling   433

and the underlying mesh. Other solutions are possible based on the ability of modern computers to crunch numbers at rates previously not possible. Techniques that involve calculations for intersecting curved surfaces and for ray tracing, which were previously considered only possible on the most powerful of computers, are now becoming routine on graphics workstations.

10.9 Suggested Readings

The use of coordinate-system–independent descriptions of curves and surfaces can be found in [Faux80]. There are a number of other methods for modeling surface patches. See [Faux80] and [Mor85]. [Bar87] provides an introduction to B splines. [Man87] discusses both the boundary-representation and constructive-solid-geometry approaches to solid modeling. The use of forward differences for curve and surface generation is presented in [Lien87]. Many variants of subdivision methods can be found in [Rog85].

Exercises

10.1 Consider a cubic parametric polynomial where we use the same values multiple times. For example, suppose we let $p_0 = p_3$. How does this choice affect the resulting spatial curve?

10.2 Show how we can change the locations p_1 and p_2 in the Bezier form without changing the derivatives at the endpoints. What effect does this change have on the resulting polynomial?

10.3 Find and plot the blending functions for the spline and Bezier polynomials.

10.4 The Bezier polynomial of degree n is given by

$$p(x) = \sum_{k=0}^{n} \binom{n}{k} t^k (1-t)^{n-k} p_k,$$

where

$$\binom{n}{k} = \frac{n!}{k!(n-k)!}$$

is the binomial coefficient and the control points are $p_0, ..., p_n$. Show why these polynomials can be expected to be smooth over the unit interval. Find an expression for the derivatives at the ends of the unit interval.

10.5 Approximate a circle with parametric cubic Hermite, Bezier, and B-spline polynomials.

10.6 Write an interactive curve-design program that uses Bezier curves. Your program should allow you to enter the interpolated points and then to manipulate the shape of the curve by altering the control points that determine the derivatives at the endpoints.

10.7 Why is the forward-difference method sensitive to error buildup?

10.8 What is the effect of changing the range of the parameter t in a parametric polynomial from the unit interval to any other interval?

10.9 Consider modeling with parametric quadric surfaces. Find an implicit equation in parameter space that describes the curve of intersection between two surfaces.

10.10 Develop a z-buffer algorithm for quadric shapes.

10.11 Suppose the control points p_0, p_1, p_2, and p_3 determine a cubic Bezier polynomial $p(t)$. Using these four points, determine seven other control points $q_0, ..., q_6$ such that the first four (q_0 through q_3) and last four (q_3 through q_6) determine two cubic Bezier polynomials, each of which is identical to $p(t)$ over one-half of the interval $0 \le t \le 1$.

10.12 Using Exercise 10.11, develop a recursive-subdivision method for approximating a Bezier curve with a polyline.

10.13 Show that the coefficients of a cubic B-spline surface patch are given by

$$\mathbf{C} = \mathbf{M}_S \mathbf{P} \mathbf{M}_S^T,$$

where $\mathbf{P}$ is a matrix of the control-point data, and $\mathbf{M}_S$ is the B-spline geometry matrix.

10.14 Develop an appropriate data structure to store a model of a solid object using a CSG representation.

A

GKS
Functions
Used in Text

Control Functions

1. Open GKS

```
void
gopen_gks(err_file, memory_units)
Gchar *err_file; /* name of error file */
size_t memory_units; /* bytes of memory available for
        buffer space */
```

2. Close GKS

```
void
gclose_gks()
```

3. Open workstation

```
void
```

```
gopen_ws(ws_id, conn_id, ws_type)
Gint ws_id;   /* workstation identifier */
Gchar *conn_id;   /* connection identifier */
Gint ws_type; /* workstation type */
```

4. Close workstation

```
void
gclose_ws(ws_id)
Gint ws_id; /* workstation identifier */
```

5. Activate workstation

```
void
gactivate_ws(ws_id)
Gint ws_id; /* workstation identifier */
```

6. Deactivate workstation

```
void
gdeactivate_ws(ws_id)
Gint ws_id; /* workstation identifier */
```

7. Redraw all segments on workstation

```
void
gredraw_all_seg_ws(ws_id)
Gint ws_id; /* workstation identifier */
```

8. Update workstation

```
void
gupd_ws(ws_id, regen_flag)
Gint ws_id; /* workstation identifier */
Gregen regen_flag;   /* update regeneration flag*/
```

9. Set deferral state

```
void
gset_defer_st(ws_id, def_state)
Gint ws_id; /* workstation identifier */
Gdefer_state *defer_state;   /* deferral mode  */
```

■ **Primitives**

1. Polyline

```
void
gpolyline(num_points, points)
Gint num_pts; /* number of points */
Gpt *array_pt; /* array of points */
```

2. Polymarker

```
void
gpolymarker(num_pts, array_pt)
Gint num_pts; /* number of points */
Gpt *array_pt; /* array of points */
```

3. Text

```
void
gtext(text_pos, char_string)
Gpt *text_pos; /* text position */
Gchar *char_string;  /* character string */
```

4. Fill area

```
void
gfill_area(num_points, array_pt)
Gint num_points; /* number of points */
Gpt *array_pt; /* array of points */
```

5. Cell array

```
void
gcell_array(rectangle, dim, colr)
Grect *rectangle; /* cell rectangle */
Gdim *dim; /* colr index array dimensions */
Gint *colr; /* colour index array */
```

6. Generalized drawing primitive

```
void
ggdp(num_pts, array_pt, gdp_id, gdp_data)
Gint num_points; /* number of points */
Gpt *array_pt; /* array of points */
Gint gdp_id; /* GDP function identifier */
Ggdp_data *gdp_data; /* GDP data record */
```

Primitive Attributes

1. Set polyline index

```
void
gset_line_ind(index)
Gint index; /* polyline index  */
```

2. Set linetype

```
void
gset_linetype(type)
Gint type; /* linetype     */
```

3. Set linewidth scale factor

```
void
gset_linewidth(width)
Gfloat width; /* linewidth */
```

4. Set polyline colour index

```
void
gset_line_colr_ind(index)
Gint index; /* polyline colour index  */
```

5. Set polymarker index

```
void
gset_marker_ind(index)
Gint index; /* polymarker index */
```

6. Set marker type

```
void
gset_marker_type(markertype)
Gint markertype; /* marker type */
```

7. Set markersize scale factor

```
void
gset_marker_size(scale)
Gfloat scale;   /* marker-size scale factor */
```

8. Set polymarker colour index

```
void
gset_marker_colr_ind(index)
Gint index; /* polymarker colour index  */
```

9. Set text index

```
void
gset_text_ind(index)
Gint index; /* text index */
```

10. Set text font and precision

```
void
gset_fontprec(fontprec)
Gfontprec *fontprec; /* text font and precision */
```

11. Set character expansion factor

```
void
gset_expan(exp_factor)
Gfloat exp_factor; /* character expansion factor */
```

12. Set character spacing

```
void
gset_space(spacing)
Gfloat spacing; /* character spacing */
```

13. Set text colour index

```
void
gset_text_colr_ind(index)
Gint index; /* text colour index */
```

14. Set character height

```
void
gset_char_ht(height)
Gfloat height; /* character height */
```

15. Set character up vector

```
void
gset_char_up_vec(up_vect)
Gvec *up_vect; /* character up vector */
```

16. Set text path

```
void
gset_text_path(path)
Gtext_path path; /* text path */
```

17. Set text alignment

```
void
gset_text_align(align)
Gtext_align *align; /* text alignment   */
```

18. Set fill area index

```
void
gset_fill_ind(index)
Gint index; /* fill area index */
```

19. Set fill area interior style

```
void
gset_fill_int_style(style)
Gfill_int_style style; /* fill area interior style  */
```

20. Set fill area interior style index

```
void
gset_fill_style_ind(index)
Gint index; /* fill area style index */
```

21. Set fill area colour index

```
void
gset_fill_colr_ind(index)
Gint index; /* fill area colour index  */
```

22. Set aspect source flags

```
void
gset_asf(asf_flags)
Gasfs *asf_flags; /* aspect source flags */
```

23. Set pick identifier

```
void
gset_pick_id(pick_id)
Gint pk_id; /* pick identifier */
```

24. Set colour representation

```
void
gset_colr_rep(ws_id, index, colr_rep)
Gint ws_id; /* workstation identifier */
```

```
Gint index; /* colour bundle index */
Gcolr_rep *colr_rep; /* colour representation */
```

■ Transformation Functions

1. Set window

```
void
gset_win(tran_num,win_lim)
Gint tran_num; /* transformation number */
Glim *win_lim /* window limits */
```

2. Set viewport

```
void
gset_vp(tran_num,vp_lim)
Gint tran_num; /* transformation number */
Glim *vp_lim /* viewport limits */
```

3. Set viewport input priority

```
void
gset_vp_in_pri(index, ref_index, priority)
Gint index; /* view index */
Gint ref_index; /* reference view index */
Gpri priority;   /* relative priority   */
```

4. Select normalization transformation

```
void
gsel_norm_tran(norm_tran_num)
Gint norm_tran_num; /* normalization transformation
        number */
```

5. Set clipping indicator

```
void
gset_clip_ind(clip_ind)
Gclip_ind clip_ind; /* clip_indicator */
```

6. Set workstation window

```
void
gset_ws_win(ws_id, window)
Gint ws_id; /* workstation identifier */
Glim *window; /* workstation window limits */
```

7. Set workstation viewport

```
void
gset_ws_vp(ws_id, viewport)
Gint ws_id; /* workstation identifier */
Glim *viewport;  /* workstation viewport limits  */
```

■ Segments

1. Create segment

```
void
gcreate_seg(seg_id)
Gint seg_id; /* segment name */
```

2. Close segment

```
void
gclose_seg()
```

3. Rename segment

```
void
grename_seg(old_seg_name,new_seg_name)
Gint old_seg_name; /* old segment name */
Gint new_seg_name; /* new segment name */
```

4. Delete segment

```
void
gdel_seg(seg_id)
Gint seg_id; /* segment name */
```

■ Segment Attributes

1. Set segment transformation

```
void
gset_seg_tran(seg_name,tran_matrix)
Gint seg_name; /* segment name */
Gfloat tran_matrix[2][3]; /* transformation matrix */
```

2. Set visibility

```
void
gset_vis(seg_name, seg_vis)
```

```
Gint seg_name; /* segment name */
Gseg_vis seg_vis; /* visibility */
```

3. Set highlighting

```
void
gset_high(seg_name, seg_highl)
Gint seg_name; /* segment name */
Gseg_highl seg_highl; /* highlighting */
```

4. Set segment priority

```
void
gset_seg_pri(seg_name,seg_pri)
Gint seg_name; /* segment name */
Gfloat seg_pri; /* segment priority */
```

5. Set detectability

```
void
gset_det(seg_name,seg_det)
Gint seg_name; /* segment name */
Gseg_det seg_det; /* detectability */
```

■ **Input Functions**

1. Initialize locator

```
void
ginit_loc(ws_id, loc_dev, init_norm_tran_num,
        init_loc_pos, pet, echo_area, loc_data_rec)
Gint ws_id; /* workstation identifier */
Gint loc_dev; /* locator device number         */
Gint init_norm_tran_num; /* initial transformation
        number */
Gpt *init_loc_pos;   /* initial locator position */
Gint pet; /* prompt and echo type */
Glim *echo_area; /* echo area */
Gloc_data *loc_data_rec; /* data record   */
```

2. Initialize pick

```
void
ginit_pick(ws_id, pick_dev, init_status, pet,
        echo_area, pick_data_rec)
```

```
Gint ws_id; /* workstation identifier */
Gint pick_dev; /* pick device number  */
Gin_stat init_status; /* initial pick status  */
Gint pet; /* prompt and echo type */
Glim *echo_area; /* echo area */
Gpick_data *pick_data_rec; /* data record  */
```

3. Initialize string

```
void
ginit_string(ws_id, string_dev, init_string,
        pet, echo_area, string_rec)
Gint ws_id; /* workstation identifier */
Gint string_dev; /* string device number */
Gchar *init_string;  /* initial string  */
Gint pet; /* prompt and echo type */
Glim *echo_area; /* echo area */
Gstring_data *string_rec; /* data record  */
```

4. Set locator mode

```
void
gset_locator_mode(ws_id, loc_dev, mode, echo_switch)
Gint ws_id; /* workstation identifier */
Gint loc_dev; /* locator device number       */
Gin_mode mode;  /* operating mode    */
Gecho_sw echo_switch; /* echo switch */
```

5. Request locator

```
void
greq_loc(ws_id, loc_dev, status, norm_tran_num,
        loc_pos)
Gint ws_id; /* workstation identifier */
Gint loc_dev; /* locator device number */
Gin_st *status;  /* input status */
Gint *norm_tran_num; /* normalization transformation
        number */
Gpt *loc_pos; /* locator position */
```

6. Request pick

```
void
greq_pick(ws_id, pick_dev, status, pick)
Gint ws_id; /* workstation identifier */
Gint pick_dev; /* pick device number  */
```

```
Gin_st *status; /* pick status    */
Gpick *pick;  /* requested pick */
```

7. Request string

```
void
greq_string(ws_id, string_dev, status, string)
Gint ws_id; /* workstation identifier */
Gint string_dev; /* string device number */
Gin_st *status;  /* input status */
Gchar *string; /* requested string */
```

8. Sample locator

```
void
gsample_loc(ws_id, loc_dev, norm_tran_num, loc_pos)
Gint ws_id; /* workstation identifier */
Gint loc_dev; /* locator device number */
Gint *norm_tran_num; /* normalization transformation
        number */
Gpt *loc_pos; /* locator position */
```

9. Await event

```
void
gawait_ev(timeout, ws_id, class, input_dev)
Gfloat timeout; /* timeout (seconds)  */
Gint *ws_id; /* workstation identifier */
Gin_class *class; /* device class  */
Gint *input_dev; /* logical input device number   */
```

10. Flush device events

```
void
gflush_ev(ws_id, class, input_dev)
Gint ws_id; /* workstation identifier */
Gflush_class class; /* device class */
Gint input_dev; /* logical input device number   */
```

11. Get locator

```
void
gget_locator(norm_tran_num, loc_pos)
Gint *norm_tran_num; /* normalization transformation
        number */
Gpt *loc_pos; /* locator position */
```

12. Get pick

```
void
gget_pick(status, pick)
Gin_st *status; /* pick status */
Gpick *pick;   /* pick */
```

13. Get string

```
void
gget_string(string)
Gchar *string; /* string */
```

■ Metafile Functions

1. Write item to metafile

```
void
gwrite_item(ws_id, item_type, length, item_data_rec)
Gint ws_id; /* workstation identifier */
Gint item_type; /* item type */
Gint length; /* item data record length */
Gitem_data *item_data_rec; /* item data record */
```

2. Get item type from metafile

```
void
gget_item_type(ws_id, item_type, length)
Gint ws_id; /* workstation identifier */
Gint *item_type; /* item type */
Gint *length; /* item data record length */
```

3. Read item from metafile

```
void
gread_item(ws_id, max_length, item_data_rec)
Gint ws_id; /* workstation identifier */
Gint max_length; /* max item data record length */
Gitem_data *item_data_rec; /* item data record */
```

4. Interpret item

```
void
ginterpret_item(type, length, item_data_rec)
Gint type; /* item type */
Gint length; /* item data record length */
Gitem_data *item_data_rec; /* item data record */
```

B

GKS Data Types Used in Text

▪ Fundamental Types

```
typedef int Gint;

typedef float Gfloat;

typedef char Gchar;
```

▪ Other Types, in Alphabetical Order

1. Aspect Source Flag

```
typedef enum {
    GBUNDLE,
    GINDIVIDUAL
} Gasf;
```

2. Aspect Source Flag

```
            typedef struct {
                Gasf linetype; /* line type asf*/
                Gasf lidewidth;  /* linewidth asf */
                Gasf line_colr; /* polyline color asf */
                Gasf marker_type; /* marker type asf */
                Gasf marker_size; /* marker size asf */
                Gasf marker_colr; /* polymarker colour asf */
                Gasf fontprec; /* text font and precision asf */
                Gasf expan; /* character expansion asf */
                Gasf space; /* character spacing asf */
                Gasf text_colr; /text colour asf */
                Gasf fill_int_style; /fill area interior style
                   asf */
                Gasf fill_style_ind; /* fill area style index
                   asf */
                Gasf fill_colr; /* fill area colour asf */
            } Gasfs;
```

3. Clipping Indicator

```
        typedef enum {
            GCLIP,
            GNOCLIP
        } Gclip_ind;
```

4. Colour Representation

```
        typedef struct {
            Gfloat x; /* red */
            Gfloat y; /* green */
            Gfloat z; /* blue */
        } Gcolr_rep;
```

5. Connection Identifier

```
        typedef Gchar *Gconn_id;
```

6. Dimension

```
        typedef struct {
            Gint x_dim;
            Gint y_dim;
        } Gdim;
```

7. Echo Switch

```
        typedef enum {
```

```
        GECHO,
        GNO_ECHO
    } Gecho_sw;
```

8. Fill Area Interior Style

```
typedef enum {
    GHOLLOW;
    GSOLID;
    GPAT;
    GHATCH;
} Gfill_int_style;
```

9. Flush Class

```
typedef enum {
    GLOC_FLUSH,
    GSTROKE_FLUSH,
    GVAL_FLUSH,
    GCHOICE_FLUSH,
    GPICK_FLUSH,
    GSTRING_FLUSH
} Gflush_class;
```

10. Text Font and Precision

```
typedef struct {
    Gint font; /* font */
    Gtext_prec prec; /* text precision */
} Gfontprec;
```

11. Input Class

```
typedef enum {
    GNONE,
    GLOCATOR,
    GSTROKE,
    GVALUATOR,
    GCHOICE,
    GPICK,
    GSTRING
} Gin_class;
```

12. Input Mode

```
typedef enum {
    GREQ,
```

```
            GSAMPLE,
            GEV
      } Gin_mode;
```

13. Input Status

```
typedef enum {
      GOK,
      GNONE,
      GNO_IN
} Gin_st;
```

14. Coordinate Limits

```
typedef struct {
      Gfloat      xmin;     /* x min */
      Gfloat      xmax;     /* x max */
      Gfloat      ymin;     /* y min */
      Gfloat      ymax;     /* y max */
} Glim;
```

15. Pick Data

```
typedef struct {
      Gint seg_name;
      Gint pick_id;
} Gpick;
```

16. Viewport Priority

```
typedef enum {
      GHIGHER,
      GLOWER
} Gpri;
```

17. Coordinate Point

```
typedef struct {
      Gfloat      x;        /* x coordinate */
      Gfloat      y;        /* y coordinate */
} Gpt;
```

18. Coordinate Rectangle

```
typedef struct {
      Gpt p;
      Gpt q;
} Grect;
```

19. Regeneration Flag

```
typedef enum {
    GPERFORM,
    GPOSTPONE
} Gregen_flag;
```

20. Segment Detectability

```
typedef enum {
    GUNDET,
    GDET
} Gseg_det;
```

21. Segment Highlighting

```
typedef enum {
    GNORMAL,
    GHIGHL
} Gseg_highl;
```

22. Segment Visibility

```
typedef enum {
    GVIS,
    GINVIS
} Gseg_vis;
```

23. Text Alignment

```
typedef struct {
    Gtext_hor  horizontal;  /* horizontal component */
    Gtext_ver  vertical;    /* vertical component */
} Gtext_align;
```

24. Text Horizontal Alignment

```
typedef enum {
    GNORMAL_HOR,
    GLEFT_HOR,
    GCENTRE_HOR,
    GRIGHT_HOR
} Gtext_hor;
```

25. Text Path

```
typedef enum {
    GRIGHT_PATH,
```

```
        GLEFT_PATH,
        GUP_PATH,
        GDOWN_PATH
    } Gtext_path;
```

26. Text Precision

```
typedef enum {
    GSTRING_PREC,
    GCHAR_PREC,
    GSTROKE_PREC
} Gtext_prec;
```

27. Text Vertical Alignment

```
tyepdef enum {
    GNORMAL_VERT,
    GTOP_VERT,
    GCAP_VERT,
    GHALF_VERT,
    GBASE_VERT,
    GBOTTOM_VERT
} Gtext_vert;
```

28. Vector

```
typedef struct {
    Gfloat x;
    Gfloat y;
} Gvec;
```

29. Workstation Type

```
typedef Gint Gws_type;
```

Types such as `item_data`, used in the metafiles functions, and `pick_data`, used to initialize the pick, are implementation dependent.

C

Self-Scaling Plotter

```c
#include <gks.h>    /* typedefs */
#include <stdio.h> /* standard I/O */

#define BLUE 1
#define GREEN 2
#define MAGENTA 3
#define DASHED 5
#define WKSID 1
#define WSTYPE 45    /* local defintion */
#define CONNID "0" /* local id */

init()
{

    FILE *fp, *fpopen();
    fp = fopen( "errors", "w" );
    gopen_gks( fp, 0 ); /* No Buffer Space Needed */
    gopen_ws( WKSID, CONNID, WSTYPE);
```

```
            gactivate_ws( WKSID );
    }

    finish()
    {
        int status;
        Gchar response;
        /* Request character from user to pause*/
        greq_string( WKSID, 1, status, &response );
        gdeactivate_ws( WKSID );
        gclose_ws( WKSID );
        gclose_gks();
    }

    bounds(data, n, xmax, xmin, ymax, ymin)
        Gpt data[];
        Gfloat *xmin,*xmax,*ymin,*ymax;
        Gint n;
    {
        int i;
        *xmax = *xmin = data[0].x;
        *ymax = *ymin = data[0].y;
        for(i=0;i<n;i++) {

if( *xmax< data[i].x )
    *xmax=data[i].x;
else if( *xmin> data[i].x )
    *xmin=data[i].x;

if( *ymax< data[i].y )
    *ymax=data[i].y;
else if( *ymin> data[i].y )
    *ymin=data[i].y;
        }
    }

    plot(data,n,xlabel,ylabel,title)
        Gpt data[];
        Gint n ;
        Gchar *xlabel, *ylabel, *title;
    {
        static Gtext_align center_text = { GCENTRE_HOR,
            GHALF_VERT };
        static Gfontprec duplex = { 1, GCHAR_PREC };
        static Glim viewport1 = { .1, 1.0, .1, .9 };
```

```
Glim window1;
Gpt axes[3], textloc, charup;
Gfloat xmin, xmax, ymin, ymax;
static Gcolr_rep green = { 0.0, 1.0, 0.0};
static Gcolr_rep blue = { 0.0, 0.0, 1.0};
static Gcolr_rep magenta = { 1.0, 0.0, 1.0};


/* Find min and max of data */

bounds(data, n, &xmax, &xmin, &ymax, &ymin);

/* Define and select transformation 1
using viewport1, which will leave room for labels */

window1.xmin = xmin;
window1.ymin = ymin;
window1.xmax = xmax;
window1.ymax = ymax;
gset_win(1, &window1);
gset_vp(1, &viewport1);

gsel_norm_tran(1);

/* Set the color representation */

gset_colr_rep(WKSID, BLUE, &blue);
gset_colr_rep(WKSID, GREEN, &green);
gset_colr_rep(WKSID, MAGENTA, &magenta);


/* Define axes */

axes[0].x = xmax;
axes[2].y = ymax;
axes[0].y = axes[1].y = ymin;

axes[1].x = axes[2].x = xmin;


/* Form fill area by adding two additional points */

data[n].x = data[n-1].x;
data[n].y = ymin;
data[n+1].x = data[0].x;
```

```
                  data[n+1].y = ymin;

                  /* Set the fill area representation to hatch,
                  select pattern 3 in magenta*/

                  gset_fill_int_style(GHATCH);
                  gset_fill_style_ind(3);
                  gset_fill_colr_ind(MAGENTA);
                  gfill_area(n+2,data);

                  /* Set the polyline color index corresponding to blue and
                  draw axes set line to be twice default thickness */

                  gset_linewidth(2.0);
                  gset_line_colr_ind(BLUE);

                  gpolyline( 3, axes);

                  /* Draw dashed polyline on top of fill area */

                  gset_linetype(DASHED);
                  gpolyline(n,data);

                  /* Select normalization transform 0 for labels */

                  gsel_norm_tran(0);

                  /*Set the font type to software font 1 with
                  character precision.  Set character height to be
                  1/20 of workstation display. Center strings.*/

                  gset_text_prec(&duplex);
                  gset_char_ht(.05);
                  gset_text_align(&center_text);

                  /* Add the x label and title */

                  gset_line_colr_ind(GREEN);

                  textloc.x = 0.5;
                  textloc.y = 0.05;
                  gtext( &textloc ,xlabel);

                  textloc.x = 0.5;
                  textloc.y = 0.95;
```

```
    gtext( &textloc, title);

    /* Change the character up vector
    and add the y label */

    charup.x = -1.0;
    charup.y =  0.0;
    gset_char_up_vec(&charup);

    textloc.x = 0.05;
    textloc.y = 0.5;
    gtext( &textloc, ylabel);

}
```

[Abel81]   Abelson, H. and A. diSessa, *Turtle Graphics*, MIT Press, Cambridge, MA, 1981.

[Akel88]   Akeley, K. and T. Jermoluk, "High Performance Polygon Rendering," *Computer Graphics*, 22(4), 239–246, 1988.

[Aman87]   Amantides, J., "Realism in Computer Graphics: A Survey," *IEEE Computer Graphics and Applications*, 7(1), 44–56, 1987.

[Bar87]   Bartels, R. H., Beatty, J. C., and Barsky, B. A. *An Introduction to Splines for use in Computer Graphics and Geometric Modeling*, Morgan Kaufmann, Los Altos, CA, 1987.

[Bres63]   Bresenham, J. E., "Algorithm for Computer Control of a Digital Plotter," *IBM Systems Journal*, 4(1), pp. 25–30, 1965.

[Bres87]   Bresenham, J. E., "Ambiguities in Incremental Line Rastering," *IEEE Computer Graphics and Applications*, 7(5), pp. 31–43, 1987.

[Bono85]   Bono, P. R., "A Survey of Graphics Standards and Their Role in Information Exchange," *Computer*, 18(10), 63–75, 1985.

[Bow83]   Bowyer, A. and J. Woodwark, *A Programmer's Geometry*, Butterworth, London, 1983.

[Brown85]   Brown, M. D. and M. Hech, *Understanding PHIGS*, Megatek, San Diego, CA, 1985.

[Carl78]   Carlbom, I. and J. Paciorek, "Geometric Projection and Viewing Transformations," *Computing Surveys*, 1(4), 465–502, 1978.

[Cat75]   Catmull, E., "A Hidden-Surface Algorithm with Antialiasing," *Computer Graphics*, 12(3), 6–11, 1975.

[Cat75b]   Catmull, E., "Computer Display of Curved Surfaces," *Proceedings of the IEEE Conference Computer Graphics, Pattern Recognition and Data Structures*, Los Angeles, CA, p. 11, May 1975.

[CG]   *Computer Graphics*, ACM Special Interest Group on Graphics (SIGGRAPH) Association for Computing Machinery.

[CGM86]   "Metafile for the Storage and Transfer of Picture Description Information," ISO/DP 8632 International Standards Organization, 1986.

[Clark82]   Clark, J. E., "The Geometry Engine: A VLSI Geometry System for Graphics," *Computer Graphics*, 10(3), 127–133, 1982.

[Cook82]   Cook, R. L. and K. E. Torrance, "A Reflectance Model for Computer Graphics," *ACM Transactions on Graphics*, 1(1), 7–24, 1982.

[Corn70]   Cornsweet, T. N., *Visual Perception*, Academic Press, New York, 1970.

[Crow77]   Crow, F. C., "The Aliasing Problem in Computer Generated Images," *Graphics and Image Processing*, 20(11), 799–805, 1977.

[Crow81]   Crow, F. C., "A Comparison of Antialiasing Techniques," *IEEE Computer Graphics and Applications*, 1(1), 40–49, 1981.

[Dun83]   Dunlavey, M. R., "Efficient Polygon Filling Algorithms for Raster Displays," *ACM Transactions on Graphics*, 2(4), 264–273, 1983.

[Ear85]   Earnshaw, R. A., *Fundamental Algorithms for Computer Graphics*, Springer-Verlag, Berlin, 1985.

[End84]   Enderle, G., K. Kansy, and G. Pfaff, *Computer Graphics Programming: GKS—The Graphics Standard*, Springer-Verlag, Berlin, 1984.

[Faux80]   Faux, I.D. and M.J. Pratt, *Computational Geometry for Design and Manufacturing*, Halsted, Chichester, England, 1980.

[Foley82]   Foley, J.D. and A. van Dam, *Fundamentals of Interactive Computer Graphics*, Addison-Wesley, Reading, MA, 1982.

[GKS84]   *Graphical Kernel System*, ISO 7492, International Standards Organization, 1985. (Also ANSI X3.124–1985, American National Standards Institute)

[GKS86]   *Graphical Kernel System for Three Dimensions*, ISO 8805, International Standards Organization, 1986.

[Gold83]   Goldberg, A. and D. Robson, *Smalltalk–80: The Language and Its Implementation*, Addison-Wesley, Reading, MA, 1983.

[Goral84]   Goral, C.M., K.E. Torrance, D.P. Greenberg, and B. Battaile, "Modeling the Interaction of Light Between Diffuse Surfaces," *Computer Graphics (SIGGRAPH 84)*, 18(3), 213–222, 1984.

[Guib82]   Guibas, L. and J. Stolfi, "A Language for Bitmap Manipulation," *ACM Transactions on Graphics*, 1(3), 191–214, 1982.

[Gour71]   Gourand, H., "Computer Display of Curved Surfaces," *IEEE Transactions on Computers*, C-20(6), pp. 623–628, 1971.

[GSPC79]   Graphics Standards Planning Committee, "Status Report of the Computer Graphics Standards Planning Committee," *Computer Graphics*, 13(3), 1979.

[Hall83]   Hall, R. and D.P. Greenberg, "A Testbed for Realistic Image Synthesis," *IEEE Computer Graphics and Applications*, 3(8), 1–20, 1983.

[Har83]   Harrington, S., *Computer Graphics: A Programming Approach*, McGraw-Hill, New York, 1983.

[Hearn86]   Hearn, D. and M.P. Baker, *Computer Graphics*, Prentice-Hall, Englewood Cliffs, NJ, 1986.

[Hend86]   Henderson, L., M. Journey, and C. Osland, "The Computer Graphics Metafile," *IEEE Computer Graphics and Applications*, 6(8), 24–32, 1986.

[Hop83]   Hopgood, F. R. A., D. A. Duce, J. A. Gallop, and D. C. Sutcliffe, *Introduction to the Graphical Kernel System: GKS*, Academic Press, London, 1983.

[IGES86]   *Initial Graphics Exchange Specification, Version 3.0*, NB-SIR 86–3359, National Bureau of Standards, Gaithersburg, MD, 1986.

[Ing81]   Ingalls, D., "The Smalltalk Graphics Kernel," *Byte*, 6(8), 1981.

[Joy88]   Joy, K. I., C. W. Grant, N. L. Max, and L. Hatfield, *Computer Graphics: Image Synthesis*, Computer Society Press, Washington, DC, 1988.

[Judd75]   Judd, D. B. and G. Wyszecki, *Color in Business, Science and Industry*, Wiley, New York, 1975.

[Ker88]   Kernigan, B. W. and D. M. Ritchie, *The C Programming Language*, Prentice-Hall, Engelwood Cliffs, NJ, 1988.

[Krebs79]   Krebs, M. and J. Wolf, "Design Principles for the Use of Color in Displays," *Proceedings of the Society for Information Display*, 20, 10–15, 1979.

[Liang84]   Liang, Y. and B. Barsky, "A New Concept and Method for Line Clipping," *ACM Transactions on Graphics*, 3(1), 1–22, 1984.

[Lien87]   Lien, A., M. Shantz, and V. Pratt, "Adaptive Forward Differencing for Rendering Curves and Surfaces," *Computer Graphics*, 21(4), 119–128, 1987.

[Mach83]   Machover, C., "An Updated Guide to Sources of Information about Computer Graphics," *IEEE Computer Graphics and Applications*, 1983.

[Mag87]   Magnenat-Thalman, N. and D. Thalman, *Image Synthesis*, Springer-Verlag, Berlin, 1987.

[Man87]   Mantyla, M., *Solid Modeling*, Computer Science Press, Rockville, MD, 1987.

[Mort85]   Mortenson, M., *Geometric Modeling*, Wiley, New York, 1985.

[Murch84]   Murch, G., "Physiological Principles for the Effective use of Color," *IEEE Computer Graphics and Applications*, 4(11), 49–54, 1984.

[Myers88]   Myers, B.A., "A Taxonomy of Window Manager-User Interfaces," *IEEE Computer Graphics and Applications*, 8(5), 65–84, 1988.

[New73]   Newman. W.M. and R.F. Sproull, *Principles of Interactive Computer Graphics*, McGraw-Hill, New York, 1973.

[Paper81]   Papert, S., *LOGO: A Language for Learning*, Creative Computer Press, Middletown, NJ, 1981.

[Pav82]   Pavlides, T., *Algorithms for Graphics and Image Processing*, Springer-Verlag, Berlin, 1982.

[PHIGS86]   Programmer's Hierarchical Interactive Graphics System, ISO TC97 SC21/N819, International Standards Organization, June 1986.

[PHIGS88]   PHIGS+ Committee, "PHIGS+ Functional Description, Revision 3.0," *Computer Graphics*, 22(3), 125–215, 1988.

[Pike84]   Pike, R., L. Guibas, and D. Ingalls, "Bitmap Graphics," *Computer Graphics*, 18(3), 135–160, 1984.

[Phong75]   Phong, B.T., "Illumination for Computer Generated Scenes," *Communications of the ACM*, 18(6), 311–317, 1975.

[Post85]   *PostScript Language Reference Manual*, Adobe Systems Inc., Addison-Wesley, Reading, MA, 1985.

[Pratt78]   Pratt, W.K., *Digital Image Processing*, Wiley, New York, 1978.

[Reis81]   Reisenfeld, R.F., "Homogeneous Coordinates and Projective Planes in Computer Graphics," *IEEE Computer Graphics and Applications*, 1(1), 50–56, 1981.

[Rog76]   Rogers, D.F. and A.J. Alan, *Mathematical Elements for Computer Graphics*, McGraw-Hill, New York, 1976.

[Rog85]   Rogers, D.F., *Procedural Elements for Computer Graphics*, McGraw-Hill, New York, 1985.

[Rog87]   Rogers, D.F. and D.A. Earnshaw (eds), *Techniques for Computer Graphics*, Springer-Verlag, Berlin, 1987.

[Sal87]   Salmon, R. and M. Slater, *Computer Graphics: Systems and Concepts*, Addison-Wesley, Wokingham, England, 1987.

[Sch83]   Schachter, B.J. (ed), *Computer Image Generation*, Wiley, New York, 1983.

[Schei86]   Scheifler, R. W. and J. Gettys, "The X Window System," *ACM Transactions on Graphics,* 5(2), 79–109, 1986.

[Schnei87]   Schneiderman, B., *Designing the User Interface: Strategies for Effective Human–Computer Interaction,* Addison-Wesley, Reading, MA, 1987.

[Smith78]   Smith, A. R., "Color Gamut Transform Pairs," *Computer Graphics (SIGGRAPH)*, 12(3), 12–19, 1978.

[Smith84]   Smith, B. and J. Wellington, "IGES: A Key Interface Specification for CAD/CAM System Integration," *Proceedings of Computer Graphics 84*, 548–555, 1984.

[Smith82]   Smith, D. C., C. Irby, R. Kimball, B. Verplank, and E. Harslen, "Designing the Star Interface," *Byte*, April, 242–282, 1982.

[Spr68]   Sproull, R. F. and I. E. Sutherland, "A Clipping Divider," *1968 Fall Joint Computer Conference*, 765–775, Thompson Books, Washington D.C. 1968.

[Spr85]   Sproull, R. F., W. R. Sutherland, and M. K. Ulner, *Device Independent Graphics*, McGraw-Hill, New York, 1985.

[Suth63]   Sutherland, I. E., "SKETCHPAD: A Man–Machine Graphical Communication System," *AFIPS Spring Joint Computer Conference*, 329–346, Spartan Books, Baltimore, MD, 1963.

[Suth74]   Sutherland, I. E. and G. W. Hodgeman, "Reentrant Polygon Clipping," *Communications of the ACM*, 17(1), 32–42, 1974.

[Suth74b]   Sutherland, I. E., R. F. Sproull, and R. A. Schumacker, "A Characterization of Ten Hidden-Surface Algorithms," *Computer Surveys*, 6(1), 1–55, 1974.

[Tufte83]   Tufte, E. R., *The Visual Display of Quantitative Information,* Graphics Press, Chesire, CN, 1983.

[Whit80]   Whitted, T., "An Improved Illumination Model for Shaded Display," *Communications of ACM*, 23(6), 343–348, 1980.

[Wysz82]   Wyszecki, G. and W. S. Stiles, *Color Science*, Wiley, New York, 1982.

FUNCTION INDEX

467

SUBJECT INDEX

Display list, 246
  operations, 297
Display memory, 7, 11
Display processor, 6, 246–248
  unit (DPU), 7
Display surface, 57
Dragging, 129
Dual ported memory, 254

Echo, 121
  area, 141
Edges, 88, 189, 357
  flag, 277
Eight-fold symmetry, 400
Erasing, 263
Error file, 77
Error handling, 48, 55
Evaluation procedures, 175–177, 311–312
Event mode input, 144–145
Event queue, 144
Execute structure, 201
Exclusive OR, 261–265
Explicit form, 39, 301, 388. *See also* Curves
  and surfaces
Extent, 93, 227
Extrusion, 431

Feedback, 151
Fill, 265, 274–282, 371
  edge flag, 277–288
  flood, 279–280
  painter's algorithm, 279
  priority, 278–279
  recursive, 279
  scan line, 282
  singularities, 277
  sort, 281–282
Fill area, 60, 88–90, 305
  attributes, 89
  GKS, 275
  set, 103
Fixed point, 165
Flood fill, 279–280

Format, 45, 47
Forward differences, 413, 429, 434
Frame buffer, 7, 11, 236, 254
Frucstrum, 325
Functionality, 45

Generalized drawing primitive, 90
Geometric attribute, 80
Geometry, 271
  engine, 250
Gouraud, 382
Graphical Kernel System (GKS), 8, 17, 46,
  53–54, 100
  levels, 60
  three dimensional (GKS-3D), 319
  functions, 60
  history, 54
  metafile (GKSM), 97
  model, 203
  transformation, 174
Graphical devices, 128–129, 152
Graphical object, 110
Graphical pipeline, 213–215, 319, 332–333
Graphics software, 11–13
Graphics system, 9–11
Graphics workstation, 249–250
Gray scale, 291
Grid, 15

Halftone, 297
Hatch, 89
Help, 150
Hermite polynomial, 405–406
Hermite geometry matrix, 405
Hidden line removal, 361
Hidden surface removal, 352, 361–372,
  425–427
  back face removal, 365–366
  depth sort, 366–388
  image space methods, 363–369
  object space methods, 363, 369–372
  painter's algorithm, 427

Metafile, 62, 96–100
  Computer Graphics Metafile (CGM), 97, 100
  functions, 63
  GKS, 97
Mode selection, 135
Modeling, 181–207
  hierarchical, 184
  PHIGS, 205–207
  solid, 252
  wire frame, 351
Modeling coordinates, 182, 320
Mouse, 3, 11, 127

National Television Systems Committee (NTSC), 289
Node, 189
Normal, 303, 353
Normalization, 318–325, 365, 371
Normalization transformation, 69–71
Normalized projection coordinates (NPC), 341, 343
Normalization transformation index, 70
Normalized device coordinates (NDC), 28

Object, 110, 430–434
  extruded, 431
  of revolution, 431
Object space, 363
Oblique view, 330, 341–343
Oblique projection matrix, 342
Open graphics system, 77
Orthogonal, 41
  view, 343
Orthogonal projection matrix, 341
Orthogonality, principle of, 15
Outcode, 222
Output devices, 9
Output functions, 60–61. *See also* Primitives

Palette, color, 292

Pan, 175–176
Packed pixel, 255
Painter's algorithm, 279
Parametric form, 43, 388. *See also* Curves and surfaces
Parent, 189
Pattern, 89
Pen plotter, 23
  model, 64
Perspective, 330–332, 343–345
Perspective normalization matrix, 345
Perspective transformation, 344
PHIGS. *See* Programmer's Hierarchical Interactive Graphics Standard
Phong, 381–382
Pick, 63, 116, 118, 129–136
  identifier, 130–132
  initialization, 135
Picture display, 10
Picture formation processing, 10
Pipeline (graphical), 213, 319, 332
Pitch, 347
Pixel, 7, 236, 254–260
  destination, 259
  multiple bit, 291
  plane, 256
  source, 259
  swapping, 255–260
Plane, 302
Point, 36–37, 306
Polygon, 88, 268–274, 353–385
  back facing, 365
  clipping, 272–274
  convex, 273, 365
  mesh, 270–271, 356–361
  normal, 353–356
  rasterization, 268–274
  rendering, 372–384
  representation, 269, 353–356
  shading, 382
Polyhedron, 360
  regular, 360
Polyline, 45, 49, 60, 66–69, 304. *See also* Line segment
Polymarker, 60, 87–88